ST/CTC/156

United Nations Conference on Trade and Development
Programme on Transnational Corporations

World Investment Report 1993
Transnational Corporations and Integrated International Production

United Nations New York, 1993

NOTE

The UNCTAD Programme on Transnational Corporations of the United Nations serves as the focal point within the United Nations Secretariat for all matters related to transnational corporations. In the past, the Programme on Transnational Corporations was carried out by the United Nations Centre on Transnational Corporations (1975-1992) and by the Transnational Corporations and Management Division of the United Nations Department of Economic and Social Development (1992-1993). In 1993, the Programme was transferred to the United Nations Conference on Trade and Development. The objectives of the work programme include to further the understanding of the nature of transnational corporations and of their economic, legal, political and social effects on home and host countries and in international relations, particularly between developed and developing countries; to secure effective international arrangements aimed at enhancing the contribution of transnational corporations to national development and world economic growth; and to strengthen the negotiating capacity of host countries, in particular developing countries, in their dealings with transnational corporations.

The *World Investment Report* is published annually by the UNCTAD Programme on Transnational Corporations to contribute to a better understanding of transnational corporations, their activities and their impact.

The term "country" as used in this report also refers, as appropriate, to territories or areas; the designations employed and the presentation of the material do not imply the expression of any opinion whatsoever on the part of the Secretariat of the United Nations concerning the legal status of any country, territory, city or area or of its authorities, or concerning the delimitation of its frontiers or boundaries. In addition, the designations of country groups are intended solely for statistical or analytical convenience and do not necessarily express a judgement about the stage of development reached by a particular country or area in the development process.

The following symbols have been used in the tables:

Two dots (..) indicate that data are not available or are not separately reported. Rows in tables have been omitted in those cases where no data are available for any of the elements in the row;

A dash (—) indicates that the item is equal to zero or its value is negligible;

A blank in a table indicates that the item is not applicable;

A slash (/) between dates representing years, e.g., 1988/89, indicates a financial year;

Use of a hyphen (-) between dates representing years, e.g., 1985-1989, signifies the full period involved, including the beginning and end years.

Reference to "dollars" ($) means United States dollars, unless otherwise indicated.

Annual rates of growth or change, unless otherwise stated, refer to annual compound rates.

Details and percentages in tables do not necessarily add to totals because of rounding.

The material contained in this study may be freely quoted with appropriate acknowledgement.

ST/CTC/156

UNITED NATIONS PUBLICATION
Sales No. E.93.II.A.14

ISBN 92-1-104417-0

Manufactured in the United States of America

PREFACE

The continuing expansion of transnational corporations, the regionalization and globalization of firms, the emergence of an integrated international production system and some legal and policy implications of these processes are the focus of the ***World Investment Report 1993.***

There are some 37,000 transnational corporations in the world, with over 170,000 foreign affiliates. This volume analyzes their evolving strategies and changing organizational structures, and the implications of the increasing functional, cross-national integration of their activities for the location of international production.

In spite of an overall decline in world-wide flows of foreign direct investment in the early 1990s, there are many features of the world economic environment pointing to a continuing and important role for transnational corporations. World investment continues to drive international trade and world output. Flows of foreign direct investment to developing countries—with the exception of Africa—are continuing to rise. Transnational corporations are continuing to invest in the newly opened economies of Central and Eastern Europe. And transnational corporations from developing countries are expanding their activities abroad.

The early 1990s have also witnessed increasing cross-national economic integration, with the single market of the European Community, the European Economic Area, the North American Free Trade Agreement, MERCOSUR and ASEAN as the most visible examples. Perhaps of greater significance is the emergence of an integrated international production system, brought about by the activities of transnational corporations which are increasingly integrating across borders the functions required to produce goods and services. This integration presents opportunities and challenges for both host and home countries, and, in particular, raises important issues for developing countries that are seeking to improve their development prospects by integrating their economies more closely into the world economy. It also raises a number of new policy issues, such as the definition of the nationality of the transnational firm, the determination of the tax base of the firm and the complex relationships between parent firms and their foreign affiliates.

Policy and regulatory frameworks need to adapt to the emerging integrated international production system, if the benefits of regionalization and globalization are to be spread as widely as possible. The analysis and evidence presented in the ***World Investment Report 1993*** should assist policy makers in formulating policies, especially in light of the emerging integrated international production system. It should also contribute to a greater awareness of the need for harmonization of policies among host countries in order to avoid policy competition as each country seeks to be the location of choice in the emerging system of integrated international production.

The *Report* was prepared by staff of the Programme on Transnational Corporations (the former Centre on Transnational Corporations), which was transferred to UNCTAD earlier this year.

Kenneth K.S. Dadzie
Secretary-General
United Nations Conference on Trade and Development

New York, July 1993

The ***World Investment Report 1993*** was prepared by a team led by Karl P. Sauvant and comprising Victoria Aranda, Persephone Economou, John Gara, David Gold, Khalil Hamdani, Azizul Islam, Hiroshi Kawamura, Peter Koudal, Richard Kozul-Wright, Padma Mallampally, Paz Estrella Tolentino, Jörg Weber and Zbigniew Zimny. Some of this staff is now with the Department for Economic and Social Information and Policy Analysis. Specific inputs were received from Marita Andersson, Ricardo Bielschowsky, Cornelia Fischer, Masataka Fujita, Michael Mortimore and Fiorina Mugione. Principal research assistance was provided by Mohamed Chiraz Baly and Dorothy Woo. Research assistance was also provided by Tracy L. Casteel, Udo Mandler, Daniela Maiorino, Franziska Rahner, Thomas Theuringer, Reiner Walleser and Herold E. Weiss. The *Report* was copy-edited by Betty Hamnett. Production of the *Report* was carried out by Medy Almario, Marie Antoine, Marie-Erdwine Antoine, Juliet Capili, Kanayalal Israni, Ditas G. Miranda, Teresita Sabico, Wilma V. Soto and Helen Thacker. It was desktop-published by Valerian Monteiro.

Experts from within and outside of the United Nations system provided substantial inputs that were utilized for the *Report*. Major inputs were received from Jag Alexeyev, Arghyrios Fatouros and Edward Saperstein. Inputs were also received from Manuel Agosin, Gillian Dell, DeAnne Julius, M. Ishaq Nadiri and Peter Petri.

A number of experts were consulted and commented on various chapters. Comments, including during expert group meetings, were received during various stages of preparation from Carlos Alfaro, Rory Allan, David Aronofsky, Samuel K. B. Asante, Reinhart Augustin, John Beck, Phillip Blumberg, Aad Cooiman, Lorraine Eden, William Egelhoff, Magnus Ericsson, David Gill, Berthold Goldman, Karl Hofstetter, Ivan Ivanov, D. C. Kelly, John Kline, Bruce Kogut, Sanjaya Lall, Fernando de Mateo, Allen Morrison, Maurice Odle, Goran Ohlin, Jeffrey Owens, Richard Pomp, Kendahl Roth, Andreas Lowenfeld, John Stopford, Osvaldo Sunkel, J. J. G. M. Vermeere, Thomas Waelde, Cynthia Day Wallace and Obie Wichard. The *Report* benefited from overall advice from John H. Dunning, Senior Economic Adviser.

Executives of a number of companies extended their cooperation by providing information and insights. They included the Ford Motor Company, Siemens, companies in the list of the largest 100 transnational corporations and many others.

The ***World Investment Report 1993*** was edited by Rupert Pennant-Rea.

CONTENTS

Page

Page

Page

Page

Page

Page

List of boxes

Page

List of figures

Page

List of tables

Page

INTRODUCTION

Transnational corporations (TNCs) are a powerful force for binding national economies together. Through complex corporate strategies and intricate network structures, TNCs engage in international production characterized by a sophisticated intra-firm division of labour for each corporate function. As a result, about one third of the world's private sector productive assets are under the common governance of TNCs, with varying degrees of integration.

The growing influence of TNCs can be seen in the increase in the stock of foreign direct investment (FDI) and the growth in the number of TNCs and their foreign affiliates. Part One of the present report documents those changes. During the 1980s, and especially after 1982, annual FDI flows grew rapidly. By 1992, the global stock of FDI had reached approximately $2 trillion, which generated about $5.5 trillion in sales by foreign affiliates. The pace of growth slowed during 1991 and 1992, but that is probably a temporary phenomenon, largely due to recession in the biggest economies.

The universe of TNCs is large, diverse and expanding: Chapter I provides an overview of its dimensions and characteristics. By the early 1990s, there were 37,000 TNCs in the world, with over 170,000 foreign affiliates. There were 24,000 TNCs based in 14 major home developed economies, up from 7,000 in 1970. Even those figures understate the number of firms that operate as TNCs, both because of measurement difficulties, and because firms carry out their transnational activities and exert control over foreign productive assets through a variety of non-equity arrangements—subcontracting, franchising, licensing, and the like—as well as through the formation of strategic alliances. These forms of international expansion occur with little or no FDI, and are therefore only partially captured by FDI data or by firm-level data defined by equity participation. More than 90 per cent of TNCs are headquartered in the developed countries and less than 1 per cent are from Central and Eastern Europe. Those from developing countries account for approximately 8 per cent of all TNCs and 5 per cent of the global stock of FDI.

The TNC universe is highly concentrated in terms of the share of foreign assets controlled by the largest firms. Roughly 1 per cent of parent TNCs own half of the FDI stock or total affiliate assets. The largest 100 TNCs accounted for roughly $280 billion of the world stock of outward investment in 1990, 14 per cent of the total.

The continuing growth of FDI is being facilitated by developments in the policy framework. At the multilateral level, examples include the adoption of the Guidelines on the Treatment of Foreign Direct Investment by the World Bank. They propose general standards of fair and equitable treatment, national treatment and most-favoured-nation treatment. Those standards apply, in principle, to all activities of foreign investors, from setting up abroad to the ultimate disposal of an investment. Elsewhere, the United Nations Conference on Environment and Development (UNCED), held in Rio de Janeiro in June 1992, adopted the *Agenda for the 21st Century*. It considers generic management issues and recommends that corporations establish world-wide corporate policies on sustainable development. These include policies to facilitate the transfer of clean technology to developing countries, to go beyond the existing practices and adopt no less stringent standards of operation as in their home country, and to report annually on their environmental records. These developments at the multilateral level, combined with an initiative of the OECD to examine the feasibility of a "wider" investment instrument, suggest that the search for a more comprehensive approach to FDI and the activities of TNCs continues.

At the bilateral and national levels, too, policy developments continued in 1992. The number of bilateral investment treaties concluded by OECD countries reached 506 at the end of 1992, with a marked growth in the participation of Latin American countries and the newly independent states in Central and Eastern Europe. Nationally, all 79 new legislative measures adopted in 1992 in 43 countries were intended to liberalize the rules on FDI; in 1991, 80 of 82 measures were more liberal (as reported in the *World Investment Report 1992: Transnational Corporations as Engines of Growth*). Other significant policy changes included legislative actions to increase intellectual property protection and to provide the legal conditions for the participation of TNCs in the privatization of state industries, a major source of FDI growth.

Foreign direct investment in the 1980s was increasingly concentrated within the Triad (the European Community, Japan and the United States), as described in the *World Investment Report 1991: The Triad in Foreign Direct Investment*. In the early 1990s, however, FDI flows to developed countries declined, while those to developing countries increased, especially in Asia and Latin America and the Caribbean, in response to rapid economic growth and fewer restrictions.

Chapter II looks at the regional distribution of FDI. The decline of FDI inflows to developed countries can be attributed, in part, to slow growth and recession in the European Community, Japan and North America. The attractiveness of these economies as hosts was further reduced since domestic profitability also declined. In addition, recession has reduced the ability and willingness of TNCs from these economies to expand abroad. Japan in particular saw its FDI outflows decline substantially as domestic financial weaknesses on top of declining profitability hampered the ability of Japanese TNCs to invest abroad.

At the same time, FDI to developing countries expanded as a result of the resurgence of strong economic performance in a wide spectrum of developing countries in Asia and Latin America, renewed opportunities from the exploitation of natural resources in Africa and countries' continuing efforts to liberalize and privatize. The growth of TNC activities in Latin America and Asia has been further stimulated by progress towards a North American Free Trade Agreement and, in Asia, by various governmental initiatives to promote trade and FDI. The general trend towards liberalization and privatization has also been evident in Central and Eastern Europe where inflows continue to grow.

The rapid increase in FDI throughout the world has been accompanied by a pronounced change in its sectoral composition, from the primary sector and resource-based manufacturing towards services and technology-intensive manufacturing. Those trends are elaborated in detail in chapter III. Undoubtedly, the growth of services FDI reflects structural changes in domestic economic activity and advances in information technology. However, its initial growth was constrained by restrictive practices introduced for strategic, political or cultural reasons. Consequently, the recent wave of liberalization has had a particularly marked effect on services FDI, which is likely to continue during the coming decade. Significant capital-intensive service industries (such as telecommunications and air transportation) have only recently opened up to FDI, providing new opportunities for TNCs.

The stock of FDI in the primary sector is now dwarfed by that in other sectors. However, it still grew quite impressively during the 1980s. Indeed, in developed market economies, its inward stock grew faster than in any other sector and faster than the stock of primary sector inward FDI to developing countries. This unexpected development was brought about by the combined effect of intense merger activity, notably in petroleum, and the search for safer investment locations. However, as more developing countries introduce open and stable FDI regimes, there are signs that locational decisions in the primary sector are again emphasizing natural advantages. But the continuing uncertainty in some resource-rich in economies in transition, particularly the Russian Federation and southern Africa, will affect future flows of FDI in this sector.

The stock of FDI in the secondary sector has declined, relative to services, although in developing countries in 1990 its stock was still considerably larger than that in other sectors. The significant changes in manufacturing have been more qualitative in their nature. In particular, there has been a shift from labour-intensive manufacturing towards more capital-intensive industries, both across and within countries. During the 1980s, this was most pronounced in the inward stock of FDI in the newly industrializing economies. Furthermore, increasing technological demands in much of manufacturing are leading to new forms of corporate activity. Non- and low-equity FDI have become established means to control assets abroad, and strategic alliances have expanded, particularly in those industries with short product cycles and high research-and-development costs.

In addition to discussing the regional and sectoral aspects of the growth of FDI, Part One of the present report also analyses patterns in the long-term growth of global FDI. The decline in world-wide FDI flows in 1991 and 1992 has marked the end of a period of constantly and rapidly rising flows that began in 1982. This slow-down raises the question, examined in chapter IV, of the extent to which the surge in FDI flows in the 1980s was the result of short-term factors—the strong growth of the world economy and the boom in mergers and acquisitions activity—or whether the influence of long-term factors is also changing the underlying trend.

The pattern of FDI flows in the second half of the 1980s was the result of an inter-play between short and long-term factors. Similar to domestic investment, FDI flows are strongly correlated with the growth of gross national product. The strong growth of the world economy in the 1980s boosted the growth of FDI flows from the major home countries. The mergers-and-acquisitions boom also promoted the surge in FDI. The impact of those short-term factors amplified the effect of long-term factors—policy-related developments and changes in the structure of the world economy as a result of the operations of TNCs. Policy-related developments included the liberalization of trade and investment regimes, especially in the developing countries; the spread of privatization allowing TNCs to enter previously closed industries; changes in the exchange rate between the dollar and the yen, prompting a wave of Japanese FDI; and regional integration schemes, notably the European Community, that induced considerable intra- and interregional investments. Structural factors—the size of international production and its increasingly integrated nature—also influenced the underlying trend.

These long-term factors suggest that the scope for rapid growth of FDI flows remains substantial, over and above the stimulus to those flows from a recovery in the world economy. Imbalances across countries and regions—for example, the low level of FDI flows to Japan—also indicate that there is plenty of room for further growth. The report therefore projects that FDI flows will continue to grow, although cyclical factors will result in short-term fluctuations during the 1990s.

Such projections do not fully reflect the role of TNCs in influencing world development. As discussed in the *World Investment Report 1992*, TNCs have an impact because they embody a package of potentially growth-enhancing attributes, including technology, managerial and organizational know-how, and access to international markets. These are becoming increasingly potent features of the growing integration of the world economy.

* * * * *

The ability of TNCs to contribute to international economic integration is a result both of their inherent attributes and of how they respond to the economic and policy environment in which they operate. Their strategies and structures are described in Part Two, which analyses the emergence of integrated international production by TNCs. Chapter V examines the evolution of strategies of TNCs, as firms respond to various pressures and opportunities, including improvements in information technologies, the convergence of demand patterns across countries, the intensification of competition and the opening of markets to international trade and FDI. The new strategies imply significant changes in how production is organized across borders; they have led firms to locate a wider range of their value-adding activities abroad.

The strategies of TNCs increasingly involve more complex forms of cross-border integration. Under the simplest strategies—stand-alone affiliates or multi-domestic affiliates engaged in international production while serving a single host economy or host region—affiliates have a high degree of autonomy from the parent firm. They are responsible for most of the activities that comprise their value chain, and in some instances can act as self-contained entities.

As trade barriers fall, as communications technologies improve, and as international competition intensifies, firms are turning to outsourcing for parts of their value-adding operations. They are strengthening the links with their foreign affiliates and with independent firms operating as subcontractors, licensees etc. However, these links are only for specific activities. Outsourcing is based largely upon the cost advantages of a particular host country for a particular component. The affiliate or subcontractor engaged in outsourcing cannot stand alone. It depends upon the parent firm for a number of key activities, while the parent firm depends on the affiliate for part of its overall value chain.

More recently, many TNCs have moved beyond these "simple integration" strategies. They are now treating all activities across the entire value chain as potential candidates for being performed by one or more affiliates. This new approach—"complex integration"—is made possible by huge improvements in communication and information technologies, which allow TNCs to coordinate a growing number of activities in a widening array of locations. This, in turn, changes the way in which TNCs structure their activities. In a number of instances, indeed, information technology is leading to a "re-engineering" of relationships within firms.

Complex integration is also being driven by the tendency for markets to converge. More products are sold in the same or similar form in a growing number of national markets. In addition, competition forces firms to seek cost savings and profits from all segments of their value chains. As a result, companies are arranging certain functions—research and development, procurement, accounting, data entry and processing, as well as activities for specific products or product lines, such as component manufacturing and assembly—in a way that requires close links between parent firms and foreign affiliates, among foreign affiliates themselves and between parents and affiliates and firms linked via alliances. With that type of integration, separate activities performed in international locations are valued according to how they contribute to the objectives of the firm as a whole, rather than their profitability at the host country location.

Integration is also occurring across geographical lines. Multidomestic strategies are being superseded by regional and global strategies. The institution or strengthening of regional integration agreements has helped foster regional strategies of TNCs, an issue analysed in last year's report. Some TNCs are beginning to pursue global strategies that include several major regions and cover the allocation of many elements in their value chains. Thus, activities such as research and development or procurement may be situated in an affiliate in a host country or region and linked to operations elsewhere to produce goods and services that are then sold in many markets.

Integration is proceeding at different rates across industries and functions. The cross-national division of labour has undoubtedly proceeded most rapidly in certain manufacturing industries, such as automobiles and electronics, and in services industries, such as air transport. Research and development, spurred by advances in information technologies, are increasingly spanning natural borders, both within firms and between firms through strategic alliances. But a truly global research-and-development and manufacturing system is still restricted to a relatively small number of firms. Financial management is probably the most global of the major corporate functions, stimulated by electronic transfers and the 24-hour trading day. Marketing has also taken advantage of communications technologies, but is still subject to national, regional and cultural differences in consumer tastes and habits. Such activities as data processing and software-writing can take place almost anywhere in the world. On the other hand, regulatory differences mean that accounting and legal reporting are still largely nationally based. In principle, however, virtually every corporate function can be located anywhere and carried out in an integrated manner for a corporate system as a whole. To the extent that this is the most cost-effective way of organizing production—as it seems to be—it becomes a benchmark for firms that have not yet seized this opportunity or have not yet been driven by competitive pressures to re-engineer themselves.

The strategies adopted by TNCs go together with changes in organizational structures, an issue examined in chapter VI. In particular, complex strategies have led to more complex mechanisms for organizing international production. Within firms, the decentralization of functional activities has led to a greater use of regional headquarters to manage regional activities, product headquarters located in host economies to manage the regional or global organization of particular products, and functional headquarters in host economies to manage firm-wide activities for a specific function. The dispersion of activities along the value chain leads to a dispersion of responsibility for those functions.

In addition, the growth of strategic alliances has led to cross-firm linkages geared to specific activities frequently limited to well-defined periods of time. Strategic alliances usually involve shared functional responsibility and can blur the boundaries of the firm. The multiplicity of intra- and interfirm linkages, combining horizontal and vertical lines of authority and resource flows between units and across countries, can best be described in terms of networks. The growth of such networks is a major source of the deepening of economic linkages between countries.

Although the nature of integration by TNCs has tended to become more complex, many firms continue to maintain older and simpler ways of organizing their international production. This is partly because the conditions leading towards complex integration are still evolving, and also because many of the simpler organizational forms remain useful. In addition, many firms will be unable or unwilling to adapt to changing conditions, but will continue to survive for some time.

Complex strategies, pursued with greater functional integration both within and across firms and over a wide geographical area, combined with network structures of organizing activities, describe integrated international production *at the level of the firm*. The aggregation of the activities of those TNCs that are involved in such production creates a system of integrated international production *at the level of countries*. For Japan and the United States, between a quarter and a third of private-sector productive assets are potentially under the common governance of TNCs pursuing integrated international production. For the world as a whole, this percentage may be one-third. Chapter VII considers the characteristics of this form of economic integration and its impact on developing countries.

Integration can occur at different levels. Economic growth, the reduction in tariff barriers during the post-war period and the recent spread of regional integration agreements have stimulated the exchange of goods and services among countries. This "shallow" form of integration opens many areas of an economy to the influence of international economic developments. The conditions that stimulate shallow integration also encourage TNCs to establish cross-border production systems that lead to "deep" integration, which is integration at the level of the production of goods and services as a result of complex corporate strategies and network structures.

Economic integration is an evolutionary process. Links between countries move from a relatively shallow type, to somewhat deeper (but still limited) integration through international production by TNCs pursuing multi-domestic or simple integration strategies, to links that are deeper, richer and more complex. These last describe integrated international production.

The power of TNCs in stimulating deep integration stems from their role as central organizers of a broad range of economic activities. They are helped in this by the liberalization by many host countries of regulations on foreign control of assets. In addition, the proliferation of regional integration agreements—most prominently the Single Market within the European Community—stimulates deep integration, as they increasingly contain provisions liberalizing *both* trade and FDI. Thus, these agreements, described frequently as free-trade agreement, are *also* "free-production agreements" among national economies. As a result, the division of labour across countries increases, and trade and technology flows, especially intra-firm, but also interfirm, expand.

Just how many countries will be affected by this new system remains unclear. Foreign direct investment has tended to be concentrated among the industrialized economies, particularly the Triad, with a clustering of developing countries and economies in transition around each Triad member. To some extent, this is because FDI follows trade, which is itself regionally concentrated. However, trade is more concentrated than FDI within regions. This suggests that trade may have played a prominent role in intraregional integration, whereas FDI has a greater capacity for promoting global integration. The emergence of integrated international production, which is likely to be more widely dispersed, should further strengthen the potential of FDI as a force for global integration. If that happens, trade may also begin to show more cross-regional patterns, given the linkages between FDI and trade.

The extent to which individual countries become part of, and benefit from, the emerging integrated international production system depends upon the interaction of their location-specific advantages with the changing firm-specific advantages that TNCs enjoy in the context of integrating their functional activities on a regional or global basis. The emergence of complex integration strategies and structures implies changes in the nature of the ownership, internalization and locational advantages of TNCs. In particular, ownership advantages are becoming system-wide in nature and are exploited through either intra-firm or interfirm mechanisms. The result is a broader range of opportunities for host countries to attract TNC activities, but also higher requirements in terms of human resources and infrastructure, as well as open frameworks for trade and investment. Given the differentiation that prevails as regards attributes of developing host countries, the types of investments they can attract are likely to differ; it should also be recognized that the emerging international production system may leave many developing countries largely untouched for the time being.

For those countries that do become part of the system, participation in the international division of labour is increasingly determined and coordinated by TNCs and their affiliates. The possibility to attract specific corporate functions may allow a host country to realize its own comparative advantages better. However, to reap the full benefits, developing countries must build up their indigenous human resources through education and training and their physical and technical infrastructure through investment.

*****

All these changes raise a wide range of policy issues, some of which are examined in Part Three. It deals with corporate nationality, parent-affiliate relations and responsibilities, the international allocation of the taxable income of TNCs and policy options for host countries to maximize the benefits from integrated production. As regards the first three of these issues in particular, the more sophisticated forms of division of labour between foreign affiliates and their parent firms and among foreign affiliates located in a number of countries, a certain decline of economic autonomy of the constituent parts of integrated TNC systems and a certain dispersion of authority throughout those systems are beginning to strain some traditional concepts and approaches.

Chapter VIII looks at the meaning and relevance of the concept of the nationality of corporations. The established approach in national and international law attributes nationality to corporations in accordance with certain criteria. This is done to ascertain what laws are applicable to corporations or to determine the Government that may exercise diplomatic protection on their behalf. Under conditions of integrated international production, this approach is becoming more difficult to apply and also less meaningful. Increasingly elaborate interpretations are needed to keep legal and policy prescriptions in touch with business realities. The growing use of the national treatment standard and of the broad provisions of investment-protection treaties may, in the long run, decrease the practical value of corporate nationality as a legal concept. Yet, informal understandings to clarify the issues and outline principles and procedures for avoiding or resolving conflicts could help to deal with emerging problems.

A second area where integrated international production affects the status and operations of TNCs concerns the relations between parent firms and their foreign affiliates. The traditional legal view is that each affiliate within a larger corporate group is a separate entity with its own rights and responsibilities. In reality, however, the concept of separate corporate personality does not accurately reflect the functional ties between affiliates as a business group, and can hinder the attribution of responsibility among them. In the case of a TNC, the fact that individual affiliates have their assets and operations in several countries poses further jurisdictional and procedural problems that do not confront a domestic company.

Integrated international production compounds those problems. As foreign affiliates become integrated parts of regional and global corporate systems, they may lose autonomy over both managerial and operational aspects. In such an environment, the concept of "parental responsibility" may need to be re-evaluated. A preliminary issue for legal and policy analysis, discussed in chapter IX, is how much responsibility should be shouldered by the parent.

Integrated international production can produce a network structure in which the concept of the parent firm itself takes on a different, more limited meaning. The parent may become more of a coordinating agent for certain corporate activities, which have been dispersed to regional, product-line or functional headquarters or to individual affiliates. The right thing to do may therefore be to focus on relations and responsibilities among all members within a corporate group, rather than on the parent firm or affiliate responsibility; perhaps the concept of "group responsibility" deserves further exploration.

The increasingly complex nature of corporate activities has already resulted in the adoption of group concepts in various areas of law. The practice differs from jurisdiction to jurisdiction, depending on the specific concerns to be tackled. This risks increasing the number of conflicting requirements being imposed on TNCs by States. It would be useful if those countries already experimenting with specific aspects of group concepts were to cooperate whenever some legal uniformity is possible.

Public opinion seems to be relevant to the issue of corporate responsibility. In the public's perception, the business of a parent company and that of its affiliates are typically one and the same. Also, TNCs do recognize that their reputations rest on the behaviour of affiliates as well as parents. Although parent companies have refused to accept legal responsibility for the actions of their affiliates, they have nevertheless been actively involved in out-of-court settlements of law suits brought against their affiliates, especially when environmental catastrophes are involved. Thus, while the law still wrestles with how to allocate responsibility between the TNC parent and its affiliates, solutions may be shaped by public opinion.

The deepening of TNC linkages also raises questions about where groups of associated enterprises earn taxable income, how it is distributed, and how the revenue from taxing their income is ultimately allocated among countries. These questions are discussed in chapter X.

The prevailing conventional approach to the allocation of business income for tax purposes has been to treat the parent firm and its foreign affiliates as separate and independent enterprises, and to apply the arm's-length standard for determining the allocation of taxable income from transactions involving related or unrelated parties. Given the widespread use of various intra-firm arrangements under conditions that differ from those prevailing between independent parties, a number of tests have been developed over the years aimed at determining whether related-party transactions conform with arm's length standards for tax purposes. However, with the growing complexity of the intra-firm division of labour, it is harder to identify separate costs and earnings for individual transactions and to compare them with unrelated-party transactions.

Those difficulties have led authorities to explore other approaches and methods for allocating income. Overall, the general norm appears to be to use the separate enterprise approach when comparable prices exist, and to use an apportionment approach that takes the TNC system as a whole when they do not exist. Finding satisfactory solutions matters as much to Governments as to TNCs. Governments need to prevent an erosion of their revenue base while, at the same time, providing a climate that attracts and retains FDI.

Apart from the legal and policy issues addressed in chapters VIII to X, integrated international production has also implications for the national policy framework concerning TNCs. The rapid growth of FDI during the 1980s has made Governments more aware of the benefits that FDI can bring to an economy in terms of capital, technology, management and access to established distribution networks. In the resulting competition to attract TNCs, FDI regimes in many countries have become broadly similar. In particular, differences regarding right of establishment, fair and equitable treatment, national treatment, nationalisation, compensation, dispute settlement and the repatriation of earnings become less effective as a means to capture FDI. Instead, the nature of the overall policy framework and the economic conditions of production become the key to locational decisions. Possibilities for pro-active policies in this respect are the focus of chapter XI.

There is general agreement that efficient economic institutions and a stable macroeconomic climate are preconditions for attracting FDI. Beyond that, Governments must provide efficient infrastructure and facilitate international trade exports to allow firms to bind into the international production system. However, since integrated international production involves more sophisticated corporate strategies and structures, government policies need to become more sophisticated too. In particular, since every part of the value chain can potentially be located anywhere in the world, Governments need to focus their promotional strategies on attracting those functions in which their countries have a comparative advantage. Furthermore, Governments could give more attention to reducing transactions costs for potential investors, providing post-approval support services and attracting specific TNCs of particular value to the national economy.

Last year's report suggested that policy discussions—nationally, regionally and multilaterally—might benefit from greater attention to FDI issues. As host countries, especially developing countries, seek to boost their competitive position in a world economy that is becoming integrated at the production level, their ability to dovetail their domestic economies to the strategies and structures of TNCs becomes increasingly critical. At the international level, the need to avoid "policy competition" among host countries, as each seeks to attract TNC activities, expands the range of policy issues on the international agenda and may lead to a greater concern for policy harmonization.

PART ONE

RECENT TRENDS

CHAPTER I

GLOBAL TRENDS IN FOREIGN DIRECT INVESTMENT

The stock of foreign direct investment (FDI), a measure of the productive capacity of transnational corporations (TNCs) in foreign countries, reached some $2 trillion in 1992 (table I.1). Over 170,000 foreign affiliates of some 37,000 parent firms generated approximately $5.5 trillion in world-wide sales in 1990. This compares with world exports of goods and non-factor services of $4 trillion, of which one third took the form of intra-firm trade. Annual world-wide flows of FDI grew rapidly during the second half of the 1980s (table I.2 and annex table 1), but then declined in 1991 and, based on preliminary data, again in 1992.[1] Even so, annual flows of FDI remain substantial, and have contributed to a significant growth in the global stock of FDI. Their growth will be stimulated by the further liberalization of FDI regulations that took place in 1992.

A. Trends

World-wide outflows of FDI declined in 1991 for the first time since 1982, largely because of the economic slow-down in the major developed countries. They totalled $180 billion, down from over $230 billion in 1990. The two main components of this decline were a fall in outflows from Japan (which accounted for more than one third of the world-wide decline and almost half of the decline from the five major home countries), and sizeable falls in outflows from Western Europe (accounting for about 60 per cent of the world-wide decline), largely because of the performance of France, Germany, the Netherlands and Sweden. Outflows from the United States and the United Kingdom did not change in 1990 and 1991 (table I.3). Preliminary estimates for 1992 show that world-wide outflows, including total outflows from the five major sources of FDI, have declined further.

Outflows of FDI from developing countries also declined in 1991, after several years of strong growth (table I.4), particularly from the Asian newly industrializing economies (chapter II). The share of developing countries in FDI outflows was over 3 per cent in 1986-1990, well up on their 0.7 per cent share in 1970-1975. The estimated stock of FDI from developing countries was $110 billion by the late 1980s, accounting for between 8 and 10 per cent of the world total (TCMD, 1993b).[2] Many more developing countries are now involved in FDI, and the geographical spread of their investments has also widened. It now includes developed countries, in which FDI from developing countries accounted for some 5 per cent of the total stock of inward investment in the late 1980s.

Despite the decline of world-wide FDI flows in 1991, FDI flows into developing countries continued to grow (table I.4 and annex table 1). Developing countries received over 25 per cent of all inflows in 1991, much

Table I.1. Stock of foreign direct investment, by country and region, 1987-1992
(Billions of dollars)

Region/country	Year					
	1987	*1988*	*1989*	*1990*	*1991*	*1992*[a]
A. Outward						
France	41	56	75	110	134	151
Germany, Federal Republic of	91	104	122	140	169	186
Japan	78	112	156	204	235	251
United Kingdom	135	172	208	226	244	259
United States	339	353	379	408	438	474
World	1 000	1 169	1 382	1 616	1 799	1 949
B. Inward						
Developed countries	787	920	1 088	1 260	1 369	..
Western Europe	357	419	507	616	702	..
North America	342	405	476	528	544	..
Other developed countries	88	96	105	116	123	..
Developing economies	212	241	270	300	338	..
Africa	22	25	30	32	35	..
Latin America and the Caribbean	84	95	104	114	129	..
East, South and South-East Asia	106	121	136	154	174	..
Central and Eastern Europe	..	..	..	..	..	..
World	999	1 161	1 357	1 560	1 709	..

Sources: UNCTAD, 1993e; and annex table 2.

Note: The levels of world-wide inward and outward FDI stocks should balance, in principle; however, in practice, they do not. Several reasons have been cited as the cause for the discrepancy, including differences in the treatment of unremitted branch profits between inward and outward direct investment; treatment of unrealized capital gains and losses; the recording of transactions of "offshore" enterprises; differences in the recording of reinvested earnings between inward and outward direct investment; differences in the method of collection, valuation and reporting of FDI between countries; and differences in the treatment of real estate and construction investment; and differences in the threshold definition between inward and outward direct investment (which, however, has not been found to be a significant source of the discrepancy).

a Estimated.

Table I.2. World-wide foreign direct investment and selected economic indicators, 1991, and growth rates for 1981-1985, 1986-1990 and 1991
(Billions of dollars and percentage)

Indicator	Value at current prices, 1991	Annual growth[a] (Percentage) 1981-1985	1986-1990	1991
All countries[b]				
Foreign-direct-investment outflows	180	4	24	-22
Foreign-direct-investment stock	1 800	7	16	11
Sales of transnational corporations	5 500[c]	2[d]	15	..
Gross domestic product at market prices	21 500	2	9	3
Gross domestic investment	4 900	0.5	10	3
Exports of goods and non-factor services	4 000	-0.2	12	2
Royalties and fees receipts	34	0.1	19	4
Developed countries				
Foreign-direct-investment outflows	177	3	24	-21
Gross domestic product at market prices	17 200	3	10	5
Gross domestic investment	3 800	2	11	5
Exports of goods and non-factor services	3 000	2	12	1
Royalty and fees receipts	33	0.2	19	5
Developing economies				
Foreign-direct-investment inflows	39	-4	17	24
Gross domestic product at market prices	3 400	0.2	8	-2
Gross domestic investment	800	-3	9	-2
Exports of goods and non-factor services	930	-3	13	4
Royalty and fees payments	2	-1	23	-26

Sources: UNCTAD, Programme on Transnational Corporations, based on International Monetary Fund (IMF), balance-of-payments tape, retrieved in February 1993; World Bank, 1992c; and unpublished data provided by the World Bank, International Economics Department.

a Growth rates in all tables in this volume were calculated at an annual compounded rate, derived from a semi-logarithmic regression equation.
b Data on developed and developing economies do not equal those for all countries because of the inclusion of Central and Eastern Europe in the item on "all countries".
c For 1990.
d For 1982-1985.

more than their share in 1986-1991 and equal to their share in the first half of the 1980s. In 1992, their inflows of FDI have increased further, to an estimated $40 billion. All parts of the developing world benefited from this increase. The strong growth of inflows to East, South and South-East Asia persisted. Sustained profitability of investments in South and South-East Asia is expected to result in further growth of inflows in the 1990s, particularly from Japan, as the region develops an integrated production structure.[3] There has been a substantial increase in inflows to Latin America and the Caribbean as well. Transnational corporations have been attracted to that region by economic recovery, liberalization in FDI policies and, in many countries, privatization opportunities. Privatization, in fact, is increasing opportunities throughout the developing world (box I.1). Africa too, had an increase in FDI inflows in 1991, largely from mining companies. Despite this widespread growth,

Table I.3. Outflows of foreign direct investment from the five major home countries, 1987-1992
(Billions of dollars and percentage)

Country	*1987*	*1988*	*1989*	*1990*	*1991*	*1992*[a]	*1981-1985*	*1986-1990*	*1991*	*1992*	*1981-1985*	*1986-1990*	*1991*	*1992*
	(Billions of dollars)						*Share in total (percentage)*				*Growth rate (percentage)*			
France	9	14	19	35	24	17[b]	6	10	13	11	-17	45	-31	-29
Germany, Federal Republic of	9	13	18	28	21	17	9	9	12	11	13	27	-24	-19
Japan[c]	20	34	44	48	31	16[b]	11	19	17	11	8	32	-36	-48
United Kingdom	31	37	35	18	18	15	19	17	10	10	-2	2	2	-17
United States[d]	26	14	26	29	29	36	23	13	16	24	-5	16	-0.4	24
Total	95	112	142	158	123	101	68	68	67	67	.01	23	-22	-18

Sources: UNCTAD, Programme on Transnational Corporations, based on TCMD, 1993c; and IMF, balance-of-payments tape, retrieved in February 1993.

a Based on preliminary estimates.
b Estimate based on outflows in the first three quarters of 1992.
c Data for Japan do not include reinvested earnings.
d Excluding outflows to the finance (except banking), insurance and real estate industries of the Netherlands Antilles. Also excludes currency-translation adjustments.

Table I.4. Inflows and outflows of foreign direct investment, 1987-1992
(Billions of dollars and percentage)

Country	*1987*	*1988*	*1989*	*1990*	*1991*	*1992*[a]	*1981-1985*	*1986-1990*	*1991*	*1992*	*1981-1985*	*1986-1990*	*1991*	*1992*
	(Billions of dollars)						*Share in total (percentage)*				*Growth rate (percentage)*			
Developed countries														
Inflows	109	132	167	172	108	86	74	83	74	68	0.2	24	-37	-20
Outflows	132	162	203	225	177	145	98	97	97	97	3	24	-21	-18
Developing economies														
Inflows	25	30	29	31	39	40	26	17	26	32	-4	14	21	3
Outflows	2	6	10	9	5	5	2	3	3	3	33	45	-39	0
All countries														
Inflows	135	162	196	203	149	126	100	100	100	100	-0.9	22	-27	-15
Outflows	135	168	213	234	183	150	100	100	100	100	4	24	-22	-18

Sources: UNCTAD, Programme on Transnational Corporations, based on UNCTAD, 1993c; 1993d, 1993e, UNCTC, 1992b; TCMD, 1993c; TCMD and ECE, 1992; World Bank Group, 1992c; IMF, balance-of-payments tape, retrieved on 17 February 1993, and OECD estimates.

a Based on preliminary estimates.

Box I.1. Foreign direct investment and privatization

The change in government attitudes to TNCs is best illustrated by what has happened to the nationalization of foreign affiliates and the privatization of state-owned enterprises.

The last significant wave of expropriations of FDI began in the mid-1960s and reached its peak in the early 1970s, with the actions of OPEC countries (figure 1). It was driven largely by two beliefs. First, that control over natural resources and key industries is a prerequisite for greater independence in managing national economic development. And secondly, that control is best achieved by public ownership.

By the mid-1970s, these beliefs were starting to fade, and expropriations were declining. Most developing countries were heavily in debt, and needed foreign capital; and their state-owned enterprises were performing badly. In many countries, FDI started to be seen as a means to acquire capital, technology, management and other skills from abroad. It also started to be seen as a natural marriage partner in a privatization programme.

Although privatization has been embraced throughout the world, it has taken different forms in different countries. Developed countries, with established capital markets and more reliable methods of valuation, have gone for large offerings. Developing countries have favoured a larger number of smaller privatizations.

All sectors have seen some privatization but industrial enterprises, particularly in developing countries, have been the most popular target to date. This pattern may soon give way to a greater emphasis on service companies. In developed countries, a willingness to canvas new ways of delivering "public goods" is opening more capital-intensive service activities, such as public utilities and telecommunications, to privatization. And many developing countries and formerly centrally planned economies, which had historically neglected their service industries are now seeking rapid modernization, in which privatization will probably have a central role.

A comprehensive picture of TNC participation in worldwide privatization is difficult to obtain. However, the involvement appears strongest in Western Europe and Latin America, often through joint ventures with domestic firms. In Central and Eastern Europe, where markets are close by, TNCs have taken a prominent and, oftentimes, strategic role.

It would be wrong, however, to rule out a possible reversal of this trend. As the influence of short-term imperatives recedes, the desire of Governments to regain greater control over decision-making could return. This is particularly likely if economic growth remains weak, FDI proves a disappointment in transferring technology and skills, or if world markets are closed by protectionism. Policy makers and TNCs must ensure that FDI, including investments acquired through privatization, fully contributes to sustained long-term development.

Figure 1. Changing moods: the number of nationalization acts and privatization activities, 1960-1992[a]

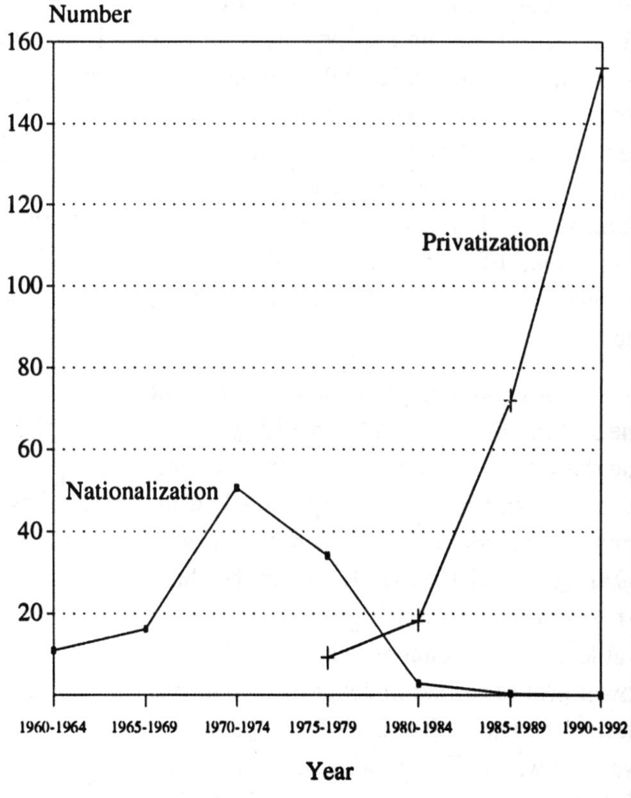

Sources: UNCTAD, Programme on Transnational Corporations, data bank; Minor, 1993a and 1993b; and the World Bank, 1992b, chapter 7.

a Nationalization numbers refer to the average number of acts per year during the period indicated. The number of privatization activities refers to the average number of firms privatized per year during the period indicated.

the distribution of FDI flows to developing countries has not changed. The 10 largest host countries continue to receive two thirds of all inflows (annex table 4). Foreign direct investment flows to the least developed countries grew by 12 per cent in 1991 to $183 million—less than a fifth of the inflows to Hong Kong.

Foreign direct investment in Central and Eastern Europe increased during 1991 and the first half of 1992 to reach an estimated $12 billion in total capital commitments. These investments are attracted by large local markets and the proximity to Western Europe, and helped by a further liberalization of their FDI regimes. The region's main drawbacks continue to be the decline in GDP and the difficulties of the transition from centrally planned to market economies. However, with developing countries, FDI is unevenly distributed among the countries of Central and Eastern Europe.

Geographical patterns aside, one of the striking features of FDI in 1991 was that the share of FDI financed through new equity capital and inter company loans had increased considerably between the periods 1981-1985 and 1986-1991, while the share of reinvested earnings has declined (table I.5). This change may be due to the lower profits earned in developed countries during the late 1980s. Significantly, too, inward flows of FDI to these countries owed little to reinvested earnings in 1990-1991 (figure I.1), a period marked by somewhat lower rates of return on business capital and negative reinvested earnings on FDI.[4] Generally, the longstanding foreign inves-

Table I.5. Share of reinvested earnings in outward foreign-direct-investment flows, 1981-1985, 1986-1990 and 1991
(Percentage)

Home country	*1981-1985*	*1986-1990*	*1991*
Australia	23	32	35
Finland	-19	5	-
Germany, Federal Republic of	5	13	17
Israel	10	33	11
Netherlands	29	21	-
New Zealand	96	43	77
Sweden	25	19	18
Switzerland	61[a]	35	20
United Kingdom	50	45	68
United States	116[b]	71	61
Total, above	60	39	38

Sources: UNCTAD, Programme on Transnational Corporations, based on TCMD, 1993c; IMF, balance-of-payments tape, retrieved in February 1993.

a For 1983-1984.

b A share higher than 100 per cent is obtained when one of the other two components of FDI flows (equity capital or intra-company loans) is negative.

Figure I.1. Share of reinvested earnings in inward foreign-direct-investment flows, 1982-1991
(Percentage)

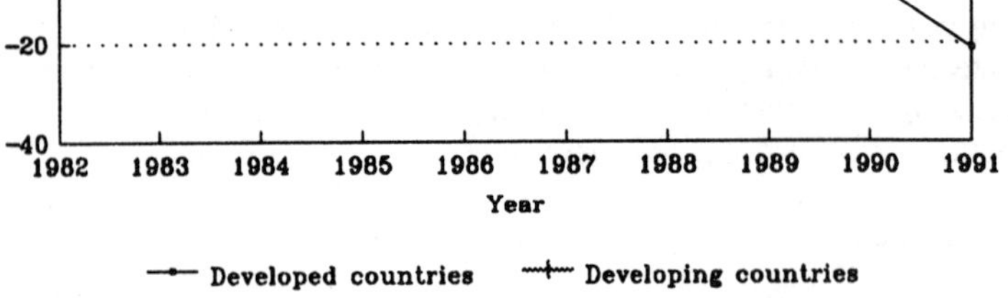

Source: UNCTAD, Programme on Transnational Corporations, based on UNCTAD, 1993e.

tors—such as the United Kingdom and the United States—have a higher proportion of reinvested earnings in their FDI outflows than do the newer home countries.

In terms of inflows, reinvested earnings are a considerably larger component of FDI in developing countries than in developed countries (figure I.1). In the latter group, inward FDI is financed overwhelmingly from funds brought in from abroad, whereas in developing countries, FDI depends more on profits earned there.[5] It is not clear whether that contrast is due to the difference in profits earned in two regions or to different rates of profit repatriation, dependent, *inter alia*, on policies of host countries. If majority-owned foreign affiliates of non-bank United States parent firms are any guide, they earned much higher profit rates in developing countries: 8 per cent in the period 1983-1990, compared with 5 per cent in developed countries (United States Department of Commerce, 1992b and various earlier issues).[6] At any rate, the share of reinvested earnings in the FDI inflows of both developed and developing countries in the early 1990s have declined from their levels a decade earlier; and other components of FDI (equity capital or intra-company loans) constitute the greater part of FDI inflows.

B. The universe of transnational corporations

The number of TNCs has been increasing steadily. Those that are based in 14 major developed home countries have more than tripled during the past two decades, from slightly more than 7,000 in 1969 (DESA, 1973) to nearly 24,000 in 1990.[7] Companies from developed countries continue to dominate the TNC universe, though a growing number of firms headquartered in developing countries and some firms from Central and Eastern Europe joined them especially during the 1980s. Furthermore, even though the share of foreign assets controlled by the largest firms is still very high, the role of small and medium-size enterprises is significant and growing.

1. Size and characteristics

(a) *Parent transnational corporations*

According to estimates based largely on national official sources of almost all developed countries and a number of other countries, the number of parent TNCs in the world at the beginning of the 1990s was almost 37,000, controlling some 170,000 foreign affiliates (table I.6).[8] This 37,000 figure covers only those firms that have equity stakes in enterprises abroad, of either more than 50 per cent (wholly- and majority-owned foreign affiliates or subsidiaries, and branches that are legally part of the parent firm), or between 10 and 50 per cent (minority-owned foreign affiliates, or associates). It does not, therefore, include firms that control assets abroad through various non-equity ties (for example, management contracts, transfer-of-technology contracts, sub-contracting agreements, franchising) and that are linked with other firms through strategic alliances. No data are available on those, but estimates are that strategic alliances number in the thousands and subcontracting agreements alone in the hundreds of thousands (Hagedoorn, 1992; Dunning, 1992).[9] The estimate of 37,000 does, however, include firms that are themselves affiliates of parent TNCs based in other countries.[10] Overall, even if

Table I.6. Number of parent transnational corporations and foreign affiliates, by area and country, early 1990s
(Number)

Area/economy	*Parent corporations based in country*	*Foreign affiliates located in country*[a]	*Year*
Developed countries	33 500	81 800	
Australia	1 036	695	1992
Austria	679	2 221	1990
Belgium and Luxembourg	96	1 121	1978
Canada	1 308[b]	5 874	1991
Denmark	800	647[c]	1992
Finland	1 300	1 000	1992
France	2 056	6 870	1990
Germany, Federal Republic of	6 984	11 821	1990
Greece	..	798	1981
Iceland	14[d]	28	1991
Ireland	30	956	1992
Italy	263	1 438	1992
Japan	3 529[e]	3 150	1992
Netherlands	1 426	2 014	1992
New Zealand	201	1 078	1991
Norway	1 321	2 854[f]	1990
Portugal	684	6 680	1992
South Africa	..	1 884	1978
Spain	744	6 232[g]	1992
Sweden	3 529	2 400	1991
Switzerland	3 000	4 000	1985
Turkey	..	267	1989
United Kingdom	1 500[h]	2 900[i]	1991
United States	3 000[j]	14 900[k]	1990
Developing economies[l]	2 700	71 300	
Brazil	566	7 110[c]	1992
China	379	15 966[f]	1989
Colombia	..	1 041	1987
Hong Kong	500[m]	2 828	1991
India	187	926[f]	1991
Indonesia	..	1 064	1988
Mexico	..	8 953	1989
Oman	..	1 489	1989
Pakistan	57	560[g]	1988
Philippines	..	1 952	1987
Republic of Korea	1 049	3 671	1991
Saudi Arabia	..	1 461	1989
Singapore	..	10 709	1986
Taiwan Province of China	..	5 733	1990
Former Yugoslavia	112	3 900	1991

/.....

(Table I.6, cont'd.)

Area/economy	*Parent corporations based in country*	*Foreign affiliates located in country*[a]	*Year*
Central and Eastern Europe[n]	400	21 800	
Bulgaria	26	114[b]	1991
Commonwealth of Independent States[o]	68[e]	3 900	1992
Former Czechoslovakia	26[e]	800	1992
Hungary	66[e]	2 400	1992
Poland	58[e]	3 800	1992
Romania	20[e]	6 900	1992
World	36 600	174 900	

Sources: UNCTAD, Programme on Transnational Corporations, based on UNCTC, 1992b; TCMD, 1993c; TCMD and ECE, 1992; and national official and secondary sources.

a Represents the number of affiliates in the country shown.
b For 1990.
c For 1986.
d For 1989.
e For 1991.
f For 1988.
g For 1987.
h Represents at total of 24 bank parents in 1991, and about 1,500 non-bank, non-oil and non-insurance concerns with direct investments above £20 million in 1981.
i Represents a total of 2,419 manufacturing affiliates in 1990 and 518 bank affiliates in 1992.
j Represents a total of 2,183 non-bank parent corporations in 1990 and 89 bank parent corporations in 1989 with at least one foreign affiliate whose assets, sales or net income exceeded $3 million, and 723 non-bank and bank parent corporations in 1989 whose affiliate(s) had assets, sales and net income under $3 million.
k Represents a total of 10,142 non-bank affiliates in 1990 and 467 bank affiliates in 1987 whose assets, sales or net income exceeded $1 million, and 4,336 bank and non-bank affiliates in 1987 with assets, sales and net income under $1 million. Each affiliate represents a fully consolidated United States business enterprise, which may consist of a number of individual companies. 10,142 non-bank affiliates represented 31,388 companies in 1990.
l Includes the largest host countries and countries for which data on parent corporations could be obtained.
m For 1982.
n Data for affiliates are estimated using number of joint-venture registrations and available information on the number of registrations, , that are operational.
o Relates to the whole of the economic territory of the former USSR.

only ultimate parent companies are counted, along with corporations with non-equity ties abroad, the world-wide total most probably exceeds 37,000.

Over 90 per cent of TNCs originate in developed countries. About 1 per cent of parent corporations are based in Central and Eastern Europe, and the remainder are headquartered in developing countries. That pattern reflects decades of capital accumulation, economic growth and technological change that have strengthened the competitive advantages of developed-country firms. The five major home countries—France, Germany, Japan, the United Kingdom and the United States—are home to over half the developed-country total. Among developing countries, parent TNCs are based mainly in the newly industrializing and larger economies. Judging from the data for Japan and the United States, nearly 60 per cent of all parent TNCs are in manufacturing, 37 per cent are in services, and 3 per cent in the primary sector.

(b) Foreign affiliates

The world-wide total of foreign affiliates of TNCs is estimated at over 170,000.[11] Developed countries are host to more than 46 per cent of them, with the five major home countries—France, the Federal Republic of Germany, Japan, the United Kingdom and the United States—hosting almost half of that share. Some 41 per cent of foreign affiliates are in developing host countries, and 13 per cent in Central and Eastern Europe.

Below the surface of these aggregates, the pattern is mixed and shifting. For example, the number of foreign affiliates of United States TNCs decreased from 33,650 to 27,086 between 1982 and 1989; employment in foreign affiliates also decreased slightly during the same period, even though both United States TNCs' assets abroad and total United States FDI increased. This suggests that United States TNCs bolstered their equity stakes in foreign affiliates, as well as the capital-intensity of their foreign operations (United States Department of Commerce, 1985; 1992a). For the Federal Republic of Germany, by contrast, the rapid increase in its FDI stock and in the foreign assets of German TNCs was accompanied by an increase in the number of foreign affiliates of German TNCs from 14,657 in 1984 to 19,352 in 1990, as well as a rise in employment in foreign affiliates of 34 per cent (Rutter, 1992; Deutsche Bundesbank, various issues; Statisches Bundesant, 1991). In other words, FDI from the Federal Republic of Germany was used partly to increase equity and control in existing foreign affiliates, as well as to expand production through establishing new affiliates.

By sector, services account for the bulk of foreign affiliates. Judging by the distribution of TNCs from the Federal Republic of Germany, Japan and the United States, services affiliates make up around 60 per cent of the total, compared with 36 per cent for manufacturing and only a small proportion in the primary sector (table I.7). As discussed in chapter III, this pattern reflects the increasing importance of services in the world economy and in FDI.

2. Concentration

Although the universe of TNCs is large, it is also highly concentrated. Judging from data for selected home countries, roughly 1 per cent of parent TNCs own about half of the stock of FDI of their home countries (table I.8). Even so, small and medium-size enterprises do play some role. Data for the United States and Japan in the 1980s show a mixed picture (table I.9); but other figures for Japan indicate that the share of small and medium-size enterprises in its total FDI outflows increased from 6 per cent in the mid-1970s to 15 per cent in the mid-1980s (Fujita, 1993). This may mean that larger TNCs from Japan, with more extensive overseas operations, invest more in existing affiliates, while small and medium-size enterprises tend to expand by setting up new affiliates.

3. The top 100 transnational corporations

Since TNC activity is so concentrated among relatively few companies, it is instructive to look at them in some detail. The largest 100 TNCs (excluding those in banking and finance), *ranked by the size of their foreign assets*, had about $3.2 trillion in global assets in 1990, of which an estimated $1.2 trillion was outside their own home countries (table I.10), and accounted for about one third of the world-wide outward stock of FDI, based on available firm-level FDI data on 53 of the 100 largest companies. These 53 firms from France, the Federal Republic of Germany, the Netherlands and the United States accounted for roughly $280 billion in world-wide FDI, about one third of the combined outward FDI stock of their home countries. Assuming that other home countries have a similar FDI concentration, then the largest 100 TNCs account for about one third of the world-wide FDI stock.

Even within this group of the 100 largest TNCs, there is a notable concentration of foreign activity. The five major home countries (France, Federal Republic of Germany, Japan, the United Kingdom and the United States) together account for almost three quarters of the TNCs in the top 100. United States corporations account for the largest number of firms (27), as well as one third of the foreign assets. This pre-eminence can be traced back to an early lead in FDI after the Second World War, as well as rapid technical progress and the large and growing home market in the United States, all of which helped United States corporations to compete abroad. The foreign assets of another third of the top 100's foreign assets are controlled by firms from France, Japan and the United Kingdom. The largest ten TNCs controlled over one quarter of the group's total assets, and a third of its foreign assets in 1990 (table I.11); the same is broadly true of foreign and total sales.

Table I.7. Distribution of outward affiliates of major investing countries, by sector
(Number and percentage)

			Sectors			
Country	*Year*		*All*	*Primary*	*Manufacturing*	*Services*
Germany, Federal Republic of[a]	1984	Number	14 657	558	4 936	9 163
		Percentage	100	4	34	63
	1990	Number	19 352	422	5 729	13 201
		Percentage	100	2	30	68
Japan[b]	1980	Number	3 567	194	1 587	1 786
		Percentage	100	5	44	50
	1990	Number	7 986	194	3 408	4 384
		Percentage	100	2	43	55
United States[c]	1982	Number	18 339	995	7 005	10 339
		Percentage	100	5	38	56
	1989	Number	18 899	785	7 552	10 562
		Percentage	100	4	40	56

Sources: UNCTAD, Programme on Transnational Corporations, based on Deutsche Bundesbank, 1992, Japan, Ministry of International Trade and Industry, 1983 and 1992a; United States Department of Commerce, 1985 and 1992a.

a Includes only affiliates whose balance sheet total exceeds DM 500,000.
b Includes only non-bank affiliates that responded to a questionnaire on FDI and that continued their foreign operations.
c Includes only affiliates whose assets, sales or income exceeded $3 million.

Table I.8. Concentration of ownership of foreign affiliate assets or foreign direct investment
(Number and percentage)

Country	*Year*	*Number of parent companies*	*Percentage of parent companies*	*Percentage of total foreign affiliate assets*	*Percentage of total foreign direct investment*
Austria	1990	41	6	65[a]	..
		95	14	84[a]	..
		312	46	98[a]	..
Brazil	1991	11	2	..	35[b]
		28	5	..	52[b]
Finland	1991	80	6	..	90
France	1990	10	0.5	..	25
		32	1.6	..	50
		223	10.8	..	90
Germany, Federal Republic of[c]	1990	10	0.1	32	35
		20	0.3	42	45
		50	0.7	69	58
	1985	27	0.5	..	50
	1976	31	0.9	..	50
Italy	1989	3[d]	..	51[e]	..
		5[d]	..	76[e]	..
		10[d]	..	84[e]	..
Netherlands[f]	1990	10	1.0	..	45
		100	9.5	..	77
New Zealand	1990-1991	12	6	..	97[b]
Spain	1991	..	8	..	92
Sweden	1991	18	0.5	51	..
		51	1.5	75	..
United States[g]	1990	22	1	45	..
		44	2	57	..
		109	5	75	..
		218	10	86	..
		437	20	94	..
		546	25	96	..
		1 091	50	99	..

Source: UNCTAD, Programme on Transnational Corporations, based on unpublished data from national and other official sources.

a Represents percentage of affiliate nominal capital.
b Represents the share of FDI flows, not stock.
c Concentration ratios for TNCs with overseas affiliates whose balance sheet total exceeded DM 500,000.
d Number of financial or holding company parent groups.
e Refers to sales.
f Concentration ratios for TNCs with participation of F1.1 million or more.
g Concentration ratios for non-bank parents of non-bank affiliates whose assets, sales or income exceeded $3 million.

As for industrial distribution, 12 petroleum companies control over $250 billion in foreign assets, 21 per cent of the total of the top 100. The petroleum industry has always involved large resource-seeking foreign investors. On the other hand, automotive companies have expanded abroad in search of lower labour costs and to get around trade barriers. The petroleum, automotive, chemical and pharmaceutical industries together account for over half of the foreign assets of the largest 100 TNCs. However, this does not necessarily mean that they are the most "transnationalized" industries of all. The list does not include financial firms (especially banks and insurance companies), because of difficulties in comparing their assets and sales figures with those of other firms. In addition, there are many other industries where the largest companies are highly transnationalized; however, owing to the size of the industries and the firms in them, they are not large enough to be included in this list.

Table I.9. Small and medium-size transnational corporations and their affiliates as a proportion of all transnational corporations from Japan and the United States

(Percentage)

Item	*Japan*[a]		*United States*[b]	
	1980	*1990*	*1982*	*1990*
Share of small and medium-size TNCs in total for all TNCs in terms of:				
Number of parent firms[c]	31.0	21.2	23.5	28.3
Number of affiliates	..	..	5.2	7.1
Assets of affiliates	..	..	1.7	4.0
Number of new equity investments[d]	41.3	53.8[e]	..	..

Sources: UNCTAD, Programme on Transnational Corporations, based on unpublished data from the United States Department of Commerce; Japan Ministry of International Trade and Industry, 1983 and 1992a; Small and Medium Enterprise Agency.

a Data do not cover banking and insurance industries. The definition of small and medium-size enterprises adopted by the Small and Medium Enterprise Agency of Japan is as follows: in wholesale trade, enterprises with capital less than 30 million yen and employment less than 100; in retail trade and other services, enterprises with capital less than 100 million yen and employment less than 50; and in other industries, enterprises with capital less than 100 million yen and employment less than 300.

b United States small and medium-size TNCs are non-bank parents of non-bank affiliates with affiliate assets, sales or income greater than $3 million with fewer than 500 employees at the parent firm.

c Data on Japanese small and medium-size parent TNCs, obtained from the Ministry of International Trade and Industry, are defined only in terms of the capital criteria in footnote a.

d New equity investments refer to investments in initial capital acquisition (thus excluding additional investments by the same company in the same affiliate) and establishment of new subsidiaries. Loan investments, which are an important component of FDI, are also excluded.

e For 1989.

C. The policy framework

Several changes in the policy framework for TNCs during 1992 may well facilitate the future growth of FDI. At the multilateral level, the most significant changes were the adoption of the Guidelines on the Treatment of Foreign Direct Investment by the World Bank (World Bank Group, 1992b), whose underlying principle is to encourage the admission of foreign investors, and various developments in the United Nations, which aim to protect the environment.[12]

The Guidelines on the Treatment of Foreign Direct Investment were submitted to the Development Committee of the Boards of Governors of the World Bank and the International Monetary Fund on 21 September 1992, after consultations with interested Governments, other international organizations, business groups and international law associations. The Development Committee decided to bring them to the attention of the members of the World Bank as "useful parameters in the admission and treatment of private foreign investment in their

Table I.10. The largest 100 non-financial transnational corporations, ranked by foreign assets, 1990
(Billions of dollars and number of employees)

Rank	Corporation	Country	Industry[a]	Foreign assets	Total assets	Foreign sales	Total sales	Foreign employment	Total employment
1	Royal Dutch Shell	United Kingdom/ Netherlands	Petroleum refining	69.2[b]	106.4	47.1[b]	106.5	99 000	137 000
2	Ford	United States	Motor vehicles and parts	55.2	173.7	47.3	97.7	188 904	370 383
3	GM	United States	Motor vehicles and parts	52.6	180.2	37.3	122.0	251 130	767 200
4	Exxon	United States	Petroleum refining	51.6	87.7	90.5	115.8	65 000	104 000
5	IBM	United States	Computers	45.7	87.6	41.9	69.0	167 868	373 816
6	British Petroleum	United Kingdom	Petroleum refining	31.6	59.3	43.3	59.3	87 200	118 050
7	Asea Brown Boveri	Switzerland	Industrial and farm equipment	26.9	30.2	25.6[d]	26.7	200 177	215 154
8	Nestle	Switzerland	Food	..[c]	28.0	35.8	36.5	192 070	199 021
9	Philips Electronics	Netherlands	Electronics	23.3	30.6	28.8[d]	30.8	217 149	272 800
10	Mobil	United States	Petroleum refining	22.3	41.7	44.3	57.8	27 593	67 300
11	Unilever	United Kingdom/ Netherlands	Food	..[c]	24.7	16.7[b]	39.6	261 000	304 000
12	Matsushita Electric	Japan	Electronics	..[c]	62.0	21.0	46.8	67 000	210 848
13	Fiat	Italy	Motor vehicles and parts	19.5	66.3	20.7[d]	47.5	66 712	303 238
14	Siemens	Germany	Electronics	..[c]	43.1	14.7[d]	39.2	143 000	373 000
15	Sony	Japan	Electronics	..[c]	32.6	12.7	20.9	62 100	112 900
16	Volkswagen	Germany	Motor vehicles and parts	..[c]	42.0	25.5[d]	42.1	95 934	268 744
17	Elf Aquitaine	France	Petroleum refining	17.0	42.6	11.4[d]	32.4	33 957	90 000
18	Mitsubishi	Japan	Trading	16.7	73.8	45.5	129.3	..	32 417
19	GE	United States	Electronics	16.5	153.9	8.3	57.7	62 580	298 000
20	Du Pont	United States	Chemicals	16.0	38.9	17.5	37.8	36 400	124 900
21	Alcatel Alsthom	France	Electronics	15.3	38.2	13.0	26.6	112 966	205 500
22	Mitsui	Japan	Trading	15.0	60.8	48.1	136.2	..	9 094
23	News Corporation	Australia	Publishing and printing	14.6	20.7	4.6	5.7	..	38 432
24	Bayer	Germany	Chemicals	14.2	25.4	20.3	25.9	80 000	171 000
25	B.A.T. Industries	United Kingdom	Tobacco	..[c]	48.1	16.5[d]	22.9	..	217 373
26	FerruzziMontedison	Italy	Food	13.4	30.8	8.0	14.0	22 300	44 949
27	Rhone-Poulenc	France	Chemicals	13.0	21.3	11.1	14.4	50 525	91 571
28	BASF	Germany	Chemicals	..[c]	24.3	19.1[d]	29.0	46 059	134 647
29	Toyota	Japan	Motor vehicles and parts	12.8	55.1	24.8	60.1	11 326	96 849
30	Philip Morris	United States	Food	12.5	46.6	10.5	51.2	66 000	168 000
31	Hoechst	Germany	Chemicals	..[c]	22.9	20.7[d]	27.8	82 169	172 890
32	Roche Holding	Switzerland	Pharmaceuticals	..[c]	17.8	6.7[d]	7.0	41 802	52 685
33	Ciba-Geigy	Switzerland	Chemicals	..[c]	20.5	7.9[bd]	14.3	69 702	94 141
34	Hanson	United Kingdom	Building materials	11.1	27.6	6.3	13.4	52 000	80 000
35	Michelin	France	Rubber and plastics	..[c]	14.9	9.1	11.5	111 533	140 829
36	Dow Chemical	United States	Chemicals	10.9	24.0	10.3	19.8	28 612	62 080
37	Total	France	Petroleum refining	..[c]	20.6	17.1	23.6	23 824	46 024
38	Amoco	United States	Petroleum refining	10.6	32.2	8.5	28.0	10 560	54 524
39	ICI	United Kingdom	Chemicals	10.5	20.8	17.7	23.0	78 400	132 100
40	C. Itoh	Japan	Trading	10.5	58.4	48.3	151.1	3 620	9 643
41	Grand Metropolitan	United Kingdom	Food	10.4	17.7	9.7	16.0	..	138 149
42	Saint-Gobain	France	Building materials	9.9	17.6	7.8	12.7	69 651	104 987
43	Volvo	Sweden	Motor vehicles and parts	9.7	18.1	12.2[d]	14.1	20 346	68 800
44	Petrofina	Belgium	Petroleum refining	..[c]	12.3	5.7	17.4	..	23 800
45	Generale Des Eaux	France	Construction	9.0[g]	27.7	5.5[d]	21.5	55 983	173 000
46	Nissan Motor	Japan	Motor vehicles and parts	..[c]	36.4	16.8	35.7	30 050	129 546
47	RTZ	United Kingdom	Mining and crude-oil production	8.4	9.3	7.3	9.3	58 153	73 612
48	Chevron	United States	Petroleum refining	8.4	35.1	9.8	38.6	10 953	54 208
49	Solvay	Belgium	Chemicals	8.1[g]	8.9	7.2	7.7	36 578	45 671
50	Xerox	United States	Scientific and photographic equipment	8.0	31.5	7.5	18.4	..	110 000
51	Texaco	United States	Petroleum refining	7.8	26.0	18.0	40.9	..	39 199
52	Electrolux	Sweden	Electronics	7.8	11.7	11.9[d]	13.9	123 337	150 892
53	ITT	United States	Diversified services	7.5	49.0	6.5	20.6	..	114 000
54	Daimler-Benz	Germany	Transport and communication	..[c]	45.1	30.2[d]	52.9	73 381	376 785
55	Renault	France	Motor vehicles and parts	7.4	23.5	12.2	30.2	42 492	157 378
56	Thomson	France	Electronics	7.4	20.5	9.8[d]	13.9	55 225	105 460
57	Thomson Corporation	Canada	Publishing and printing	7.4	7.9	4.8	5.3	38 700	44 800

/.....

(Table I.10, cont'd.)

Rank	*Corporation*	*Country*	*Industry*[a]	*Foreign assets*	*Total assets*	*Foreign sales*	*Total sales*	*Foreign employment*	*Total employment*
58	Stora	Sweden	Forestry products	7.3	15.0	8.9[d]	11.1	47 544	69 691
59	Pechiney	France	Metals	7.3	14.2	8.6	14.2	39 458	70 965
60	olderbank	Switzerland	Building materials	6.9[g]	7.4	3.4[d]	3.8	27 754	29 557
61	Alcan Aluminium	Canada	Metal products	6.8	10.6	7.6	8.9	41 040	55 500
62	Sandoz	Switzerland	Pharmaceuticals	6.7	10.1	8.7[d]	9.0	42 449	52 400
63	Honda	Japan	Motor vehicles and parts	6.7	18.0	16.1	26.9	23 760[e]	79 200
64	Toshiba	Japan	Electronics	..[c]	39.2	10.3	33.3	27 000	162 000
65	ENI	Italy	Petroleum refining	6.5	60.3	15.6	41.8	22 131	130 745
66	Procter & Gamble	United States	Soaps and cosmetics	6.5	18.5	9.6	24.1	45 278	92 625
67	Eastman Kodak	United States	Scientific and photographic equipment	6.4	24.1	8.2	18.9	54 100	134 450
68	Marubeni	Japan	Trading	6.3	54.9	38.1	131.0	3 500	9 905
69	Glaxo Holdings	United Kingdom	Pharmaceuticals	6.1	8.6	5.1[d]	5.7	20 934	33 225
70	Fletcher Challenge	New Zealand	Forestry products	5.9	10.4	4.9	7.3	..	40 000
71	Nissho Iwai	Japan	Trading	..[c]	38.8	27.5	94.4	2 073	7 350
72	Seagram	Canada	Beverages	5.7	10.2	4.6[d]	4.8	9 328	17 600
73	Chrysler	United States	Motor vehicles and parts	5.7	46.4	8.5	30.6	30 820	109 943
74	Tenneco	United States	Industrial and farm equipment	5.6	19.0	4.6	14.5	..	92 000
75	Usinor-Sacilor	France	Metals	..[c]	20.8	7.3	17.6	31 025	97 300
76	Hewlett-Packard	United States	Computers	5.3	11.4	7.2	13.2	35 000[f]	92 200
77	Akzo	Netherlands	Chemicals	5.3	8.1	6.3	9.5	47 700	69 800
78	Smithkline Beecham	United Kingdom	Pharmaceuticals	5.2	7.5	7.4	8.5	46 413	57 300
79	Bridgestone	Japan	Rubber and plastics	..[c]	13.0	7.6	13.2	56 000	87 234
80	Alcoa	United States	Metals	5.1	11.4	4.3	10.7	27 391	63 700
81	Digital Equipment	United States	Computers	5.1	11.7	7.1	12.9	..	124 000
82	Olivetti	Italy	Computers	5.0	12.4	4.8[d]	7.5	26 690	53 679
83	SKF	Sweden	Metal products	5.0	5.5	4.5[d]	4.7	48 075	53 995
84	L'air Liquide	France	Chemicals	4.9	7.1	2.9	5.4	17 000	28 000
85	Atlantic Richfield	United States	Petroleum refining	4.9	23.9	3.9	18.8	..	27 300
86	GTE	United States	Telecommunications	4.9	33.8	3.0	18.4	35 000	177 000
87	Mannesmann	Germany	Industrial and farm equipment	4.9	15.3	9.0	14.8	34 021	123 997
88	Robert Bosch	Germany	Motor vehicles and parts	..[c]	15.8	10.0[bd]	19.7	62 087	179 636
89	SCA	Sweden	Paper and packaging	4.8	8.6	4.2[d]	5.3	19 590	30 139
90	Peugeot	France	Motor vehicles and parts	4.8	22.6	15.8	29.5	31 820	159 100
91	3M	United States	Scientific and photographic equipment	4.7	11.1	6.2[d]	13.0	39 000	89 601
92	McDonald's	United States	Restaurants	4.6	10.7	6.5	18.8	..	177 000
93	Cable and Wireless	United Kingdom	Telecommunications	4.6	7.2	3.3	3.8	28 261	37 681
94	United Technologies	United States	Aerospace	4.4	15.9	7.8	21.4	84 500	192 600
95	Lonrho	United Kingdom	Trading	..[c]	7.0	5.6	9.3	127 369	142 159
96	Johnson & Johnson	United States	Pharmaceuticals	4.4	9.5	5.8	11.2	44 369[e]	84 902
97	BHP	Australia	Metals	4.3	16.2	3.2	10.8	..	52 000
98	Norsk Hydro	Norway	Chemicals	4.3	12.0	5.9	9.8	16 745	33 042
99	Veba	Germany	Trading	..[c]	30.8	9.5	32.9	14 696	106 877
100	LVMH Moet-Hennessy	France	Beverages	4.2	8.8	2.6	3.7	..	14 297

Source: UNCTAD, Programme on Transnational Corporations, based on company annual financial statements, Worldscope company accounts database, unpublished sources from companies, The Industrial Institute for Economic and Social Research (IUI, Stockholm, Sweden), and Stopford, 1992. The Worldscope database uses standardized data definitions to adjust for differences in accounting terminology. Data for United States companies with fiscal year-end up to 10 February 1991, as well as for non-United States companies with fiscal year-end until 15 January 1991, are classified as 1990 data.

a Industry classification of companies follows that in the Fortune Global 500 list in *Fortune*, 29 July 1991, and the Fortune Global Service 500 list in *Fortune*, 26 August 1991, except for Akzo, Daimler-Benz, GTE, ITT McDonald's and SCA corporations. In the Fortune classification, companies are included in the industry or service that represents the greatest volume of their sales; industry groups are based on categories established by the United States Office of Management and Budget. Several companies, however, are highly diversified. These companies include 3M, Ferruzzi Montedison, GE, Grand Metropolitan, Hanson, ITT, Sandoz, Tenneco, United Technologies and Veba.

b Excludes other European countries.

c Data for foreign assets not available; ranking is according to foreign assets estimated by the Transnational Corporations and Management Division on the basis of the ratio of foreign to total employment, foreign to total fixed assets or other similar ratios.

d Includes export sales which are not separately reported.

e For 1992; previous data not available.

f For 1993; previous data not available.

g Company's own estimate.

Table I.11. Transnationalization and concentration ratios for the largest 100 transnational corporations, by foreign assets and foreign sales, 1990
(Percentage and billions of dollars)

Item	Share in top 100 (Percentage)		Share in top 100 (Percentage)		Share of foreign in total assets	Share of foreign in total sales
	Total assets	Foreign assets[a]	Total sales	Foreign sales	(Percentage)	
Top 10	25.8	33.5	23.2	29.4	49.1	61.2
Top 25	50.0	54.4	46.0	49.2	41.1	51.7
Top 50	70.9	76.3	68.7	70.9	41.0	49.9
Top 100 Percentage	100.0	100.0	100.0	100.0	37.8	48.4
Value (Billion dollars)	3 198.6	1 208.5	3 107.1	1 502.4		

Source: Table I.10.

a Estimates for foreign assets were used where the data were missing.

Table I.12. Bilateral investment treaties concluded by developed countries, January 1993

Country	Total number concluded until mid-1991	Treaties concluded between mid-1991 and end-1992: Africa	Asia	Latin America and the Caribbean	West Asia	Central and Eastern Europe	Total number as of 1 January 1993
Australia	2		2			3	7
Austria	10	2	1	1			14
Belgium-Luxembourg	29	1	1	3			34
Canada	3			2		1	6
Denmark	13	1	1	1		4	20
Finland	9					10	19
France	44		2	1	1	4	52
Germany, Federal Republic of	73		1	3		4	81
Greece	3				1	2	6
Iceland							
Ireland							
Italy	22		1			2	25
Japan	3						3
Netherlands	32	2		4		2	40
New Zealand	1						1
Norway	9					3	12
Portugal	3		1			1	5
Spain	5		1	3			9
Sweden	16		1	1		3	21
Switzerland	51			1		3	56
Turkey	12		1	1		8	22
United Kingdom	49				1		50
United States	13		1	1		7	22
Total	402	6	15	22	3	57	506[a]

Source: UNCTAD, Programme on Transnational Corporations, based on information provided by Governments.

a Including a bilateral investment protection treaty between Japan and Turkey.

territories" (World Bank Group, 1992b, p. 36). They are a set of recommendations for implementation on a voluntary basis, which can be applied to all countries (box I.2). To the extent that they are adopted by individual countries, the World Bank Guidelines may help to develop an international standard for FDI. However, they do not explicitly deal with standards of corporate conduct,[13] because it was thought that the formulation of such

Box I.2. The World Bank Guidelines on the Treatment of Foreign Direct Investment

The Guidelines provide a voluntary framework for the treatment of FDI. They cover the admission of FDI, general standards of treatment, transfer of capital and revenues, expropriation and compensation and settlement of disputes between host countries and investors. Overall, they are a synthesis of the existing instruments and the "best practices" that tend to stimulate FDI.

The Guidelines contain prescriptions to governments of host countries on how they should treat private foreign investors; they do not deal with the obligations of foreign investors, except in very general ways. Guideline 1 says that the framework applies to existing and new investments "which are established and operating in good faith and in full conformity with the laws and regulations of the host State".

Guideline II states that States are encouraged to admit foreign investors, while recognizing the possibility of some exceptions and emphasizing the importance of providing information to investors about investment conditions. States are also advised to avoid complicated procedural regulations or conditions on admission. Yet their right to regulate is preserved, especially when this is required by public order.

Guideline III endorses the general standards of fair and equitable treatment, and national and non-discriminatory treatment. These standards should be applied, in principle, to all activities of a foreign investor after admission or establishment. They apply to all States without prejudice to the provisions of applicable international instruments and to firmly established rules of customary international law. In addition, this Guideline elaborates on several specific aspects of FDI treatment that are particularly important: timely issuance of authorizations; flexibility in relation to employment policy; facilitation of transfer of funds and repatriation of the investment; prevention and control of corrupt practices and promotion of accountability and transparency in FDI operations; "best practices" in relation to fiscal incentives; and "best practices" by home countries on the facilitation and promotion of FDI to developing countries.

The provisions on expropriation (Guideline IV) are fairly detailed. Expropriation includes indirect or "creeping" expropriation. In the light of practice, this Guideline recognizes the right of a State to expropriate, but only if this is done in accordance with applicable legal procedures, in the pursuance in good faith of a public purpose, without discrimination on the basis of nationality and against the payment of appropriate compensation. The Guideline recommends the use of detailed and practical compensation formulae, adaptable to each case, and drawing mainly from international arbitration awards. Compensation should generally be deemed prompt, adequate and effective; the meaning of each of these terms is described in considerable detail. However, investors may be entitled to lesser (or no) compensation if they breach the law of the host State; and the Guideline also recognizes that, in the case of comprehensive non-discriminatory nationalizations effected in the process of large scale social reforms under exceptional circumstances of revolution, war and similar exigencies, compensation may be determined by inter-State negotiations or by international arbitration.

Guideline V deals with the settlement of disputes between the host States and foreign investors. It provides that these disputes be settled through negotiations between them and, failing this, through national courts or through other agreed mechanisms including conciliation and binding international arbitration. It stresses the independence of the arbitration procedure, which means basically that the majority of the arbitrators should not be appointed by one party. The Guidelines encourage the use of ICSID mechanisms in case of agreement on independent arbitration.

Source: World Bank Group, 1992b.

Box I.3. Minimum standards for the supervision of banks

Transnational banks are not just an important source of capital for FDI, they are also active participants in investment projects around the world. In 1975, the Governors of the Central Banks of the Group of Ten industrialized countries established the Basel Committee on Banking Regulations and Supervisory Practices (now the Basel Committee on Banking Supervision) to strengthen collaboration among national authorities in their prudential supervision of international banking. During that year, the Committee obtained the agreement of the Governors to a paper setting out principles for the supervision of foreign establishments of banks; those arrangements, which were revised in 1983, are now better known as the Basel Concordat. In 1988, the Committee concluded an agreement to establish a common measurement system and a minimum standard for capital adequacy of international banks; this became known as the Basel Capital Accord. The Accord was revised in November 1991 to ensure greater consistency in respect of the inclusion of general provisions/general loan-loss reserves in capital. In 1989, the Committee released the Statement of Principles on Money-Laundering (to which the World Bank Guidelines made reference). More recently, it has been drawing up regulatory proposals dealing with netting, market risks and interest-rate risks.

In July 1992, in the aftermath of the BCCI affair, the Committee issued a set of minimum standards for international cooperation in the supervision of banks, designed to reinforce the Basel Concordat. Those standards can be summarized as follows:

- All international banking groups and international banks should be supervised by a home-country authority that capably performs consolidated supervision. In home countries where supervisory responsibility is shared among two or more authorities, the word "authority" is used to include all relevant authorities in any one country;
- The creation of across-border banking establishments should receive the prior consent of both the host-country supervisory authority as well as the bank's (and, if different, the banking group's) home-country supervisory authority;
- Supervisory authorities should possess the right to gather information from the cross-border banking establishments of the banks or banking groups for which they are the home-country supervisor;
- If a host-country authority determines that any one of the foregoing minimum standards is not met to its satisfaction, that authority could impose restrictive measures necessary to satisfy its prudential concerns consistent with the minimum standards, including the prohibition of the creation of banking establishments.

If these minimum standards are not met with respect to a particular bank or banking group, and the relevant home-country authorities are unwilling or unable to initiate the effort to take measures to meet the standards, the host-country authority should prevent the creation in its jurisdiction of any cross-border establishments by that bank or banking group. However, in its sole discretion, a host-country authority may choose to permit the creation of establishments by such a bank or banking group, subject to whatever prudential restrictions on the scope and nature of the establishment's operations which the host-country authority deems necessary and appropriate to cover its prudential concerns, provided that the host-country authority itself also accepts the responsibility to perform adequate supervision of the bank's or banking group's local establishments on a "stand-alone" consolidated basis.

Source: Basel Committee on Banking Supervision, 1992.

standards was being undertaken by other bodies such as the United Nations Commission on Transnational Corporations.

Further progress on international investment cooperation was made at the United Nations Conference on Environment and Development (UNCED), held in Rio de Janeiro in June 1992. The conference's main document—*Agenda for the 21st Century* (UNCED, 1992)—contains numerous recommendations with implica-

Figure I.2. Network of tax conventions between OECD countries, 1 January 1992

	Finland	Norway	France	Germany	United Kingdom	Belgium	Denmark	Sweden	Italy	Austria	Netherlands	United States	Switzerland	Canada	Japan	Ireland	Australia	Spain	New Zealand	Luxembourg	Greece	Portugal	Turkey	Iceland
Finland		■	■	■	■	■	■	■	■	■	■	■	□	□	■	■	■	■	■	■	■	■	■	■
Norway	■		■	□	■	■	■	■	■	■	■	■	■	■	■	■	■	■	■	■	■	■	■	■
France	■	■		■	■	■	■	□	■	■	■	■	■	■	■	■	■	■	■	■	■	■	■	◆
Germany	□	□	■		■	■	■	■	◆	■	■	■	■	■	■	■	■	■	■	■	■	■	■	■
United Kingdom	■	■	■	■		■	■	■	■	■	■	■	■	■	■	■	■	■	■	■	■	■	■	■
Belgium	■	■	■	■	■		■	◆	■	■	■	■	■	■	■	■	■	■	■	■	■	■	■	◆
Denmark	■	■	■	■	■	■		■	■	■	■	□	■	■	■	■	■	■	■	■	◆	■	◆	■
Sweden	■	■	□	■	■	◆	■		■	■	□	■	■	■	■	■	■	■	■	■	■	◆	■	■
Italy	■	■	■	◆	■	■	■	■		■	□	■	■	■	■	■	◆	■	■	■	■	■	◆	◆
Austria	■	■	■	■	■	■	■	■	■		■	■	■	■	■	■	■	■	■	■	■	■	■	■
Netherlands	■	■	■	■	■	■	■	□	□	■		■	■	■	■	■	■	■	■	■	■	◆	■	◆
United States	■	■	■	■	■	■	■	□	■	■	◆		■	■	■	■	■	■	■	■	■	■	■	■
Switzerland	□	■	■	■	■	■	■	■	■	■	■	■		■	■	■	■	■	■	■	■	■	◆	■
Canada	□	■	■	■	■	■	■	■	■	■	■	■	■		■	■	■	■	■	■	◆	◆	◆	◆
Japan	■	■	■	■	■	■	■	■	■	■	■	■	■	■		■	■	■	■	■	◆	◆	◆	◆
Ireland	■	■	■	■	■	■	■	■	◆	■	■	■	■	■	■		■	◆	■	■	◆	◆	◆	◆
Australia	■	■	■	■	■	■	■	■	■	■	■	■	■	■	■	■		◆	■	◆	◆	◆	◆	◆
Spain	■	■	■	■	■	■	■	■	■	■	■	■	■	■	■	◆	◆		◆	■	◆	■	◆	◆
New Zealand	■	■	■	■	■	■	■	■	■	■	◆	■	■	■	■	■	■	◆		◆	◆	◆	◆	◆
Luxembourg	■	■	■	■	■	■	■	■	■	■	■	■	◆	■	◆	■	◆	■	◆		◆	◆	◆	◆
Greece	■	■	■	■	■	■	◆	■	■	■	■	■	■	◆	◆	◆	◆	◆	◆	◆		◆	◆	◆
Portugal	■	■	■	■	■	■	■	◆	■	■	◆	◆	■	◆	◆	◆	◆	■	◆	◆	◆		◆	◆
Turkey	■	■	■	■	■	■	◆	■	◆	■	■	◆	◆	◆	◆	◆	◆	◆	◆	◆	◆	◆		◆
Iceland	■	■	◆	■	■	◆	■	■	◆	◆	◆	■	■	◆	◆	◆	◆	◆	◆	◆	◆	◆	◆	
Treaties in force	23	23	22	22	23	21	21	21	19	21	21	21	21	19	18	17	17	17	16	15	12	11	9	8

■ **Conventions in force** □ **New convention signed** (old convention still in force) ◆ **Convention signed** (no previous convention

Source: OECD, 1992b, p. A-33.

Table I.13. Main changes in investment regimes in 1992

Region/Country	Operational conditions: More liberal	Operational conditions: Less liberal	Foreign ownership/ sectoral restrictions: More liberal	Foreign ownership/ sectoral restrictions: Less liberal	Approval procedures: More liberal	Approval procedures: Less liberal	Incentives: More liberal	Incentives: Less liberal	Guarantees: More liberal	Guarantees: Less liberal	Controls: More liberal	Controls: Less liberal
Africa												
Burundi							x					
Egypt	x		x		x		x				x	
Ethiopia			x		x		x		x			
Malawi	x		x		x		x		x			
Morocco	x						x					
Tunisia							x					
Asia												
China			x				x					
Democratic People's Republic of Korea	x		x		x		x					
India	x		x		x				x		x	
Indonesia			x									
Malaysia			x				x					
Republic of Korea			x		x		x				x	
Viet Nam	x		x				x		x			
Central and Eastern Europe												
Albania			x		x				x			
Azerbaijan	x		x		x				x			
Belarus							x		x			
Bulgaria			x		x							
Kazakhstan									x			
Lithuania	x				x		x					
Republic of Moldova			x								x	
Romania							x					
Russian Federation	x		x		x							
Tajikistan	x		x		x		x					
Turkmenistan							x					
Ukraine	x		x		x		x		x		x	
Uzbekistan			x				x				x	
Latin America and the Caribbean												
Argentina							x					
Cuba			x									
Guatemala							x				x	
Honduras			x		x				x		x	
Mexico			x		x		x		x			
Nicaragua									x		x	
Paraguay									x		x	
Peru			x				x					
Sao Tome and Principe	x				x		x					
Venezuela			x		x		x		x		x	

/.....

(Table I.13, cont'd.)

Region/Country	*Type of measure*											
	Operational conditions		*Foreign ownership/ sectoral restrictions*		*Approval procedures*		*Incentives*		*Guarantees*		*Controls*	
	More liberal	*Less liberal*	*More liberal*	*Less liberal*	*More liberal*	*Less liberal*	*More liberal*	*Less liberal*	*More liberal*	*Less liberal*	*More liberal*	*Less liberal*
West Asia												
Iran, Islamic Republic of			x						x		x	
United Arab Emirates			x		x							
Developed countries												
Australia					x							
Canada			x									
Finland			x		x							
France					x							
Japan			x									
Sweden			x		x							

Source: UNCTAD, Programme on Transnational Corporations, drawing from various national sources.

tions for TNCs.[14] In a chapter on "Business and industry", *Agenda 21* calls on corporations to establish world-wide policies on sustainable development; to help the transfer of clean technology to developing countries; to adopt environmental standards at least as stringent as those they employ in their home countries; and to report annually on their environmental records. The chapters on environmentally sound management of toxic chemicals and environmentally sound management of hazardous wastes recommend that foreign affiliates be sensitive to local conditions; apply a "responsible care" approach to chemicals, based on the full life-cycle of products; be open in describing their management of hazardous waste; and provide information to developing countries that are short of technical expertise. Lastly, *Agenda 21*, in a chapter on integrating environment and development in decision-making, favours greater use of market mechanisms, corporate self-regulation and voluntary initiatives (such as industry association guidelines) to achieve sustainable development. These recommendations, together with some legally binding conventions on specific aspects of environmental protection, provide norms to which various FDI instruments make reference. Environmental considerations are now an integral part of the international framework on FDI.

Less progress has been made on another part of the global framework, the United Nations Code of Conduct on Transnational Corporations. After informal consultations held from 21 to 23 July 1992, delegations concluded that, at present, no consensus was possible on the draft Code. They favoured a fresh approach, which could include the preparation of guidelines and/or any other international instruments on FDI.[15] For the time being, this brings to a formal end the most comprehensive effort to create a global and balanced framework for FDI. However, it is generally recognized that the Code negotiations, which lasted for more than 15 years and involved all countries, did much to clarify the principles and standards for FDI.

The cessation of the Code negotiations does not, however, mean that the need to elaborate international standards for FDI has diminished (Kline, 1993; Fatouros, 1993; Rubin and Wallace, 1993). That, certainly, is the implication of the adoption of the World Bank Guidelines and of the progress made in the Uruguay Round. In the OECD, too, the Council, in June 1992, invited the Secretary-General to prepare a study to explore the advantage and feasibility of a "Wider Investment Instrument" (OECD, 1992a), an instrument that combines, among other things, the liberalization codes, the OECD Guidelines for TNCs and the decisions on national treatment and incentives and disincentives. The two committees currently dealing with investment issues (the Committee on International Investment and Multinational Enterprises and the Committee on Capital Movements and Invisible Transactions[16]) suggested that the feasibility study address the purpose of a wider instrument, including such issues as the utility of such an agreement; how to correct deficiencies and adjust the national treatment commitments to the same level as that provided by the (binding) liberalization codes; achieving higher levels of liberalization; providing for investment protection; ensuring that there are no gaps and conflicts with other investment instruments; extending the geographical scope to non-member countries; providing for dispute settlement between States and investors; and binding the subnational units of federal countries.

There seems to be a perception among OECD countries that a wider investment instrument would improve the existing instruments and lead to a greater liberalization of FDI flows than that which currently exists among OECD countries. Although it would be negotiated among OECD members, they are likely to take account of the possible eventual participation of non-members and the institutional implications this would have. Hence, although the discussions about a wider instrument are still at an early stage, they may evolve into the first comprehensive instrument on TNCs, albeit in a less-than-global form.

At a regional level, too, much is going on. The *World Investment Report 1992* (TCMD, 1992a) discussed the creation of the European Economic Area (EEA), which involves extending certain aspects of European Community principles and undertakings to the members of the European Free Trade Association (EFTA). This will create a single home base for TNCs headquartered in the EEA. Furthermore, the EC has negotiated or is negotiating association agreements with individual countries in Central Europe as well as with groups of developing countries (for example, North Africa, the Gulf Cooperation Council, ASEAN and the Andean Pact).[17] Most of those agreements include provisions on capital movements, the establishment of firms and the protection and promotion of FDI. Elsewhere, one of the principal regional developments in 1992 was the signing, on 12 August, of the North American Free Trade Agreement (NAFTA) between Canada, Mexico and the United States (see chapter II).

The regional arrangements continue to be supplemented by bilateral treaties for the promotion and protection of FDI and for the avoidance of double taxation. The number of bilateral investment treaties concluded by OECD countries reached 506 at the end of 1992 (table I.12 and annex table 5), with a marked growth in the participation of Latin American countries and the newly independent States in Central and Eastern Europe. In 1992 alone, OECD member countries concluded at least 72 bilateral investment treaties. The number of double taxation treaties now exceeds 1,200, and the network among OECD countries is almost complete (figure I.2). Those treaties are of great importance for TNCs and for Governments, as they influence, among other things, the allocation of profits between host and home countries. To shift the balance towards countries where profits are generated, recent bilateral treaties and the 1992 revision of the 1977 OECD Model Treaty have expanded the definition of permanent establishment; they also seek to limit the extension of tax-treaty benefits to residents of third countries.

Almost all these instruments and discussions are based on a common purpose: to reduce national barriers and protect FDI. They deal mainly with conditions of entry and establishment, operational conditions, transfer of payments and repatriation of capital and the settlement of disputes. But instruments granting an unconditional right to establishment are still rare. Instead, an increasingly common approach is to extend the standards of national and most-favoured-nation treatment and non-discrimination (qualified sometimes by reciprocity requirements) to cover the establishment of the investment, as well as its operational conditions. This is accompanied by an attempt to limit or eliminate performance requirements that may be placed on TNCs.

As in the past, international agreements also contain derogations or exceptions to the general principles by adding a list of exempted activities and industries. And the new instruments continue to provide guarantees of protection for TNCs, both in general terms and in specific areas (notably the transfer of funds and the repatriation of the investment, expropriation, state contracts and the settlement of investment disputes).

Where agreements try to set standards and principles for the activities of TNCs, they tend to concentrate on specific issues like environmental protection and banking and financial markets supervision (box I.3). In those and other areas, the emphasis is on developing preventive measures, mostly by way of requirements on information-disclosure and auditing. Attempts to lay down standards for the full range of TNC activities have been less successful. Apart from a general obligation to act in good faith, the overall regulation of TNC activities in host countries tends to be seen as a matter better left to those countries. In this respect, national FDI regimes have continued to be liberalized during 1992 (table I.13 and annex table 6). In fact, all the 79 new legislative measures adopted in 43 countries were in the direction of liberalization. A number of Governments also took measures to increase the protection of intellectual property and to allow TNCs to participate in the privatization of state industries.

Notes

1 In SDR terms, the rate of annual growth of world-wide outflows, gross domestic product, gross domestic investment, exports of goods and non-factor services, sales, royalty-and-fees receipts during the period 1986-1990 were 21 per cent, 6 per cent, 7 per cent, 12 per cent, 12 per cent and 16 per cent, respectively. Hence, in SDR terms, world-wide outflows grew almost twice as fast as world-wide exports, three times as fast as world-wide gross domestic product and gross domestic investment, and considerably faster than royalties and fees receipts. World-wide sales of TNCs grew twice faster than world-wide gross domestic product and gross domestic investment, and as fast as world-wide exports.

2 A significant proportion of FDI by developing countries may not represent genuine investment—that is, transfer of capital, skills, know-how and control. For example, more than one-third of FDI by developing countries originates from offshore investment sites and

tax havens such as Bermuda, the Cayman Islands, Liberia, the Netherlands Antilles and Panama. The exclusion of these countries reduces the outward investment stock of developing countries to $80 billion in the late 1980s.

3 A survey undertaken by Japan's Export-Import Bank of 115 major Japanese companies indicated that, although they would direct the biggest single share (26 per cent) of their foreign investment to the European Community between early 1992 and March 1994, the member countries of the Association of South-East Asian Nations come close behind. Asia plus Oceania will absorb half of the total. See Anthony Rowley, "Japan looks closer to home", *Far Eastern Economic Review*, 16 January 1992, p. 40, and David Dodwell, "Trade surplus likely to fuel Japanese investment in the Pacific", *Financial Times*, 3 December 1991.

4 The rate of return in the business sector in the OECD declined to 20.3 per cent in 1990 and 1991 from 20.7 per cent in 1988 and 20.6 per cent in 1989. See table on rates of return on capital in the business sector, *OECD Economic Outlook*, appearing in various issues.

5 It may be presumed that, in the developed countries, profits earned from FDI activities in one country or area may be used to finance FDI in another country or area. This may also hold true of the other components of FDI, equity capital and short- and long-term capital.

6 Profit rates are defined here as the share of net income to total income.

7 Data relate to 14 countries for which information was available for both 1969 and 1990. Those are Austria, Belgium, Denmark, France, Federal Republic of Germany, Italy, Japan, Luxembourg, Norway, Portugal, Spain, Sweden, United Kingdom and United States. Data for 1990 are from table I.6.

8 Although the data in table I.6 provide a good picture of the number of companies involved in FDI activities and their spread, data limitations should be noted. Several countries do not report the number of TNCs or foreign affiliates, while others report only those with sales or assets above a minimum size, or exclude firms in certain industries. This would suggest that the number of parents and affiliates is an underestimate.

9 According to the MERIT-CATI Data Bank in the Netherlands, the total number of cooperative agreements is estimated at about 10,000, involving some 3,500 different parent companies during the period 1980 to 1989.

10 It could be argued that a problem of double-counting would arise only if majority-owned affiliates (subsidiaries) of foreign enterprises were counted as parents originating in the host country. Minority-owned affiliates could be considered as legitimate parent TNCs because the influence of foreign firms is not necessarily dominant, and because their accounts are not always consolidated with those of their ultimate parents.

11 This estimate is based on the number of inward foreign affiliates. The total of inward affiliates is a better estimate of the number of affiliates than the sum of outward affiliates, which tends to be an overestimate. For example, if a United States corporation holds a 30 per cent stake in a French company, the latter is counted as an outward foreign affiliate of the United States. If the French company holds a 40 per cent stake in a Brazilian company, then the latter is a direct affiliate of the French parent, as well as an indirect affiliate of the United States parent. In this case, the United States and France would report a total of three foreign affiliates of their own transnational corporations; however, France and Brazil together would report two inward affiliates, which is the actual number.

12 Negotiations of international agreements on trade (including FDI) in services, trade-related investment measures and trade-related intellectual property continued in the context of the Uruguay Round without, however, coming to a conclusion. See TCMD (1992a).

13 In the World Bank Group (1992b, p. 9), the World Bank noted: "This report covers general principles suggested to guide governmental behavior toward foreign investors; it does not include rules of good conduct on the part of the foreign investors. A set of rules for the latter purpose was reflected in negotiated provisions of the UNCTC draft Code of Conduct, which is now being reviewed 'in the light of the changed international economic environment'."

14 Although *Agenda 21* contains no chapter addressing TNCs specifically, it contains numerous more or less explicit references to these firms and their activities, including, for example, "foreign direct investment", "multinational enterprises" and "business and industry, including transnational corporations".

15 "Report by the President of the forty-sixth session of the General Assembly" (United Nations document, A/47/446, of 15 September 1992), annex.

16 Currently, the role of these Committees is to ensure the progressive liberalization of Government policies on FDI under the OECD Liberalisation Codes and the National Treatment Instrument, and to monitor various arrangements for cooperation on a wide range of investment issues under the OECD Declaration and Decisions on International Investment and Multinational Enterprises (of which the National Treatment Instrument is also part). (The instruments are reprinted in UNCTAD, 1993b.) Among the main tools to carry out the Committees' mandate are the examinations of member countries' reservations/exceptions to these instruments, which often lead to the formulation of Council recommendations inviting the member country to act in a particular way. In 1993, for the first time, country examinations will be published to bring transparency on member countries' position under the Codes, and to provide an analysis of member countries' policies on investment issues.

17 See, for example, the Association Agreement with Poland, concluded on 22 November 1991 (Commission of the European Community, *Official Journal of the European Community*, No. L 114/92).

CHAPTER II

REGIONAL TRENDS

While chapter I dealt with overall trends, this chapter examines in greater detail recent trends in FDI within regions, focusing on issues of particular importance to each region.

A. Developed countries

Outflows of foreign direct investment (FDI) from the developed countries declined in 1991 and 1992 (figure II.1). The economic slow-down and financial system weaknesses in a number of countries prompted transnational corporations (TNCs) to concentrate on improving the efficiency of their existing investments, rather than investing heavily in new assets. As mentioned in chapter I, the decline in outflows was accounted for largely by Japan and Western Europe. Despite the recent decline in their outflows, developed countries continue to account for over 97 per cent of world-wide outflows of FDI.

One reason for the fall in outflows in 1991 in the developed countries was the significant reduction in cross-border mergers and acquisitions. For example, in the United States, takeover activities in 1991 have further declined and those of a large-scale nature have been undertaken essentially by domestic firms.[1] Even French companies, which had made substantial overseas acquisitions between 1987 and 1990, have slowed down these activities sharply between 1990 and 1991.[2] The factors that had stimulated mergers and acquisitions earlier in the 1980s became less powerful at the turn of the decade. Tighter monetary policies, higher interest rates in most developed countries and higher stock-market valuations made acquisitions more costly. Slower economic growth contributed to some well-publicized corporate failures of TNCs, such as the Campeau Corporation (Canada). And any wave of regional restructuring is liable to be followed by consolidation, as TNCs concentrate on managing their newly re-organized networks.

Figure II.1. Outflows of foreign direct investment from developed regions and country, 1981-1991
(Billions of dollars)

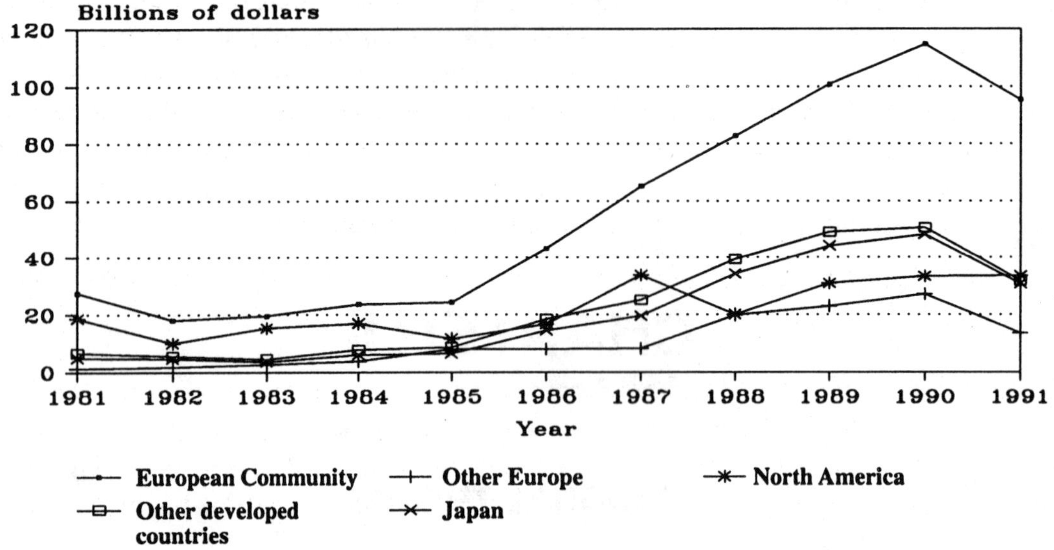

Source: United Nations, Transnational Corporations and Management Division, 1993c.

As mentioned, it was Japan that did the most to make 1991 a sluggish year for outflows. Its outward investment declined for the first time since 1983, and preliminary estimates show that the decline continued in 1992. Domestic economic slowdown, declining profitability and difficulties in financial markets left Japanese companies with less capital to invest abroad; indeed, some were obliged to sell foreign assets to cover losses at home. In addition, the drive of Japanese TNCs to set up manufacturing bases in North America and the European Community in automobiles, steel and electronics abated, at least for the time being.[3] Outflows from most of Western Europe also declined in 1991 and 1992. Less favourable prospects for economic growth, together with the need to consolidate and streamline investments after a period of large-scale FDI, reduced the incentive for firms to keep expanding their investments abroad so rapidly (Rutter, 1992). Only Denmark, Norway, Portugal and Spain showed a growth of outflows in 1991.

Similarly, investment *inflows* to the developed countries fell in 1991 and 1992. This was mainly owing to the United States (where inflows declined by 75 per cent in 1991 and turned negative at $4 billion in 1992, representing net capital outflows) and, to a lesser extent, the European Community (EC) (table II.1). The share of intra-regional investment in total FDI in EC continued to increase, with the level estimated to have reached at least $300 billion in 1991, up from a level of $220 billion in 1989. The members of the European Free Trade Association (EFTA) also experienced a decline in inflows. Inflows in Japan remained small. Several factors were clearly at work in the case of the United States: sluggish economic growth; declining profitability; and poor business performance in banking, finance and real estate industries, where FDI has been significant (Rutter, 1992). Even TNCs from Japan, the most dynamic source of new inflows into the United States, have recently become cautious.[4]

The 1991 inflows to Western Europe declined below their 1989 level, owing both to reduced FDI in EC (particularly in Germany, Italy, the Netherlands, Spain and the United Kingdom) and, to a lesser extent, in EFTA; in the case of EFTA, the decline continued sharply in 1992. Again, there were several reasons for this: sagging business confidence in the face of recession, uncertainties over plans for European integration and the fact that many foreign companies (particularly Japanese firms) had already established a foothold within EC.[5] However, the general EC trend towards liberalization of FDI policies facilitated many ground-breaking alliances with foreign firms in previously protected state industries, such as in France.[6] Privatization as an instrument of economic liberalization has also attracted foreign participation in several Western European countries (for example, Italy),[7] though others (e.g., Greece and Portugal) had less foreign participation in privatized industries.[8]

Although FDI in EFTA declined in 1991, the prospects of the European Economic Area—with most EFTA countries (Austria, Finland, Norway and Sweden) planning to join EC—continue to attract TNCs. In particular, FDI inflows to Sweden more than trebled in 1991 as a result of significant acquisitions by foreign companies and the growth of joint ventures and strategic alliances between domestic and foreign companies. The adoption of a free market strategy in 1992, including privatization and the lifting of legal restrictions that hamper new FDI, is likely further to increase FDI in Sweden.[9] The liberalizing trend was apparent in Switzerland also, with increasing amounts of foreign capital being needed to bolster the weakened Swiss capital market. It remains to be seen how far the rejection of the European Economic Area agreement in December 1992 will influence the attractiveness of Switzerland as an investment location.

Table II.1. Inflows of foreign direct investment to the developed countries, by region, 1987-1992, and shares, 1981-1985, 1986-1990, 1991 and 1992

(Billions of dollars and percentage)

Region	*1987*	*1988*	*1989*	*1990*	*1991*	*1992*[a]	*1981-1985*	*1986-1990*	*1991*	*1992*
	(Billions of dollars)						*Share in total (Percentage)*			
Western Europe of which:	41	60	88	109	84	77	42	50	78	90
European Community	38	57	81	99	75	76	38	46	70	88
EFTA[b]	4	3	7	10	9	1	4	5	8	1
North America	62	63	71	52	16	.002	50	44	15	.002
of which: United States	58	59	68	45	11	-4	51	41	11	-5
Other developed regions	6	8	8	11	8	9	8	6	7	10
of which: Japan	1	-0.5	-1.1	1.8	1.4	1.4	3	0.2	1	2
Total, above	109	132	167	172	108	86	100	100	100	100

Source: UNCTAD, Programme on Transnational Corporations, based on TCMD, 1993c; International Monetary Fund, balance-of-payments tape, retrieved on 17 February 1993; and Organisation for Economic Co-operation and Development estimates.

a Estimated.
b Including some other Western Europe.

The low level of FDI in Japan continued in the early 1990s for several reasons. At the macro level, the factors inhibiting inward investment include government preference of licensing over FDI, an ineffective liberalization process, difficulties in acquisitions and keiretsu relationships. There are also various problems facing individual companies in doing business in Japan, some of which are uniquely rooted in Japanese business practices and some of which are common problems in doing business in a foreign environment (box II.1).

Despite the decline in FDI inflows in the developed countries, they made up almost three quarters of world-wide inflows in 1991. The Triad—consisting of EC, Japan and the United States—accounted for approximately three fifths of world-wide inflows, a proportion well below the 70 per cent of the 1980s, and 86 per cent of outflows, compared with 81 per cent in the 1980s. As a host region of FDI in 1991, the Triad diminished; as a home region, it became more important. But the expanded Triad—consisting of Japan, North America and Western Europe—accounted for 70 per cent of global inflows and 96 per cent of outflows in 1991. Cross-holdings of stocks of FDI within the expanded Triad amounted to $640 billion in 1990 (figure II.2).

Box II.1. Why is foreign direct investment in Japan so low?

In 1990, Japan's stock of inward FDI was the fourteenth largest in the world, up from its position as twenty-first largest in 1980. Despite this rise, Japan's share in still very low. Moreover, the level of inward stock in Japan was still only one fifteenth of Japan's outward stock of FDI as of March 1992.

Historically, the Government of Japan has aimed to promote indigenous technical and managerial strengths by importing foreign technology, primarily in the form of licensing. As recently as 1987-1991, the value of Japan's technological imports (defined as payments of royalties and licence fees to foreign owners of patents, copyrights and other non-financial intangible assets) was nearly ten times greater than inflows of FDI.[a] The value of those technological imports was two or three times that of other major developed countries, such as France, Germany, the United Kingdom and the United States, indicating a sustained preference for licensing over FDI for technology acquisition in Japan.

The liberalization of inward FDI policies starting in 1967 has not led to any significant growth of such investment in Japan because of the slow implementation process. For example, only industries that have achieved international competitiveness have been gradually liberalized for foreign competition. Although full liberalization was achieved in principle in 1976, FDI remains closed in four industry groups—agriculture, forestry and fisheries, mining, oil exploration and leather and leather products. Until 1990, the Foreign Exchange and Foreign Trade Control Law enabled the Government to restrict inward FDI on the grounds that the investment might adversely affect similar domestic business activities or the smooth performance of the Japanese economy. The restrictions also played a part in retarding FDI inflows.

Difficulties faced by foreign firms in merger-and-acquisition activities in Japan also constitute another reason for the low level of inward FDI (Lawrence, 1992). Hostile take-overs (take-over bid system) were institutionally difficult until 1990, as prior notification was required. Thus, targeted companies could prepare in time to defend themselves from an impending take-over. Apart from this factor, the practice of shareholdings owned by financial companies and *keiretsu* firms, lifetime employment and the seniority system may have made mergers and acquisitions difficult for foreign firms.

/.....

B. Developing countries

Except for 1989, *inflows* of FDI to developing countries increased steadily between 1984 and 1992. Most remarkably, while inflows to the developed countries declined in 1991, they grew by more than 20 per cent to the developing countries, to $39 billion. As mentioned in the preceding chapter, developing countries made up more than one quarter of global inflows in 1991, a much larger share than in 1986-1991, and equal to their share in the first half of the 1980s. In 1992, FDI into developing countries increased further to at least $40 billion.

The growth of inflows has affected all developing regions and is associated with continued strong economic expansion in Asia and the Pacific, recovery in some Latin American countries (Argentina, Chile and Venezuela), and the trend towards liberalization. Although East, South and South-East Asia continues to account for over half of the inflows to developing countries, the region's share fell in 1991. On the other hand, inflows to Latin America and the Caribbean grew significantly in 1991, and those to Africa were up by more than 20 per cent. Even flows to the least developed countries rose marginally, though they accounted for just 0.5 per cent of the developing countries' total inflows. A large proportion of that total is still going to a small number of countries (table II.2), although the share obtained by the ten largest host countries fell from over 70 per cent during the period 1981-1985 to 64 per cent during the period 1986-1990.

(Box II.1, cont'd.)

Certain aspects of *keiretsu* relationships promote preferential group trade and negatively affect FDI in Japan (Lawrence, 1992). Anti-competitive and exclusive business practices decrease the transparency of business transactions and place non-*keiretsu* firms and, in particular, foreign firms in a disadvantageous position. Other problems inhibiting inward FDI at a company level include, among others, high costs of doing business and staffing problems, as well as the complex, multi-layered distribution system.[b] Those problems are more profound in Japan than in other countries as they are related to the uniqueness of Japanese business practices.

Even so, FDI into Japan is increasing. Inflows in the first half of 1992 were almost double those in the same period in 1991.[c] It also seems that mergers and acquisitions by foreign firms are behind the increase in inflows, prompted by the lower acquisition cost of Japanese firms,[d] some of which can be bought at less than half the cost of acquisition in 1990. The decline in Japanese real estate and stock prices over the past two years and the restructuring of Japanese industries have provided foreign firms with their best opportunity in years to set up, expand or acquire business in Japan. Moreover, the Government of Japan has recently committed itself to boost inward investment, and this is likely to change the attitude of foreign investors.[e]

---

a Data on payments of royalties and fees are from the International Monetary Fund, balance-of-payments tape, retrieved in November 1992. They include payments to both affiliated and non-affiliated foreigners by domestic firms and TNCs.

b Quoted in "Trade and investment in Japan: the current environment", *Center for Industrial and Technological Cooperation (CITEC) News* (Tokyo, Japan, External Trade Organization, September 1992), p. 1; Japan, Ministry of International Trade and Industry, 1992c, table 60, pp. 166-167.

c *Nihon Keizai Shimbun*, 19 August 1992, p. 5. Data on inward FDI here are formulated on the notification basis (*ex post facto* reports since April 1991) reported by the Ministry of Finance. As the data exclude withdrawals and cancellations of FDI after reporting, they are normally larger than the data on inflows reported in the balance of payments.

d In the first half of 1992, the number of mergers and acquisitions of Japanese companies by overseas corporations more than doubled to 16 transactions, compared to the previous year. The number of acquisitions by United States companies rose to 10 from three in the same period last year, while those from Europe halved to two deals. The value of the transactions, however, fell 43 per cent to $105 million in the first half of 1992. See also Emiko Terazono, "Foreigners find Japanese companies attractive", *Financial Times*, 2 July 1992.

e "Japan's trade surpluses: the long-term solution", *The Economist*, 13 June 1992; and "Japan mulls tax incentives for foreign-based firms", *The Wall Street Journal*, 9 September 1991.

Figure II.2. Intra-Triad foreign direct investment, 1990
(Billions of dollars)

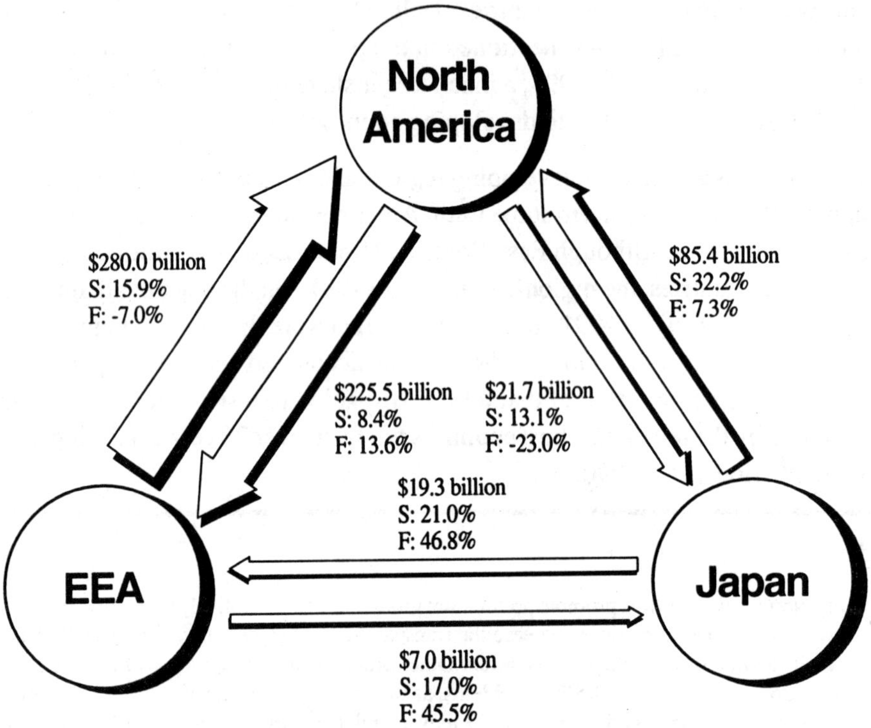

Source: UNCTAD, Programme on Transnational Corporations, foreign-direct-investment database.

Note: Dollar figures show estimated values of stock of FDI based on data on inward and outward investment from North America and the European Economic Area (EEA), excluding Iceland and Liechtenstein. Intra-North American investment and intra-EEA investment have been netted out. Percentages show average annual growth rates for stocks (1980-1990) and flows (1985-1991). North America includes Canada and the United States. The European Economic Area includes the European Community (EC) and the European Free Trade Association, excluding Iceland and Liechtenstein.

Although they fell in 1991, *outflows* from developing countries grew almost twice as fast as those from the developed countries during the period 1986-1990. Their share of world-wide investment outflows remains small, and comes largely from a few countries in the Asia-Pacific region.

The 1992 programme for the single EC market may have a bearing on FDI and trade in developing countries in the 1990s. For example, although it is primarily intended to remove internal non-tariff barriers, its effect may be to increase the competitiveness of European-based firms, and thus influence adversely less-efficient producers in developing countries. Moreover, many developing countries are anxious that the implementation of the programme may cause EC to become more protectionist. In addition, any EC tendency to tighten European sourcing policies and rules of origin could divert trade and investment to EC and away from developing countries. Similarly, EC technical, health and safety standards might serve to exclude some developing countries from exporting to the European market. More generally, the expectation that EC integration would promote faster economic growth could increase the attractiveness of EC to foreign investors, diverting FDI away from developing countries (TCMD, 1993a; UNCTC, 1990).

Some of those concerns are exaggerated or unfounded. The single market programme is unlikely to divert much trade and investment from developing countries, largely because they are determined by the availability of natural resources, large and rapidly growing domestic markets and lower production costs for exports. In particular, export-oriented FDI in developing countries is not likely to be affected, since few of those investments are intended to serve EC.[10] More importantly, the single market is geared more to improving the competitiveness of EC in world markets than to increasing protectionism from outside competition. Indeed, FDI inflows into developing countries since the mid-1980s, when the single market programme was announced, continued to rise.[11]

Table II.2. Inflows of foreign direct investment to developing economies, by region, 1981-1985, 1986-1990 and 1991

(Billions of dollars and percentage)

	Average (Billions of dollars)				*Share in total (Percentage)*				*Growth rate (Percentage)*			
Country/economy	*1981-1985*	*1986-1990*	*1991*	*1992* [a]	*1981-1985*	*1986-1990*	*1991*	*1992*	*1981-1985*	*1986-1990*	*1991*	*1992*
All countries	50	155	149	126	100	100	100	100	-1	22	-27	-15
Developing countries	14	26	39	40	26	17	26	32	-4	14	24	3
Africa	2	3	3	2	3	2	2	2	12	6	21	-33
East, South and South-East Asia	5	13	20	21	10	9	13	17	-3	21	8	5
Latin America and the Caribbean	6	9	15	16	12	6	10	13	-10	9	53	7
Oceania	0.1	0.2	0.1	0.5	0.3	0.1	0.1	0.4	-2	27	-57	400
West Asia	0.4	0.4	0.8	0.8	1	0.3	0.5	0.6	7	27	61	0
Other [b]	0.03	0.05	0.1	0.1	0.1	0.03	0.1	0.08	-10	103	35	0
Least developed countries	0.2	0.1	0.2	..	0.3	0.1	0.1	..	-0.4	1	12	..
Ten largest host developing economies	9[c]	17[d]	25[e]	26[e]	18[b]	11[c]	16[d]	21[e]	-9[b]	18[c]	44[d]	4

Source: UNCTAD, Programme on Transnational Corporations, based on UNCTAD, 1993c, 1993d; UNCTC 1992b; TCMD, 1993c; TCMD and ECE, 1992; International Monetary Fund, balance-of-payments tape, retrieved on 17 February 1993; and Organisation for Economic Co-operation and Development estimates.

a Estimated.
b Malta and Yugoslavia.
c Argentina, Brazil, China, Colombia, Egypt, Hong Kong, Malaysia, Mexico, Nigeria and Singapore.
d Argentina, Brazil, China, Egypt, Hong Kong, Mexico, Nigeria, Singapore, Taiwan Province of China and Thailand.
e Argentina, Brazil, China, Indonesia, Malaysia, Mexico, Republic of Korea, Taiwan Province of China, Thailand and Venezuela.

This finding confirms recent studies, which concluded that, given all the factors that drive FDI in developing countries, the potential effects of the single market are relatively unimportant.[12] On the contrary, if the single market speeds up EC economic growth, it would increase the resources to finance outward FDI from Europe, and increase European demand for goods produced in developing countries. It would also mean that certain types of industry, involving less skill, capital and technology, would be transferred to developing countries from EC. The precise impact will have to depend on external trade policies of the EC which will greatly influence its economic relations with the developing world.

1. Asia and the Pacific

Investment *inflows* to Asia and the Pacific rose by 8 per cent in 1991, to reach $20 billion (table II.2). In 1992, inflows to the region reached at least $21 billion. They were attracted by strong economic growth, especially in the newly industrializing economies and Indonesia, Malaysia and Thailand. That group accounted for about three quarters of FDI inflows to the region in 1991. However, the two biggest countries in the region are now making their presence felt. India liberalized its FDI regime and obtained a notable increase in inflows, while China became the region's single largest recipient of FDI (figure II.3). Some countries, such as Malaysia and

Figure II.3. Foreign-direct-investment inflows to Asia, 1981-1991
(Billions of dollars)

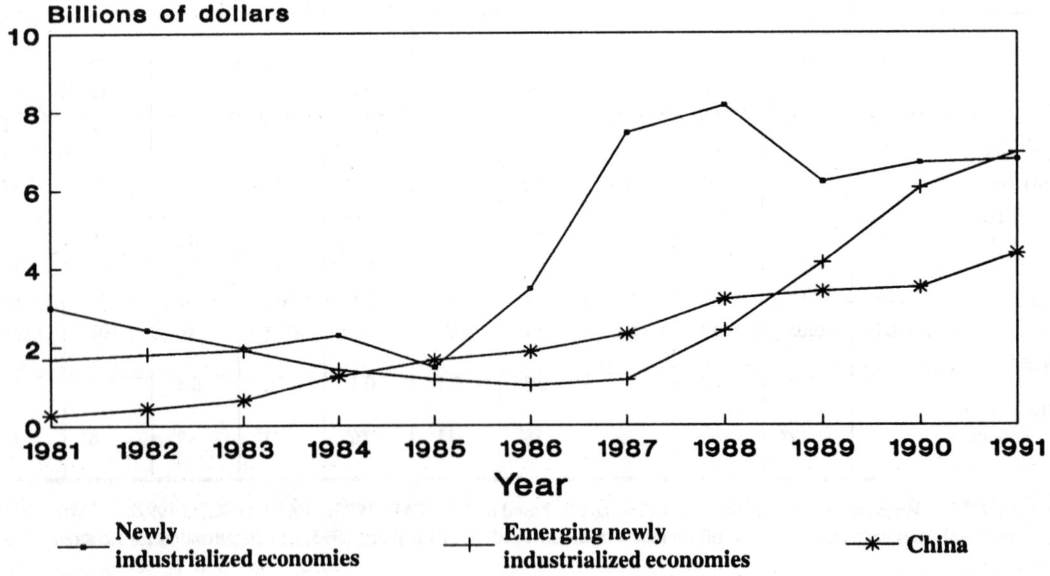

Source: UNCTAD, Programme on Transnational Corporations, based on UNCTC, 1992b; and foreign-direct-investment database.

a Indonesia, Malaysia, Thailand.

Thailand, have been seeking to raise the quality of FDI, so as to increase domestic linkages and promote technologically-advanced industries. And the natural-resource industries of some newly opening economies in Asia (Viet Nam and, to a lesser extent, Cambodia) have attracted investments from several TNCs from Japan and the newly industrializing economies.[13] Japan continues to be a major source of FDI in Asia and the Pacific, although its outflows there fell in 1991. Its investments in Asia remain very profitable, which is likely to ensure that growth will resume.[14] Faced with the rising cost of capital at home, however, Japanese TNCs may increasingly rely on local finance for their investments.[15]

Although the newly industrializing economies continue to be significant recipients of investment flows, their rising labour costs have led some TNCs to relocate to China and South Asia, where production costs are lower and the FDI climate is improving. For example, India's liberalization of its FDI regime has resulted in a significant increase in investments there; the value of foreign equity in joint ventures approved in the first seven months of 1992, at slightly over $1 billion, was almost three times greater than in the whole of 1991.[16] As for China, in 1991, it became the second largest recipient of inflows among *all* developing countries, exceeded only by Mexico. There are signs that this trend will continue: investment in China on a *contract* basis during the first half of 1992 was about $15 billion, compared to $12 billion in the whole of 1991.[17] The principal reasons for the increase in inflows to China are the same as those for many countries in the region as a whole: rapid economic growth, low costs, a large domestic market and rising per capita incomes.[18] However, some factors particular to China have also been at work: it has improved its relationship with some of its neighbours (Indonesia, Singapore and Taiwan Province of China), and its most- favoured-nation status with the United States has been renewed. All in all, it seems that the effect of the Tiananmen Square incident on corporate decisions on investing in China is diminishing.[19] For example, Motorola has revived plans for a manufacturing plant of semiconductors and communications equipment that would supply mostly the domestic market, a project that was suspended in 1989.[20]

The industrial composition of FDI inflows may also change as countries seek to upgrade the quality of their inward investment. Malaysia, for example, wants to broaden and deepen its industrial base; promote capital-intensive and technologically sophisticated industries; develop intermediate and capital-goods industries; and promote linkages between foreign and domestic companies. In order to achieve those objectives, it has revised its tax-incentive system to encourage FDI in higher value-added industries and services, and has included proposals to offer incentives to affiliates to increase linkages with domestic producers via local procurement, staff training and the transfer of technology.[21] In Thailand, a similar pattern is occurring: some industrial upgrading towards more technologically intensive investments is already being undertaken by foreign oil and gas companies and some computer firms.

Investment *outflows* from East, South and South-East Asia fell by a third in 1991. This reflected a decline of about 65 per cent in outflows from Taiwan Province of China between 1990 and 1991, with a further decline registered for 1992.[22] Even then, its outflows were more than 30 times their annual average during the first half of the 1980s. Together with the Republic of Korea, it remains a net exporter of FDI (figure II.4). The burst of outward investment during the period 1988-1990 by TNCs from Taiwan Province of China was mainly in response to rising production costs and labour shortages at home, and was concentrated largely in manufacturing plants in member states of ASEAN and China. In the future, investment outflows from Taiwan Province of China

Figure II.4. The Republic of Korea and Taiwan Province of China: foreign-direct-investment flows, 1981-1991
(Millions and billions of dollars)

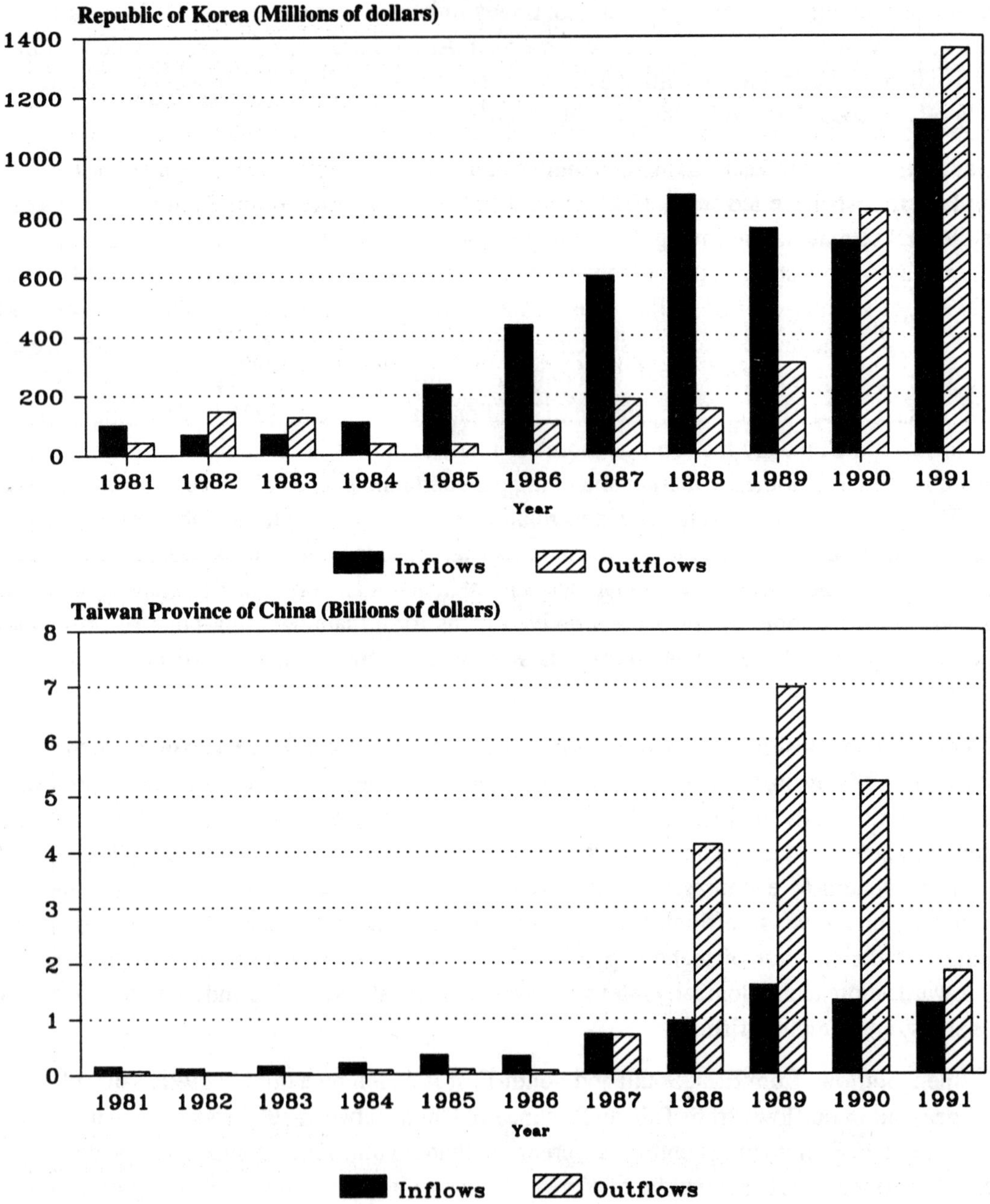

Source: UNCTAD, Programme on Transnational Corporations, based on UNCTC, 1992b; and UNCTAD, Programme on Transnational Corporations, foreign-direct-investment database.

are likely to grow again, driven by the desire to acquire technology, establish marketing and distribution channels in developed countries, and take advantage of expanding consumer markets and lower production costs in developing countries.

Outflows from the Republic of Korea and Singapore continued to grow in 1991.[23] In addition, TNCs from some other Asian countries, such as Thailand (which only a few years ago had very little investment abroad), are shifting assembly and other labour-intensive operations to neighbouring countries with lower labour costs.[24] Therefore, in spite of the overall decline in investment outflows in 1991 and 1992, several Asian economies are building up a network of investment in manufactured goods within the region. This is particularly true of Malaysia, Singapore, Taiwan Province of China and Thailand (table II.3), while South Asia has yet to play a major intraregional role.

Table II.3. Selected host economies in Asia: Intra- and extraregional investment inflows, 1985-1987 and 1988-1990[a]
(Percentage share of total)

	Intraregional				*Extraregional*	
	Total		*Of which: Japan*			
Host economy	*1985-1987*	*1988-1990*	*1985-1987*	*1988-1990*	*1985-1987*	*1988-1990*
Bangladesh	10	11	6	4	90	89
China	77	72	12	12	23	28
India[b]	11	8	10	5	89	92
Indonesia	51	50	31	18	49	50
Republic of Korea	58	52	53	49	29	48
Malaysia	38	67	19	25	62	33
Pakistan	1	2	1	2	99	98
Philippines	21	23	14	14	79	77
Singapore[c]	10	47[d]	22	35[d]	90	53[d]
Taiwan Province of China	40	47	29	32	60	53
Thailand	55	77	38	45	45	23

Sources: UNCTAD, Programme on Transnational Corporations, based on UNCTC, 1992b; and UNCTAD, Programme on Transnational Corporations, foreign-direct-investment database.

a Intraregional investment inflows refers to investment from the entire Asia-Pacific region, including Japan. Extraregional invesstment inflows refers to investment from sources other than the Asia-Pacific region.

b Excludes FDI by non-resident Indians.

c Flows estimated as the difference in year-end values of foreign direct equity investments in two consecutive years.

d For 1988-1989.

2. Latin America and the Caribbean

In Latin America and the Caribbean region, FDI inflows have risen in every year since 1988 (UNCTAD, 1993c). The main reasons seem to have been a recovery in several economies as a result of fiscal discipline, the restructuring of the external debt with private sector creditors, and the continuing trend towards economic liberalization. Furthermore, specific measures such as debt-equity swaps and, recently, privatization helped to stimulate investment inflows by expanding the range of profitable investment opportunities in the region. Even though reforms have occurred throughout the region, inflows continue to be concentrated in a handful of countries: Argentina, Brazil, Chile, Mexico and, as of 1991, Venezuela (Aspe, Bianchi and Cavallo, 1992).

In 1992, the chief policy development affecting FDI in this region was the signing of the North American Free Trade Agreement (NAFTA) by Canada, Mexico and the United States. It is expected that NAFTA will take effect on 1 January 1994 and create the largest free trade zone on the American continent and the second largest in the world (after the European Economic Area). NAFTA is also remarkable because it involves both a developing country and developed countries; other integration efforts have joined only countries at a similar level of development. It will also most likely increase the volume of FDI flows, both within the integrating area and as regards flows from outside the area; in addition, the sectoral composition of FDI flows, especially into Mexico, is likely to change as new industries are opened to foreign competition.

The North American Free Trade Agreement introduces liberalization to several interrelated areas: trade barriers (tariffs and non-tariffs) for goods; technical barriers to trade; government procurement; investment, services and related matters (that is, competition policy and temporary entry of business persons); and intellectual property. It also contains special rules for some strategic industries (financial services, transportation, telecommunications) and pays attention to regulatory aspects, such as environmental protection, product standards and industrial policies. Key aspects of the investment regime include a considerable broadening of the definition of investment; the right of establishment and commercial presence on a non-discriminatory basis, and of temporary entry for executive staff; freedom from restrictions on monetary movements; abolition of the main types of performance requirements; national and most-favoured-nation treatment for FDI operations; and guarantees for the protection of FDI against non-commercial risks (notably expropriation and state contracts), including provisions for arbitration (see box II.2). The approach of NAFTA is to lay down generic rules, to which specific exceptions and reservations are appended in separate schedules. As with other instruments of economic integration, its commitments are legally binding.

The establishment of NAFTA reinforces moves to liberalize FDI policies in other parts of Latin America. This trend, evident since the late 1980s, has enabled TNCs to engage in new activities in the region, with the pattern varying from country to country. In Mexico, for example, much recent FDI has gone into restructuring the motor industry, although TNCs have also entered various service industries, such as tourism and telecommunications (Mortimore and Huss, 1991; Perez, 1990; UNCTC, 1992a; Unger, 1990; de Maria y Campo, 1992; Secretaria de Comercio y Fomento Industrial, UNCTAD and UNDP, 1991). Chile has had FDI across much of its economy: new exporters in natural resources (forestry, fish products, gold mining etc.), substantial expansion of traditional mining activities (copper), and liberalized services industries (finance, airlines, telecommunications etc.) (Behrens, 1992; Rozas, 1992; Ffrench-Davis, Leiva and Madrid, 1991). Recent increases in investment

Box II.2. The provisions on foreign direct investment of the North American Free Trade Agreement

The main objectives of the North American Free Trade Agreement (NAFTA) include increased investment opportunities and the promotion of fair competition within the North American region. The Agreement dedicates much of its provisions to the regulation of investment, services and related matters (part five). In fact, NAFTA introduces substantial changes to the approach taken on these issues in its predecessor agreement, the Free Trade Agreement between Canada and the United States, in a way that underlines the growing importance of FDI and services in the process of international economic integration (Gestrin and Rugman, 1993).

The investments covered under NAFTA include portfolio investments (e.g., equity and debt securities), certain loans, intangible property and property interests, and contracts where the remuneration depends substantially on the production, revenues or profits of an enterprise (chapter 11). Companies in a NAFTA country owned by non-party nationals are generally entitled to protections under the Agreement when investing in another NAFTA country. However, a party may deny the benefits of NAFTA to enterprises or investments of another party if they are owned or controlled by investors of a non-party and the enterprise has no substantial business in the territory of the party under whose laws it is constituted or organized.

National treatment is an important principle of NAFTA: it stipulates that each party shall grant investors and investments of another party treatment no less favourable than that it accords, in like circumstances, to its own investors. In addition, NAFTA prescribes most-favoured-nation treatment among the parties and in relation to third countries. The standard of treatment to be granted to investors and their investments under NAFTA is whichever is the better of those two. These standards are complemented by the "minimum standard" for FDI prescribed by international law, typically including fair and equitable treatment and full protection under the law. All three standards apply in principle to all aspects of investment operations (including the entry of the company and the establishment of foreign affiliates), and they cover measures imposed at the federal, state, provincial and local levels. On the other hand, where NAFTA permits investments to be denied admission, the decision cannot be reviewed by an arbitration panel. The general non-discrimination standards are subject to reservations included in some annexes to the Agreement (see below).

The Agreement also prohibits the imposition or enforcement of performance requirements on TNCs upon establishment and throughout the life of an investment. It lists the measures considered to be performance requirements (e.g., export and/or import requirements, local content, domestic purchasing, trade balancing, licensing of technology, exclusive sales, exchange control requirements), including some that do not appear in the Draft Final Act of the Uruguay Round (see TCMD 1992a). In addition, some performance requirements (e.g., local content, domestic purchasing, exchange and trade balancing) are not allowed as conditions for granting subsidies or other incentives. However, the agreement does allow the granting of incentives or advantages tied to the compliance with certain specific requirements, such as training or employment of workers, construction or expansion of facilities and research and development. Furthermore, countries of host Governments may lay down requirements for the organization of an investment according to their own laws and regulations, provided those do not impair the substance of the protection offered by the Agreement. Likewise, the parties are able to request from TNCs information on their investment for statistical and general information purposes.

The Agreement does not allow restrictions on the nationality of the senior management of NAFTA investments. However, the parties are entitled to require that a majority of the board of directors or any board committee be of a particular nationality or reside in the territory of the party, so long as this does not undermine the investors' capabilities to control their investments.

The Agreement provides that all transfers of payments shall be made freely and without delay. Transfers are defined broadly to include profits, dividends, interests, royalties and management fees, technical assistance, as well as the proceeds from the sale of all or any part of an investment, or from its partial or complete liquidation. Moreover, transfers are to be permitted in freely usable currencies at the market rate of exchange prevailing on the date of transfer. Such transfers may be prevented through the application, in good faith, of insolvency laws, securities regulations, the enforcement of judgements in adjudicatory proceedings and similar situations.

The Agreement also deals with expropriation, which is defined broadly to include any measures that are tantamount to nationalization or expropriation of an investment. The parties are permitted to expropriate or nationalize only for a public purpose, on a non-discriminatory basis, in accordance with due process of law and with payment of prompt, adequate and effective compensation. The standards for compensation are laid out in detail; in addition to prescribing the valuation criteria to be used, the Agreement provides that compensation is to be paid without delay, and the payment is to be fully realizable and freely transferable.

/.....

(Box II.2, cont'd.)

The North American Free Trade Agreement stipulates that all investment in the territories of its parties should be undertaken in a manner sensitive to environmental concerns. Thus, nothing in the Agreement is to be interpreted as preventing the parties from maintaining or enforcing any measure consistent with the Agreement that is considered appropriate in the area of environmental, health and safety laws.

The Agreement includes detailed provisions on the settlement of disputes between private investors and any of the NAFTA parties. An attempt should be made first to settle those disputes through consultation and negotiation; if those options fail, the Agreement establishes the conditions under which arbitration may proceed, in order to ensure equal treatment among investors in accordance with the principle of international reciprocity and due process before an impartial tribunal. The dispute-settlement procedures may be based on the Rules of the International Convention for the Settlement of Investment Disputes (ICSID) or its Additional Facility, or on the Arbitration Rules of the United Nations International Commission on Trade Law (UNCITRAL).

Other aspects of NAFTA closely related to investment issues are those dealing with cross-border trade in services (chapter 12). The provisions of NAFTA in this area apply to all aspects of services operations (e.g., the production, distribution, marketing, purchase, use, sale and delivery of services, and access to, and use of, distribution and transportation systems in connection with the provision of services) and to the presence in a party's territory of a service provider of another party. In all of these respects, each party is obliged to provide the better of national treatment and most-favoured-nation treatment. Moreover, under NAFTA, local establishment of services firms cannot be imposed as a condition for the cross-border provision of services. Those basic principles are developed in annexes dealing with specific industries—e.g., professional services and transportation. To ensure that licensing or certification requirements do not constitute unnecessary barriers to trade, the annex prescribes for professional services a set of criteria, emphasizing mutual recognition and transparency. In addition, some indivudual service industries are dealt with in separate chapters of the Agreement (i.e., telecommunications, in chapter 13, and financial services, in chapter 14).

Chapter 15 of NAFTA sets out disciplines on the operations of State-sanctioned monopolies and state enterprises in general. For those entities, all sales must be made on a non-discriminatory basis. In addition, there are limits on anti-competitive practices (such as cross-subsidiarization).

Another important aspect of NAFTA is the regulation of temporary entry of people pursuing business and investment opportunities. Under certain conditions, citizens of each party are allowed to enter the other countries on a temporary basis without the need to meet labour market requirements, for which the respective countries retain regulatory authority; so those provisions do not create a free movement of labour. The four categories of people eligible for temporary entry are visitors engaged in international business activities set out in appendix 1603.A.1 (including international transit and international services providers); traders and investors carrying out substantial operations between the relevant countries; intra-company transferees engaged in managerial, executive or specialized expert activities; and professionals listed in Appendix 1603.D.1 entering the country to provide professional services on a temporary basis. However, temporary entry for professionals does not entail the recognition of licences and certificates.

The North American Free Trade Agreement allows reservations to be lodged against some of the core obligations contained in its investment and various services chapters. These reservations are set out in seven annexes. Annex 1 lists existing measures that derogate from the obligations relating to national treatment, most-favoured-nation treatment, local presence and performance and nationality requirements. These are subject to stand-still obligations. Annex 2 relates to the same chapters and provisions, but includes a list of sectors in which the federal Governments of the parties are allowed to maintain existing measures, as well as to adopt new ones or make them more restrictive. Annex 3 contains a list of 11 sectors reserved for Mexicans by virtue of the country's constitution. Annex 4 deals with areas in which the Governments reserve the right to negotiate bilateral or multilateral agreements that run counter to the most-favoured-nation standard. (It should be noted also that bilateral double taxation treaties take precedence over NAFTA, so there is a possibility of discriminatory treatment for income and capital taxes.) Annex 5 deals with non-discriminatory quantitative restrictions for transparency (e.g., telecommunications, media, transportation). Annex 6 contains a list of non-discriminatory measures on the provision of services which the parties undertake to liberalize (e.g., performance requirements, licensing requirements). Annex 7 deals with reservations on financial services.

The North American Free Trade Agreement represents a major step forward in the liberalization of sectoral restrictions, and a significant strengthening of the international regime for the treatment of FDI. Its adoption is likely to give impetus to further integration and liberalization efforts throughout the world.

inflows to Argentina and Venezuela have also been concentrated in liberalized services (telecommunications, air transport) (Herrera, 1992). By contrast, Brazil's limited inflows in recent years have been geared towards modernizing the manufacturing operations of foreign affiliates already in the country (Bielschowsky, 1992; Fritsch and Franco, 1991).

Across the region, FDI regimes have continued to be liberalized by simplifying authorization and registration procedures, easing sectoral restrictions, relaxing limits on profit remittances, capital repatriation and technology payments and improving the protection of intellectual property. The larger countries have also done much to encourage FDI through their programmes of external debt conversion (Mortimore, 1991; TCMD, 1993d) and (more recently) of privatization (figure II.5). In Jamaica, for example, 90 per cent of the state-owned enterprises have been subject to privatization (the largest proportion in any developing country), of which almost one quarter involved foreign participation. That process may have accounted for as much as 40 per cent of FDI inflows into Jamaica (Odle, 1993). It is noteworthy that virtually all the region's privatizations of telecommunications and air transport involved foreign capital from Spain, particularly from the state-owned Telefónica de España and Iberia.

In spite of these developments, it is worth noting that Latin Amarica and the Caribbean have benefited very little from the growth of FDI from Japan and the Asian newly industrializing economies. As of fiscal year 1991, only 7 per cent of FDI by Japanese manufacturers, and less than 13 per cent total FDI by all Japanese TNCs had gone to Latin America. Furthermore, although sales by Japanese manufacturing affiliates operating in Latin

Figure II.5. Foreign-direct-investment inflows in Latin America, 1985-1991[a]
(Billions of dollars)

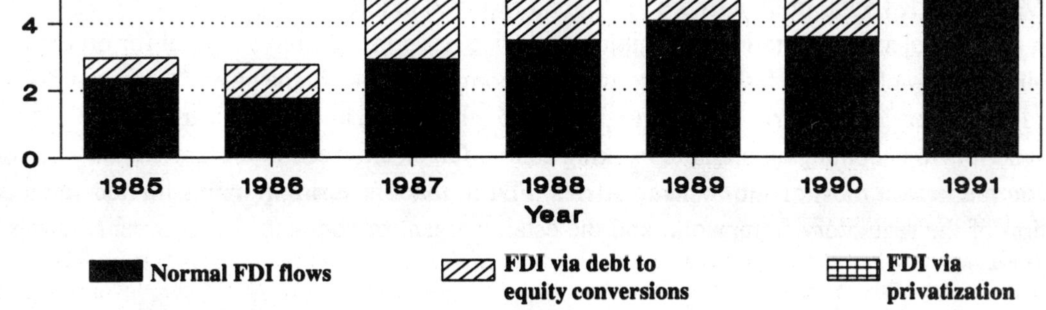

Source: UNCTAD, Programme on Transnational Corporations, based on UNCTAD, 1993c.

a Includes Argentina, Brazil, Chile, Mexico and Venezuela, which accounted for three quarters of total FDI in the region in 1991.

America rose from $2 billion to over $6 billion between 1982 and 1990, the region's share of their global sales fell from 8 per cent to just over 3 percent (Japan, MITI, 1986, 1992b). Recent Japanese investment in the region has been concentrated in a few special activities, such as the *maquiladora* and motor industries in Mexico, and some mining, forestry and fishing projects in Chile and Venezuela. While Japanese TNCs have traditionally been active in Brazilian manufacturing, they have recently tended to rationalize their operations or to withdraw slowly. Similarly, only modest amounts of FDI from the Asian newly industrializing economies have gone into the region. In the past few years, almost 100 Korean textile companies have invested about $100 million in Central America, to take advantage of its unused quotas for the United States market under the Caribbean Basin Initiative. Taiwanese investors have also set up shops in the industrial parks bordering the Canal in Panama.[25]

The region's future pattern of FDI will depend on several factors. One is how far Brazil, once the largest recipient of FDI in the region, manages to stabilize its economy. Another is the effect of NAFTA: Mexico has become more attractive as a low-cost sourcing base for United States TNCs and as a location for third-country investors seeking access to the North American market (United States, International Trade Commission, 1991; Erzan and Yeats, 1992). A third factor could be the growth of intra-regional investments, which are already a force in some Asia-Pacific countries, but are still negligible in Latin America and the Caribbean. This contrast shows up in the level of FDI *outflows* from the region which, during the period 1981-1991, totalled only $4.1 billion, some 13 per cent of the outflows from the Asia-Pacific region.[26]

3. Africa

Investment *inflows* to Africa rose to $2.5 billion in 1991, an increase of 21 per cent from 1990 (figure II.6) (UNCTAD, 1993d). The 1991 total, however, was still below the annual average for the period 1985-1990, which was about $2.7 billion. The bulk of FDI has been in oil-exporting countries, although the share of non-oil producing countries has risen from 20 per cent during the period 1986-1988 to 28 per cent during the period 1989-1991 (figure II.6). That change reflects primarily a sharp rise in inflows to Morocco, where economic growth has been robust, FDI legislation has been liberal and the country has enjoyed duty-free access to the European Community for manufacturing goods produced with a minimum of 40 per cent local content.[27]

Africa's main attraction for foreign investors is still its natural resources. In Angola, for example, investment flows in 1991 exceeded $660 million (more than it had received in total during the period 1985-1990), with the bulk going into petroleum exploration and mining.[28] Africa has considerable potential for oil exploration, and several countries now offer more favourable terms to oil companies than in the past.[29] Some countries have also encouraged FDI in services: Mauritius, for example, has sought foreign investors in banking and finance in recent years, with a view to becoming an offshore banking centre. Given slow economic growth and the small size of the domestic markets in most of sub-Saharan Africa, FDI in manufacturing remains limited. This is despite a liberalization of the regulatory framework, and the establishment of "one-stop" investment centres in several countries.

Investment *outflows* from Africa are negligible. However, increased investment outflows from South Africa in 1992 could bring benefits to the southern African region[30] in a fashion similar to that of Japanese investments

Figure II.6. Foreign-direct-investment inflows to Africa, 1981-1991
(Billions of dollars)

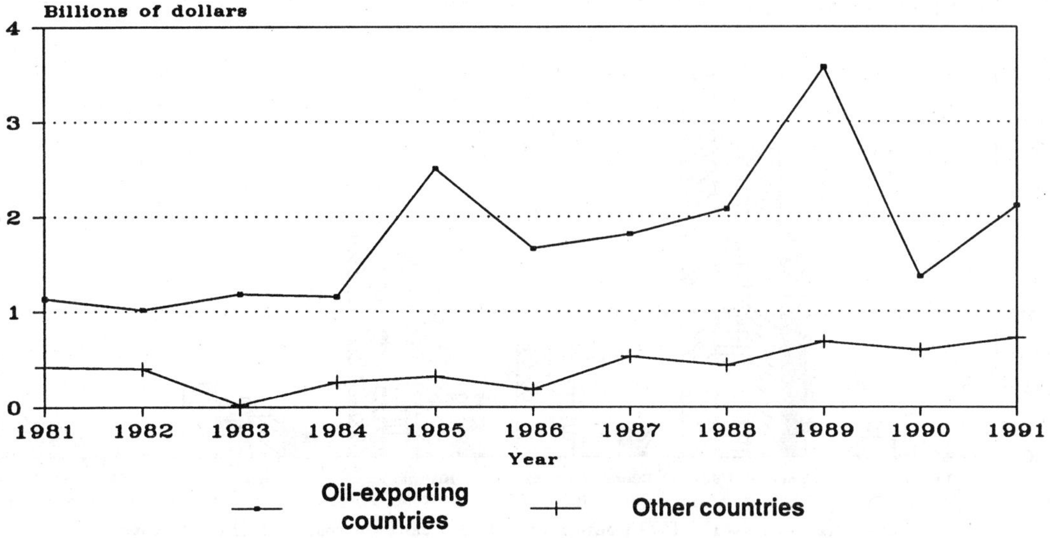

Source: UNCTAD, Programme on Transnational Corporations, based on UNCTAD, 1993d.

in Asia (Vascianne, 1992). However, there are significant differences between the two. For example, the inherent attractions of most southern African countries are their natural resources and cheap labour—and South Africa, unlike Japan, has plenty of both. Economic relations between South Africa and its neighbours have also been cramped by the long years of apartheid, but are almost certain to grow once political relations are fully normalized.

C. Central and Eastern Europe

The number of foreign investment registrations and the amount of foreign capital committed to Central and Eastern Europe continued to grow in 1991 and the first half of 1992 (figure II.7), with Western Europe remaining the main source of investment (TCMD and ECE, 1992). As a result, the region's share of world-wide FDI has risen. The pace of FDI seems to be slowing down, however, and its distribution across the region remains very uneven. Every country in Central and Eastern Europe puts great emphasis on the role of FDI in the transition from central planning to a market economy; since actual inflows of FDI have been small, however, those expectations may be unreasonably high. Apart from some well-publicized cases of investments by large TNCs,[31] most investment projects in the region range from $45,000 to $1.5 million.

During the first half of 1992, the number of FDI registrations in the countries of Central and Eastern Europe (excluding the former Yugoslavia) increased by 50 per cent, reaching some 46,000 foreign affiliates with an estimated $11.7 billion of capital committed (table II.4). According to data from OECD, by the end of 1992 the

Figure II.7. Cumulative foreign direct investment in Central and Eastern Europe, 1991 and 1992
(Billions of dollars)

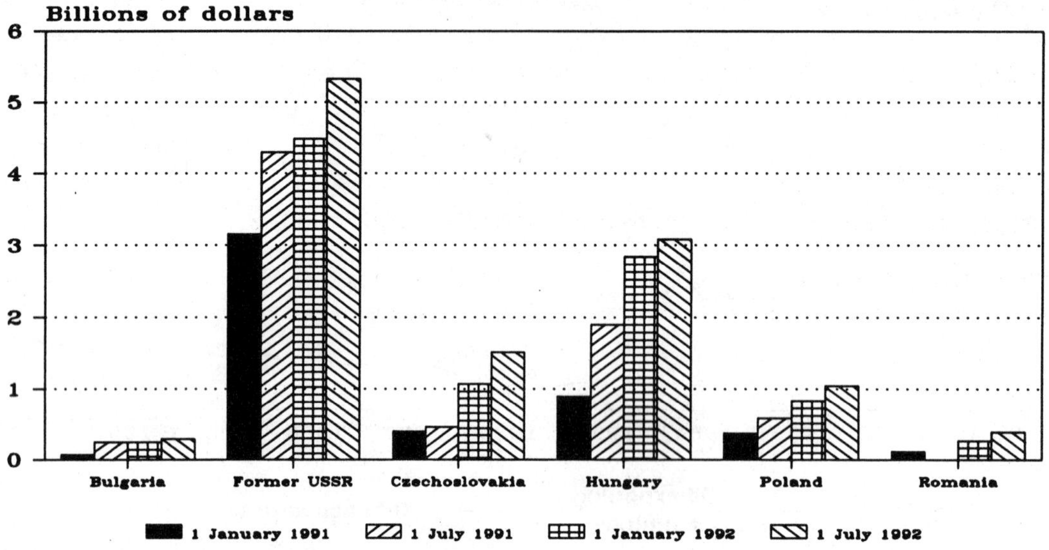

Source: UNCTAD, Programme on Transnational Corporations, based on TCMD and ECE, 1992.

Table II.4. Cumulative number of foreign investment registrations in Central and Eastern Europe, by host country, 1 January and 1 July 1992

Host country	*1 January 1992*	*1 July 1992*
Albania	55[a]	70[b]
Bulgaria	900	1 080
Czechoslovakia	4 000	4 800
Hungary	9 117	11 196
Poland	4 796	7 648
Romania	8 022	13 432
Former Union of Soviet Socialist Republic	4 208	7 792
of which: Commonwealth of Independent States[c]	2 593	4 632
Total	31 098	46 018

Sources: UNCTAD, Programme on Transnational Corporations, based on TCMD and ECE, 1992; and Alter, 1993.

a As of 1 April 1992.
b As of 1 October 1992.
c Excludes Estonia, Latvia, Lithuania and Georgia.

number had risen to 60,000, with a total capital commitment of $14 billion (Alter, 1993). Western European investors provided the largest share of FDI in the region, particularly in Hungary, Romania, Poland and the former USSR. Within the latter, investment continues to be concentrated in the Russian Federation, but figures for Estonia, Latvia and Lithuania are also increasing (World Bank Group, 1992a). This is partly because the Russian Federation (and, to a much lesser extent, Ukraine) has become a significant investor in the Baltic States and the other republics of the former USSR, usually through joint-venture agreements that preserve old supplier and customer links (TCMD and ECE, 1992, p. 20).[32] In the former USSR, it was predominantly enterprises from Russia that had (limited) investments abroad (TCMD, 1992b). They are still investing abroad, especially in Western Europe, and their investments would appear to be increasing.[33]

Within the region, the pattern of FDI inflows still strongly favours a few countries. The Czech and Slovak Republic, Hungary and Poland have made progress with economic reform; they are close to the EC, with which they have concluded association agreements.[34] All of those factors have helped them to attract FDI. Within the former USSR, the Asian republics lag behind the European republics in attracting FDI. Putting all the figures together, Hungary and the republics of the former USSR have accounted for 72 per cent of the foreign capital commitments to the economies of Central and Eastern Europe (excluding the former Yugoslavia) and 41 per cent of the number of registered foreign affiliates.

For the region as a whole, it is instructive to note that, although the number of registrations of foreign affiliates has increased rapidly, the value of capital commitments has grown much more slowly. This may be because some foreign investors hold back in the face of continuing political and economic instability, or because the registered foreign investment projects serve merely as devices to benefit from favourable tax treatment granted to foreign affiliates (World Bank Group, 1992a). By 1991, the ratio of operational to registered joint ventures was estimated to be 41 per cent for Hungary and 35 per cent for the former USSR (Marton, 1993; World Bank Group, 1992a). In 1992, however, the ratio increased to 40 per cent in the former USSR, so the number of projects actually realized may be starting to pick up (World Bank Group, 1992a).

Despite the small amount of FDI thus far, it is beginning to contribute to structural changes. The performance of joint ventures between foreign and domestic firms has been particularly remarkable: their record of sales, profits and foreign-currency earnings per employee has been well above that of domestically-owned enterprises.[35] The sectoral distribution of FDI in the region illustrates the role of TNCs in triggering structural changes. Manufacturing is the single largest type of FDI in most countries. Investment in high-technology industries involving computer and computer-related technologies and telecommunications, where some local expertise exists, has been particularly important (TCMD and ECE, 1992). Although the primary sector has attracted relatively little foreign investment thus far, several TNCs are interested in the potential for petroleum exploration and exploitation in the former USSR, which is expected to be a major source of foreign-currency earnings for the new republics.[36] As for services, they were traditionally neglected in centrally planned economies, but are now considered to be central to the success of the transition process. They are attracting a lot of interest from TNCs, particularly in Hungary (TCMD and ECE, 1992).

The contribution of TNCs to economic reform is also apparent from the way they are clustered in export industries. This is helping to integrate the region into the world economy and to increase foreign exchange earnings. In Hungary, for example, foreign affiliates account for more than 16 per cent of non-rouble exports

(Marton, 1993). It is through TNCs that host countries obtain speedy access to marketing and distribution facilities, particularly in Western Europe; and it is through the perception of closer association with the European Community (including possible membership) that more TNCs are then encouraged to invest in the region.[37] Only through such a virtuous circle will FDI play its part in providing the amount of foreign finance that the region requires.[38]

Notes

1 Takeover activities in the United States amounted to $116.7 billion in 1991, representing a decline from $169.4 billion in 1990 and the $263.8 billion record in 1988. See Martin Dickson, "Mergers and acquisitions: steady stream of smaller deals", *Financial Times*, 11 June 1992.

2 The value of foreign takeovers by the largest 50 French firms declined by 24 per cent to 80 billion French francs by 1991, putting an end to four years of straight growth. See William Dawkins, "Exports revival", *Financial Times*, 22 June 1992.

3 "Japanese capital flows: inward bound", *The Economist*, 8 February 1992; "Japan's direct investment slows", *The Wall Street Journal*, 8 June 1992.

4 The United States affiliates of Japanese companies are cautious about re-investment in plant and equipment and long-term plans, because of low profitability. Sixty-three per cent of 264 Japanese affiliates in the United States cited earnings as their biggest concern; and half plan no change in future capital spending, while 19 per cent plan cuts. See James Sterngold, "Japanese shifting their investments back toward home", *The New York Times*, 22 March 1992, and "Japanese wary on U.S. operations", *The Wall Street Journal*, 9 June 1992.

5 See Lionel Barber, "Big stake in EC's future", *Financial Times Survey: Japan and The European Community*, 13 November 1992; Michiyo Nakamoto, "Investment in manufacturing: time for rigorous assessment", *Financial Times Survey*, op. cit.; Daniel Green, "Fears over long-term impact", *Financial Times Survey*, op. cit.

6 Some examples of new alliances established are those between Renault, a state-owned automobile company, and Volvo, the Swedish car maker; the stakes taken in Bull, the state-owned French computer group, by Nippon Electric Corporation of Japan and International Business Machine (IBM) of the United States; and the share swap being negotiated between Banque Nationale de Paris and Dresdner Bank of Germany. See William Dawkins, "Revising the borders", *Financial Times*, 22 June 1992.

7 See Robert Graham, "The Italian auction begins", *Financial Times*, 20 July 1992; Heig Simonian, "Privatization encounters barriers", *Financial Times*, 7 July 1992; Tim Carrington, "Italy braces for privatization measures", *The Wall Street Journal*, 12 June 1992.

8 The slow pace in which the privatization programme has been implemented in Greece has resulted in limited investments by foreign entities. The exception was Heracles General Cement, Europe's biggest cement exporter, sold for 124 billion drachmas to a joint venture between Calcestruzzi (52.5 per cent), the construction arm of Italy's Feruzzi group, and the National Bank of Greece. In addition, although the Government of Portugal has pursued an ambitious programme of economic liberalization and privatization (with the dismantling of state monopolies and the liberalization of financial markets), the state continues to play a dominant role in the economy. Foreign control of privatized companies is not generally authorized, while foreign participation cannot exceed 40 per cent of the voting capital. Hence, in all but two privatizations, foreign participation has been limited to between 2 and 35 per cent. See Kerin Hope, "Privatization: quickening pace of sales", *Financial Times*, 15 June 1992, and Andrew Jack, "Privatization: the state prevails", *Financial Times*, 4 March 1992.

9 The number of Swedes employed by foreign companies has tripled. An estimated 135 Swedish companies employing 40,000 workers were acquired by foreign concerns since the late 1980s. See Robert Taylor, "Sweden to launch strategy to attract foreign investors", *Financial Times*, 18 February 1992.

10 Of 18 FDI cases by companies engaged in the production of automobiles, engineering products, chemicals and pharmaceuticals, only three cases were concerned with exporting from the domestic market, and in only one was the investment motivated by exports to the EC (and Latin America). For 17 of the 18 cases, the main objective of FDI was import-substituting, made in response to the imposition of high tariffs and import quotas (Buckley and Artisien, 1987).

11 Even export-oriented FDI in developing countries that could have been negatively affected by the single EC market, owing to possible investment diversion to the southern members of the EC (Greece, Portugal and Spain), did not suffer because of the rising costs of labour and stricter pollution standards in the latter (Agarwal, 1992).

12 However, although the overall effect of the single market is very small, its specific effect on some developing countries like Cyprus, Malta, Mauritius and Tunisia may be substantial (TCMD, 1993a and Cable, 1988).

13 "Japanese prepare for the Vietnam gold rush", *The Wall Street Journal*, 21 February 1992. As of 31 August 1992, Taiwan Province of China was the largest foreign investor in Viet Nam. See Alexander Nicoll, "Vietnam looks for gains from US election", *Financial Times*, 3 November 1992, and Victor Mallet, "Cambodians rush headlong to market", *Financial Times*, 28 November 1991.

14 "Japanese investment in Asia: the second wave", *The Economist*, 7 November 1992, pp. 87-88.

15 These would not be reflected in FDI data compiled for the balance of payments.

16 Consulate General of India, unpublished data. See also "Foreign investment: more, but still not enough", *Financial Times*, 26 June 1992.

17 Foreign direct investment on a contract basis differs from investment actually made. In 1991, for example, FDI totalling $4.4 billion was actually made from the $12 billion contracted.

18 James McGregor, "Foreign firms in China are preparing for expected consumer spending surge", *The Asian Wall Street Journal Weekly*, 23 March 1992; Robert Thomson, "Honda announced first motorcycle venture in China", *Financial Times*, 27 May 1992.

19 It should also be noted that investment inflows did not decline in the aftermath of the Tiananmen Square incident in 1989, which might suggest that these investments would have increased sooner, were it not for the incident.

20 Michiyo Nakamoto, "Motorola builds semiconductor plant in China", *Financial Times*, 19 May 1992.

21 "Bank Negara signals shift in foreign investment focus", *East Asian Executive Reports*, May 1992, pp. 13-14; Jon Liden, "Foreign investment: a more selective approach", *Euromoney* (Malaysia supplement), August 1992, pp. 51-53, 56-57.

22 Outflows of FDI from Taiwan Province of China to China and Viet Nam, however, continued to grow in 1992 despite the overall decline in their total outflows in 1992.

23 Urban C. Lehner, "With Japan's backing, Indonesia gains a larger role in regional economy", *The Wall Street Journal*, 10 January 1992.

24 "Thai group invests $1 billion in China", *Financial Times*, 7/8 November 1992. Thai firms have also begun to invest in Laos and other neighbouring countries.

25 See "Asian tigers leap into Central America", *Business Latin America*, 16 December 1991, pp. 401-402; and "Bienvenidos, invasores", *America Economia*, No. 65 (September 1992), p. 77.

26 Data do not include outflows from Mexico which are not available.

27 Claude Clement, "U.S. and Morocco expand commercial ties: Morocco gives priority to tourism development", *Business America*, 112 (4 November 1991), pp. 2-8; and "Morocco's investment rules", *Middle East Executive Reports*, 113 (November 1990), pp. 16-21.

28 Caroline Southey, "The oil industry: key to Angola's survival since independence", *Financial Times*, 12 May 1992; Griffin (1991); "Industry poised to boost production on Angola/Cabinda acreage", *Oil and Gas Journal*, 90 (10 February 1992), pp. 36-37. A record level of petroleum exploration activity in Angola was recorded in 1991. Several transnational petroleum corporations (e.g., Chevron, Elf, Texaco, Petrofina and Agip) have been active in this country.

29 Martin Quinlan, "Energy finance: Africa woos the energy giants", *Euromoney*, Energy Finance Supplement (June-July 1990), pp. 63-64.

30 Philip Gawith, "South Africa investment up—but so are the outflows", *Financial Times*, 26 November 1992; and Patti Waldmeir, "Pretoria acts on exchange control curbs", *Financial Times*, 1 December 1992. Some of the South African TNCs that have recently invested abroad include Sappi, Mondi and First National Bank. There is also a proposed takeover of Del Monte Foods International by the Royal Group and Anglo American.

31 For example, in terms of capital committed, Volkswagen AG is investing $6.6 billion in the Czech and Slovak Federal Republic, Fiat is investing $2 billion in Poland, Chevron is investing $1.5 billion in Kazakhstan, General Motors is investing $289 million in Hungary and Pilkington is investing $140 million in Poland. See TCMD and ECE (1992) as well as Steve Levine, "Kazakhs move slowly to negotiate deals that will unlock their riches", *Financial Times*, 8 April 1993.

32 According to the national statistics of Latvia and Lithuania, the Russian Federation's share of registered foreign affiliates was 32 per cent in both countries. The share of registered foreign affiliates of corporations headquartered in Ukraine was 4 per cent in Lithuania and 3 per cent in Latvia.

33 For example, a Moscow-based firm recently purchased part of the German company, United Cellulose Works of Pirna (Saxony). See German Information Center, "First Russian firm buys Eastern German company", *The Week in Germany*, 16 October 1992, p. 5.

34 The flow of FDI to the Czech and Slovak Federal Republic will probably be affected by the break-up of the country. According to the Czech Republic Industry Minister, approximately 20 per cent of foreign firms had canceled ongoing negotiations with Czech firms and about 40 per cent had put talks on hold because of the political uncertainties (see Bureau of National Affairs, *Eastern Europe Reporter*, 2 (20 July 1992), p. 592. The agreement on the dissolution of the Czech and Slovak Federal Republic concluded on 20 July 1992 stipulates, however, that the two states will maintain close cooperation in foreign policy, defense and trade, including the creation of a free-trade zone ensuring the free flow of labour and capital. For the time being, Slovakia has received less than 20 per cent of total FDI in the Czech and Slovak Federal Republic (see Bureau of National Affairs, *Eastern Europe Reporter*, 2 (3 August 1992), p. 650).

35 See Nicolas Denton, "A kiss of life from across the border", *Financial Times*, 4 December 1992.

36 See Leyla Boulton, "The lure of oil's final frontier", *Financial Times*, 6 March 1992.

37 For example, the global rivalry between Coca-Cola and Pepsi Cola and between Ford and General Motors seems to have been carried over into the Hungarian market. See Bureau of National Affairs, *Eastern Europe Reporter, Special Report: Hungary*, 2 (20 July 1992), pp. 613-616.

38 The capital needed for privatizations in Latin America, South-East Asia and Central and Eastern Europe has recently been estimated at $500 billion. A similar amount is required for the former Soviet Union. See William B. Rhodes, Vice Chairperson of Citibank, in *The Economist*, 12 September 1992, p. 21.

CHAPTER III

SECTORAL TRENDS

A. Overall trends

The rapid growth of foreign direct investment (FDI) has been accompanied by big changes in its sectoral composition (table III.1). During the 1950s, FDI was concentrated in the primary sector and resource-based manufacturing; today, it is mainly in services and in technology-intensive manufacturing. The shift towards services accelerated during the 1980s. They represented a quarter of the world stock of FDI at the beginning of the 1970s; 20 years later, their share was close to 50 per cent, and they were accounting for 55 to 60 per cent of annual flows.

This growth in services should not be allowed to obscure the strength of FDI in other sectors. In manufacturing, both the outward and inward stock of FDI in developed countries grew significantly during the second half of the 1980s. Moreover, in the early 1990s it was still manufacturing that had the largest inward stock of FDI in the main developing countries. As for the primary sector, it showed the fastest growth in the inward stock of FDI in developed countries during the 1980s (table III.1).

1. Explaining sectoral shifts

Shifts in the pattern of both inward and outward FDI broadly reflect structural changes in the nature of economic activity (Ozawa, 1992), with the primary sector declining in relative terms while services increase. However, the main home and host countries became predominantly service economies some time ago, whereas the surge of services FDI is relatively recent. Clearly, the FDI changes happened with a lag.

The nature of that lag reflects the different sectoral roles of trade and FDI as conduits of international integration. Where goods are concerned, by and large trade has preceded FDI as the main way of delivering them to foreign markets. In the case of services, this sequence was not really feasible, because so many of them are non-tradable. As a result, FDI was the only means to participate in international service transactions. But in many important service industries, and in both developed and developing countries, FDI was initially prohibited for strategic, political or cultural reasons. Consequently, the rise of FDI in services had to wait for the liberalization of major service industries to catch up with the domestic process of structural change.

In general, the pace and sequence of liberalization has depended on the size of the economy, the speed of technological and business change at the firm, industry and national levels, and political circumstances. With services, liberalization has followed distinct stages. Banking and other financial services have, historically, been the most international services and the earliest targets of liberalization. Over the post-war period, the growth of FDI in trade-related services has gradually caught up with the expansion of world trade. Now, with the liberalization of producer services, FDI is beginning to respond to the broader needs of transnational corporations (TNCs) competing in a global market-place.

Table III.1. Sectoral distribution of foreign-direct-investment stock for the largest developed home countries and the largest developed and developing host countries, 1970-1990

(Billions of dollars and percentage)

Group of countries and sectors	*1970*	*1975*	*1980*	*1985*	*1990*	*1971-1975*	*1976-1980*	*1981-1985*	*1986-1990*	*1981-1990*	*1970*	*1975*	*1980*	*1985*	*1990*
	Billions of dollars					*Average annual growth rate in per cent*					*Share in percentage*				
A. Outward stock															
Developed countries[a]															
Primary	29	58	88	115	160	14.0	8.7	5.5	6.8	6.2	22.7	25.3	18.5	18.5	11.2
Secondary	58	103	208	240	556	11.7	15.1	2.9	18.3	10.3	45.2	45.0	43.8	38.7	38.7
Tertiary	41	68	179	265	720	10.4	21.4	8.2	22.1	14.9	31.4	27.7	37.7	42.8	50.1
Total	129	229	475	620	1 436	11.7	15.7	5.5	18.3	11.7	100.0	100.0	100.0	100.0	100.0
B. Inward stock															
Developed countries[b]															
Primary	12	17	18	39	94	4.7	5.9	16.7	19.2	18.0	16.2	12.1	6.7	9.2	9.1
Secondary	44	79	148	195	439	10.7	13.4	5.7	17.6	11.5	60.2	56.5	55.2	46.2	42.5
Tertiary	17	44	102	188	499	16.5	18.3	13.0	21.6	17.2	23.7	31.4	38.1	44.5	48.4
Total	73	140	268	422	1 032	11.3	13.9	9.5	19.6	14.4	100.0	100.0	100.0	100.0	100.0
Developing countries/ economies[c]															
Primary	..	7	17	31	46	..	19.4	12.8	8.2	10.5	..	20.6	22.7	24.0	21.9
Secondary	..	19	41	64	102	..	16.6	9.3	9.8	9.5	..	55.9	54.6	49.6	48.6
Tertiary	..	8	17	34	62	..	16.3	14.9	12.8	13.8	..	23.5	22.7	26.4	29.5
Total	..	34	75	129	210	..	17.1	11.4	10.2	10.8	..	100.0	100.0	100.0	100.0

Source: UNCTAD, Programme on Transnational Corporations, foreign-direct-investment database.

a Australia, Canada, France, Federal Republic of Germany, Italy, Japan, Netherlands, United Kingdom and the United States; together these countries accounted for almost 90 per cent of outward FDI stock in 1990. 1970 and 1971-1975 growth data exclude Australia and France.

b Australia, Canada, France, Federal Republic of Germany, Italy, Japan, Netherlands, Spain, United Kingdom and the United States; together these countries accounted for approximately 72 per cent of total inward FDI stock in 1990. 1970 and 1971-1975 growth data exclude Australia, France and Spain.

c Argentina, Brazil, Chile, China, Colombia, Hong Kong, Indonesia, Malaysia, Mexico, Nigeria, Philippines, Republic of Korea, Singapore, Taiwan Province of China, Thailand and Venezuela; together these countries accounted for 68 per cent of total inward FDI in developing countries.

In addition to liberalization, technological change has become an increasingly important influence on FDI across sectors (and also within sectors). The outstanding development in recent decades has been the widespread application of micro-electronics-based technologies. These new technologies have been accompanied by innovations in the organization and management of production, which encourage closer cooperation between companies and customers and place a premium on the flexibility of firms and the quality of products. By the very nature of those technologies, TNCs have been well placed to benefit from their wider application.

The new technological paradigm, based on information processing and dissemination, has been particularly suited to manufacturing and services. Computer technology was initially adopted in mature manufacturing industries in response to, among other things, the competitive pressures of freer trade. But it spread quickly to services, and made possible the creation of new activities.[1] A prominent example is telecommunication services, which were long based on electro-mechanical technology, but have been transformed by computers, micro-electronics, fibre optics and satellites into a modern service industry. Similar changes have happened in financial services, advertising, design, retailing and tourism.

Information technology has therefore been central to a new form of dynamism in economic life. It has ensured that all activities can be based on more and better knowledge. It has created new markets and made other markets more accessible. It has thereby increased competitive pressures in most types of economic activity. Such competition spurs further technological change to produce information more cheaply and disseminate it more rapidly.

2. The sectoral dimensions of the activities of transnational corporations

The sectoral composition of FDI is only one measure of the economic influence of TNCs. The size of individual TNCs, their job-creating capacities, their ownership structure, their contribution to trade and technology transfer—all these can and do vary from one sector to another.

- The size of individual TNCs reflects several influences that vary between sectors. Transnational corporations in the primary sector are still among the largest of all: taking all resource-based activities (the primary sector plus food, drink, tobacco and paper), they account for one quarter of the largest 100 TNCs. By contrast, TNCs in services are noticeable by their absence from that list (see table I.10).[2] The smaller size of services-sector TNCs indicates the limited scale economies in many business services and the more restrictive FDI regulations in many capital-intensive services.
- On its own, size does not automatically translate into jobs. For firms from the primary sector, their weight among the top 100 TNCs is significantly reduced when measured by employment—which simply reflects their capital intensity. Also, despite the labour-intensive nature of many service companies, FDI in services does not create more employment than FDI in other sectors. Rather, the capital- and asset-intensity of FDI in services is comparable to industrial affiliates (table III.2). However, service affiliates do have a skill level closer to that of their parents and, on average, higher than affiliates in either the manufacturing or primary sectors, although this reflects their larger presence in developed economies.

Table III.2. Characteristics of United States transnational corporations, by sector, 1982 and 1989

Variable	1982 Services	1982 Manufacturing	1982 Primary	1989 Services	1989 Manufacturing	1989 Primary
R&D intensity						
1. R&D expenditures as percentage of sales						
Parents[a]	0.53	3.01	0.64	0.47	3.33	0.72
Affiliates[b]	0.10	1.15	0.15	0.31	1.12	0.15
In developed countries	0.14	1.31	0.20	0.36	1.27	0.11
In developing countries[c]	0.02	0.46	0.02	0.05	0.30	0.32
2. R&D employment as percentage of total employment						
Parents[a]	0.78	4.91	2.30	0.75	5.46	3.24
Affiliates[b]	0.76	2.27	0.68	0.83	2.42	0.62
Skill level (Compensation per employee, thousands of dollars)						
Parents[a]	24.2	29.8	36.0	30.6	38.9	47.1
Affiliates[b]	18.8	16.9	22.4	27.1	25.2	24.8
In developed countries[d]	19.1	20.6	31.0	29.6	33.3	42.3
In developing countries[c]	15.0	8.7	16.6	13.8	9.5	20.7
Capital intensity						
1. Physical capital intensity[e] (thousands of dollars)						
Parents[f]	52	30	191	62	47	337
Affiliates[b]						
By industry of parent	21	20	173	26	31	398
By industry of affiliates	26	20	143	30	31	258
2. Assets per employee						
Parents[f]	192	97	385	316	186	757
Affiliates[b]	215	57	300	371	114	428
In developed countries[d]	173	65	532	349	147	884
In developing countries[c]	348	39	142	485	52	190
Trade (Percentage of sales)						
Parents[a]						
Total exports	4.3	10.3	2.1	2.8	11.6	2.6
Exports to affiliates	0.4	3.9	0.6	0.4	5.3	0.8
Imports from affiliates	0.5	2.6	2.4	0.4	4.2	2.2
Affiliates[b]						
Total exports[g]	30.6	33.9	32.7	27.2	37.8	25.5
Exports to parents						
Sales to United States parents	5.6	8.3	15.9	5.4	12.2	8.4
United States imports[h]						
Industry of affiliate	2.0	8.4	6.3	1.6	11.2	7.0
Industry of parent	2.7	6.8	4.7	2.8	9.0	3.8
Imports from parents						
Industry of affiliate	4.7	10.7	0.6	6.9	11.3	0.8
Industry of parent	2.5	10.9	0.9	2.5	12.0	1.4

Source: United States Department of Commerce, 1985, 1992a.

a Non-bank United States parent firms with non-bank affiliates.
b Majority-owned non-bank affiliates of non-bank United States parent firms.
c 1989 developing country data include Israel, New Zealand and South Africa.
d 1989 developed country data include non-allocated international transactions.
e Net property, plant and equipment per employee.
f Non-bank United States parent firms with majority-owned nonbank affiliates.
g Sales to the United States and countries other than home country.
h United States imports shipped by affiliates to United States parent firms.

- Also in terms of their ownership structure, TNCs vary from sector to sector. Those operating with natural resources have traditionally been involved in international joint ventures and strategic alliances. More recently, in manufacturing and services, new types of non-equity relations have evolved. Manufacturers have been drawn to subcontracting, networking and international research-and-development consortia, while service companies are active in franchising, financial consortia, management contracts and professional partnerships. Those developments reflect not only the rising costs of research and development and the risks associated with shorter product cycles, but also the increasing importance of non-tangible assets that can be supplied without foreign equity capital.

- The nature of TNC linkages with the global economy also differs across sectors. As goods are tradable and many services are not, service companies and their foreign affiliates are not big exporters. Moreover, both primary sector and manufacturing activities are better suited to developing an intra-firm division of labour. Service firms can build transnational networks among their affiliates, but they cannot split their activities in the same way as their industrial counterparts do. Consequently, intra-firm trade in the services sector is considerably lower than in manufacturing. However, the lower tradability of many services means that a given amount of FDI in services involves a greater use of soft technology and skills than the same amount of FDI in manufacturing or the primary sector.

  When affiliates in the different sectors are compared with their parent companies, it is the service affiliates that are most like their parent firms in terms of skill profile, research-and-development expenditures and asset-intensity (table III.2). In other words, service affiliates are more like miniature versions of their parent firms rather than specialized elements in a world-wide production network; they are more complete and free standing than manufacturing affiliates.

B. The primary sector

1. Introduction

Primary activities can be divided into renewable resources (agriculture, fishing and forestry) and non-renewable (mining and quarrying and petroleum). Of the two, non-renewable resources dominate FDI.[3]

For historical, technical and financial reasons, FDI has featured disproportionately in the development of the primary sector. Few firms in developing countries have the resources and know-how to conduct large-scale exploration or exploit the commercial potential of deposits.[4] Consequently, although geography is still the main determinant of FDI in this sector, the sensitive issues of control and the depletion of finite resources, combined with the size and visibility of TNCs, imply that bargaining between foreign investors and national Governments will strongly influence the scale and scope of FDI (McKern, 1993).

During the 1950s, investment was dominated by a small group of large and experienced TNCs, predominantly of Anglo-Saxon origin. This pattern has been changing, however, not least because many developing countries have sought to capture more of the expected economic rents from their natural resources, including through nationalizations (Kennedy, 1992). The most visible changes occurred in the petroleum industry, where expropriations by OPEC nations significantly reduced the TNC role in production.[5] However, similar developments occurred in many areas of mineral extraction (UNCTC, 1983, pp. 205-209), creating some of the world's largest mineral companies (Ericsson and Tegen, 1993, p. 5). At the same time, new firms from resource-dependent developed economies (notably Germany and Japan) entered into the development of natural resources.

Contrary to predictions of increasing scarcity, the price of many primary resources has fallen sharply in real (and often nominal) terms (TCMD, 1992a, p. 133). Each extra dollar of GNP needs a smaller amount of raw materials, a trend that has caused difficulty for many developing countries. None the less, comparative advantage dictates that resource-rich countries will still have to develop their primary sector, both as a source of fiscal revenue and foreign exchange and as the starting point for sustainable growth and development (box III.1).

Box. III.1. Resource-led growth and foreign direct investment: the example of Botswana

Africa has long been particularly dependent on FDI for the development of its natural resources.[a] One country that has managed this relationship successfully is Botswana. At independence in 1966, it was one of the world's poorest countries. Since then, it has been one of the world's fastest growing economies, with annual growth averaging 14 per cent during the period 1965-1980 and 11 per cent during the period 1980-1990. Employment growth in the formal sector has been equally impressive, averaging 10 per cent a year since 1972. By 1990, with a per capita income of $2,040, Botswana was comfortably a middle-income economy.

The country's success has been based almost exclusively on the expansion of mining and quarrying. Their share of GDP rose from only 1 per cent in the early 1970s to over 50 per cent in 1988-1989. Government revenues from mineral taxes and royalties have risen steadily, to over 50 per cent of the total. Although the country contains deposits of gold, copper, coal and soda-ash, it is diamonds that have predominated;[b] they accounted for well over three quarters of total exports during the 1980s.

With limited domestic resources and mining know-how, the Government of Botswana had to attract FDI. Circumstances ensured that capital, entrepreneurship and technology would come from South Africa, and from one TNC in particular: De Beers of South Africa. From the opening of the first mine in 1971, all Botswana diamond mines have been owned by Debswana, a 50:50 venture between De Beers and the government. A similar equity arrangement was devised for sorting; marketing is exclusively controlled by De Beer's Central Selling Organization. In addition, import licences have been freely available and exchange controls are liberal. As a result, inward FDI has risen from 8 per cent of GDP in 1971 to 30 per cent in 1980, falling back to 17 per cent in 1989.

Stable internal politics and good governance have also done much to ensure that the local economy has benefited from FDI:

- Diamond contracts were renegotiated after the second mine was developed. The aim was to increase Government revenues, but also to continue longer-term contractual agreements with De Beers and ensure a degree of price stability (Lewis, 1988, p. 1592).
- The Government has based its fiscal policy on longer-term expectations of mineral taxes and royalties.
- Botswana has avoided direct state investment in the mining industry, and has been able to ensure that a rising share of government expenditures has gone to improving human capital through better health-care provision and expanded educational opportunities. Those trends are forecast to continue in the most recent development plan (Harvey, 1991).

/.....

2. Recent trends

The share of the primary sector in the total outward stock of leading developed countries declined during the 1980s, from 18 per cent in 1980 to 11 per cent in 1990.[6] The dominance of the four leading developed countries—Japan, the Netherlands, the United Kingdom and the United States—increased slightly, and more noticeably in the case of the United Kingdom, which became the leading home country. But a more interesting development in the 1980s was the rapid growth of the primary sector's inflows of FDI into developed countries. Although its inward stock in 1990 was considerably smaller than that of manufacturing and services, during the 1980s it outgrew both (see table III.1). Moreover, because it grew considerably faster than the inward stock in developing countries, the developed countries' share of the primary sector's stock of inward FDI rose from 52 per cent in 1980 to 67 per cent in 1990. Consequently, whereas the primary sector's share of the total stock of FDI remained unchanged in developing countries, in developed countries it actually rose from 7 per cent to 9 per cent;[7] reversing the declining trend in the 1970s (see table III.1).

This unexpected shift was driven by particularly rapid growth in the developed countries' inward stock of petroleum during the first half of the 1980s (40 per cent) and in mining and quarrying in the second half

(Box III.1, cont'd.)

- Externally, Botswana's status as a small open economy, heavily dependent upon imports, has led it to build up foreign reserves when export earnings were strong for use when revenues fell. Combined with an effective monetary policy to curb inflation, this has ensured a relatively stable exchange rate. Botswana has therefore been able to avoid the potentially varying effect that large and fluctuating export earnings would have on the rest of the economy—the so-called "Dutch disease" (Hill, 1992).[c]

Despite Botswana's success, doubts about resource-led development remain. The future of the economy continues to depend on prospects in the world diamond market. The Central Bank of Botswana anticipates slower growth in the 1990s as diamond prices fall. It has stressed the need to diversify output—particularly in favour of manufacturing, which has had a declining share in GDP (though its employment total has increased). Moreover, the economy is still handicapped by poor infrastructure, lack of skilled manpower and the small domestic market; and political developments in South Africa add to the uncertainty of the region.

In recent years, Botswana has tried to diversify the range of activities based on diamonds: cutting and polishing have both involved large amounts of FDI, with the single biggest investment coming from a United States company, Lazare Kaplan International, and including a minority government holding (15 per cent). Elsewhere in the primary sector, diversification has been achieved through a soda-ash project which began operating in 1991. Much of the capital has been provided by three South African corporations. However, not much FDI has yet been attracted to manufacturing or services; their combined share has remained at only around 7 per cent of total inward stock during the 1980s. Botswana's next challenge is to transfer its experience in managing the development of its primary sector to organizing the expansion of the rest of the economy.

---

a Cantwell (1991a), table 9.5, estimated that, in 1982, the share of FDI stock in the primary sector in Africa was in excess of 50 per cent, compared to 12 per cent for Asia and Pacific and 20 per cent for Latin America and the Caribbean.

b Botswana is the third largest producer of diamonds in volume terms (after Zaire and Australia) and the largest in value terms (Blomström and Norberg, 1990, pp. 15-16).

c The monopolized nature of the world diamond market has added to price stability. Moreover, external stability has also derived from Botswana's membership in the Southern African Custom Union (Blomström and Norberg, 1990, pp. 39 and 42-43).

(23 per cent). It is clear that TNCs were still, in part, reacting against the policies of nationalization pursued by the Governments of many developing countries in the 1970s, and were putting more weight on the stability and credibility of the host Governments countries. However, FDI flows have also been directly influenced by purely economic factors, including the scale of investment, changes in technology, financial expectations and market prospects. Moreover, TNCs have continued to move into higher-value added transportation, processing and marketing activities. All these developments have biased FDI flows towards developed countries.

Expectations of higher oil prices stimulated investment in the first half of the 1980s. Some developed countries were the main beneficiaries (primarily the United Kingdom, Norway and also the United States); so too were a few developing countries, such as Indonesia, Malaysia, the Philippines and Thailand.[8] Companies also responded to the rising costs and greater risks of oil exploration by increasing their cross-border mergers and acquisitions during the late 1970s and the first half of the 1980s, particularly in the United States, and involving, primarily, Western European TNCs (UNCTC, 1988a, pp. 62-65). Some oil companies, notably British Petroleum, also acquired mining companies in an attempt to diversify production. Under similar market pressures, horizontal and vertical integration has also taken place among mining companies and many spent money to boost productivity (Ericsson and Tegen, 1993, p. 6).

In the primary sector, low equity forms of FDI have been commonplace. This has been particularly true of late arrivals, such as German and Japanese TNCs (Ozawa, 1982). Significantly, Japan is still alone among the developed countries in having most of its primary sector investment stock located in developing countries. During the 1980s, however, Japanese companies in the primary sector also participated in new ventures through equity rather than just through long-term contracts, and particularly during the second half of the 1980s, built a stronger presence in developed countries (Ericsson and Tegen, 1993, p. 7).

Although technological advances have been less pronounced than in other sectors, some new technologies developed in response to declining mineral prices have increased FDI including to developing countries. In gold mining, new technologies have encouraged the entry of smaller producers, and in copper mining, new extraction methods have made the development of low-cost ore deposits, in such countries as Chile and Mexico, more attractive.

3. Prospects

Although predictions must come with the usual qualifications and caveats, three factors are likely to affect FDI in the primary sector during the 1990s. First, the FDI associated with the mergers and acquisitions of petroleum and mining companies is being replaced by a retreat to core business activities; even by the mid-1980s petroleum companies were abandoning their mining investments.[9] This will result in a reduction in FDI flows to developed countries, because it is the developing countries (and the Commonwealth of Independent States) which will offer the best opportunities for privatization and new activity. Examples include Algeria's recent production-sharing agreements in the Hassi Messaoud fields, the intention of the Government of Argentina to privatize its oil industry and Peru's privatizations in copper and iron-ore mining; and these are likely to be repeated in other countries.[10] Given the trend to privatization and the scarcity of domestic capital in many developing countries, the share of mineral production controlled by TNCs is likely to increase. However, many of the most successful mining companies remain state controlled and, even if privatization accelerates, the State will retain a significant role in the industry (Ericsson and Tegen, 1993, pp. 6-7).

Second, and more importantly, prospects for FDI in the oil industry will depend critically on conditions in world energy markets.[11] The declining influence of OPEC should be set against the fact that most experts believe world demand for oil and gas will grow during the 1990s. Capacity constraints in the more mature fields will almost certainly require the opening of new fields. Already, in their search for oil and gas, the big TNCs are moving away from the North Sea and North America (where production costs are high) into more uncertain regions in Asia, Latin America and Eastern Europe. Undoubtedly, the attractiveness of these regions for inward FDI will improve as privatization gathers pace, liberalization is extended and contractual rights are firmed up. However, given the preference of oil investors for regions with proved reserves, production, including through FDI, is likely to expand in the OPEC countries.[12]

Similar movements, also driven by cost considerations, can be expected in mining. Prices there seem set to continue their secular decline of the past two decades. In addition, further expansion to ensure profitable operations will attract FDI back to the most promising areas, which include many developing countries. South African mining companies are set to expand into the underexplored countries of southern Africa, such as Angola, Mozambique and Namibia, where they might face increasing competition from Australian companies. And the dominance of United States TNCs in Latin America is likely to be challenged by European firms.

Thirdly, the opening up of the former socialist countries to FDI is likely to provide significant opportunities, particularly in mining and petroleum. Developing the Russian oil industry could involve, according to one estimate, $70 billion of FDI (box III.2).[13] Given the political and economic instability of the region, the poorly defined legal regimes and the longer-term horizon required for much FDI in this sector, TNCs have so far responded cautiously to the opportunities. Moreover, foreign ownership remains a sensitive issue, adding to investor uncertainty.

In many regions of the former Soviet Union, however, only the top geological layer has been explored and many experts believe there is a high probability of discovering large new fields. As the major oil companies prefer to explore areas with known potential, the attraction of the former Soviet Union once the investment climate is clearer, may very well result in some developing countries seeing declines in oil FDI.

C. The secondary sector

1. Introduction

Despite a relative decline in the 1980s, manufacturing still accounted for almost 40 per cent of outward FDI from developed countries in 1990. Within the sector, three notable changes took place during the 1980s:

- In both inward and outward FDI, a move to capital- and technology-intensive industries, and away from resource- and labour-intensive activities.
- New forms of investment have evolved, particularly low-equity and non-equity arrangements and strategic alliances among TNCs from different countries.
- The emergence of corporate networks, often taking a markedly regional form.

Each of these developments is considered in more detail below.

2. Recent trends

(a) *More capital- and technology-intensive manufacturing*

This category of manufacturing increased its share of the sector's outward FDI from 46 per cent in 1980 to 51 per cent in 1990 (table III.3).[14] However, the significance of this change is more readily discernable in inward FDI. The five largest industries for inward manufacturing FDI since the mid-1970s have been chemicals, food, beverages and tobacco, electrical equipment, metals and mechanical equipment. These contain a mixture of technologies and of capital intensities. None the less, the overall pattern was clear (albeit with noticeable regional differences).

Box III.2. Prospects for foreign direct investment in the oil industry in the former Soviet Union

During the 1970s and 1980s the Soviet Union became the world's largest oil producer, with output peaking at 12.8 million barrels per day in 1988. However, investment has plummeted since 1989, and output has fallen sharply.[a] With estimated potential production of 20m barrels a day (only slightly less than the current output of OPEC), there is a strong case for FDI to play a part in reviving and modernizing oil production in the former Soviet Union. One recent estimate suggests that oil companies would spend up to $70 billion developing the industry.[b]

To date, FDI has been hindered by various obstacles. In the first place, the scale of the task now seems larger than originally thought. The inherent risk of oil development is magnified in the former Soviet Union by widespread fragmentation of the infrastructural network, the lack of managerial skills and environmental obstacles. Longer-term commitments have been further hampered by the slow pace of legislative and political reform.[c]

Moreover, the structure of the post-Soviet industry is only just beginning to take shape. Legislation in November 1992 created three regionally based companies—Lukoil, Yukos and Surgutneftegaz—involved in all stages of production. Although these vertically integrated companies will be mainly privately owned, the Government intends to keep some control over the equity, and will not allow the pipeline systems to be privatized. The extent of foreign participation (if any) remains uncertain and many officials continue to favour non-equity involvement. To date, the actual amounts of FDI in the oil industry in the former Soviet Union have been very small.[d]

Despite these difficulties, prospects for FDI have been improving, as the problems of restructuring become more apparent and the authorities recognize the potential contribution that TNCs would make. The smaller countries of the former Soviet Union have been particularly accommodating. In the race to attract western investment, Kazakhstan has some of the largest deals pending. It has persuaded foreign investors of its fiscal and legal credibility, offers light oil-industry taxes and has achieved some political stability.

/.....

In the developed countries, the largest share of FDI still goes to natural-resource and labour-intensive industries. However, this share has fallen steadily since the mid-1970s and more rapidly during the second half of the 1980s (figure III.1) Inward FDI in the capital- and technology- intensive industries grew fastest in 1975-1980 at more than 21 per cent a year, compared with 17 per cent for the natural-resource and labour-intensive industries. The share of the former in manufacturing's inward stock of FDI increased correspondingly, from 27 per cent to more than 38 per cent; by 1990 it stood at 40 per cent. Between 1980 and 1990, the share of capital- and technology-intensive industries in FDI rose faster in developing than developed countries; in particular, the electrical equipment industry is considerably more important in developing countries, accounting for more than 12 per cent of their inward stock of manufacturing FDI in 1990, compared with only 7 per cent in developed countries.

The category of capital- and technology-intensive industries is particularly significant in the newly industrialized economies, such as Hong Kong, the Republic of Korea, Singapore, Taiwan Province of China and Thailand (figure III.1). In the newly industrialized economies, inward FDI in manufacturing grew at 16 per cent annually in 1975-1990, compared with 9 per cent for other developing countries; and the capital- and technology-intensive industries grew at 18 per cent annually, compared with 14 per cent for natural-resource- and labour-intensive industries. By comparison, in developing countries other than the Asian newly industrialized economies, inward FDI grew at roughly the same rate in both categories.

The gradual move of FDI away from labour-intensive, low-cost, low-skill manufacturing and towards more capital-, knowledge- and skill-intensive industries reflects the spread of new technologies, especially those

(Box III.2, cont'd.)

Elf was involved in the earliest deals (after lengthy negotiations) and Chevron is negotiating to invest $10 billion to develop the Tenzig and Korolev fields, with estimated recoverable reserves of 6 billion and 9 billion barrels. Further deals are expected on the Caspian Sea. Uzbekistan recently reached agreement with the Stan Cornelius Consortium (a group of United States investors) to develop its Mingbulak field, which has estimated reserves of 800 million barrels; and the autonomous region of Komi has recently concluded deals with Conoco, Total and Occidental Petroleum.

To date most involvement has been through joint ventures with local producers. In many cases, and in light of the scale and risks involved, TNCs have formed collaborative ventures. For example, the 3M group consisting of Marathon Oil, McDermott and Japan's Mitsui has been instrumental in studying the Sakhlin Island fields, and Phibro Energy and Anglo Suisse have collaborated with local producers to pump Siberian crude oil. However, in many of these cases further expansion will require cooperative agreements at the Government level.

---

a Investment declined by one third between 1989 and 1991; see "West needed to plug leaks in former Soviet oil sector", *Financial Times*, 24 July 1992, p. 32. Recent estimates by Russian officials do not anticipate output from their fields—which hold 90 per cent of proved reserves in the former Soviet Union—to exceed 1992 levels until well into the next century. See "Russian energy projections", *Eastern European Markets*, 19 February 1993, 13.

b Ann Imse,"American know-how and Russian oil", *The New York Times Magazine*, 7 March 1993.

c Territorial disputes are pervasive, such as in Azerbaijan, which has deals pending with Amoco to develop fields in the Caspian Sea. Also the development of the large Sakhalin field has been delayed by a dispute with Japan over the Kurile Islands.

d According to a recent study, less than one per cent of the assets of the Russian oil sector at the beginning of 1992 could be attributed to foreign firms; see "Russia's cold shoulder", *The Economist*, 13 March 1993.

involving electronics and informatics. These technologies have reduced the labour content of production and increased the knowledge component.[15] Furthermore, an expanding range of smaller manufactured products and lighter materials has increased the opportunities for FDI, because transportation costs have fallen. However, the increasing popularity of a "best practice" approach has worked to increase the concentration of FDI. Computer-aided-manufacturing and computer-aided-design, plus just-in-time production, are steering TNCs to locate in developed countries and those developing countries (such as the Asian newly industrialized economies) which have built up their human skills and physical infrastructure.

The trend to knowledge- and skill-intensive manufacturing takes place not only among broadly classified industries, but also within the same industries. As the competitive advantages of firms come to depend on their ability to innovate, FDI in certain research-intensive industries (such as pharmaceuticals, computer and office equipment, special industry machinery and electronic components and accessories) has grown faster than that in less research-intensive manufacturing. That is clearly revealed in the United States inward and outward data for 1982-1991 (table III.4).

Table III.3. Industrial distribution of foreign-direct-investment stock in the manufacturing sector for the nine largest home countries, by group of industries, 1975-1990[a]
(Billions of dollars and percentage)

	Amount (Billions of dollars)				*Share (Percentage)*			
Sector/industry	*1975*	*1980*	*1985*	*1990*	*1975*	*1980*	*1985*	*1990*
Natural-resource and labour-intensive industries	32.1	97.6	103.6	214.0	31.1	46.9	43.2	38.5
Food, beverages and tobacco	12.6	25.2	26.1	67.8	12.2	12.1	10.9	12.2
Textiles, leather and clothing	1.3	5.5	4.4	8.7	1.3	2.6	1.8	1.6
Paper	2.6	8.8	11.4	37.0	2.5	4.2	4.8	6.7
Coal and petroleum	1.3	23.3	22.0	24.5	1.3	11.2	9.2	4.4
Rubber	0.1	4.7	4.0	9.0	0.1	2.3	1.7	1.6
Non-metallic minerals	0.2	3.2	8.5	7.0	0.2	1.5	3.5	1.3
Metals	14.0	26.9	27.2	60.0	13.6	12.9	11.3	10.8
Capital- and technology-intensive industries	51.2	95.5	115.4	284.6	49.6	45.9	48.1	51.2
Chemicals	18.8	40.2	48.2	112.3	18.2	19.3	20.1	20.2
Mechanical equipment	18.2	22.0	26.6	56.8	17.6	10.6	11.1	10.2
Electrical equipment	3.6	15.0	19.9	62.4	3.5	7.2	8.3	11.2
Motor vehicles	10.2	16.6	16.5	40.1	9.9	8.0	6.9	7.2
Other transport equipment	0.4	1.7	4.2	13.0	0.4	0.8	1.7	2.3
Other manufacturing	19.2	14.8	20.9	55.8	18.6	7.1	8.7	10.0
Total [b]	103.2	207.9	239.9	555.6	100.0	100.0	100.0	100.0

Source: UNCTAD, Programme on Transnational Corporations, based on TCMD, 1993c.

a Australia, Canada, France, Federal Republic of Germany, Italy, Japan, Netherlands, United Kingdom and the United States. These countries accounted for 90 per cent of the world-wide outward FDI stock in 1990.

b Total may not add up because of unallocated industries.

Figure III.1. Distribution of the inward foreign-direct-investment stock in the manufacturing sector, by groups of industries and countries, 1975-1990
(Percentage share)

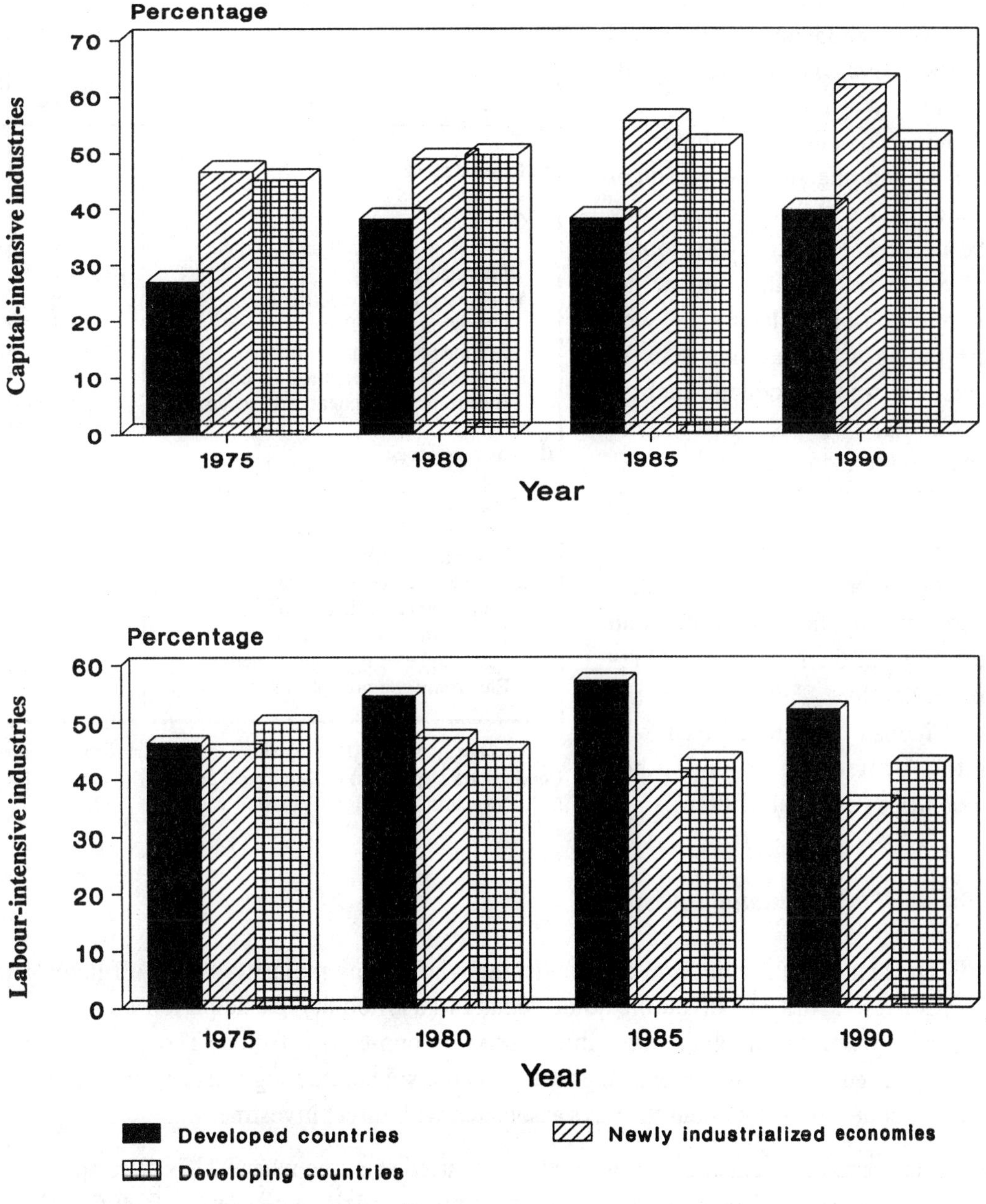

Source: UNCTAD, Programme on Transnational Corporations, based on UNCTAD, 1993c, 1993d; UNCTC, 1992b; TCMD, 1993c.

This upgrading can also be seen in the Asian newly industrialized economies, particularly Taiwan Province of China and the Republic of Korea. In the 1970s and 1980s, they were assembly sites for the intermediate products of TNCs from Japan and the United States. Now they have advanced to the full-production stage in semiconductors, consumer electronics, computers, computerized design and manufacturing, often as a result of the activities of TNCs.[16] Similar upgrading seems to be occurring in other developing countries of South-East Asia, from the assembly of simple consumer electronics, such as transistor radios and television sets, to more complex electronic products, such as television monitors, videocassette recorders and computers and semiconductors.[17]

The presence of strong domestic industries based on indigenous research capacities enables firms to extend their outward FDI more rapidly, because it offers an attractive location for their international research and production. This explains the growing intra-industry nature of FDI witnessed in the United States and other developed countries (Cantwell, 1991b).

Table III.4. Growth of inward and outward foreign-direct-investment stock in research-intensive manufacturing industries for the United States, 1982-1991
(Millions of dollars and percentage)

Industry/activity	*Growth rate (Percentage)* 1982-1991	*Value (Millions of dollars)* 1991
A. Inward stock		
Chemicals	14.6	49 133
Industrial chemicals and synthetics	12.4	27 611
Pharmaceuticals	24.7	13 125
Machinery, except electrical	12.8	10 450
Computer and office equipment	17.4	2 907
Special industry machinery	15.8	1 795
Electric and electronic equipment	14.5	17 188
Electronic components and accessories	7.8	4 327
B. Outward stock		
Chemicals	9.2	40 229
Industrial chemicals and synthetics	8.8	18 734
Pharmaceuticals	13.0	10 902
Machinery, except electrical	8.9	29 781
Computer and office equipment	11.9	20 649
Special industry machinery	7.1	931
Electric and electronic equipment	8.6	15 334
Electronic components and accessories	15.7	7 678

Sources: UNCTAD, Programme on Transnational Corporations, based on United States Department of Commerce, *Survey of Current Business* (Washington, D.C., Government Printing Office), various issues.

(b) New forms of transnational investment

Not all TNC activity takes the form of establishing wholly- and majority-owned affiliates. Particularly in developing countries, TNCs are favouring joint ventures (with equity participation coming in the form of capitalization of technology or other intangible assets) or non-equity forms. The latter includes licensing agreements, original-equipment-manufacturing arrangements, subcontracting and turnkey contracts, all of which allow firms to maintain control without the risks associated with direct investment.

Some of those arrangements were known and widely used at a time when TNCs were not very popular and their activities were restricted. Yet, they seem to have maintained their share of manufacturing FDI, to judge by United States figures (figure III.2). This suggests that the reasons for using them have changed. To take an example from manufacturing in developing countries, non-equity links are increasingly common in the international sourcing of components. Many of these forms of FDI establish close and longer-term relationships with domestic firms, often to the point of quasi-integration. They seem particularly suited to small and medium-size TNCs from developing countries, in such industries as consumer electronics, textiles and clothing, and footwear.

Minority joint ventures and licensing with TNCs have also been prominent in the automotive-assembly industry of developing countries (including several North African, ASEAN and Latin American countries, the Islamic Republic of Iran and Nigeria), particularly because of government restrictions on foreign ownership. In the mid-1980s, almost 3 million vehicles were produced or assembled in 47 developing countries, of which 47 per cent were under non-equity arrangements and 53 per cent under equity FDI (UNCTC, 1988a). Process industries, such as chemicals and petroleum, have also been successfully established in many developing countries through turnkey and engineering contracts (Oman, 1984).

Because manufacturing in the developed countries is often in the innovation phase, TNCs are more likely to retain control through wholly- or majority-owned affiliates. However, non-equity arrangements are also increasingly motivated by similar influences. Increasingly, they involve strategic alliances in high-technology industries (and even in mature industries that seek technological infusion). Their main motive is to share the risks of new research and the costs of developing new products, and to get quicker access to rapidly changing technologies. More importantly, strategic alliances bring technological cross-fertilization, as technologies origi-

Figure III.2. Majority- and minority-owned manufacturing affiliates of the United States transnational corporations, by assets and sales, 1977, 1982 and 1989

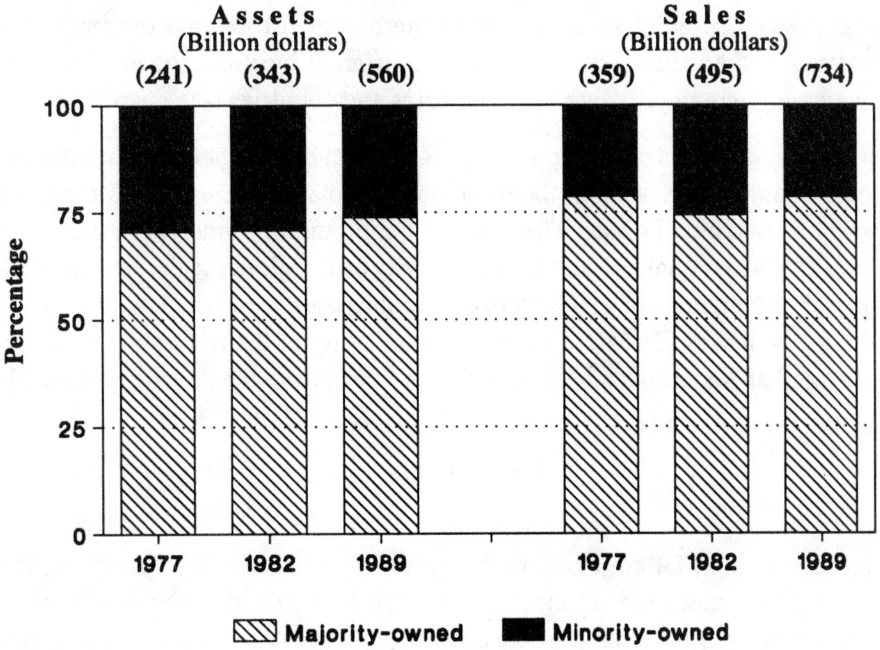

Source: UNCTAD, Programme on Transnational Corporations, based on United States Department of Commerce, 1981, 1985 and 1992a.

originally developed for one industry are increasingly applicable to others. These agreements have been boosted by the need not to break anti-monopoly laws (as in the United States), as well as to consolidate manufacturing production and to gain competitive advantages in regional markets (Gross, 1989).[18] In some cases, they have been promoted directly, to support collective efforts in research, development and manufacturing (as in the European Community). Some of these cooperation agreements may involve equity participation, but they stop short of outright mergers or acquisitions.

The adoption of new technologies and organizational methods in manufacturing have altered the sourcing and locational patterns of TNCs in favour of quality, reliability and proximity to the site of final manufacture. Technological changes have extended the life of a number of sunset industries in developed economies, by reducing labour costs and improving supplies through more integrated management strategies. Although TNCs in the consumer electronics and motor industries still engage in outsourcing (particularly of materials or standardized parts and components), increasingly they prefer to establish either joint ventures or other forms of cooperative relations with their suppliers (Dunning, 1988; Tolentino, 1993). These changes clearly work against those developing countries whose comparative advantage lies in labour-intensive assembly operations, which are farther away from developed country markets and which do not have large internal markets of their own. Moreover, the more technologically complex forms of production by TNCs take place in developing countries too, the establishment of wholly- or majority-owned affiliates will matter more.

(c) *The growth of corporate networks*

With the spread of non-equity and collaborative arrangements, the shape of TNC networks has changed considerably (Dunning, 1985). The links between parent firms and their foreign affiliates, and between foreign affiliates at different stages of the value-added chain and in different locations, have become closer and more complex, leading to increasing interdependence between firms and countries (see chapters V to VII).[19]

The integration of production has often happened on a regional basis. That trend has been enhanced by the development of regional arrangements, such as the formation of the Single European Market and NAFTA, and the gradual emergence of a trade bloc in Asia. The expanded opportunities inherent in such arrangements have led many manufacturing TNCs to organize much of their activity on a regional scale. Another factor contributing to regional integration is the emergence of TNCs from developing countries, which tend to be a growing source of FDI in other developing countries (TCMD, 1993c). Because many of them are still in their infancy, they are establishing minority-owned affiliates to a greater extent than TNCs from the developed countries.[20]

3. Prospects

The trends in manufacturing FDI are likely to strengthen over time. In the first place, many developing countries (and the transition economies of Central and Eastern Europe) will probably move towards greater capital- and technology-intensity. Some countries are already pursuing policies to upgrade their economies and to attract TNCs in the newer growth industries. Malaysia is an excellent case in point (see chapter II): its recent change in policy is directed to attract FDI into higher-end electronics (Astbury, 1991).

Secondly, the move to regionally integrated strategies of TNCs will gather pace if Europe, North America and Asia do indeed set up trade blocs. Corporate strategies of globalization through regionalization are still at an early stage, but will become increasingly significant. Two of the most likely changes relate to the role of Japan in Asia and the role of the United States in Latin America, initially in Mexico. Japan is likely to strengthen its position as the largest source of FDI in an increasing number of Asian countries, particularly in manufacturing.[21] Asia offers a horizontal division of labour, allowing factories in Japan to specialize in manufacturing high-end products while relying on a steady supply of goods from their foreign affiliates and local companies in Asia. Similar developments are likely to affect Mexico in relation to North American TNCs.

Thirdly, TNCs will probably expand the range of ways they enter foreign markets, so their networks will become increasingly widespread and complex. However, much will depend on the stability of the host economy, and the adoption of an appropriate policy framework, including measures to improve physical infrastructure and increased training (Konopacki, 1992).[22]

Lastly, as developing countries get richer, more of their firms are expected to become TNCs, and their existing TNCs will increase the scale and complexity of their overseas manufacturing (TCMD, 1993b; Tolentino, 1993). Indeed, a two-tier pattern of cross-border FDI in manufacturing is already taking place in Asia: from Japan into the Asian newly industrializing economies, and from all of them to China, Indonesia, Malaysia, the Philippines and Thailand (Lall, 1991; Levin, 1991). However, some of these firms, particularly from Taiwan Province of China, are getting into developed country markets through higher-value electronics such as computers and petrochemicals.[23]

D. The tertiary sector

1. Recent trends

Although services have grown rapidly in the outward and inward FDI of most developed countries and in the inward FDI of many developing countries, their strongest growth has been in the Triad countries. This has changed their position in world-wide FDI (see annex tables). In the case of the United States, it has been services are primarily responsible for making that country the largest host to FDI. Japan owes its remarkable rise among home countries to an explosion of investment in financial, trading and transportation services, as well as real estate. Similarly, the emergence of the European Community as a major FDI Triad partner is largely owing to the expansion of services within the European Community (in response to the creation of the single market) as well as in the United States (in part owing to the strength of European currencies).

The rapid growth of FDI in services has come not only from transnational service corporations (TSCs), but also from substantial investment in service activities by transnational industrial corporations. Other factors have also played a role: the establishment of holding companies and regional headquarters, investment in real estate, and the setting up of financial affiliates in tax havens and of transportation affiliates in countries offering flags of convenience.

The share of TSCs in the services stock of FDI differs among the four major home countries. In Germany and the United Kingdom, TSCs have been the dominant force; their share has been high—over 80 per cent—and rising. In the United States, by contrast, TSCs account for less then half of FDI in services and their share has declined (table III.5). Japan falls in between; affiliates of services parents account for two thirds of all affiliates in services.

Within the services sector, finance- and trade-related activities account for two thirds of the FDI stock for developed countries and the majority of the stock in many host developing countries. This is not surprising, given that financial TNCs (banks, insurance companies) and trading companies (for example, Japanese *sogo shosha*) are among the most prominent TSCs, that manufacturing and petroleum companies have invested heavily in wholesale and marketing affiliates and that all kinds of TNCs tend to establish their own finance-related foreign affiliates.[24] In addition, other service industries in which TNCs are prominent are either small (such as advertising), or rely heavily on non-equity forms of investment (such as the hotel and restaurant industry), or both (accounting and business consultancy). There are, however, some exceptions, such as real estate (relatively large in inward FDI into France and the United States and in outward FDI from Japan) and construction (sizeable in some host developing countries). Most importantly, in those capital-intensive service industries—telecom-

Table III.5. Sources of services foreign direct investment in the four largest home countries, 1976-1990[a]
(Number and percentage)

	United States[b]			*Federal Republic of Germany*[c]			*Japan*[d]			*United Kingdom*	
Item	*1977*	*1982*	*1989*	*1976*	*1984*	*1990*	*1977*	*1984*	*1990*	*1981*[e]	*1987*
Number of TNCs:											
Total	3 540	2 245	2 272	2 589	3 910	4 917	1 223	1 488	1 616	..	..
Services	1 204	925	901	1 097	1 841	2 523	409	541	575	..	..
Number of foreign affiliates:											
Total	24 666	18 339	18 899	9 059	14 657	19 352	3 589	4 937	7 986	..	..
Controlled by service parents	7 317	5 212	5 318	..	..		1 538	1 916	2 965	..	..
In services	13 595	10 339	10 562	5 267	9 429	13 201	1 586	2 671	4 384	..	..
Stock of FDI as percentage of total FDI stocks:											
Controlled by service TNCs	21	19	22	29	32	46	..	..	..	24	33
In services	41	38	49	42	47	56	38	52[f]	67	34	39

Source: UNCTAD, Programme on Transnational Corporations, based on official sources.

a These countries account for 80 to 85 per cent of the FDI stock in services of the largest ten home countries.

b Services include holding companies. The substantial decline in the total number of United States TNCs and their affiliates is most likely a result of changed reporting procedures. The cut-off point below which full data for foreign affiliates do not have to be reported was increased from $500,000 in 1977 to $3 million in 1982 and in 1989.

c Excluding individuals. Services include holding companies.

d Does not include banks and insurance companies.

e Does not include oil, banking and insurance.

f 1985.

munications, various kinds of transportation and public utilities—which could rival finance and trading, FDI has so far been restricted in most countries.

2. New areas for foreign direct investment in services

These old restrictions are starting to change, which in time will alter the pattern of FDI. Already, some capital-intensive service industries are opening up to FDI.

(a) Air transportation

This is one of the most rapidly changing industries in terms of FDI, with a surge of equity investments taking place since the second half of the 1980s (table III.6). However, most countries continue to restrict FDI to minority equity holdings. The most active investors are airlines from Western Europe, pursuing different geographical strategies. For example, Air France has expanded its equity links to other airlines primarily in Europe, Iberia Airlines has done so in Latin America, while the expansion of British Airways has shown the most global reach.

Although a few United States airlines have bought equity stakes in foreign airlines, more often they have been the target of others; as a result of which the United States has become the major host country. Latin American and Central and Eastern European countries have attracted FDI through privatization.[25]

In addition to minority equity holdings, there has been a proliferation of strategic alliances among major airlines from both developed and developing countries. Most of these alliances have eschewed ownership, though the case of Delta Air Lines, Swissair and Singapore Airlines has involved cross-share-holdings of up to 5 per cent. One quite common form of alliance is the linking of airline computer-reservation systems, which are an important marketing tool and can capture travelers by directing them to partner airlines.[26] One example is the current merger between the European COVIA-APOLLO and the United States GALLILEO computer-reservation systems. If approved by the United States and European regulatory bodies, it would establish the first reservation network between European and United States airlines with a global scope (see box VI.4).[27] Other non-equity arrangements common in air transportation include technical cooperation and service contracts, especially between airlines from developed and developing countries.

Deregulation has been a big influence on the way the airline industry has opened up to FDI. It began in the United States in the late 1970s, but did not initially affect FDI. Foreign airlines were not allowed to hold more than 25 per cent of the equity of a domestic airline, and any acquisition was subject to approval by the United States Department of Transportation. The surge of FDI occurred only after policy changes began to extend to international traffic as a result of:

- The intention of the European Community to deregulate and liberalize intra-EC traffic within the Single Market programme, followed by the first steps to achieve this goal;
- Further liberalization of United States air-transport services in 1991. The aim was to attract FDI to an industry financially exhausted after years of competition. The ceiling on foreign equity in domestic

Table III.6. Foreign direct investment in the airline industry, 1987-1993

Year	*Foreign investor*	*Home country*	*Recipient company*	*Host country*	*Share of equity*	
					Millions of dollars	*Percentage*
1993	Aeromexico	Mexico	Aeroperu	Peru	54	70
	Air Canada	Canada	Continental Airlines	United States	235	27.5
	Air Lanka[a]	Sri Lanka	Vada-Bosnaair	Macedonia	..	..
	Baltic International[a]	United States	Baltic International Airlines	Latvia	..	..
	British Airways	United Kingdom	USAir	United States	300	24
	Sun Air[a]	Denmark	Blue Sky	Poland	..	..
	Viennair[a]	Austria	Danube Air	Hungary	..	..
1992	Air France	France	Czechoslovak Airlines[b]	Czechoslovakia	30	19.1
			Sabena World Airlines	Belgium	178	37.5
	Alitalia[c]	Italy	Malev Hungarian Airlines	Hungary	77	30
	American Airlines[a]	United States	Canadian Airlines International	Canada	192	33.3
	Austrian Airlines	Austria	Albanian Airlines	Albania	..	..
	British Airways	United Kingdom	Deutsche BA[d]	Germany	..	49
			Qantas Airways	Australia	450	25
			Touraine Air Transport	France	25	49
			Trans World Airlines[a]	United States	..	..
	Iberia Lineas Aereas de Espana[e]	Spain	Aerolinas Argentinas	Argentina	..	30
			Ladeco Linea Aerea del Cobre	Chile	..	35
			Lan-Chile	Chile	..	30
			Viasa Internacional de Aviacíon	Venezuela	145	45
	Korean Air[a]	Republic of Korea	Pakistan International Airlines	Pakistan	..	..
	Lufthansa German Airlines	Germany	Luxair	Luxembourg	..	13
	T. Roche	France	Ada Air	Albania	..	..
	Xabre Group[f]		Mexicana	Mexico	..	48
1991	El Al Airline	Israel	North American Airlines	United States	..	24.9
	Japan Airlines	Japan	Air New Zealand	New Zealand	..	8
	Singapore Airlines	Singapore	Swissair	Switzerland	..	3
	Swissair	Switzerland	Singapore Airlines	Singapore	..	1
1990	British Airways	United Kingdom	Air Russia[g]	Russia	32.5	31
	China International Trust and Investment Corporation	People's Republic of China	Dragonair	Hong Kong	..	38
	Crossair	Switzerland	Tatra Air	Czechoslovakia	..	..
	Delta Air Lines	United States	Swissair	Switzerland	..	5
	Swissair	Switzerland	Delta Air Lines	United States	..	5
	Taca International Airlines	El Salvador	Aviateca	Guatemala	..	30
			Lacsa	Costa Rica	..	10
			Nica	Nicaragua	..	49
			Sahsa	Honduras	..	40
1989	Air France	France	Austrian Airlines	Austria	..	2
			Euskal Air	Spain	..	20
	Delta Air Lines	United States	Singapore Airlines	Singapore	..	3

/.....

(Table III.6, cont'd.)

Year	Foreign investor	Home country	Recipient company	Host country	Share of equity	
					Millions of dollars	*Per-centage*
1989 (cont'd.)	Finnair	Finland	Scandinavian Airline Systems	Sweden, Norway, Denmark	..	5
	Japan Airlines	Japan	Hawaiian Airlines	United States	..	20
	KLM Royal Dutch Airlines[h]	Netherlands	Northwest Airlines	United States	400	20
	Lufthansa German Airlines	Germany	Austrian Airlines	Austria	..	10
			Sunexpress	Turkey	..	40
	Sabena World Airlines	Belgium	Universaire	Italy	..	49
	Singapore Airlines	Singapore	Delta Air Lines	United States	..	5
	Scandinavian Airline Systems	Sweden, Norway, Denmark	Lan-Chile	Chile	..	30
			Finnair	Finland		5
1988	American Airlines	United States	Air New Zealand	New Zealand	..	8
	All Nippon Airways	Japan	Austrian Airlines	Austria	..	10
	Ansett Australia	Australia	Ladeco Linea Aerea del Cobre	Chile	..	25
	Qantas Airways	Australia	Air New Zealand	New Zealand	..	20
	Scandinavian Airline Systems	Sweden, Norway, Denmark	British Midland Airways	United Kingdom	..	49
			Continental Airlines	United States	..	17
	Swissair	Switzerland	Austrian Airlines	Austria	..	10
1987	Ansett Australia	Australia	America West Airlines	United States	..	20
	KLM Royal Dutch Airlines	Netherlands	Air UK	United Kingdom	..	15

Sources: UNCTAD, Programme on Transnational Corporations, based on various reports.

a Case is pending; the year indicates the opening of negotiations.
b In addition, the European Bank for Reconstruction and Development invested $30 million and holds an equity share of 19.1 per cent.
c Additional 5 per cent bought by SIMEST, a recently created Italian state agency to promote investment abroad.
d Deutsche BA was set up by British Airways and three German banks.
e Iberia is also considering investing in the state-owned airlines of Costa Rica, Dominican Republic, Ecuador, Paraguay, Peru and Uruguay (see *The Economist*, 29 February 1992).
f Grubo Xabre is part of the Falcon group, a multinational consortium including individual investors and the Chase Manhattan Bank.
g Air Russia is a joint venture between British Airways and Aeroflot.
h KLM owns 20 per cent of the common stock and 10.5 per cent of the voting stock in Northwest Airline's parent, the Wings Holdings Inc.

airlines was raised to 49 per cent, with the limit on the voting stock of a foreign investor remaining at 25 per cent;[28]

- Negotiations to liberalize services within the Uruguay Round, and the possibility that a General Agreement on Trade in Services would cover air transportation;

- The growing interest of some countries in liberalizing (if not abolishing) bilateral air-service agreements that guarantee market shares and revenues. Changes in that direction have already been concluded between the United States and the Netherlands; it provides airlines of both countries with unlimited access to each other's airports. Other similar negotiations are taking place.

These regulatory changes are starting to create more intensive competition for market share. The recent FDI agreements with certain United States airlines, some of which are still being negotiated or are awaiting approval, need to be seen in this light. Furthermore, competition within the European Community may lead to the privatization of some state-owned carriers, thus increasing the potential for FDI from within and outside the Community.[29] Many other countries, especially in developing regions and in Central and Eastern Europe, need more efficient air-transport services, so they are seeking investments and know-how that TNCs from developed countries can provide.

(b) Telecommunications

Telecommunications companies are among the largest in nearly all countries, but the industry has historically been so closed to FDI that most countries have not even singled it out in their FDI statistics. Recently, however, because of technological and regulatory changes as well as privatization, telecommunications has been transformed. Its restructuring has led to the opening up of several regions and market segments to FDI, as well as to the emergence of TNCs (and the potential for a wide-ranging globalization of the industry).

Technological change—the birth of telematics as a result of the marriage between computer and communications technology—has been a major factor behind the industry's restructuring. It has broadly expanded the range of applications of telecommunication services, and moved the industry to the centre of national attention. The availability, price and quality of telecommunications services affect so many economic activities that pressure on governments to improve those services has vastly increased. In addition, some new technologies have been decentralizing in nature (for example, satellite transmissions, cellular phones), and have therefore deprived more and more the industry of its natural monopoly status—and governments of their ability to keep the whole industry under control.

The privatization of telecommunications monopolies in developing countries, especially in Latin American countries such as Argentina, Chile, Mexico and Venezuela, has been accompanied by the liberalization of FDI rules. As a result, telecommunications TNCs from France, Italy, Spain and the United States have acquired stakes in firms in those countries.[30] As the privatization trend continues, it will bring FDI to the indebted, capital-poor countries of Africa, Central and Eastern Europe and Latin America, which need both capital and know-how to modernize their telecommunications infrastructure.[31]

Among developed countries a group of large public and private telecommunication companies are increasingly competing with each other in markets for new services. The most important single group of services at stake, where competition is most intense, are those involving the management and operation of the international communication networks of TNCs headquartered in the Triad region, where 75 per cent of the world telecommunication activity is concentrated.[32] Competition for a share of this market explains the increasing intensity of cross-border acquisitions and alliances among the big companies (table III.7), and offers the greatest potential for globalization; projections to the end of the century suggest that there will be five or six global telecommunication companies carrying voice as well as data, and serving households as well as offices.[33]

For the time being, however, global networks owned and operated by TNCs are the exception rather than the rule. This is partly because in many countries it is not yet possible for TNCs to own and operate the necessary physical assets and/or to have access to the necessary international telecommunication traffic rights. Another reason is that the creation of truly global super carriers providing the whole range of modern telecommunication services is hugely expensive. In terms of both capital outlays and risk, it is still beyond the finances and capabilities of even the largest firms.[34] The big companies have therefore begun to build alliances coordinating their services across separate telecommunication regimes. They are establishing global networking as a substitute for global networks.[35]

Table III.7. Telecommunications: cross-border acquisitions of companies,1985-1990
(Number and millions of dollars)

Year	*Number of acquisitions*	*Value (Millions of dollars)*
1985	5	399
1986	7	132
1987	7	63
1988	11	117
1989	50	2 694
1990	67	16 539[a]

Source: *Financial Times Survey, World Telecommunications*, 7 October 1991.

a The high value in 1990 is owing to privatizations that occurred in that year ($9.9 billion). Investment by foreign companies in the United States represented only 2.8 per cent of the value of cross-border deals in 1990.

In addition to telecommunication services for TNCs, a vast range of new, specialized services and markets is opening up to competition and FDI. They include cellular communication, private data transmissions, cable television, satellite-based data transmission, paging-services systems and new long-distance networks linking cities. These are attractive areas for TNCs, because they offer opportunities for rapid growth, as well as the possibility to exploit technological advantages, not only through risky capital investment, but also through non-equity arrangements such as licensing and franchising.[36]

As with the airline industry, the same factors that generated the initial impetus for FDI in telecommunications will not only continue, but are likely to intensify. This will keep the telecommunications industry in the forefront of FDI activities in the services sector. It is notable that, in the United States, where overall outward FDI has been decelerating, the outward stock of FDI in telecommunications increased nearly eightfold between 1989 and 1991, from $560 million to $4.4 billion.

3. Prospects

The internationalization of service industries through FDI is still in its early phases, and its growth will be maintained or even increased during the 1990s (UNCTC, 1991a, pp. 21-22). One reason is that demand for modern services, supplied mostly by TNCs, is growing rapidly everywhere. In addition, the countries of Central and Eastern Europe will need to make full use of such services as banking, insurance, telecommunications, accounting, and legal services in their transition to a market economy. Secondly, the liberalization of FDI in services is relatively recent, but it is spreading to more countries and more industries, including capital-intensive infrastructure services, such as telecommunications, transportation and public utilities, in which private ownership (local or foreign) was previously not allowed. Opening those industries to FDI, mostly through joint ventures, has been closely related to privatization. Furthermore, TSCs as a group are much less transnationalized than industrial firms, suggesting there is still considerable potential for rapid growth in services FDI.

Although there is little doubt that those and other factors will lead to more transnationalization of services in the near term, technological developments may, in the longer run, alter the ways in which services are delivered to foreign markets. The limited tradability of many services has been a big reason for the rapid growth of FDI. The convergence of computer and telecommunication technologies eases this constraint considerably, because transborder flows of data permit instantaneous, long-distance, interactive transactions (Sauvant, 1990). By collapsing time and space, they make it possible for certain services to be produced in one place and consumed in another. The result is an increased transportability (and therefore tradability) of some services, especially information-intensive services, which may reduce the need for FDI. Or it may prompt TSCs to split their production processes into parts and, like manufacturing companies, allocate labour-intensive operations to foreign affiliates to take advantage of lower wages and other costs. That kind of development would result in both increased FDI and intra-firm trade in services.

E. Conclusions

Governments of host countries, including those of developing countries, increasingly recognize the potential contribution of TNCs to economic development, so they are pursuing policies to attract FDI. In doing so, they should keep in mind the structural changes described in this chapter.

- As the competitive advantage of resource-intensive, low-cost, low-skill activities declines, countries must be able to attract higher value-added FDI. If they fail to do so, they will pay the price in terms of slower economic growth. Although host developing countries, whose main locational advantages are based on low-cost and low-skilled labour, should continue to attract all kinds of FDI, their Governments must place increasing importance on higher value-added FDI to help upgrade existing industries, create new industries and encourage the entry of new firms. This will require, among other things, investments to raise the level of local skills, improve infrastructure and increase the supply of certain producer services. In addition, given the small size of many developing country markets and the increasing importance of regionally-based TNC strategies, governments of host countries need to participate in regional integration schemes so as to take full advantage of the potential contribution of TNCs. Many developing countries should also pay closer attention to the needs of smaller TNCs, particularly those from other developing countries.

- Policies designed to attract FDI must take into account that TNCs deliver a *package* of tangible and intangible assets. These include technological and managerial capabilities, access to distribution networks, responsiveness to changing demand patterns, training and capital; in this package, the capital component—traditionally seen as the principal benefit of FDI—is of diminishing significance

(TCMD, 1992a). Non-equity linkages with TNCs, ranging from subcontracting through franchising to licensing, therefore provide host countries with many of the same tangible and intangible assets. Removing legal obstacles to non-equity arrangements, ensuring adequate information and producing a suitably qualified labour force are all, at least in part, government responsibilities.

- Whether involving equity or non-equity links, policies to attract FDI must reflect the sectoral changes discussed in this chapter. Foreign direct investment will continue to be of importance for the development of the primary sector. Indeed, after a period of troubled relations, many Governments in developing countries are now willing to cooperate with TNCs in large natural resource projects (UNCTC, 1988a, pp. 321-326; Wälde, 1991). In manufacturing, attracting higher value-added FDI will be an integral component of upgrading production towards capital- and technology-intensive activities. As for services, any failure to appreciate their growing role in FDI would leave countries competing for less than half the annual flows of FDI and missing its fastest growing bit. Moreover, obtaining the range of skills provided by service TNCs will be essential for attracting FDI to other sectors of the economy.

As the growth of services has been increasingly propelled by soft technologies (especially those related to information technologies), the process of technology transfer has also shifted from harder to softer technologies, in which the contribution of TNCs is crucial. The recent emphasis on intellectual property rights to stimulate technology transfer is appropriate for some industries, but it should not obscure the fact that the informal knowledge associated with the application of new technologies often matters more (TCMD, 1993b). In fact, because formal and informal knowledge is complementary and increasingly difficult to separate, intellectual property rights alone are unlikely to create the right environment to transfer technology through TNCs (David, 1992). Governments need to devise new incentives and suitable training schemes (including with TNCs) to facilitate the diffusion of know-how (see box XI.4).

Technology is perhaps the most powerful stimulus to economic growth. Countries able to upgrade their economic structures and technological capacities in line with the needs of TNCs will therefore be better placed to participate in the international division of labour. However, devising appropriate policies is complicated by the nature of new technologies. They are redefining (and in many cases blurring) the traditional lines that divide sectors. Policies aimed at sectoral transformation are being increasingly outdated by the clustering of technology-related, cross-sectoral activities involving inter-firm alliances of TNCs.

The pace of structural change, however, has been forced not only by new technologies, but also by the opening of markets to competitive pressures. In that respect, privatization has been particularly significant, not just because it offers an immediate investment opportunity for TNCs, but also because it is a symbol of market-friendly reforms. Although the number of privatization measures has risen steadily over the past decade, they have been uneven at the sectoral level, with the primary and services sectors lagging behind the secondary sector. Consequently, the potential for further privatization (and hence FDI) in those sectors is significant: witness the large privatization in telecommunications and air transportation, both capital-intensive service industries, that is now taking place.

Privatization, however, should not be seen as an all-purpose panacea. On its own, it will not solve such problems as limited competition in some markets, the widespread presence of externalities and the need for longer-term planning, particularly in industries with large capital requirements or characterized by a natural monopoly. In addition, as experience with privatization accumulates, it may be the case that the managerial, technological and entrepreneurial capabilities required to enhance competitiveness do not automatically follow a switch in ownership. Consequently, privatization measures, particularly in service industries, may increasingly be only part of wider policy objectives, including the appropriate forms of regulating such activities.[37] Indeed, privatization may sometimes be a less effective way to attract FDI than a joint venture or another linkage between state-owned and foreign companies. This is particularly so in countries where the political risks attached to privatization outweigh any potential economic benefits, or in countries, such as those in transition from central planning, which still cannot make markets work effectively (Murrell, 1992; Kennedy, 1992).

Liberalization, too, has increased market access by reducing tariff barriers and restrictions on investment. The impact of these measures, however, has been uneven at the sectoral level. Because manufacturing has a longer history of adapting to competition, it has often appeared as the easiest target of reforms. In spite of the widening scope of liberalization of services FDI, they are still relatively closed compared with manufacturing. This is certainly true of large domestic service industries, such as health care, education, broadcasting, and rail and road transportation; and even in the two industries where liberalization is beginning to take hold, telecommunications and air transportation, most countries are proceeding cautiously. Governments need to make further efforts to measure and evaluate the performance of service firms, and define the roles of the market and of the State.

In some areas, indeed, Governments will need to strengthen their regulatory role. One example, which will grow in prominence over the coming decade, is the environment. Multilateral and bilateral measures have placed restrictions on trade in tropical timber, and environmental concerns have been written into development finance agreements.[38] Although tighter national environmental legislation and international initiatives such as *Agenda 21* (see chapter I) will encourage all TNCs to improve their environmental practices still further, it will affect different industries in different ways. Environmental laws have already caused a decline in oil, mineral and timber exploration in North America and Australia,[39] and TNCs are anticipating higher energy taxes in developed countries. More contentious still will be the conflicting pressure on TNCs from environmental interest groups at home and from host countries in the developing world. The likely problems are already visible in the NAFTA negotiations. Because FDI in pollution-intensive industries (such as chemicals and paper and pulp) in Mexico may rise, the enforcement of environmental standards has become a sensitive issue in the supplemental agreement.[40]

* * * * *

The contribution that TNCs can make as agents of growth, structural change and international integration has made FDI a coveted tool of economic development. As developing countries have reduced their own protectionism, they have removed the purely defensive rationale for FDI. As a result, the locational options of TNCs have expanded right across the value chain, and the antagonistic relations between host countries and TNCs have been replaced by a new spirit of cooperation.

Still, it must be recognized that FDI is not a substitute for domestic-led growth. However, government policies in pursuit of growth must also incorporate the sectoral changes discussed above. Upgrading production to include more technology- and skill-intensive activities and ensuring an efficient services sector will require considerable investments in physical infrastructure and training, along with measures to stimulate entrepreneurship. These initiatives can best be pursued through an integrated policy regime which, in addition to domestic macroeconomic stabilization, includes trade and technology policies (see chapter XI).

Notes

1 Technological convergence and the greater ease of transferring technology and skills initially mastered in industrial activities may explain, in part, the high frequency of cross-sectoral investment in the services sector, that is, by TNCs from other sectors.

2 Table I.10 excludes banking corporations.

3 However, growth opportunities in some renewable resources will undoubtedly require significant amounts of FDI, as has already happened in the case of Chilean agribusiness; see "Exports add savour to Chile's fruit cocktail", *Financial Times*, 18 November 1992.

4 However a number of resource-poor newly industrializing countries in Latin America and Asia have accumulated the technological expertise to invest abroad for this purpose, see TCMD, 1993b, p. 13; and Ericsson and Tegen (1993).

5 In petroleum, between 1970 and 1979, the share of total crude oil production taken by TNCs declined from 94 per cent to 45 per cent (UNCTC, 1983, p. 197).

6 It is probably true that, with the possible exception of petroleum, the real value of the stock of outward FDI was lower at the end of the decade than at the beginning.

7 Reversing the declining trend in the 1970s, see table III.1.

8 Indicatively, in Malaysia, the Philippines and Thailand, the stock of inward FDI fell during the second half of the decade.

9 The problems of diversification are typified by the case of British Petroleum; see "BP after Horton", *The Economist*, 4 July 1992, p. 59; Ericsson and Tegen (1993), p. 6.

10 Constitutional restrictions on foreign ownership in mining and petroleum remain in a large number of developing countries, including Brazil, India, Mexico and the Philippines. However, Wälde (1991, p. 108), noted a number of cases of renegotiation involving significantly reduced Government equity stakes.

11 "Oil and gas industry", Financial Times Survey, *Financial Times*, 18 December 1991.

12 *Financial Times*, op. cit.

13 Not only is the former Soviet Union the world's leading oil producer, but the country ranks first or second in aluminum, copper, lead zinc, nickel and iron ore and is the third largest gold producer behind South Africa and the United States. As in the oil industry, state sector involvement may persist longer than expected. However, capital constraints and the desperate need for environmental clean-up will ensure a growing TNC presence, particularly by European and Asian TNCs (Ericsson and Tegen, 1993, p. 7).

14 The resource-based manufacturing industries are coal and petroleum, food, beverages and tobacco, metals, non-metallic minerals, paper, rubber and textiles, leather and clothing. The more capital- and technology-intensive manufacturing industries are chemicals, electrical equipment, mechanical equipment, motor vehicles and other transport equipment.

15 Increased capital formation in the most advanced forms of technologies has been estimated to account for 25 per cent of the productivity growth in manufacturing industries in the late 1980s (Steindel, 1992).

16 Hobday (1992); Balk (1991); Saghafi and Davidson (1989); Henderson (1989). Significantly, the activities of Japanese TNCs in South East Asia are now including research-and-development functions; see "corporate Japan in Asia," *Tokyo Business Today*, 60 (January 1992), pp. 22-26.

17 For example, Malaysia has become the world's largest exporter and the third largest producer (after Japan and the United States) of electronics and semiconductors, fueled by the activities of TNCs from Japan and, more recently, Hong Kong and Taiwan Province of China that seek lower operating costs. See Thuermer (1992) and Carl Goldstein, "Chips of change: electronics transforms the face of Malaysia's industry", *Far Eastern Economic Review*, vol. 145, No. 36 (September), pp. 98-99. In China, Hewlett-Packard (which has become the largest foreign-owned high-technology joint venture) is playing an important role in technology transfer through industrial upgrading. See Carl Goldstein, "Logging on to Asia: Persistence pays off for Hewlett-Packard", *Far Eastern Economic Review*, vol. 155, No. 17 (April), p.63.

18 See also Steward Toy, et al., "The battle for Europe, "*Business Week*, 3216 (June), pp. 44-52.

19 Indeed, recent objectives for overseas expansion by Japanese firms are closely related to locating at sites of consumption and developing marketing outlets for locally produced goods (Otaki, 1992). Similar objectives propel TNCs from the United States that are beginning to look beyond low-cost manufacturing and are attempting to tap into local, growing markets (Van Oldenborgh, 1992). Over half of 3,332 Japanese firms that had invested in a total of 13,522 foreign affiliates in 1991 cited this objective, according to a Toyo Keizai survey; see Otaki (1992), and "Corporate Japan in Asia," *Tokyo Business Today*, 60 (January 1992), pp. 22-26.

20 In fact, 20 per cent of the total number of outward affiliates of Korean TNCs and more than 26 per cent of their outward FDI stock in 1988 was in the form of minority-owned FDI. Similar trends are observed for Malaysian TNCs in terms of share of the number of outward affiliates. The importance of minority-owned foreign affiliates is most important in the case of Singapore TNCs: they accounted almost two-thirds of the total number of their outward affiliates in 1989 (TCMD, 1992a).

21 Louise de Rosario, "Drop in the bucket: Japan likely to continue pouring money into Asia", *Far Eastern Economic Review*, vol. 150, No. 51 (September), pp. 98-99; and Doi Guat Tin, E. P. Patanne and Jose Marte Abueg, "Economic Report: Philippines," *Asian Business*, vol. 27, no. 1 (January), pp. 36-48.

22 See also Doug Tsurnoka, "Fabricated future—rising costs could threaten Malaysia's chip industry", *Far Eastern Economic Review*, vol. 150, no. 20 (November), pp. 64-66.

23 Paul Handley, Doug Tsuruoka and Adam Schwarz, "Money bags move in: Taiwanese investors flock to low-wage neighbors", *Far Eastern Economic Review*, vol. 148, No. 16 (April), pp. 87-88; Jonathan Moore, "The upstart taipans; cash rich Taiwanese scour Asia for opportunities", *Far Eastern Economic Review*, vol. 148, No. 16 (April), pp. 84-87; Carl Goldstein, "Taiwan's PC gample: computer firms cosy up to China", *Far Eastern Economic Review*, vol. 155, No. 38 (September), pp. 87-88. Other significant areas of Third World TNC activity in developed countries are not geared to the manufacture of a product *per se*, but towards the acquisition of high-technology manufacturing capabilities and experience in specific manufacturing industries (Feinerman, 1991).

24 For more detail on this, see UNCTC (1988a) and UNCTC publications on services.

25 See also Rapp and Vellas (1988).

26 See also "Tangled — A survey of the airline industry", *The Economist*, 12 June 1993, pp. 20-21.

27 North-American partners are United Airlines, USAir and Air Canada, while European airlines involved are British Airways, KLM, Swissair, Alitalia, Air Lingus, Olympic Airways, TAP Air Portugal and Austrian Airlines.

28 See *The New York Times*, 24 January 1991; see also Donoghue and Nelms (1993); Flint (1993) and Kasper (1988).

29 See also Daoust (1992); Gialloreto (1992) and Crumley (1992).

30 See *Business Week*, 6 April 1992, p. 86.

31 See *Financial Times*, 7 October 1991 and 15 October 1992; *New York Times*, 10 October 1992.

32 Ibid.

33 See *The Economist: Telecommunications Survey*, 5 October 1991, p. 25.

34 See *Financial Times*, 15 October 1992, p. 3.

35 See *The Economist*, 5 October 1991, op. cit.

36 See *The Wall Street Journal*, 4 October 1991.

37 This has begun in the United Kingdom, which has most fully embraced the privatization concept among developed countries; see "Return to familiar ground", *Financial Times*, 24 March 1993.

38 See "For the chop", *The Economist*, 30 January 1993, p. 61; Wälde (1991).

39 See "In the doldrums", *The Economist*, 18 April 1992, p. 75.

40 See "Negligent neighbours", *Financial Times*, Survey of the North American Free Trade Agreement, 12 May 1993, p. 30.

CHAPTER IV

THE GROWTH OF FOREIGN DIRECT INVESTMENT IN THE 1980s: THE BULGE IN THE TREND

During the past two decades, flows of FDI have followed an upward trend averaging 13 per cent annually with year-to-year fluctuations. Two surges followed by falls stand out: during the period from 1978 to 1981, growth averaged 11 per cent per year and, from 1986 to 1990 it averaged 28 per cent per year (figure IV.1). Even excluding Japan—which became a sizeable outward investor from 1985[1]—the second period still showed remarkable growth. However, the declines in 1991 and 1992, though not uniform across all countries, may cast some doubt as to whether FDI will continue to grow at the same pace. To address this issue, the present chapter divides the various influences on FDI into three categories: short-term, policy-related and structural. The analysis seeks to explain the increase in the flows of FDI in the 1980s and their subsequent fall in the 1990s, as well as their likely future performance.

The unprecedented growth in the flow of foreign direct investment (FDI) in the periods from 1986 to 1990 and its subsequent decline raise an important question: Were the favourable conditions for FDI in that period the result of short-term stimuli causing a bulge in the underlying upward trend? In other words, did the trend undergo a temporary surge over and above what might have been expected had no short-term factors been at work? The rapid economic growth after the recession of the early 1980s, the mergers-and-acquisitions boom and the initial reaction to policy changes were powerful short-term factors for stimulating the growth of FDI flows. These factors were at work against the backdrop of long-term factors that influence the underlying trend, namely, changes in policies and pressures arising from the structural transformation of the world economy as a result of the activities of transnational corporations (TNCs). The inter-play of short-term, policy-related and structural forces created the favourable circumstances that led to the bulge in the flows of FDI. While economic growth has declined in the early 1990s and mergers-and-acquistions activity has subsided, the continuing effect of policy changes and structural pressures will, most likely, ensure the continuation of the previous trend in FDI flows over the next decade and into the next century.

A. Short-term factors

Rapid economic growth in the 1980s and the boom in mergers and acquisitions undertaken by TNCs were among the principal factors that led to a surge of FDI flows during the period from 1986 to 1990 (box IV.1). Expenditures on capital goods by foreign affiliates were similarly affected. There were, however, differences among sectors and in the method of financing FDI flows that resulted from the cyclical fluctuations in economic activity. The initial reaction by TNCs to one-time policy changes (e.g., the announcement of the Single Market by the European Community) also contributed to the rapid growth of FDI in that period. The impact of such policy changes tends to be prolonged, and it is discussed later. This one-time boost in FDI flows was, however, temporary: as economic growth receded and the conditions that led to the popularity of mergers and acquisitions ceased to exist, their stimulus to the growth of FDI abated.

Figure IV.1. Foreign-direct-investment outflows and rate of growth of real gross domestic product, 1970-1991
(Billions of dollars and percentage)

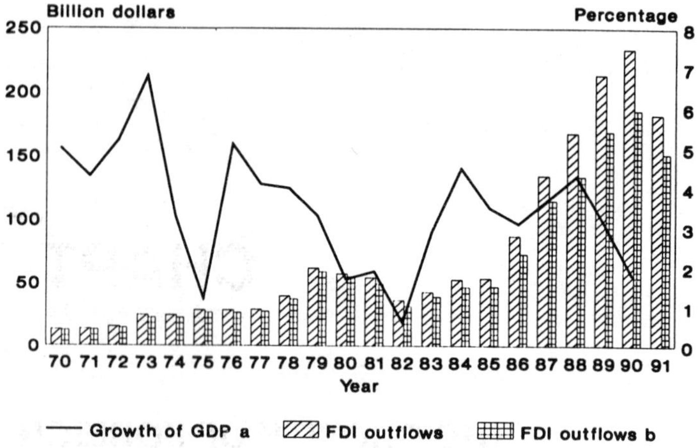

Sources: UNCTAD, Programme on Transnational Corporations, based on International Monetary Fund (IMF), balance-of-payments tape, retrieved in February 1993; OECD estimates; UNCTAD, 1993e; TCMD, 1993h; and DESD, Development Policy and Analysis Division, DPAD data bank of world development statistics.

a 1980 prices.
b Excluding Japan.

1. Business-cycles

(a) Cyclical influences on foreign-direct-investment flows and capital expenditures

The growth of FDI outflows is closely correlated with the growth of output.[2] In short, and not surprisingly, the decision by TNCs to invest abroad is affected by cyclical fluctuations in economic growth (business cycles), both at home and abroad. The impact of business cycles on global FDI flows operates through the interactions between home and host-country economic conditions. This is partly owing to the fact that, as regards the supply-side of FDI, the foreign investment decisions of TNCs are affected by the availability of investible funds from corporate profits or loans, which are themselves affected by conditions at home. However, demand-side factors also play their part: growing markets abroad can give TNCs an impetus to invest, especially if domestic conditions are deteriorating. Indeed, growing foreign markets may be particularly attractive for TNCs based in countries experiencing a cyclical downturn. In 1991, these factors helped to raise the share of developing countries in total inflows rose to 25 per cent from an average of 17 per cent during the period 1985-1990 (chapter I). Nevertheless, the interdependence of the world economy suggests that, as recession spreads, growth will slow down almost everywhere, and that will depress the flow of FDI world-wide.

A strong cyclical upswing in the developed countries after the recession of the early 1980s contributed to the growth of FDI flows (figure IV.2). Since so much of total FDI occurs between developed countries, the cyclical

Box IV.1. Foreign-direct-investment flows in the 1980s: was the surge exceptional?

Regressing the log of FDI flows on a time variable, fitting a line through the calculated values and comparing the fitted line with the actual observations shows a clear upward trend in the growth of FDI and a cyclical pattern in their movement.

$$LNFDI = 0.52 + 0.13\,(TIME)$$
$$(0.68)\;(13.52)$$
$$(R^2 = 0.90)$$

LNFDI = log of foreign-direct-investment outflows

TIME = 1970-1991

From 1970 through 1991, global FDI flows grew at an average rate of 13 per cent per year. That pattern of trend and cycles is consistent with the picture that emerges from a casual observation of the year-to-year movements in FDI flows. What is not apparent from observing FDI flows is that the bulge in the second half of the 1980s is similar to that in the late 1970s (figure 1). Instead, it is the drop in these flows in the early 1980s that appears to be an aberration in the underlying pattern. That drop may be ascribed to the severity of the economic recession in the early 1980s, which appears to have influenced FDI flows after a time lag of one to two years. In fact, the size of the drop might help explain the subsequent increase, suggesting that some "overshooting" might have taken place as FDI flows sought to resume their growth along the trend line. At the same time, important policy changes and structural re-alignments coincided with the recovery of the mid-1980s, accelerating the upward movement in FDI flows.

The cyclical pattern that emerges from comparing actual values to the time trend implies that business cycles play an important role in the investment decision of TNCs. It is also apparent that the oscillations of FDI flows around the fitted trend line were wider in the 1980s compared to the 1970s, suggesting that those flows became more prone to the influence of short-term factors that caused them to diverge from the underlying trend. Those oscillations appear to have continued into the 1990s. Given the past pattern of FDI flows, it could be expected that the upward trend will continue, as the decade proceeds, accompanied by short-term deviations.

Figure 1. Outflows of foreign direct investment, 1970-1991
(Logarithmic values)

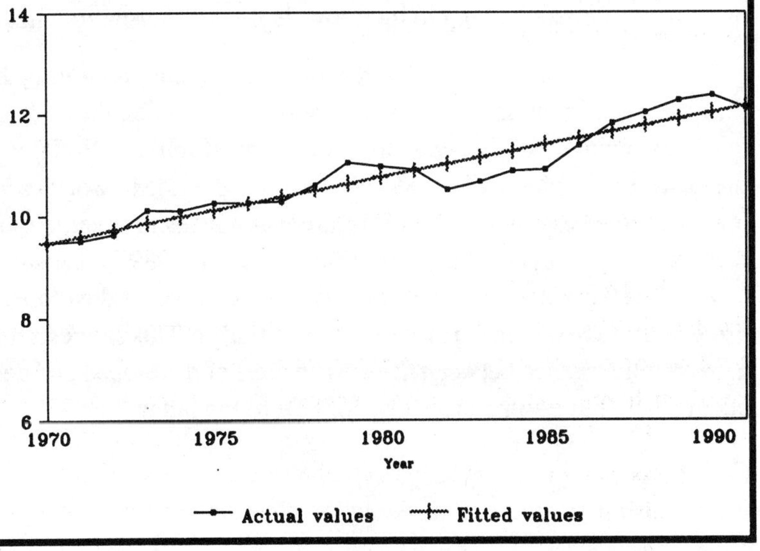

upswing helps explain the surge in investment flows in the 1980s, as well as their subsequent fall in the early 1990s. As for developing countries, FDI inflows in the 1980s also increased in response to the cyclical upswing in developed countries, where most FDI originates (figure IV.3).

Investment expenditures on capital goods (plant and equipment) by foreign affiliates is also influenced by business cycles. Taking the activities of TNCs based in the United States, the capital spending of their foreign affiliates world-wide, as well as their domestic investments, have followed a cyclical path (figure IV.4).[3] Planned and actual spending of those affiliates jumped considerably in the late 1980s in response to the earlier cyclical upswing (table IV.1), suggesting the existence of time-lags.

Figure IV.2. Foreign-direct-investment inflows to developed countries and rate of growth of real gross domestic product, 1970-1991
(Billions of dollars and percentage)

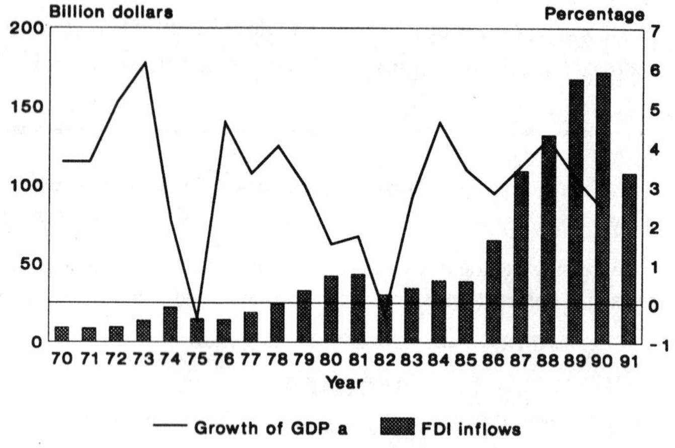

Sources: UNCTAD, Programme on Transnational Corporations, based on IMF, balance-of-payments tape, retrieved in February 1993; OECD estimates; UNCTAD, 1993e; and DESD, Development Policy and Analysis Division, DPAD data bank of world development statistics.

a 1980 prices.

When growth rates change, TNCs adjust their investment plans accordingly. That happened in the early 1980s, and again during 1991 and 1992, when growth in the United States was sluggish.[4] Japanese TNCs have also modified their spending plans, partly because deteriorating domestic economic conditions damaged their profits.[5] This climate seems to have affected small and medium-size TNCs in particular, since they are more susceptible to fluctuations in domestic demand owing to their low degree of transnationalization.

The above observations lead to some conclusions regarding the role played by business cycles in influencing the post-1985 boom in FDI flows and subsequent fall in the early 1990s. The growth of the world economy after the recession of the early 1980s appears to have stimulated FDI flows with a time-lag of about two years. Similarly, the downturn beginning in 1989-1990 led to a decline in world-wide FDI flows starting in 1991. Business cycles may also induce growth rates of different countries to diverge more by affecting some countries more severely than others. The cyclical downturn that began in 1989 is one such example: GDP growth in the early 1990s in developing countries was significantly higher than in developed countries, and the difference between their growth rates is expected to increase substantially.[6] This suggests that business cycles, to the extent that they cause a greater divergence between the growth rates of developed and developing countries than would otherwise have taken place, have stimulated flows of FDI to the latter.

(b) Sectoral differences

For FDI outflows from the major home countries, investments in services tend to be less volatile than primary- and secondary-sector investments. For the majority-owned foreign affiliates of United States services TNCs, for example, capital spending has been less volatile than that for manufacturing and petroleum firms (figure IV.5). However, the rapid economic growth of the 1980s boosted the growth of services FDI more than either primary or secondary FDI (chapter III), as TNCs sought to invest in services industries previously closed to them. This raises the question of whether business cycles affect different sectors in different ways.

Figure IV.3. Foreign-direct-investment inflows to developing countries and rate of growth of real gross domestic product, 1970-1991

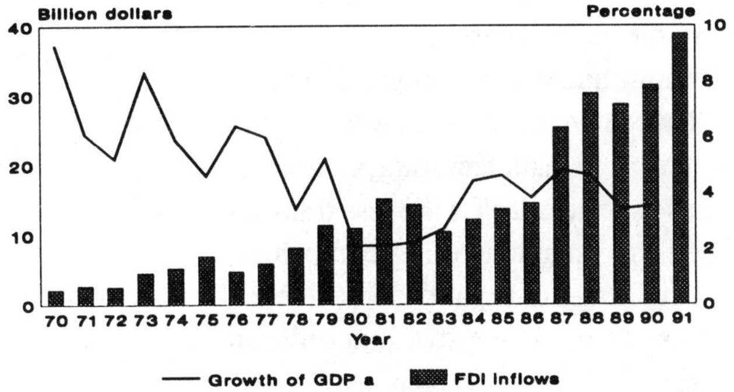

Sources: UNCTAD, Programme on Transnational Corporations, based on IMF, balance-of-payments tape, retrieved in February 1993; OECD estimates; Transnational Corporations and Management Division, UNCTAD, 1993e; and DESD, Development Policy and Analysis Division, DPAD data bank of world development statistics.

a 1980 prices.

Table IV.1. Planned and actual capital expenditures by majority-owned non-bank foreign affiliates of United States transnational corporations
(Percentage change over previous year)

Year	*World*		*Developed countries*		*Developing countries*	
	Planned	*Actual*	*Planned*	*Actual*	*Planned*	*Actual*
1974	22	23	21	26	38	28
1975	3	6	1	5	18	18
1976	-5	-8	-3	-5	-12	-19
1977	12	11	15	15	11	9
1978	15	12	14	14	25	13
1979	22	25	20	25	28	20
1980	24	30	24	29	22	38
1981	7	3	1	-2	28	23
1982	6	1	4	-2	12	11
1983	-4	-18	-1	-16	-6	-20
1984	12	-6	14	-3	10	-13
1985	15	2	15	5	15	-4
1986	2	-7	5	-2	-6	-18
1987	3	5	4	9	1	-8
1988	23	24	21	24	29	18
1989	15	13	11	11	31	18
1990	17	19	16	18	27	22
1991	3	..	1	..	10	..
1992	4	..	3	..	10	..

Sources: United States Department of Commerce, *Survey of Current Business*, various issues.

Typically, services TNCs rely more on FDI for delivering services to host countries than manufacturing TNCs, because of the non-tradable nature of their output. Consequently, a cyclical downturn is less likely to impact FDI in services to the same extent as in manufacturing. Conversely, because services TNCs are less transnationalized than manufacturing companies, they are willing to expand abroad, even during periods of slow growth, in order to attain a desired level of foreign investment. Thus, capital spending by services TNCs appears to be more resilient to business cycles than that by manufacturing firms. In addition, it may well be that, given the less-tradable nature of most services, market positions abroad have to be maintained through continuing investments, rather than by switching to exports (as can happen in manufacturing).

Figure IV.4. Actual capital expenditures by majority-owned non-bank foreign affiliates of United States transnational corporations and growth rate of real gross domestic product,[a] 1974-1991
(Billions of dollars and percentage)

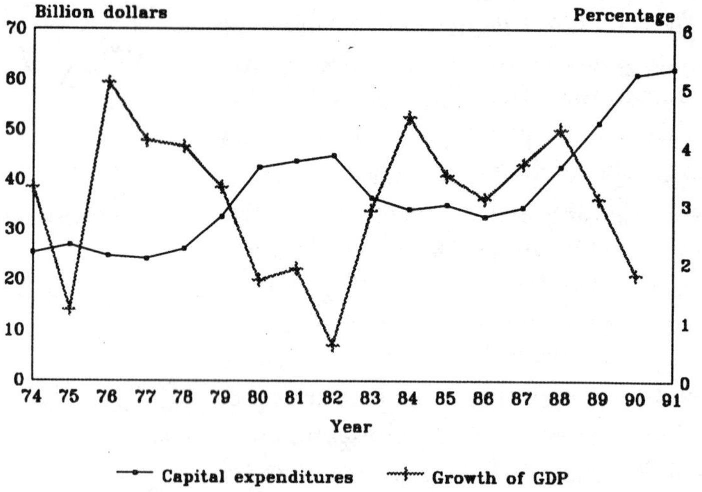

Sources: United States Department of Commerce, *Survey of Current Business*, various issues; DESD, Development Policy and Analysis Division, DPAD data bank of world development statistics.

a 1980 prices.

Figure IV.5. Actual capital expenditures by majority-owned non-bank foreign affiliates of United States transnational corporations, by sector, and growth rate of real gross domestic product of the world economy,[a] 1974-1991
(Billions of dollars and percentage)

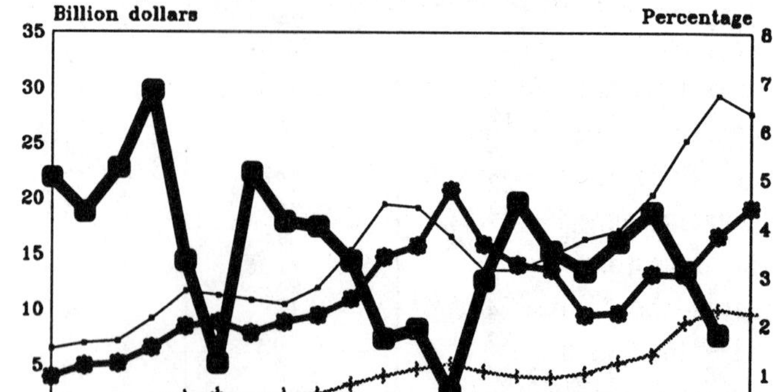

Sources: United States Department of Commerce, *Survey of Current Business*, various issues; DESD, Development Policy and Analysis Division, DPAD data bank of world development statistics.

a 1980 prices.

(c) Financing methods

The financing of FDI flows has varied significantly over time. Its variability comes through clearly in looking at investment outflows from the five largest home countries (France, the Federal Republic of Germany, Japan, the United Kingdom and the United States). During the second half of the 1980s, total outflows grew rapidly, but their components—equity, reinvested earnings and intra-company loans—did not all grow at the same rate. In particular, equity investments and intra-company loans grew faster than reinvested earnings (figure IV.6). In that period, reinvested earnings accounted for 39 per cent of total FDI outflows from developed countries, down from 60 per cent during the period 1981-1985 (table I.5).

Business cycles are likely to affect differently the shares of equity, reinvested earnings and intra-company loans in total FDI outflows.[7] During a cyclical upswing, TNCs may be inclined to finance investments abroad through equity or loans to their affiliates. Conversely, during a recession, TNCs may be inclined to change methods of financing investments abroad; for example, a decline in profits of the parent companies may induce them to use profits earned in the host country for investment purposes. On the other hand, foreign profits may be needed at home during a downturn, and this seems to be the case with the largest home countries, for which the ratio of reinvested earnings to total FDI outflows decreased in 1991 (figure IV.7).

Intra-company loans can also be affected by cyclical fluctuation in economic activity. If parent firms face favourable domestic conditions, which increase their operating profits and make them expand their investment plans at home and abroad, it is plausible to suppose that loans from parents to their affiliates will increase. That is indeed what happened with three of the largest outward investors (the Federal Republic of Germany, the United Kingdom and the United States) in the 1980s, while the reverse took place during the period 1989-1991 (figure IV.7). However, the same pattern did not occur during earlier periods of slow growth. This might suggest that the home-country cycle has become more important. Specifically for the United States, the sharp drop in operating profits of United

Figure IV.6. Foreign-direct-investment outflows from France, the Federal Republic of Germany, Japan, [a] the United Kingdom [b] and the United States, 1970-1991
(Billions of dollars and percentage)

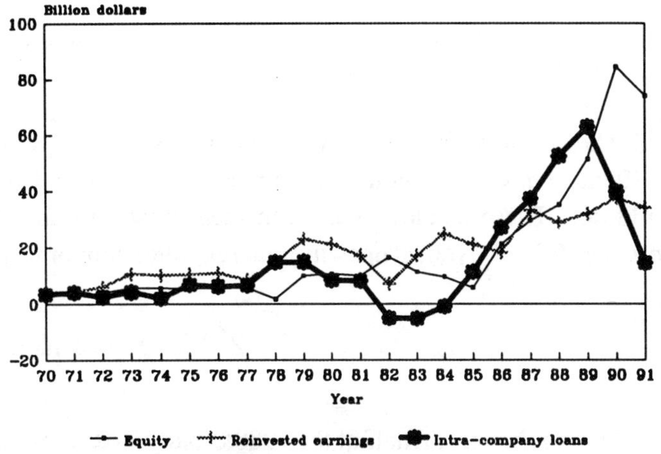

Sources: UNCTAD, Programme on Transnational Corporations, based on IMF, balance-of-payments tape, retrieved in October 1992.

a Does not include reinvested earnings.
b Does not include equity.

Figure IV.7. The ratio of reinvested earnings and of intra-company loans to foreign-direct-investment outflows for the Federal Republic of Germany, the United Kingdom and the United States, 1970-1991
(Billions of dollars and percentage)

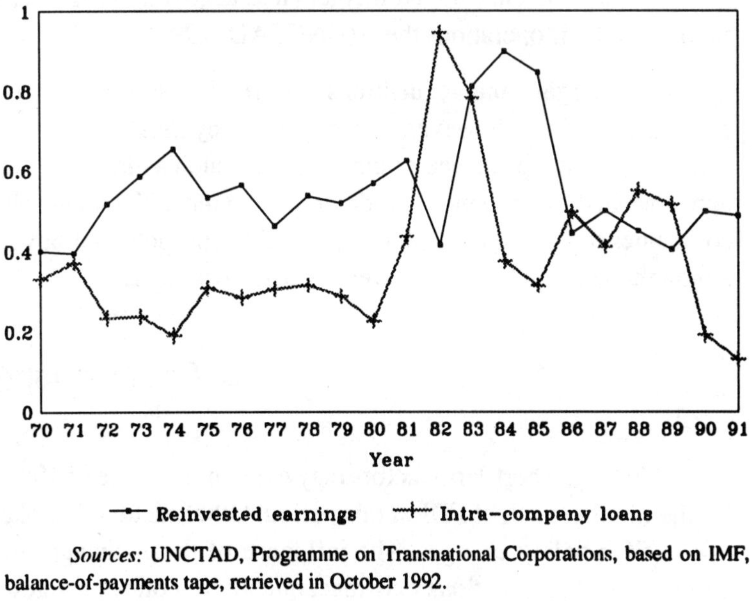

Sources: UNCTAD, Programme on Transnational Corporations, based on IMF, balance-of-payments tape, retrieved in October 1992.

States TNCs during 1990 and 1991 considerably limited their ability to lend to their affiliates abroad (Scholl *et al.*, 1992). In fact, affiliates repaid more than they received, and the share of total outflows from the United States accounted for by intra-company loans fell.

* * * * *

The strong growth of the world economy appears to have stimulated FDI flows during the second half of the 1980s and, correspondingly, the recent fall in those flows may be attributed partly to deteriorating growth conditions. These conditions are confined mostly to developed countries, which are, however, the principal sources of FDI. A cyclical upswing that rekindles economic growth would help stimulate FDI flows in the 1990s.

2. Mergers and acquisitions

During the second half of the 1980s, many TNCs saw acquisitions as a less expensive way to gain a foreign foothold than establishing new production facilities. Indeed, the majority of FDI in the United States and Western Europe took the form of acquisitions. The merger wave of the 1980s was partly a result of macroeconomic conditions in most developed countries especially the end of the recession at the beginning of that decade. That, combined with stronger international competition, created substantial excess capacity in many low- and medium-technology industries, such as petroleum and consumer durables. Other factors were easier credit, the valuation of many companies below their break-up values and innovations in corporate finance, such as the growth of the "junk" bond market and the use of leveraged buy-outs. Many TNCs sought to narrow their business base, but others thought conditions were ripe for expanding into new markets or activities. The programme for a single market in the EC encouraged mergers and acquisitions as TNCs sought a quick means to gain a foothold or to rationalize their operations there (UNCTAD, 1993f).

The mergers-and-acquisitions boom and its subsequent decline coincided with the duration of the business cycle. It is difficult, however, to separate this cyclical impact on the rise and decline of mergers-and-acquisitions activity from the influence of other factors, such as interest rates and stock-market valuations. Nevertheless, it appears that the economic slow-down was linked to the slow-down of mergers and acquisitions, because acquired companies tended to become less profitable and potential buyers were hampered by declining profits at home, although clearly other factors were also at work.

B. Policy changes

Although short-term factors may explain the surge of 1986-1990, they were not the sole reason accounting for the rapid growth of FDI in this period. Other factors that played a part included the initial reaction of TNCs to one-time policy changes. The influence of those changes on FDI flows, however, is of a longer duration. Transnational corporations may react quickly to policy changes that have an impact on their strategies, but their response usually continues long after the initial reaction to the new policy has taken place. The initial adjustment in the flow of FDI in response to policy changes was a factor that contributed to the surge of FDI. Nevertheless, it is the continuous response of TNCs to the one-time policy changes that explains partly the trend underlying the growth of FDI flows.

1. Trade liberalization

The links between FDI and international trade are close (UNCTC, 1991a; TCMD, 1993a). For the largest home countries, TNCs account for most exports and imports (80 per cent for the United States in 1989), while intra-firm trade accounts for between one fourth and one third of total international trade (TCMD, 1992a, chap. VIII). Measures to liberalize trade can boost FDI by allowing TNCs to establish production facilities in low-cost sites from which they can export their output, by allowing TNCs to outsource inputs, by enabling the formation of regional networks and by allowing the integration of production regionally or globally.

Trade liberalization, which began in the post-war period with the establishment of the General Agreement on Tariffs and Trade (GATT), accelerated in the 1980s, especially in developing countries (DIESA, 1991). In spite of the overall trend towards trade liberalization, non-tariff barriers have been used by some countries to restrict imports in selected industries. For example, through voluntary export restraints, Japan was compelled to reduce its exports of automobiles and semiconductors to the United States. Such policies have led to fears about the future imposition of non-tariff barriers in other industries and to the growing necessity to preserve market access through FDI. Non-tariff barriers, coupled with threats of other trade restrictions, encouraged Japanese automobile manufacturers during the second half of the 1980s to become established in host-country markets, especially in the United States.

2. Exchange rates

From the viewpoint of TNCs, the cost of acquiring assets in different countries depends on prevailing exchange rates. If the host country currency falls against a TNC's home-country currency, that will boost the inflow of FDI, and vice versa. For example, the decline of the dollar against the yen in the second half of the 1980s made United States assets less expensive to Japanese firms, and was one reason for the growth of Japanese investment there (Froot and Stein, 1991; Krugman and Graham, 1992).[8]

Beyond that effect, other factors were pushing in the same direction. The large rise in the yen (coupled with rising production costs and a shortage of skilled labour at home) raised the prices of Japanese exports so much that they found it difficult to retain market share. As a result, operating in the United States became an imperative for many Japanese firms.

3. Liberalization and privatization

The trend towards a liberalization of FDI policies, which accelerated during the 1980s, especially in services (UNCTC, 1988a, chap. XVII), created a new framework for TNCs and helped boost flows of FDI. There is strong evidence that the trend towards liberalization is continuing. In 1991, almost every change in the investment regimes of some 30 countries was a liberalizing change; in 1992, all countries on which regulations data could be obtained moved in that direction (annex table 6). Not only do all countries allow FDI, but they often compete to attract such investments.

Regulatory reforms to attract FDI have been complemented by privatization programmes, but mostly in the past few years. In 1990, more than 70 countries had active privatization schemes, and they sold state enterprises to the value of over $185 billion (TCMD, 1992a, p. 86). Despite the shortage of firm data on the involvement of TNCs in the process of privatization, they appear to have been sizeable buyers in Latin America and in Central and Eastern Europe (Minor, 1993a and 1993b).

4. Regional integration

The single market programme of the European Community and the Free Trade Agreement between the United States and Canada have sparked significant investment to and within the regions involved. The desire by TNCs from third countries to become regional "insiders" led to a faster growth of FDI in the European Community than would have otherwise been expected.[9] At the same time, TNCs already located there began to reorganize and rationalize their investments, taking a Community-wide approach. This led to a substantial rise in intra-regional investment flows and in cross-border mergers and acquisitions. Similar changes were made by TNCs from the United States in response to the Free Trade Agreement with Canada. Investment from outside also increased, with third-party TNCs viewing North America more and more as an integrated market (UNCTC, 1990b).

Given that these were one-time policy changes, it is plausible to suppose that the growth of investment flows to the European Community and North America (including intra-regional flows) would eventually slow down. That seems to have happened in 1991 in the case of the European Community, at least as regards investments from Japan. However, there are likely to be dynamic effects arising from the formation of the Single Market. The expansion of markets and the growth of demand are likely to present new investment opportunities and encourage new inflows of FDI, even after the completion of the Single Market by 1993.

C. Structural factors

The structure of the world economy, characterized by a large and growing stock of FDI and by international production of an increasingly integrated nature, plays a role in explaining the underlying trend of the growth of FDI flows. Its influence is long-lasting and extends beyond the second half of the 1980s, suggesting the continuation of the trend even in the absence of short-term or policy-related factors. Given the drop in FDI flows in the early 1990s, however, the growth of FDI flows will resume from a lower level.

1. The growth of the stock of foreign direct investment

The stock of global FDI has increased steadily in the post-war period and, in 1992, was estimated to have reached about $2.0 trillion in book value (table IV.2).[10] It grew by an annual average of 15 per cent during 1985-1991, compared with 10 per cent in 1980-1985.[11] Associated with that stock, world-wide sales of foreign affiliates more than doubled between 1985 and 1990 (table IV.2). The fact that a sizeable stock of FDI is already in place is likely to lead to a self-sustained growth of investment and resource flows associated with the activities of TNCs. The constantly increasing stock of FDI suggests that its capacity to generate output and income will also continue to grow. In particular, its capacity to generate earnings, a portion of which will be reinvested, may continue to increase as well.

2. The emergence of integrated international production

The sizeable stock of FDI attributable to the 37,000 TNCs, and their world-wide sales of about $5.5 trillion mean that about one third of the world's private sector productive assets are under the governance of TNCs and that, therefore, international production has become a central structural characteristic of the world economy. Partly, this is the result of the technological revolution in communications, which has greatly improved coordination and integration between parent TNCs and their affiliates. Even small and medium-size firms are now able to operate as TNCs, and to take advantage of falling transport costs to export their output. These technological developments have brought about changes in the organizational structure of TNCs, driven by heightened competition and the growing awareness among companies of the necessity to invest abroad in order to serve domestic markets better.

Table IV.2. World stock of foreign direct investment and sales of foreign affiliates, 1982-1992
(Billions of dollars)

Year	*Outward stock*	*Sales*
1982	629	2 400
1983	672	2 300
1984	725	2 500
1985	778	2 500
1986	866	2 900
1987	1 000	3 500
1988	1 169	4 200
1989	1 382	4 400
1990	1 616	5 500
1991	1 799	..
1992	1 949	..

Sources: Chapter I and UNCTAD, 1993e.

The trend to organize production on a regional or global basis implies that more and more of a country's resources (including capital) are involved in the building of an integrated production system. Within this framework, the nature of cross-border transactions is changing, even if many (especially intangible) activities are not reflected in the conventional measures of investment flows. Furthermore, TNCs have established many non-equity links, including strategic alliances, which are not captured in the FDI statistics. In other words, the rise of the international production system is creating a self-sustaining momentum, with major implications for the growth of FDI and other forms of cross-border transactions.

* * * * *

The strong economic performance of the world economy and the popularity of mergers and acquistions are the principal explanations for the bulge in the trend of FDI flows during the second half of the 1980s. These short-term factors ceased to influence favourably the growth of FDI after 1989, as deteriorating growth conditions set in, particularly in developed countries, and mergers-and-acquisitions activity dwindled. The 1980s also witnessed the continuation of the influence of two other forces: policy-related changes and pressures arising from structural changes in the world economy resulting from the actions of TNCs. Essentially, policy changes and structural changes explain the underlying trend in FDI flows, with short-term factors amplifying temporarily that trend. Given that the impact of these changes is long-term, a question arises regarding the future outlook for the flow of FDI, which is discussed below.

D. Future prospects

In general, of course, firms with tangible or intangible assets arising from ownership will continue to use them best by internalizing transaction costs and by investing in countries that offer suitable locational advantages (Dunning, 1993). This approach will ensure that firms continue to engage in international production and to locate value-adding activities abroad. However, the fall in investment flows in 1991 and 1992 raises the question of whether they will continue to increase in the future. Assuming they do, a related question is how fast that increase will be. Policy changes and structural changes in the world economy make it very likely that investment flows will continue to grow, although from a lower level than that reached in 1990. An economic upswing would amplify further the impact of those changes. The rest of this chapter is devoted to these issues.

1. The future of policy

(a) Liberalization of trade and investment

If trade liberalization continues, TNCs will have an incentive to invest in countries where costs are low and from which their output can be exported. Trade liberalization may also accelerate the organization of international production into regional or global networks of firms by allowing the movement of goods (and, increasingly, services) that is necessary for the pursuit of complex integration strategies (chapter V).

Despite progressive liberalization of FDI regimes, there is still more to be done. In services, which now account for over half of total FDI flows from the major home countries, the regulatory framework for foreign investment could be opened up further, especially in developing countries. The opening of telecommunications, transportation, public utilities, insurance and other services to FDI, coupled with the relatively low tradability of services, are likely to keep TNCs investing heavily abroad. It is also likely that privatization will play a bigger role, as some countries (especially in Latin America) are already replacing debt-to-equity conversion schemes with privatizations as the principal incentive to attract FDI.

(b) Regional integration schemes

Foreign investment will also be boosted by further regional integration in Western Europe and North America. The same is true in Asia, where TNCs are integrating their production even in the absence of a formal institutional framework. Specifically, the closer links between the European Community and the European Free Trade Association (EFTA), leading to the formation of a European Economic Area, are likely to result in greater intra- and extraregional flows of investment. Similarly, the extension of the United States-Canada Free Trade Agreement to include Mexico under the North American Free Trade Agreement (NAFTA), which has already led to substantial investment flows to Mexico ($4.8 billion in 1991), will help promote investments there. The envisioned creation of a free trade zone in the Western Hemisphere (the Enterprise for the Americas Initiative) could also aid the growth of FDI. Those effects will continue to make themselves felt. If regional integration results in permanently faster economic growth, FDI, too, will grow faster.

2. Imbalances in transnationalization

Although there is no reason why countries, industries or firms need to converge towards any particular degree of transnationalization, it is possible that international competition will force young and ambitious companies, as well as more mature TNCs, to invest abroad. At the same time, services TNCs may continue to invest abroad at a rapid rate. The degree of transnationalization in their sector may eventually catch up with that of manufacturing.

(a) Country imbalances

The imbalance between inward and outward FDI for Japan, as well as the low ratio of inward FDI stock to GDP, is not in line with the experience of the European Community and the United States (TCMD, 1992a, p. 20). This is likely to change as perceptions of foreign TNCs change or actual barriers to inward FDI come down. As for outward investment, countries tend to differ according to their position on the development path. Relatively mature investors, such as the United Kingdom, have a high degree of transnationalization of their firms. Despite the rapid growth of its outward investment between 1985 and 1990, Japan is still a relative newcomer (table IV.3) (UNCTC, 1989). It is therefore likely that investment outflows from Japan, despite their recent slow-down, will pick up again before long.

The same is true of those other countries which accelerated the pace of transnationalizing their economies in the 1980s. The Republic of Korea and Taiwan Province of China are two prominent examples. China itself is rapidly expanding its investment position abroad. Other countries in Asia and Latin America could follow suit.

It is even conceivable that some countries in Central Europe could become sizeable outward investors, once they have completed their transition to market economies.

(b) Sectoral imbalances

At the sectoral level, the degree of transnationalization varies considerably (chapter III). Services are usually behind manufacturing, despite the rapid growth of their share of GDP in many countries. Taking the case of the United States as an example, 21 per cent of the assets of its transnational services corporations were abroad in 1990, compared with 27 per cent for its manufacturing TNCs (United States Department of Commerce, 1992a). This disparity is largely due to restrictions on inward investments in services, which have only recently started to be reduced. It may therefore be expected that investment flows in services may well grow substantially over the next decade.

Table IV.3. Ratio of foreign-direct-investment outward stock to total assets of the home country, 1990
(Percentage)

Country	*Ratio*
Japan	4
United States[a]	8
Germany	15
United Kingdom[b]	26

Sources: TCMD, 1993c.

a For 1991. Foreign-direct-investment stock at historical cost adjusted for the finance (except banking), insurance and real estate industry of the Netherlands Antilles.

b Ratio of non-bank foreign-direct-investment stock to non-financial assets in 1987.

3. Projecting foreign-direct-investment flows

As with all forecasts, projections of FDI inflows must be treated with caution. They depend on certain assumptions about the future course of the independent variables in the model used for forecasting (box IV.2), and those assumptions may turn out to be wrong. Moreover, timing is crucial: forecasts will be wrong if lags are longer than expected. Thus, world-wide FDI inflows are projected to grow, but not as rapidly as in the second half of the 1980s.

Projections of FDI inflows were made in the late 1980s on the basis of data through 1988, owing to significant lags in the availability of a suitable data set. The projection are based on three methods of forecasting the independent variables (see table IV.4), and indicate that the increase between 1984 and 1988 continued in 1989—a finding confirmed by the actual behaviour of FDI flows in that year. Using this same approach, FDI, on average, is projected to grow in real terms during the first half of the 1990s in most regions, but more slowly than in 1984-1988. In particular, it is expected to grow faster in developing regions (Latin America, Africa and Asia) than in developed, albeit from a small base.[12] The highest growth rates are projected for Latin America and Africa, although the pace depends on the forecast method used. Investment inflows in Asia are also expected to grow rapidly, at about 11 per cent annually, a finding confirmed by all methods of forecasting.

In an alternative long-term "scenario" of the world economy, based on assumptions of secular growth and further rapid policy liberalization in developing countries (leading to higher incremental output-capital ratios in these countries than during the 1980s), global FDI inflows are expected to about $800 billion (in 1990 prices) by the year 2020 (box IV.3 and figures IV.8 and IV.9). The main beneficiaries of that increase will be developing countries, which are projected to receive about half those inflows, compared with their present share of 25 per cent.

Box IV.2. The determinants of foreign-direct-investment inflows: a model for projections

The Transnational Corporations and Management Division of the United Nations Department of Economic and Social Development initiated a project on projecting FDI flows for developed and developing countries, by region, and separately for the United States and Japan. The projections are based on a single-equation model reflecting the principal determinants of FDI inflows, and tested using regression analysis for 1972-1988.

$$FDI_t = a_0 + a_1 GNP_{t-1} + a_2 \Delta GNP_t + a_3 (I/GNP)_{t-1} + a_3 XR_t + a_4 V(XR)_t$$

where:

FDI_t = inflow of FDI to a region in year t;

GNP_{t-1} = gross national product in year t-1 (signifies the size of the market);

ΔGNP_t = the change in GNP between years t-1 and t;

$(I/GNP)_{t-1}$ = ratio of domestic investment to GNP in year t-1;

XR_t = the exchange rate (defined as the ratio of the domestic currency to the dollar);

$V(XR)_t$ = the squared variation of the exchange rate from its mean over the period 1972-1988.

The level of gross national product (GNP) with a one-year lag, a measure of the size of the economy of the region, captures the opportunities available to foreign investors for supplying a large market. The annual change in GNP represents the attractiveness of a growing region to foreign investors, as well as cyclical (demand or supply-induced) fluctuations in the rate of growth of GNP. Both the level and the growth rate of GNP are expected to be positively associated with the inflow of FDI. A depreciation of the exchange rate, defined as the ratio of domestic currency to the dollar, is expected to boost FDI inflows by allowing TNCs to acquire domestic assets more cheaply. On the other hand, the extent of its volatility—indicated by the variance of the exchange rate—reflects uncertainty that could hamper FDI inflows. Domestic investment as a proportion of GNP—a measure of the rate of domestic capital formation—reflects the attractiveness to foreign investors of a region which invests a large proportion of its domestic output; that variable would be expected to be positively related to FDI inflows.

To capture region-specific developments, additional independent variables have been included for Latin America and Africa. In the case of Latin America, the sum of exports and imports as a proportion of GNP (O_{t-1})—the degree of openness of the host economy of the country—and the level of external indebtedness (XDB_{t-1}) are expected to have, respectively, a positive and negative impact on FDI inflows. In the case of Africa, a dummy variable (D) has been introduced to capture unforeseen jumps in FDI inflows that occurred in 1979, 1981 and 1985, attributed to special political and economic circumstances in the region's largest recipient countries.

Source: UNCTAD, 1993a.

Table IV.4. Actual and projected growth rates of foreign-direct-investment inflows, 1972-1988 and 1989-1995
(Percentage)

Countries	*Annual average growth rates*				
	Actual		*Forecast* [a]		
	1972-1988	*1984-1988*	*1989-1995* [b]	*1989-1995* [c]	*1989-1995* [d]
Developed countries	10.4	22.0	8.3	9.6	8.1
European Community	8.6	23.8	6.3	11.1	8.5
Other developed countries	16.4	28.4	7.9	5.2	4.2
Japan	-- [e]	-- [e]	9.0	13.8	9.5
United States	42.8	44.7	8.7	6.1	5.7
Asia	12.5	21.1	11.3	11.6	11.8
Latin America	19.0	16.4	17.9	15.6	12.2
Africa	12.2	4.4	6.3	16.3	16.1

Source: UNCTAD, 1993a.

a Derived from deflated FDI flows.

b Based on least-squares estimates of the average rate of growth of the independent variables during the period 1972-1986, on the assumption that the same growth rate will continue to prevail in the forecast period 1989-1995.

c Based on forecasts generated by Project Link of the United Nations Department for Economic and Social Information and Policy Analysis, with regional growth rates of the independent variable being constructed as weighted aggregates of these variables for individual countries. The projected growth rates of FDI inflows based on Project Link forecasts of the independent variables are generally higher than those based on the other methods of forecasting.

d Based on IMF and World Bank projects of the *average* growth rates of the independent variables over the period 1990-1995 (the lack of annual forecasts does not allow cyclical fluctuations in the growth rates of these variables to be reflected).

e The growth rates are not meaningful because the underlying series becomes negative for several years.

These exercises and their projected FDI flows (figure IV.9) carry several implications. First, FDI flows will continue to grow, but with year-to-year fluctuations. The speed of their growth will depend on the rate of economic growth in host countries. The conditions that are likely to encourage FDI inflows to developing countries will also encourage domestic investment. Still, the share of FDI inflows in total investment could increase, given that, on average, the growth of FDI may exceed the growth of that investment. Secondly, the share of developing countries in global FDI inflows is expected to rise, given the higher profitability of investments there and provided that these countries continue to liberalize their FDI regimes.

* * * * *

As the importance of structural factors and policy changes increases, the long-term trend in FDI flows might also increase. Nevertheless, FDI, like domestic investment, will continue to respond to business cycles (and such fluctuations may well be transmitted faster world-wide as a result of the growing integration of national economies through integrated international production at the level of firms, discussed in chapter VII). In view of those developments, the transnationalization of the world economy is likely to increase, strengthening the role of TNCs as integrating forces and co-ordinators of cross-border transactions.

Box IV.3. A long-term scenario for foreign direct investment

It is a paradox that year-to-year changes in FDI are so volatile, whereas decisions by TNCs to make cross-border investments rest on long-term considerations. One way around the problem of cyclical volatility is to construct a long-term forecast based only on the structural parameters driving FDI. The difficulty with that approach is common to all long-term forecasts: the range of uncertainty around the future parameters increases with the forecast horizon.

Scenario planning is a technique for thinking about the uncertain, long-term future in a structured way without forecasting or assigning probabilities to the outcome. The basic difference between scenario planning and forecasting is that the former is used to rehearse what *could* happen to prepare for contingencies that one may think are unlikely, rather than to plan for what one thinks *will* happen. Some companies use scenario planning to avoid the dangers of conventional forecasting and the complacency it spawns in a world where the unthinkable is increasingly common. This approach has been used to develop a scenario for global FDI flows over the period to the year 2020.

Over such a long period, business cycles can be ignored and FDI can be considered in the context of overall economic growth and investment. Just as, for most countries, exports represent a small part of production, so FDI represents only a small part of investment. At the same time, high investment (as a share of income) both leads to and results from rapid economic growth. Though less conclusively established, a further structural assumption is that high FDI inflows (as a share of total investment) are associated with an open or opening policy framework. During the 1980s some developed countries did much to privatize and deregulate their service industries. This sector was the biggest recipient of the massive increase in their FDI flows.

Where will growth be highest and policy liberalization strongest in the 1990s? A plausible assumption is that it will be in the developing countries. The Asian region has been growing faster than the developed countries for more than two decades, and growth is accelerating in Latin America and parts of Africa. Examples of market-oriented economic reforms abound in every region: from Chile to Ghana to Poland to China. The reforms invariably include a greater role for the private sector and more open policies for trade and FDI.

A key result of successful policy liberalization is to raise the return on investment, both domestic and foreign. Countries reap greater gains in output per unit invested. Freeing business from excessive regulation and stimulating competition between firms—public and private, domestic and foreign—increase the productivity of investment. This is beginning to show up in the United Kingdom and the United States, as they recover from their recessions following major industrial restructuring, particularly in services.

An aggregate long-term measure of the return on investment for an economy as a whole is the incremental output/capital ratio. This is calculated by dividing the economic growth rate (percentage change in real GDP per year) by the investment ratio (average share of investment in GDP over the same period). It provides a rough measure of the productivity of investment, under the simplifying assumption that all of the incremental growth was due to capital accumulation. That is clearly an oversimplification because, for example, it does not take account of changes in the labour force. However, it is a useful tool for comparing aggregate investment returns for a single country, or a fixed set of countries, over different time periods.

For developing countries as a group the incremental output/capital ratio was 24 per cent over the period 1965-1980 (figure IV.8). On average, a dollar invested produced a real return to the economy as a whole of 24 per cent. Meanwhile in the slower-growing and already capital-rich developed countries, the return on investment was lower—around 19 per cent. However, this expected relationship was reversed during the 1980s, a period that has been called the "lost decade" for many developing countries. The second oil-price shock in 1979, the early-1980s recession in their main export markets, the sharp increases in interest rates and the appreciation of the dollar through 1985 culminated in the debt problems that paralysed growth in many countries. This is reflected in their incremental output/capital ratio, which fell to 13 per cent over the 1980s, even below that of the developed countries. Under those conditions it is little wonder that FDI flows to many of the developing countries were lower in real terms in the 1980s than in the 1970s.

Given the recent changes in many developing countries, it seems plausible to assume that average investment returns over the next 25 years will be more like those of the 1960s and 1970s than the very low ones of the 1980s. An iterative model relating economic growth and investments was used to derive an incremental output/capital ratio in developing countries of 21 per cent for the 1990-2020 period, somewhat below what was achieved in the 1965-1980 period, but considerably above that of the 1980s. Meanwhile, the ratio in the developed countries would continue its gentle downward drift to 13 per cent on the assumption of diminishing marginal returns.

With investment returns of 21 per cent and a slight increase in the investment ratio of developing countries to 27 per cent of GDP (it was 24 per cent in 1990 and has been over 30 per cent in the East-Asian developing countries for more than a decade),

/.....

(Box IV.3, cont'd.)

economic growth in the developing countries would average 5.7 per cent over the full period through 2020. Not every country would grow at this rate, but, equally, some would grow faster. Compared with the 1980s, this scenario suggests that growth in East Asia would slow, while growth would accelerate in Latin America and South Asia. Globally, a 5-6 per cent growth rate in the developing countries would be lower than the average 6.5 per cent achieved during the 13-year period before the first oil shock, but it would be a major improvement over the 3 per cent of the 1980s. Such growth results from the policy-induced rise in the output/capital ratio which leads to an average growth in developing country investment (including both domestic and foreign inflows) of 6.2 per cent per year.

These trends imply a widening gap between returns to investment and growth in the developing and developed countries. Provided economies are open to foreign investors, provided political risks are reduced by the willingness of developing countries to follow international norms of investor protection, and provided tax regimes on TNCs are no more onerous in the developing countries than in the developed countries, the result would be a major increase in FDI to the developing world. Under this scenario—which assumes all of the above—FDI would grow from $32 billion in 1990 to around $80 billion in the year 2000 and to nearly $400 billion by 2020 (all in 1990 dollars). In that year, it would account for half of the world FDI of nearly $800 billion, up from only one fifth in 1991.

Although those figures sound massive, they imply a surprisingly modest move towards further globalization of investment. By the year 2020, the share of FDI in total investment would have risen to 6 per cent in the developing countries and 7 per cent in the developed countries. This compares with 1990 shares of 3 per cent and 4 per cent, respectively. There is scope for the shares to be much higher; they have already reached levels of 8 per cent to 15 per cent in such open and mature international investors as the United Kingdom and the United States. The long-term future for FDI may be even more dynamic than this scenario suggests.

Source: Based on Julius, 1993.

Figure IV.8. Incremental output/capital ratio
(Percentage)

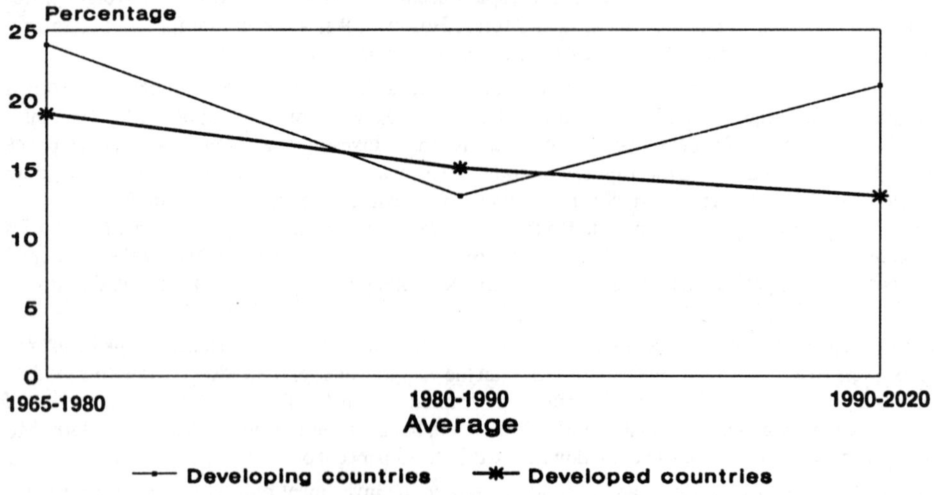

Source: Shell International Petroleum Company Limited, Group Planning.

Figure IV.9. Actual and projected inflows of foreign direct investment to developed and developing countries, 1970-1995 and 1970-2020 [a]

(Percentage)

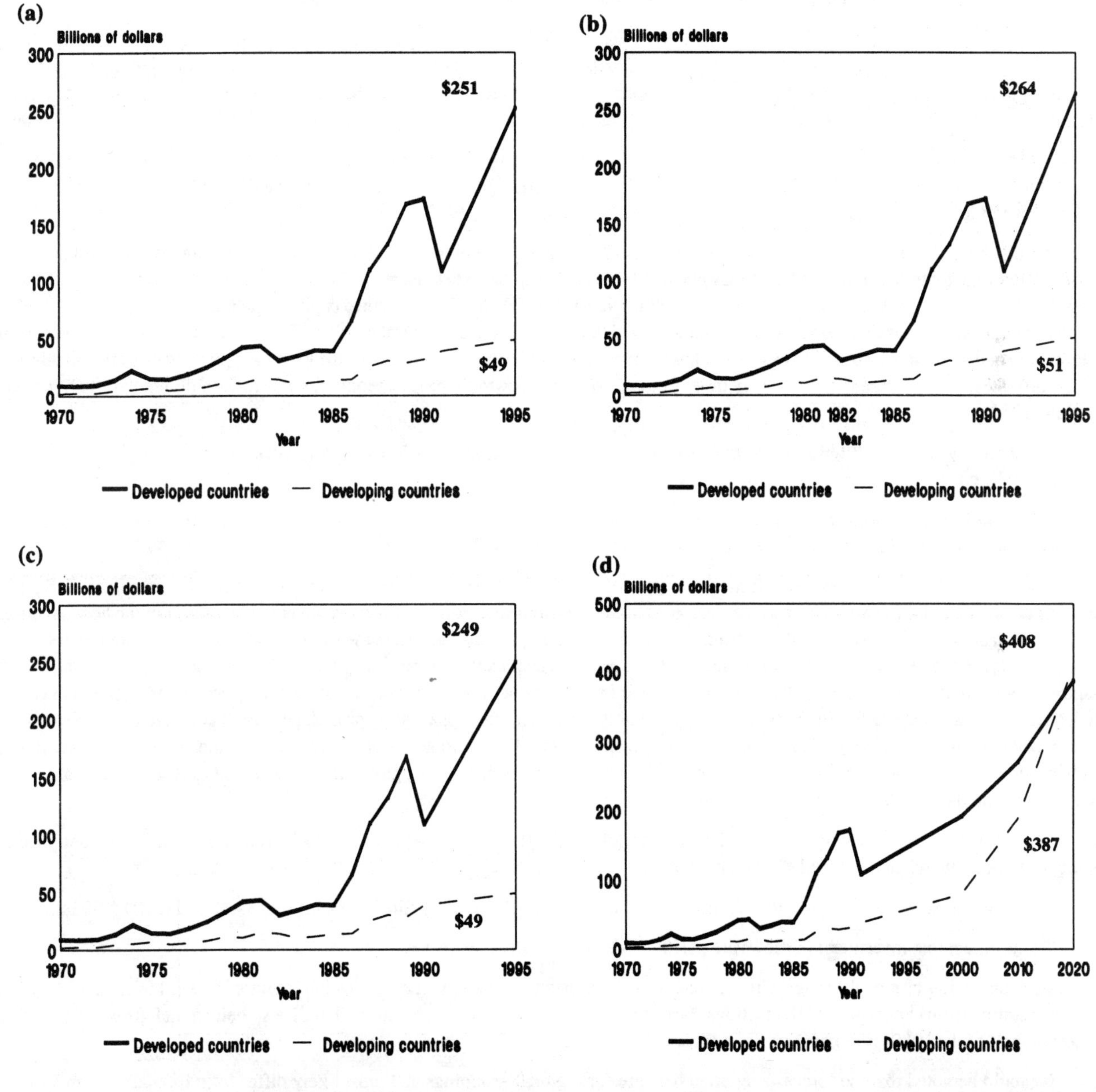

Source: Projected FDI inflows in (a) are based on least-squares estimates of the average rate of growth of the independent variables during the period 1972-1986, on the assumption that the same growth rate will continue to prevail in the forecast period 1989-1995; in (b), on forecasts generated by Project Link of the United Nations Department for Economic and Social Information and Policy Analysis, with regional growth rates of the independent variable being constructed as weighted aggregates of these variables for individual countries; in (c), on IMF and World Bank projects of the *average* growth rates of the independent variables over the period 1990-1995 and (d), on Julius, 1993.

a 1990 prices.

Notes

1 Japanese FDI outflows increased consistently from $6 billion in 1985 to $48 billion in 1990.

2 The regression equation FDI = -61.75 + 4.5 (GNP) where FDI is the percentage change in world-wide FDI ouflows and GNP is the percentage change in world-wide GNP, and R^2=0.93) shows that the growth of FDI outflows is highly correlated with the growth of GNP. The growth of aggregated FDI outflows (FDI) for France, Germany, Japan, the United Kingdom and the United States is also closely correlated with the growth of output (GNP) over 1970-1991, as shown by the estimated regression equation FDI = -55.48 + 4.23 (GNP) (R^2 = 0.89). See also Julius (1990).

3 Planned domestic capital expenditures by all United States companies are closely correlated with capital expenditures of majority-owned foreign affiliates of United States parent firms (Fahim-Nader, 1992a).

4 According to a survey taken by the United States Department of Commerce, Bureau of Economic Analysis in June 1991, majority-owned affiliates of United States TNCs planned to increase capital expenditures in 1991 by 10 per cent; in the survey taken in December 1991, that figure was revised to 3 per cent (Fahim-Nader, 1992b). Similarly, planned capital expenditures for 1992 were revised downward in the survey taken in June 1992 in comparison to the survey taken in December 1991 (Fahim-Nader, 1992a). This is similar to the experience in earlier periods of slow growth: based on a survey taken in December 1981, the growth of planned capital expenditures of these affiliates was 11 per cent; in the survey taken in June 1982, the growth of these expenditures was revised downwards to 6 per cent (Kozlow, 1982, p. 43).

5 See Anthony Rowley, "Ebbing streams: Japanese firms curtail their overseas forays", *Far Eastern Economic Review*, vol. 155 (18 June 1992), pp. 78-79.

6 Based on forecasts of the Department of Economic and Social Development, the growth of GDP (1988 prices) in developing countries is substantially higher than in developed countries in 1991 and 1992.

7 In addition to business cycles, other factors, such as the cost of capital in host countries or changes in exchange rates, may influence the mode of financing FDI flows. For example, foreign affiliates may consider it more advantageous to raise capital in the host countries if interest rates are favourable than to borrow from the parent firm. Other factors can affect the extent to which earnings are repatriated or reinvested. The cost of alternative types of capital may be one influence; exchange rates may be another. A high cost of capital in host countries, for example, may induce affiliates to reinvest their earnings rather than borrow from host-country equity markets. On the other hand, a fall in the exchange rate of a host country may discourage affiliates from repatriating profits, because that would reduce their value when translated into the currency of the home country. (Exchange-rate fluctuations also influence the valuation of reinvested earnings and hence total investment flows. The United States, for example, has excluded changes in flows attributed to sizeable exchange-rate fluctuations from the reported foreign-direct-investment data.)

8 In 1985, the average exchange rate was 239 yen per dollar; in 1986, the yen appreciated to 169 yen to the dollar and continued to appreciate until 1988, when it reached 128 yen per dollar.

9 For a discussion of the impact of the completion of the European Community Single Market by 1993, see TCMD (1993a).

10 To the extent that investment outflows are positive, the outward stock increases.

11 The conversion of global foreign-direct-investment stock data from national currencies into dollars is bound to reflect valuation changes resulting from exchange-rate fluctuations. Nevertheless, even when stocks are reported in SDRs, their annual growth rate during the second half of the 1980s is almost two times higher than that during the first half.

12 It should be noted that the forecasts reported here are for regional groupings and most likely differ from forecasts for individual countries for which there may be a considerable degree of variation.

PART TWO

INTEGRATED INTERNATIONAL PRODUCTION

A major feature of the world economy over the past decades has been the growing integration of national economies. International trade in goods and services grew faster than gross domestic product (GDP), links between national financial markets strengthened, more people moved across borders, foreign direct investment (FDI) expanded rapidly, and so did the activities of transnational corporations (TNCs). Policy changes by Governments, particularly the opening of previously closed industries to foreign corporations, the move towards stronger and wider regional trading blocs, the liberalization of restrictions on financial flows and the long-term effects of the lowering of tariff barriers have both ratified and fostered the trend to integration.

Integration can take two main forms. "Shallow" integration occurs largely through *trade* in goods and services and international movements of capital. "Deep" integration extends to the level of the *production* of goods and services and in addition, increases visible and invisible trade. Linkages between national economies are therefore increasingly influenced by the cross-border value-adding activities within TNCs and within networks established by TNCs.

As with shallow integration, changes in government policy help to foster deep integration. Yet the private sector has the lead role. By their very nature, TNCs are the agents that organize the cross-national production of value-adding activities via ownership (foreign direct investment) or other means of control. In this manner, the activities of TNCs create new parameters for Governments and, in many instances, lead rather than follow Government actions. The chapters that follow describe the evolution of the strategies and structures of TNCs and how this evolution has contributed to the growth of international economic integration.

Transnational corporations adopt *strategies* to achieve both short-term and long-term objectives—whether those be a target rate of profit on invested capital, a rising market share, or growth in shareholder value—all in the context of the economic and policy environment in which they operate.[1] The choice of strategy will differ across firms to the extent that they have different strengths, different objectives, and operate under different conditions. Transnational corporations adopt or modify organizational *structures* to carry out their basic strategies.[2] Organizational structures define lines of authority, coordinate flows of resources and establish mechanisms of accountability. Structures define how the different functional and geographical units that operate under the scope of common governance of the firm are linked together.

One example of the link between strategies and structures is the way that the multi-plant and multi-divisional organizational structures adopted by many manufacturing corporations in the United States in the first half of the twentieth century were a response to the need to manage production for a large and diverse home market (Chandler, 1962). Their successful application of the multi-divisional structure gave them a competitive advantage in managing cross-border production as they expanded abroad (Caves, 1982, pp. 74-81).

Part Two presents an analysis of both the strategies adopted by firms and the organizational structures brought about by the evolution of strategies. Chapter V describes at what is causing the cross-border integration of functions and the changing geographical scope of corporate strategies, in particular the growth of complex corporate strategies and their causes. Chapter VI analyses changes in the organizational structures of TNCs and discusses how their evolution produces a more complex and more integrated form of international production. Chapter VII discusses how the changing strategies and structures of TNCs contribute, at the aggregate level, to an increasing integration of national economies, and what this means for host developing countries in particular.

Notes

1 For analyses of strategies of transnational corporations, see Lecraw and Morrison (1993).

2 For analyses of structures of transnational corporations, see Hedlund (1993).

CHAPTER V

STRATEGIES OF TRANSNATIONAL CORPORATIONS

A. The functional scope of international production

1. The functions of the firm

Firms exist in order to organize the production and distribution of goods and services. In the absence of firms, production and distribution would be organized largely through arm's-length transactions between the owners of productive assets, labourers, distributors and consumers. Many of those transactions are handled within the firm. The extent to which a firm internalizes any of those transactions depends upon (a) its ability to achieve economies of scale in production and distribution, and (b) its ability to achieve "coordination economies". In many industries, the growth of internalized activity suggests the presence of substantial efficiency gains.[1]

A company's various functions can be described as comprising its value chain (box V.1). The firm purchases, hires and trains productive inputs, combines those inputs to create goods and services, and distributes and markets those goods and services to its customers. Corporations have departments or divisions to handle these functions, under such headings as procurement, human resource management, marketing etc. (figure V.1). In addition, large corporations require several managerial functions, including capital budgeting, cash management, accounting, information systems, strategic planning, legal and government relations.

Most firms start by serving national or sub-national markets. They build upon the competitive advantages gained at home to serve international markets, either via exports or by investing to produce abroad; the latter—called *international production*—includes all activities organized and controlled by transnational corporations (TNCs) within host economies that contribute to the value of the firm's output, including the creation of

Box V.1. The value chain of a firm

A value chain describes how a firm organizes and performs the discrete activities that add value to the goods and services it produces and sells. Some of those activities are linked together vertically and sequentially; others occur at any and all points and are linked horizontally.

Using the framework developed by Michael E. Porter (Porter 1990, pp. 40-44; Dunning, 1993, chap. 7), vertically linked activities include inbound logistics (for example, site selection), operations (for example, assembly in manufacturing), outbound logistics (for example, movement of products), marketing (for example, advertising and sales) and after-sales services. Horizontally linked activities include human resource management, research and development, procurement, finance, accounting and other management functions, sometimes called firm-wide infrastructural functions. Although every firm performs all those activities, their importance varies across companies and across products. Thus, operations and after-sales services are more important in automobiles and consumer electronics than in food and detergents. Furthermore, services firms define operations in a quite different way from manufacturing firms because the production and consumption of the service typically takes place at the same time. In addition, the importance of horizontal and vertical linkages may differ from one company to the next. The ability of a firm to identify and exploit those activities and linkages that matter most for its performance is frequently seen as a source of success (Porter, 1990, chap. 2; Prahalad and Hamel, 1993).

The activities comprising a value chain can be linked in different ways and can be more or less closely integrated, combining intra-firm, extra-firm and cross-border linkages. A corporation's strategy, its organizational structure, the external environment, demand for its output, public policies—all determine the form and closeness of the linkages.

Figure V.1. Distribution of labour costs, by function, for the global operations of Swedish manufacturing firms[a]

(Percentage)

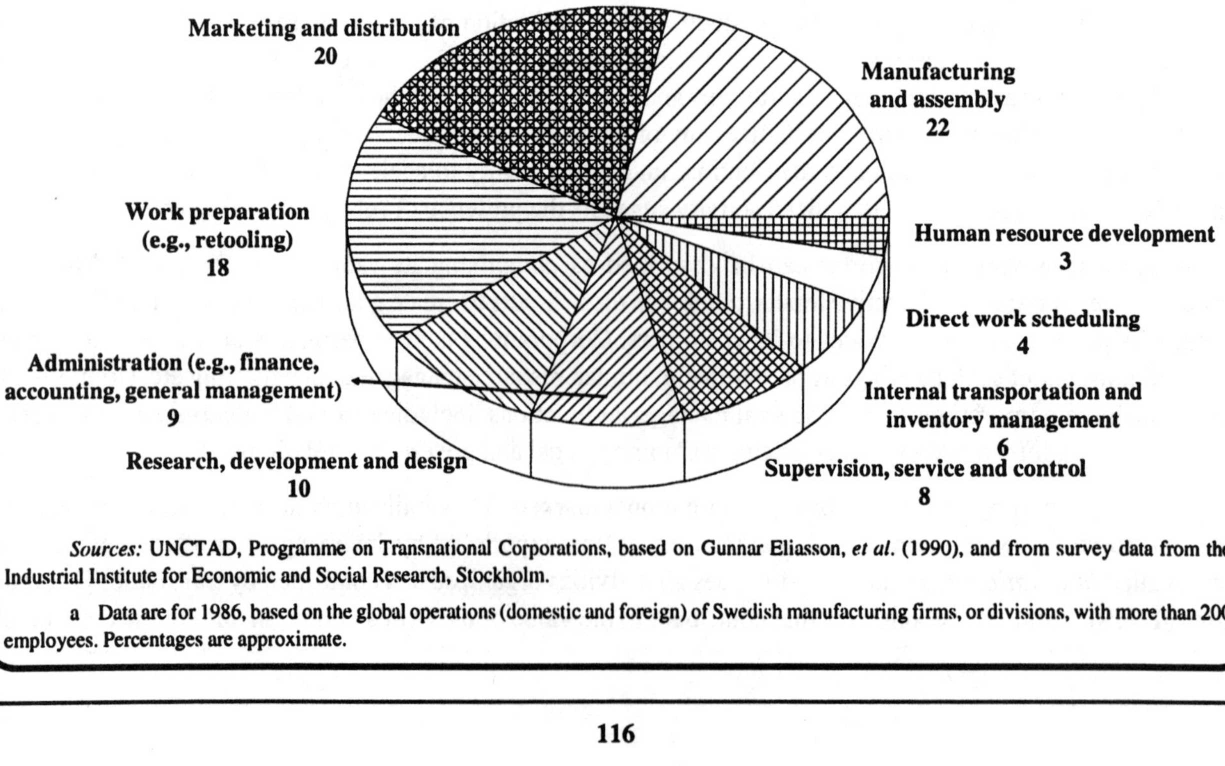

Sources: UNCTAD, Programme on Transnational Corporations, based on Gunnar Eliasson, *et al.* (1990), and from survey data from the Industrial Institute for Economic and Social Research, Stockholm.

a Data are for 1986, based on the global operations (domestic and foreign) of Swedish manufacturing firms, or divisions, with more than 200 employees. Percentages are approximate.

both goods and services and intermediate and final products. The choice between exporting or international production depends on a firm's assessment of its competitive advantages, the gains to be made from a particular location and the potential gains from internalizing cross-border activities within the organizational structure of the firm (Dunning, 1988, pp. 41-70). And the choice will often be strongly influenced by host country policies, including the degree and nature of trade barriers.

It is important to note that international production includes both goods and services. The services sector has grown rapidly throughout the world, and foreign direct investment (FDI) in services has expanded more rapidly than that in other sectors; it now accounts for over half the stock of outward FDI held by the five largest home countries. Moreover, services activities, such as research and development and marketing, are contributing a growing share of value-added within many primary and secondary industries (figure V.1). Since many services are not tradable and can be consumed only at the point where they are produced, the delivery of services via international production has grown rapidly. International production, then, involves not just the creation of goods in manufacturing processes, but all cross-border value-adding activities in extractive, manufacturing and services industries.

Firms engaged in international production need strategies and organizational structures that are suited to this form of economic activity. Strategies for organizing the cross-border production of goods and services involve choices about the international location of different activities and the degree of integration among the various entities that fall under the common governance of the firm. The range of possible strategies and structures has grown over time, as TNCs have responded differently to major changes in the international economic, technological and policy environment (table V.1). There is, however, a trend among TNCs in many industries to adopt strategies and structures that involve closer integration of their functional activities. Sometimes this involves giving primary responsibility for a corporate-wide function to an affiliate rather than the parent. Integration also

Table V.1. Evolution of the strategies and structures of transnational corporations

Form	*Types of intra-firm linkages*	*Degree of integration*	*Environment*
Stand-alone, e.g., multi-domestic	Ownership, technology	Weak	Host country accessible to FDI; significant trade barriers; costly communications and transportation
Simple integration e.g., outsourcing	Ownership, technology, markets, finance, other inputs	Strong at some points of value chain, weak in others	Open trade and FDI regime, at least bilaterally; non-equity arrangements
Complex international production, e.g., regional core networks	All functions	Potentially strong throughout value chain	Open trade and FDI regime; information technology; convergence in tastes; heightened competition

increases as the performance of corporate-wide functions is shared. For example, two or more affiliates may jointly do product-development work, which is then linked with process research and development by the parent.

2. Strategies

(a) *Stand-alone strategies*

One common form of TNC strategy is the establishment of *stand-alone affiliates*—affiliates that operate largely as independent concerns within the host economy. The main link between a parent and its foreign affiliates is control through ownership; other links include transferring technology and the supply of long-term capital (box V.2). The parent may exercise very little control over the affiliate, so long as the latter is profitable. In general, a stand-alone affiliate is responsible for most of the value-added chain in its output, though it may develop substantial links with local suppliers and subcontractors. It may also hire local workers and managers, borrow and lend with local financial intermediaries and engage in international trade with other countries. Large TNCs can control many stand-alone affiliates, each serving a separate host economy.

A stand-alone affiliate can be seen as a smaller version of the parent firm (figure V.2). It might be in manufacturing, especially where the host economy can provide resource inputs and where imports of materials and components are difficult or expensive. However, stand-alone affiliates are particularly common in services. Since many services are not tradable, affiliates need to operate as self-contained units, replicating the production organization of their parents.

Box V.2. An analysis of strategies of transnational corporations

While the strategies of most TNCs have evolved over time, this evolution does not always follow similar or precisely defined paths. The categories of functional and geographical integration described in the text are meant to capture the essence of the processes under way. But these processes are complex and no set of categories can be all encompassing.

Few stand-alone affiliates are wholly independent of their parent TNCs. In fact, many begin as closely integrated affiliates, with the parent controlling most aspects of their operations and defining their objectives. However, it can be difficult to integrate many functions owing to trade barriers and limits on the movement of resources. In addition, the absence or high cost of the appropriate technology, especially information technology, can hamper the maintenance of close linkages. An affiliate may become more independent over time, in part as it becomes more profitable. Changes in government policies can also affect the links between affiliates and their parent firms: examples include trade barriers and exchange controls. And major political events, such as wars, may push an affiliate to achieve greater independence from its parent.

Clearly, the ability to stand alone depends on the range of an affiliate's competence. If it can produce components for a parent firm's manufacturing operations, but does not perform its own research and development, raise its own financing or do its own marketing, it will remain dependent on the parent. The purpose of the categories introduced in the present chapter—stand-alone, simple integration, complex integration, multi-domestic, regional and global—is to highlight the fundamental elements in the way that TNC strategies evolve towards greater functional and geographic integration both within and across firms.

Figure V.2. Stand-alone strategy

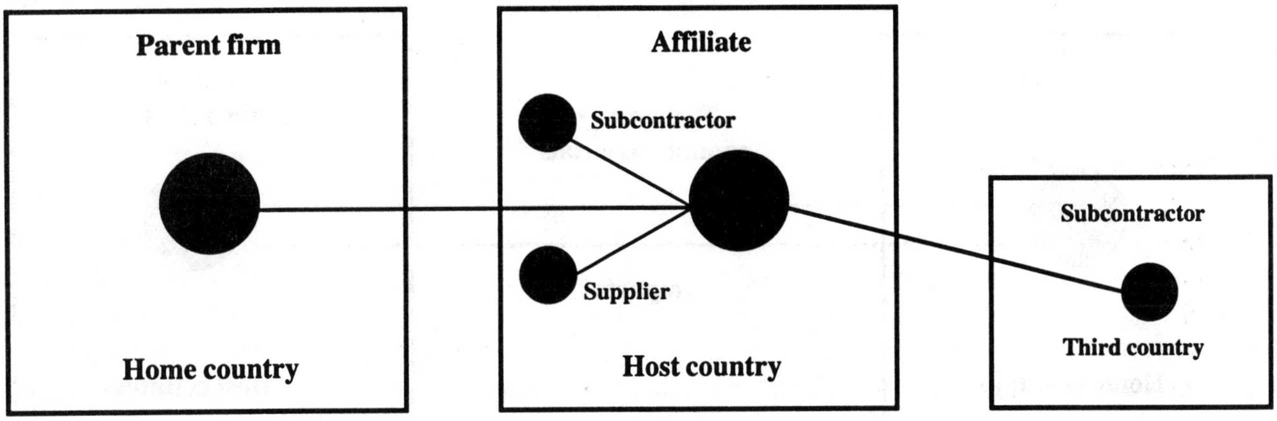

(b) Simple integration strategies

For some TNCs, their main involvement in international production is via outsourcing—some activities being performed in host countries and linked to work done elsewhere, mainly in the home country (figure V.3). In manufacturing, the clothing industry provides many examples of outsourced international production: large retail chains, such as Montgomery Ward (United States) and Marks and Spencer (United Kingdom), rely heavily on outsourced production from developing countries. In services, too, some TNCs use foreign affiliates or subcontractors to process data or write software[2], services that have become tradable due to advances in telecommunications and computer technology.

Outsourced international production represents a transfer of some value-adding activities to locations other than the home country and the primary country or countries of final sale. The primary motive for outsourcing is to utilize the locational advantages of a host country with respect to a portion of a TNC's value chain. Outsourced production is controlled by the parent TNC either through ownership of the affiliate or through non-equity arrangements with local firms, such as subcontracting, which enables a TNC to concentrate on certain parts of the value chain while subcontractors specialize in the production of other usually labour intensive parts. In effect, subcontracted firms are linking themselves with TNCs or their affiliates, thus becoming part of the production system of TNCs. Components, for example, may not only be produced by a subcontractor; they may also be designed by it according to the specification of the TNCs. The extent and nature of linkages depends on where and how the outsourced production fits into a parent firm's value chain. Firms related to the parent firm through subcontracting arrangements often cannot stand alone, but must be integrated into the parent firm's value chain through the establishment of functional linkages. Thus, *integration* of some corporate functions is required to manage outsourced international production.

Figure V.3. Outsourcing

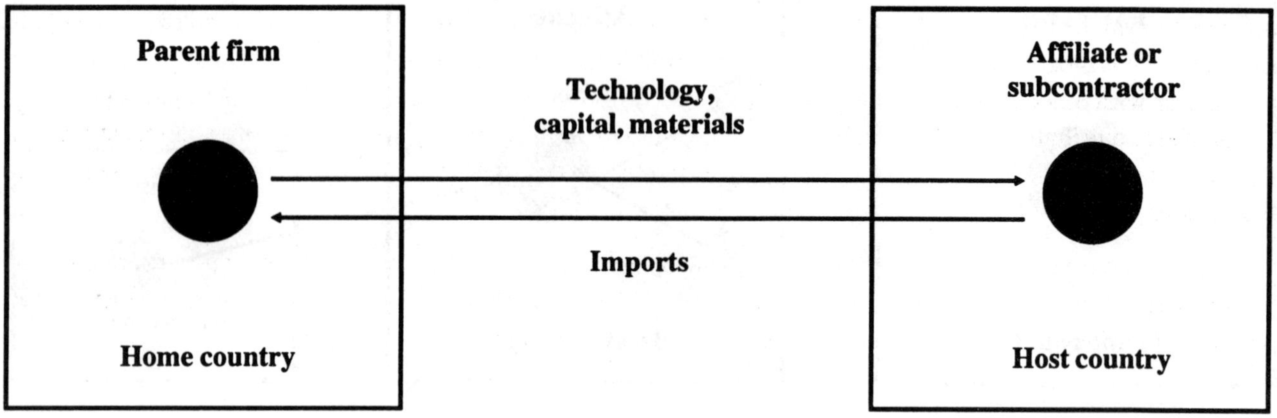

Outsourcing is predicated on the absence, reduction or elimination of trade barriers between home and host countries, on TNCs being able to invest in host countries and on transport costs being only a small proportion of the value of outsourced output. Since policy and technology are working to bring all these conditions about, the scope for outsourced international production is increasing considerably. Export-processing zones are often the base for outsourced production: the *maquiladoras* along the border between Mexico and the United States are an excellent example.

To a significant extent, outsourcing is cost-driven. Nike (United States), for example, subcontracts the manufacture of its athletic shoes and clothing to 40 separate locations, mostly in South and South-East Asia.[3] Design and marketing are done by the parent firm, with new designs relayed by satellite to a computer-aided design/computer-aided-manufacturing (CAD/CAM) facility run by a subcontractor in Taiwan Province of China. Prototypes are constructed and modified, and final plans are sent by facsimile to subcontractors throughout the region, where some Nike employees are present to ensure quality control. The output is sold world-wide. Since individual subcontractors are dependent upon the parent for design, standards and marketing, they are not capable of standing alone.

In recent years, Nike has been expanding in China, Indonesia and Thailand, which offer substantial savings on labour costs. As a result—and despite big improvements in manufacturing productivity—most subcontractors in the Republic of Korea have been unable to retain Nike's business. Nike is constantly introducing new products and operates in many price-sensitive markets. It therefore has both the opportunity and the need continually to seek out lower-cost suppliers. For some products, however, as in the electronics industry, the technological aspects of competitiveness are beginning to outweigh the cost considerations (box V.3).

(c) Complex integration strategies

In recent years it has become clear that, for some firms, international production can occur at almost any point on the value chain. *Complex integration strategy* is based upon a firm's ability to shift production or supply to wherever it is most profitable. Under complex integration, any affiliate operating anywhere may perform, either by itself or with other affiliates or the parent firm, functions for the firm as a whole. Each operation is judged in terms of its contribution to the entire value chain. Complex integration requires a willingness to locate various functional activities—not just production, but also research and development, finance, accounting etc.—wherever they can be done best to fulfil the firm's overall strategy (box V.4).

Under complex integration, there is substantial functional integration among the different processes and the different locations, although not every element of the value chain will be integrated to the same degree (figure V.4). Many firms have begun to undertake some functions in an integrated manner (box V.5).

Examples include:

- *Research and development.* A growing number of TNCs have been locating a small (but rising) portion of their research-and-development activities outside their home country. One reason is to take advantage of the skills available abroad. For example, the research by IBM on high temperature superconductivity was done in Switzerland. The growing importance of research and development has also led to more of it being located near factories and near markets. The big Japanese automobile producers, for example,

Box V.3. Outsourcing and integration in semiconductors and electronics

Outsourcing has been common in semiconductors and other electronics products, but its nature has been changing in recent years. United States-based merchant semiconductor companies expanded their output in the 1960s and 1970s in an increasingly competitive environment, so took to outsourcing in various Asian countries (UNCTC, 1986; Henderson, 1989). They did so largely through wholly-owned affiliates, as parent TNCs sought to retain close control over the underlying technology which, in this industry, is a major source of firm-specific advantages. Most corporate functions remained within the parent firm. Wafers manufactured in the United States were air-freighted to Asia, where they were assembled into circuits. The circuits were then air-freighted back to the parent firm for testing and distribution. In some cases, local firms developed the manufacturing skills and acted as subcontractors. Over time, and especially when Japanese semiconductor TNCs expanded into Asia, the Asian industry attracted more sophisticated parts of the process, including research and development and wafer fabrication. Some local firms, such as those from the Republic of Korea, have themselves become competitors in world markets.

The dissemination of semiconductor-based electronics throughout some manufacturing industries has been accompanied by widespread use of outsourcing. Contract electronics manufacturing (CEM), in which firms make semiconductor-based electronics components for use in automobiles, consumer durables, computers and other products, has grown rapidly and involves sophisticated products and manufacturing methods[a]. Many large TNCs use CEM as part of an outsourcing strategy to cut costs, but also to take advantage of the technical competence of the participating firms. Some of the producers are themselves TNCs, some are defence-contractors seeking new markets and others are high-technology start-ups. The development of CEM suggests that outsourcing may be a continuing feature of the technological division of labour, driven initially by cost considerations based on specialization.

a Paul Taylor, *et al.*, "Contract electronic manufacture", Financial Times Survey, *Financial Times*, 16 March 1993.

Box V.4. Integrated international production in accounting: the case of Swissair

In January 1993, Swissair started to transfer its revenue accounting (the calculation of amounts earned from and owed to other airlines by the carrier, which takes place on the basis of flight coupons collected) to Bombay, India, as part of its overall cost-reduction and results-enhancement programme. This activity is now undertaken by a newly established affiliate, Airline Financial Support Services India Pvt. Ltd., 75 per cent of which is owned by Swissair and the remaining 25 per cent by a local company, Tata-Consulting-Services TCS, Bombay.[a]

Airline revenue accounting involves the processing of flight coupons. Each document sold (a ticket for passenger services or an airbill for cargo services) becomes a flight coupon (sales record), which is passed on to Swissair's general ledger (formerly located at headquarters). Within the ledger, a liability per ticket number is recorded to the office issuing the document. Once the passenger/shipment is aboard, a copy of the flight coupon is picked up and sent to the general ledger, where it is recorded and processed in accordance with each step of the flight-services rendered (usually, one-way or roundtrip). Since revenues are only earned once the actual service is delivered, that is, when the flight actually takes place, each step is credited automatically to the account of the branch that originally sold the ticket, thus reducing the liability of the issuing branch.

Formerly, this accounting for documents sold was done locally in each branch, with the coupons shipped to headquarters in Zürich both in hard-copy form and via a direct electronic transmission. Beginning in October 1992, the transfer of accounting for coupon-transactions commenced with the training of personnel at the new affiliate in India. In January 1993, the affiliate began performing the revenue accounting for cargo services; it is expected to take over all passenger-related transactions in July 1993. The coupons are air-shipped to the affiliate in Bombay (either directly from each branch or via Zürich headquarters), where the entry into the general ledger is undertaken and credits and liabilities are processed. The affiliate transfers the results of these transactions to a central processing unit in Switzerland, which, while keeping the overall records, informs each branch with regard to its accounts. The Bombay office also takes care of the decodification of flight coupons (which are coded when issued with the agency/branch number, the International Air Transportation Association code and the sales personnel identification code).

In addition, the affiliate undertakes the inter-airline transfers and transactions. Since approximately 25 per cent of Swissair tickets are used on other airlines and approximately 20 per cent of Swissair flights are sold by other airlines, a considerable amount of the flight coupons are not Swissair tickets. Rather, they are issued by other airlines with which Swissair has an inter-airline cooperation agreement (currently, there are some 900 agreements in operation). These transactions require interline invoicing (debiting and crediting). While the recording of those transactions is now being processed in Bombay, the financial part takes place at the International Air Transportation Association inter-airline clearing-house in London. For example, a typical Swissair cooperation agreement involves some $2 million in debts by Swissair to another carrier and $1.5 million in credits to Swissair each month. The difference of $500,000 is being paid through the International Air Transportation Association clearing-house in London. The coupon transfer is still based on the actual delivery of coupons to the other airline's offices. Only a few airlines are currently linked electronically and can exchange coupon information on-line. Swissair's central balancing system, however, remains at its headquarters in Zürich. The central processing unit still monitors all transactions and provides data analysis, that is, further value-adding services based on flight coupons (such as branch performance evaluation). The sales part of the transaction (the money collection) remains a function of each branch office, which transfers its results and surpluses to the headquarters in Zürich.

The move of revenue accounting to the Indian affiliate involved a substantial transfer of know-how and technology to that affiliate and subcontracting of software development to local software companies. In particular, the know-how transfer to the Indian affiliate included writing working-orders, education of personnel and continuing support to facilitate independent operations, as well as the implementation of the necessary electronic data-processing equipment (local data-capturing systems, international communication installations for data-transfer and information exchange). The software used for the establishment of the new electronic link between Bombay and Zürich was principally developed by Oracle Corporation, California.

Once fully operational, the Indian affiliate will be more than a pure data-entry operation. It will also involve considerable value-adding services (proration, debiting and crediting of branch accounts, inter-airline transfer processing and billing, and decodification). While those operations are still at an infant stage, it is conceivable that these services will be sold to other airlines in the future, with the Bombay operation itself becoming a profit centre.

a Swissair press release No. 32/91 (Zürich, 10 July 1991) and information obtained from the company.

do some of their research and development in the United States, where they have begun to design models for world-wide sales. Ford has taken this kind of integration a step further with its Mondeo model, assembling a research, development and design team headed by Ford of Europe and linked to numerous sites in Europe and North America via computer-communication networks (see chapter VI). However, some research-and-development activities are harder to integrate. Rhône-Poulenc (France) has found that its pharmaceutical research is best done on a relatively small scale, and not linked with research and development in its affiliates.

- *Procurement.* ITT (United States), a producer of yellow-pages directories in eight countries, has centralized its world-wide procurement function for paper (its major input) in an affiliate in Belgium. This has enabled the firm to plan its world-wide purchasing and inventories of paper to take advantage of price fluctuations.
- *Manufacturing.* Automobile TNCs have adopted complex integration in the manufacture of components and the assembly of final products. Toyota has a network of parts and component producers in four ASEAN countries. Ford and General Motors have established cross-national networks within Europe, building on previously stand-alone affiliates which tended to be geared to a single country. Honda, Nissan and Toyota have established networks in North America and, in Nissan's case, Mexico as well. Parts and component-makers are more closely bound into the parent firm's strategies, supporting just-in-time

Figure V.4. Complex integration

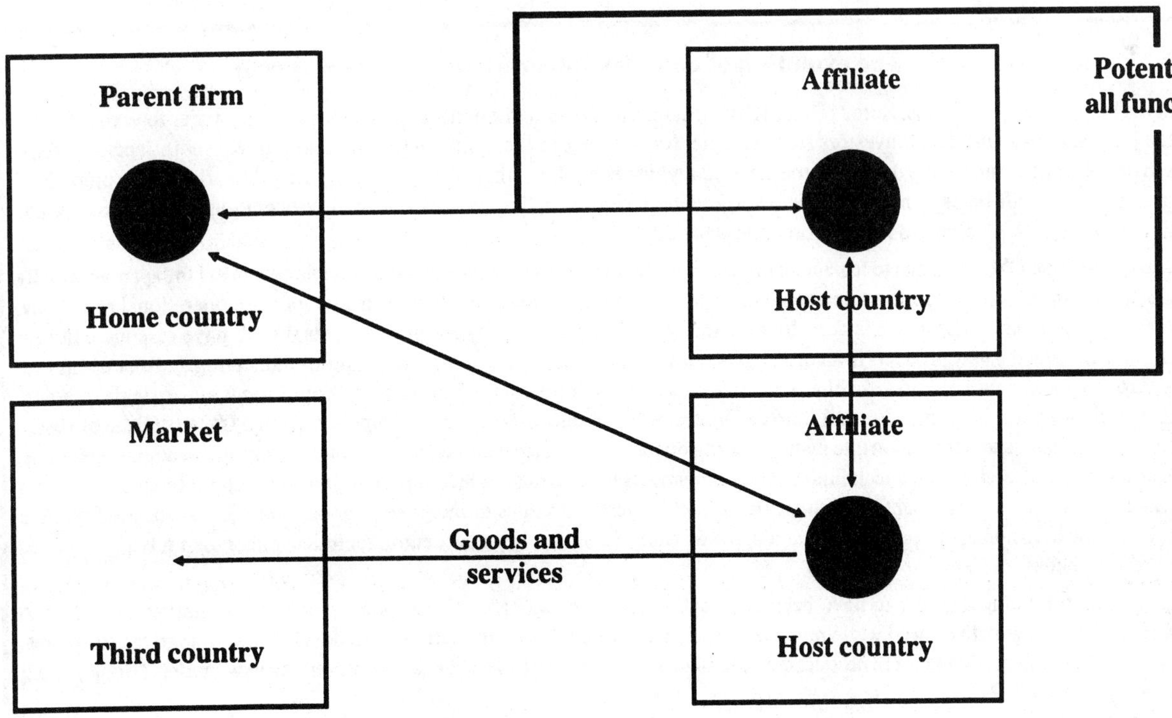

inventory systems, sharing research and development initiatives and being linked via information technology.

- *Accounting.* Owing to differences in national rules, accounting needs to be performed at the national level. However, information technology has allowed significant integration of accounting activities. For example, Swissair transferred its revenue accounting work to an affiliate in Bombay, India (box V.4). The affiliate, using technology supplied by Swissair, tracks earnings and receivables for the airline world-wide, based on the sum of coupons collected in daily operations.

- *Finance.* Liquidity management and other aspects of the finance function are, for many TNCs, being located where they best meet the needs of the firm as a whole. Taking advantage of innovations in information technology, the integration of the finance function can occur either at a home country location or with a foreign affiliate. For example, Pirelli (Italy) coordinates and guarantees its global financial commitments from a Swiss affiliate which is responsible for financing activities for the TNC as a whole. The United States affiliate of Siemens (Germany) transmits daily financial information to headquarters, where system-wide financial management occurs.

- *Training.* As one aspect of complex strategies, TNCs often try to transfer skills between parents and foreign affiliates and between affiliates. Ford (United States) and Mazda (Japan) have sent production workers from their jointly operated factory in Hermosillo, Mexico, to Japan and to Ford factories in Europe for training. The engineering team that set up the production line for Ford's Mondeo in Belgium performs the same function in the United States, and trains local engineers in the process. Motorola

Box V.5. The evolution of complex integration: the case of Xerox

At the beginning of the 1980s, Xerox (United States) essentially operated a multi-domestic strategy. Its major foreign affiliates were often joint ventures with local investors (for example, Rank Xerox in the United Kingdom and Fuji Xerox in Japan); foreign affiliates had substantial autonomy to apply the basic copying technology that had given the firm its world-wide competitive advantages. Individual affiliates controlled their own product design, supplier networks, assembly operations and marketing and distribution, usually with little regard for any corporate-wide objectives.

During the 1980s, Xerox began to feel intensified competition from lower-cost and more flexible producers in Japan, especially Canon and Ricoh. In response, it restructured some of its key functions in order to lower costs and increase operational efficiency. Research and development on products is done by functionally and geographically integrated teams, which have responsibility for developing and introducing new products in all of Xerox's sales areas. The company connected design, engineering and manufacturing activities through local area networks, so that teams with members from each of those areas could focus on a single product. Procurement is done by a group drawn from all Xerox affiliates, which reduced the number of suppliers from 5,000 to 400 (as of 1992). Xerox introduced greater standardization into manufacturing operations, so as to facilitate cross-plant cost and efficiency comparisons, and to ensure the use of best-practice techniques. The company used information technology to improve supply integration across national boundaries, and is experimenting with artificial intelligence techniques to integrate after-sales service. If successful, these techniques will allow customers to perform initial diagnostic tests via links with some central facilities, rather than relying solely on their local repair teams.

Xerox's restructuring appears to have been successful. The firm was able to recapture much of the market share lost to competitors and its cost growth slowed while revenue growth accelerated. Xerox is continuing to develop new, integrated structures, as it seeks to create greater efficiencies in product development and reduce the time and cost of introducing new models (Hoole, 1992; Howard, 1992; Dickson, 1992).

(United States), as part of its expansion in China, is sending Chinese engineering recruits to Motorola facilities in Hong Kong, Singapore and the United States for training, and is rotating top management trainees for its Chinese affiliate through almost all of its semiconductor manufacturing operations world-wide.

- *Corporate planning*. Asea Brown Boveri (ABB) (Sweden and Switzerland) conducts corporate planning through a 13 member executive committee, including the chief executive officer and 12 executives, each responsible for a business segment, a region or a corporate-wide function, and many working out of an affiliate. The committee meets every three weeks in different locations. ABB's matrix structure, with each unit reporting simultaneously to a business segment headquarters and a country headquarters, and its use of a company-wide management information system, permit a rapid two-way flow of information and allows key aspects of corporate-wide planning to take place in regional and product headquarters in host countries.
- *Legal*. General Electric (United States) has integrated its legal activities to conform with the integration of its main lines of business. Legal activities are located within the headquarters of major business segments, both in the home country and in major regions. A legal office in London handles firm-wide coordination, including international acquisition activity.

3. Complex integration and the world economy

Transnational corporations have been adopting complex integration strategies because of major changes in the world economy. These include advances in information technology, some cross-national convergence in demand patterns and an intensification of competition world-wide.

(a) *Information technology*

Advances in informatics and telecommunications have increased the capacity to process and communicate information, and have reduced costs. For example, the price of a computer with a processing power of 4.5 million instructions per second fell from $4.5 million in 1980 to $100,000 in 1990 (current prices), with a projected price of $10,000 in the year 2000 (Morton, 1991, p. 9). Such changes have allowed information technologies to be decentralized within TNCs and used throughout the value chain, which paves the way for the spread of flexible production technologies and new management and research-and-development practices.

Information technologies are also critical in coordinating activities throughout the value chain. In rather the same way as multi-plant and multi-divisional strategies created the need for greater coordination and a bigger managerial structure, so the development of complex integration strategies has increased the need for TNCs to manage their cross-border networks. Examples include Benetton (Italy) and Levi Strauss (United States) in the clothing industry and IKEA (Sweden) in the furniture industry. These are all TNCs that have used information technologies to match production more closely to demand in all the countries in which they operate. Research and development, especially in such industries as aerospace, automobiles, electronics and biotechnology, is dominated by the new information technologies.

Information technology also allows the value chains of firms under separate ownership to become more integrated. For example, one firm's shipping department may be linked electronically with another firm's purchasing department to speed the flow of goods between them. With communications technology, TNCs can combine key resources in order to pursue certain strategic objectives.

New information technologies both facilitate and require new forms of organization. The speed, ease and cheapness of communication are helping to undermine hierarchical reporting systems and have increased possibilities for horizontal communications across functional and geographical lines. To take advantage of the new technologies, firms need more flexible reporting and organizational systems; this is especially true of research and development and financial management.

(b) The role of demand

Some TNCs have shifted to complex integration because they want to serve world-wide markets. Growing consumer demand and some cross-national convergence of *consumer tastes* have contributed to that trend. As a result, an increasing number of products of identical or similar design are being sold in many markets. Examples include clothing, electronic goods, cameras and recorded music. Other products, including some automobile models, are often sold in different markets with only minor alterations.

The tendency for demand patterns to converge is due partly to a convergence in income levels since the Second World War in the more advanced economies, leading to a greater similarity in spending patterns, partly to the spread of communications technologies and an increase in tourism and educational and cultural exchanges, which increase the cross-national visibility of national consumption patterns, and partly to marketing efforts by TNCs. As products become more standardized across countries, the ability of firms to be present in multiple markets increases. It also becomes necessary for firms to be present in these markets to challenge competitors and strengthen their own positions throughout the world (Ohmae, 1985).

Despite the convergence of consumer tastes, many products remain differentiated owing to important differences in culture, economic conditions and government regulations across countries. For example, the rationalization of the white goods industry within Western Europe has been limited by differences in demand patterns with respect to the size and design of household appliances. In addition, the growth of flexible production technologies has made it possible for firms to tailor output to niche markets without suffering large penalties in terms of higher costs, as happened under mass production. Such differences in demand and production suggest that national and regional factors will continue to influence the future strategies of TNCs (box V.6).

(c) Intensified competition

One powerful force driving complex integration has been the intensification of international *competition*. Over the past 45 years, the sustained decline in tariff barriers and the spread of productivity growth have intensified competition across countries and brought many new competitors onto the world scene. The number of TNCs and their foreign affiliates has expanded enormously, and they come from an ever wider range of home countries. In 1968-1969, almost 60 per cent of the 7,000 TNCs from 14 developed economies came from just two home countries, the United Kingdom and the United States. At the beginning of the 1990s, four home countries—the

Federal Republic of Germany, Japan, Switzerland and the United States—accounted for 49 per cent of the 24,000 TNCs based in the same 14 developed economies; the United Kingdom was seventh in importance as a home country. The TNCs from developed economies concentrate their FDI mainly in other developed economies, creating a substantial TNC network that includes large amounts of intra-industry cross-investments (TCMD, 1993c).

These trends have pushed TNCs to seek new ways of gaining international competitive advantages. They have increased their efforts to cut costs by locating abroad and by paying close attention to different elements of their value chains. One example is the centralizing of procurement, often made possible by innovations in information technology. Studies indicate that TNCs with integrated procurement achieve greater long-run cost savings, through improved quality and shorter product-development schedules (Monczka and Trent, 1992). Similarily Japanese TNCs pioneered the integration of suppliers and subcontractors more closely with production and assembly, to achieve just-in-time inventory management and quality-control objectives. Now TNCs are increasing their ties with suppliers to foster a two-way flow of technological innovation. It is precisely pressures of this kind, combined with the opportunities offered by information technologies, that foster the growth of complex corporate strategies.

Box V.6. Marketing by transnational corporations: global products and local tastes

In response to an increasing uniformity of tastes for some products, TNCs sometimes opt for a concerted marketing strategy. Global brand names, such as Coca Cola (United States), McDonald's (United States), Nestlé (Switzerland), Philip Morris (United States), Procter and Gamble (United States), Toyota Motor Co. (Japan), Kellogg Co. (United States) and Unilever (United Kingdom/Netherlands) are advertised world-wide, often using the same (or a slightly modified) theme (Klein, 1991). Nestlé, for example, has restructured its operations along product lines and created a strategic business unit for each of its global brands (Nescafé, Nestlé, Friskies and Buitoni). The Buitoni unit provides guidance on marketing, including the advertising of its products to all its affiliates.[a]

Quest International, a food ingredients affiliate of Unilever that operates independently of its parent, used to have separate sales forces in each country. As its customers changed their demands, however, Quest International's various units in different countries started to work together. The company provided marketing services and intelligence to local managers selling its products, including information on new product launches (Jenster and Hover, 1992).

Even for internationally known products, however, global marketing strategies sometimes need to be modified to suit local or regional tastes. In advertising, for example, Coca-Cola has developed a pan-European television campaign with a new logo for the European market.[b] Toyota allows distributors in each country to manage their own sales efforts (with the exception of the marketing of Lexus, a luxury car, for which a more unified marketing approach was adopted).

a Suzanne Bidlake, "Nestlé adopts the personal touch", *Marketing*, 19 November 1992, pp. 24-26.

b Alison Fashey and Jennifer Lawrence, "Coke thinks regional in the U.S.", *Advertising Age*, vol. 62, Issue 50 (25 November 1991), pp. 1 and 36.

B. The geographical scope of international production

1. Multi-country strategies

In these strategies, an affiliate primarily serves the host country market while the parent TNC controls several affiliates in different markets (box V.7). The existence of trade barriers, including high local content requirements, has frequently required TNCs to adopt such strategies in order to enter specific host economies. In some industries, for example retailing and food production, these strategies are adopted because of the difficulty in achieving economies of scale and the persistence of particular national tastes and habits. Many services TNCs adopt multi-domestic strategies because what they are selling is essentially non-tradable. In addition, small and medium-size firms often concentrate their efforts on serving markets close to home.

In recent years, technological advances in transport and communications have reduced the costs of cross-national coordination. As trade barriers have been reduced and regional economic groupings formed, some TNCs have turned affiliates that previously served single countries into part of a more integrated production network to serve a larger market. That has occurred within the European Community as part of the transition to the Single Market. It has also happened in the four-nation Southern Cone Common Market—Argentina, Brazil,

Box V.7. Multi-domestic strategies of transnational corporations

Multi-domestic strategies remain important for many TNCs within the overall context of greater cross-national integration, frequently as a component of complex strategies. Unilever (United Kingdom, Netherlands), for example, seeks a balance in food, its largest product group, between centralized activities, such as research, finance and packaging, and the need to stay close to local markets. In some instances, this has been achieved by buying a local company to obtain access to a market niche. In France, Unilever acquired Boursin, to operate in a specialty-food area with a strong national base. Boursin has remained largely autonomous within the Unilever corporate structure. At the same time, while Unilever has organized its detergent business on a regional basis in Europe and North America, it has kept a national structure in Asia, largely to meet differences in consumer tastes (Maljers, 1992).

Transport costs loom large in some product areas, leading to multi-domestic manufacturing operations. Nestlé (Switzerland) has adopted global strategies for marketing its highly visible brand names. However, it manufactures chocolate in 23 countries for local distribution, due to the high cost of transporting raw materials, particularly milk and sugar (Yip and Coundouriotis, 1991). Government rules on procurement also foster multi-domestic operations. Asea Brown Boveri (Sweden and Switzerland) builds locomotives for government contracts that are designed for alpine terrain to meet stringent environmental standards in Switzerland. Yet Asea Brown Boveri also manufactures locomotives in India to comply with that country's local content requirements for government suppliers (Taylor, 1991). In the food industry, multi-domestic manufacturing is often required to satisfy national regulations.

Multi-domestic strategies are also followed to gain or protect market shares in host countries. In the case of ABB, its organizational structure allows affiliates to compete as if they were national companies in industries where local presence is helpful, while drawing upon the parent firm in such areas as core technologies, design, component manufacturing, managerial expertise and finance. The firm is organized into a matrix structure, in which affiliates are responsible to both a global manager of the business area and the head of the local affiliate. Global managers are based throughout the world—for example, the power transmission business, headquartered in Germany, oversees 25 factories in 16 countries—and are responsible for firm-wide strategies on exports, manufacturing capacity, employee development etc. At the same time, nationally-based managers are responsible for proving themselves competitive within their market areas.

Paraguay and Uruguay—in Latin America: Ford (United States) and Volkswagen (Germany) are two examples.[4] Transnational corporations are integrating affiliates in Mexico into a North American production network, in anticipation of a North American Free Trade Area.

2. Regional strategies

Many TNCs have production networks that are organized primarily along regional lines (box V.8). *Regionalized international production* includes affiliates located in various host countries within a single region, along with non-affiliated companies acting as suppliers and subcontractors. Final assembly can occur anywhere within the region, and the major market for the product is the same region. Regional networks of TNCs exist in Europe (Central and Eastern, as well as Western Europe), in North America (especially with the growth of FDI into Mexico in recent years) and in East Asia (UNCTC, 1991a, pp. 44-53). They are also reflected in FDI stocks and flows to developing countries from the three Triad regions—the European Community, Japan and the United States—which suggest a clustering of FDI along regional lines (chapter VII). United States TNCs are the biggest investors in much of Latin America and the Caribbean, Japanese TNCs are increasingly dominant in Asia, and TNCs from the European Community are strongest in Central and Eastern Europe and much of Africa (TCMD, 1992a, pp. 32-46). Similar clusters exist for strategic technology alliances (Hagedoorn and Schakenraad, 1991).

Changes in *policies* have spurred TNCs to adopt regional strategies, especially in Europe and North America. The lowering of tariff barriers, the liberalization of FDI regimes, the deregulation of many industries (especially in services) and the privatization of state-owned companies—all have helped to boost FDI. The establishment or strengthening of regional integration agreements covering both trade and FDI—including the European Community's Single Market, the European Economic Area and the North American Free Trade Agreement—have increased the incentives for TNCs to develop regional strategies. However, the regional strategies of TNCs in East Asia have largely developed in the absence of intergovernmental agreements; instead, they have been fostered by the lowering of trade barriers in the region, the increasing competitive strengths of many East-Asian countries and the shift of Japanese TNCs towards lower-cost locations after the yen rose sharply in the mid-1980s (Ostry, 1992b).

In some circumstances, regional integration agreements may also impose limits on TNC regional strategies. Regionally integrated production requires free movement of capital, technology and people, not just free movement of goods and services. On its own, trade liberalization is not enough to stimulate the fuller integration of production that could result from TNCs strategies.

3. Global strategies

Transnational corporations have often been described as having *global strategies*. According to Peter Dicken (1992, p. 1), globalization "implies a degree of functional integration between internationally dispersed economic activities"; globalization "is a more advanced and complex form of internationalization", which, in turn, involves "the increasing geographic spread of economic activities across national boundaries". The term also describes the approach of many TNCs that want to be in all the world's largest markets, in order to take advantage of the growth and convergence of demand, as well as to compete effectively with other corporations.

Box V.8. Regional strategies of transnational corporations

In Europe, many TNCs have adopted regional strategies, partly in response to the Single Market initiative, which have led to considerable restructuring and concentration of production. Unilever (the Netherlands and the United Kingdom) rationalized the manufacture of toilet soap in Europe, cutting the number of factories from 13 to four between 1973 and 1989. Its four key units, located in Austria, France, Italy and the United Kingdom, supply the entire European market and each has a separate line of products (Howelles and Wood, 1991, pp. 77-78). Unilever has also combined its 16 separate affiliates into a single cleaning and hygiene business, Lever Europe, which is responsible for product development, sales and distribution. With the new structure, Lever Europe's first new product was available almost simultaneously in 17 European countries (Williamson, 1992, p. 74). Euro-facilities were also created in food production; for example, Unilever's frozen meals are manufactured in Italy and distributed across the region.

Thomson (France) rationalized television manufacturing on a regional basis. Its plant in Germany concentrates on high feature, large-screen television sets, the one in France on high-volume products, and those in Spain and the United Kingdom assemble low-cost, smaller sets. The regional strategy adopted by Thomson separates manufacturing from marketing and distribution. The four assembly plants do not sell to retail customers. Instead, they hand their products to a separate regional marketing and distribution organization. Sourcing of raw materials and components has also often been reorganized on a regional basis. For example, Hoechst (Germany), facing the problem of lack of company-wide standards for materials and components, established a central European purchasing unit, which supplies its European affiliates.

Similar moves have also been made by non-European TNCs to reorganize their operations in Europe. Procter & Gamble (United States) coordinated its affiliates in Europe by setting up Euro Brand Teams. Each team is headed by the general manager of the affiliate that has special competence in that business. Product and advertising managers come from other affiliates, and the managers in finance, procurement and product development operate from European headquarters. Quaker (United States) created a European headquarters in Brussels, which fully integrated some functions, such as finance and procurement (including the entire supply chain). Marketing is done by individual affiliates, and adapted to local conditions. Yet, the regional headquarters is responsible for coordinating the group's strategy and does the market surveys.

Japanese TNCs follow regional strategies, mainly in the manufacturing of automobiles and electronics (Miller and Armstrong, 1992). For example, Toshiba has established a holding company in the United States, Toshiba America Inc., which has control of all affiliates there. Affiliates report both to it and to product managers in the head office. Since 1992, affiliates in Canada and Mexico also report to the President of Toshiba America, Inc.

In automobile production, Japanese firms have built a system of regional networks. In South-East Asia, some Japanese TNCs are investing in an intra-ASEAN manufacturing system. A typical case of parts procurement within the region is Mitsubishi Motors, operating in Thailand, but incorporating parts produced by Mitsubishi plants in various ASEAN countries. Nissan and Toyota have similar cross-supply arrangements. Those investments have been encouraged by the ASEAN secretariat.

The regional approach is also evident in research and development. For most TNCs, basic research laboratories are based at home and supported by smaller applied research laboratories in the major production plants abroad (Warrant, 1991, pp. 85-91). In some cases, regional units specialize in certain scientific fields or stages in the research-and-development process. For example, Du Pont (United States) has moved the headquarters of its agricultural research to Switzerland. Glaxo (United Kingdom) was able to coordinate the development of a new drug with joint research at its different sites in the United States and some European laboratories. Fujitsu develops computer systems business (hardware and applications software) from its research and development facility in the United Kingdom to serve the European market, and is planning to strengthen this function in the United States. Toyota's research-and-development organization, headed by the technical centre at Toyota headquarters, has been extended throughout Europe, Japan, and the United States. The regional centres support global product development through an exchange of information with design centres in Japan.

However, the world-wide spread of products and brand names is not necessarily accompanied by a similar geographic spread of all the activities in the value chain. Indeed, some TNCs initially aim to meet global demand by producing most of their output at home and then selling it abroad. Even then, some functions (such as finance) may be done on a globally-integrated basis.

Transnational corporations are frequently able to serve global markets with networks that are concentrated on a regional or subregional basis. Prominent examples include the largest Japanese TNCs in the automobile industry. Honda, Nissan and Toyota are all establishing regional networks for the production and distribution of automobiles in each of the major Triad regions. Each network is linked to the parent corporation through ownership and technology, and obtains materials and components from affiliates and non-affiliated firms outside its region. All sell some of their output outside their regions, and their products are quite similar across regions. However, the bulk of the value added remains within the primary region of operations. Thus, these TNCs are meeting global objectives through a regional organization of their value chains. At the same time, these same firms are introducing elements of cross-regional integration into their regional networks.

Over time, the pressures of competition are likely to ensure that TNCs spread their activities more widely across the world. At present, however, relatively few firms are integrating production beyond the regional level, and for only a limited number of corporate functions. The establishment of regional economic arrangements, in some cases with barriers to extra-regional trade, may be restricting the growth of global strategies.[5]

C. Conclusions

The present chapter has described the evolution of TNC strategies from those involving simple functional and geographical links between parent firms and their foreign affiliates towards those involving broader and more complex forms of integration. This evolution continues, as TNCs seek to protect existing competitive advantages and develop new ones. Older strategies remain, however, represented, for example, by stand-alone affiliates. And in some countries, local-content requirements mean that TNCs must serve a host country market via a multi-domestic strategy. But the same firms may serve another market through a regional strategy with complex integration of the main corporate functions.

Looking ahead, various developments could lead to less, not more, integration. For example, the spread of flexible production systems has allowed firms to use small-batch production to a much greater extent, providing a shield from global competitive pressures. Small-batch production requires less integration of manufacturing processes, reduces the minimum size of market required for profitable operations and permits firms to exploit niche strategies. Since small-batch production works well for small and medium-size firms, it is a counterweight to the forces pushing towards integrated international production. The same is true of non-tariff barriers to trade.

The picture, therefore, is mixed. Strategic evolution will not necessarily lead to most functions or most TNCs going global. The evolution of strategies is linked to changes in organizational forms, which are discussed in chapter VI. A related issue, presented in chapters VI and VII, is the link between the development of integrated strategies and structures and the growing integration of the world economy.

Notes

1 The classic statement of the economic rationale of the firm, originally published in 1937, is Coase (1988).

2 Sanita Wadekar Bhargava, "Software from India? Yes, it's for real", *Business Week*, 18 January 1993.

3 Mark Clifford, "Spring in their step", *Far Eastern Economic Review*, 5 November 1992, pp. 56-57.

4 Geri Smith and John Pearson, "The new world's newest trade bloc", *Business Week*, 4 May 1992, pp. 50-51.

5 John Griffiths, "Toyota reveals names by key European car parts supplies", *Financial Times*, 11 December 1992.

CHAPTER VI

ORGANIZATIONAL STRUCTURES OF TRANSNATIONAL CORPORATIONS

As strategies of transnational corporations (TNCs) change, so do their organizational structures. The traditional structure is based on stand-alone strategies involving affiliates linked to their parent firms via ownership and the supply of technology. The flow of resources and the functional links between parents and affiliates are limited. Decision-making lies mainly with the managers of each affiliate. Reporting arrangements are hierarchical: the top manager in each affiliate is in charge of operations and reports to the head of an international division and/or product division of the parent firm.

Simple integration strategies already imply more elaborate organizational forms. With simple integration, substantial coordination usually takes place between headquarters and foreign affiliates or subcontracting firms for some activities. The production of parts, for example, requires parts producers to match the design and quality requirements of the assembler, the parent firm. Alternatively, by improving the design of the component, the affiliate or subcontractor can influence the production of the final product. The process of contact and communication is therefore essentially two-way, although most decision-making authority still lies at the headquarters and reporting arrangements are essentially hierarchical.

Complex strategies, by contrast, typically involve multi-directional linkages and information flows between parent firms and affiliates, among affiliates (intra-firm), or with unrelated firms (inter-firm). A firm is organized so that almost any activity can, in principle, be located in an affiliate or in an unaffiliated firm. The combination of intra- and inter-firm structures creates a network, a structure in which the flow of resources and information, as well as reporting arrangements, are both hierarchical and lateral. Within a corporate system, decision-making authority is usually centralized, though not necessarily at the parent firm. Affiliates may have considerable autonomy in coordinating a particular function corporation-wide. Decision-making among TNCs engaging in value-adding partnerships for a specified period (e.g., strategic alliances for research and development) is shared among the firms involved.

Although organizational structures are supposed to help carry out strategies, they can actually be a hindrance. When the strategy changes, quite often the organization does not. Attitudes, too, may be resistant to change, especially if managers have got used to securing a particular market or group of markets. For instance, Monsanto (United States) moved the headquarters for its resins business to Belgium—near its largest and fastest growing market—because it felt that the home-country bias in the parent firm's headquarters was a barrier to developing a global approach to the business.[1] Moreover, establishing new structures can cause disruptions which may themselves lead to long-term inefficiencies. Linking strategies and structures is a complex task that is not always managed successfully.

A. Structures of transnational corporations under complex strategies

Complex integration strategies frequently require complex organizational structures. The very nature of complex integration strategies involving greater dispersion of activities than is dictated by stand-alone or simple integration strategies necessitates structures that are themselves complex. Complex structures are fluid and adaptable to changing conditions and facilitate the intra- and inter-firm flow of information and resources. With international production occurring throughout a firm's value chain, a hierarchical structure (stand-alone or simple integration) may not provide enough flexibility to deal with conditions that may change rapidly at one point of the value chain, but not at others. Similarly, basic corporate-wide functions, such as research and development, strategic planning, and marketing and finance, may be required in different amounts at different points in the value chain.

1. Intra-firm structures

Complex strategies often require intra-firm structures that foster greater functional specialization. This implies that corporate divisions in the parent firm are often organized by functions for a particular product. In other words, a point in the value chain may be located in an affiliate outside the home country, which is responsible for carrying out an activity for the TNC either world-wide or for a given region.

Under complex structures, reporting arrangements often follow a matrix form. Affiliates may report separately to different divisions of the parent firm involved in a particular activity, thus multiplying linkages within the firm. In spite of the greater geographical dispersion of activities, there is usually a high degree of centralization of decision-making, though not always in the parent firm. Decisions may also be taken in those affiliates that have corporate-wide mandates for particular functions.

In pursuing complex strategies and in adopting structures associated with them, some TNCs with substantial operations abroad have established headquarters outside their home countries to manage affiliates on the basis of a region, a product or a function (table VI.1).

Transnational corporations establish *product-line headquarters*, either regionally or globally, for important products. Those headquarters are responsible for coordinating all functions of the TNC that relate to a particular product line. Some TNCs, such as IBM, AT&T and Hewlett-Packard, have recently moved their headquarters for some leading products from the United States to Europe.

Regional headquarters are responsible for coordinating and supporting all activities of all affiliates in a region (Aoki and Tachiki, 1992). Regional headquarters are sometimes established in response to regional integration schemes. The number of Japanese TNCs that has established regional headquarters in Europe, for example, has risen in recent years (Aoki and Tachiki, 1992, p. 30) in response to the need to coordinate operations of affiliates that were established there in anticipation of the Single Market. Similarly, more United States TNCs are setting up regional headquarters in Europe in response to the unification of the European Community, with the choice of location being influenced by costs and infrastructure considerations. They can be seen as a mechanism for giving greater autonomy to the regional operations of a TNC. For instance, General Electric (United States) has recently established a regional headquarters in Asia (excluding Japan and the Republic of Korea) for its main product lines—power generation, aircraft engines and plastics—responsible for all its activities in that region. The Asian headquarters represents General Electric's first step away from a strict product-line division of operations towards a geographically-based organization of its activities for all main products.[2] Both General Motors and Ford have set up regional headquarters in Europe; these have evolved from the multi-domestic strategies pursued by them and the need to manage complex production networks covering several models of automobiles (Dicken, 1992, pp. 298-303).

Corporate units in charge of a particular function—what might be termed *functional headquarters*—are responsible for a specific activity for a TNC, which would otherwise be undertaken separately in home and host countries. An international procurement office, an affiliate that coordinates sales and marketing internationally or an affiliate in charge of providing after-sales services, are examples of functional headquarters. Often, corporate units in charge of a function cut across both regions and products. Establishing functional headquarters outside the home country for particular functions reduces the scope of responsibility that the headquarters at home assumes and allows it to focus on the overall coordination of the various dispersed functions, while retaining some key functions, such as strategic planning or finance. In turn, each headquarters in charge of a specific function regionally or globally bears the responsibility for performing that function and reports directly to the top level of management in the home country. The dispersion of activities requires that the parent firm monitors closely its functional headquarters. To achieve this, the configuration of a TNC's activities and the flow of information requires matrix forms with vertical and horizontal reporting arrangements.

Several TNCs have established functional headquarters outside their home countries, which specialize in carrying out a function for all affiliates in a specific region. The NEC Corporation (Japan), for example, has a regional headquarters in Singapore which, among other things, is in charge of research-and-development support for all affiliates in the members of the Association of South-East Asian Nations (ASEAN) through its facilities for the development of software and the design of integrated circuits (Wu, 1991, pp. 113-114). Similarly, the

Table VI.1. Selected transnational corporations with regional, product-line or functional headquarters

Parent firm	*Home country*	*Type of headquarters*	*Country/territory of location of headquarters*
		Regional headquarters	
Asea Brown Boveri	Switzerland	Asia and the Pacific North America	Hong Kong United States
British Petroleum	United Kingdom	North America Asia and the Pacific, Middle East Europe	United States Singapore Belgium
Ford Motor Company	United States	Asia and the Pacific Europe	Japan United Kingdom
General Motors	United States	Asia and the Pacific Europe	Singapore Switzerland
Hitachi	Japan	Asia Europe	Singapore United Kingdom
Nissan	Japan	North America Europe	United States Netherlands
Sony	Japan	North America Europe	United States Germany
Toshiba	Japan	North America Europe Asia and the Pacific (including Australia and New Zealand)	United States United Kingdom Japan
		Product-line headquarters	
Asea Brown Boveri	Switzerland	Power transformers	Germany
AT&T	United States	Corded telephones	France
Du Point	United States	Electronics Agricultural products, elements of fibres and polymers Lycra	Japan Switzerland Switzerland
Hewlett-Packard	United States	Desktop personal computers	France
Hyundai	Republic of Korea	Personal computers	United States
IBM	United States	Networking systems	United Kingdom
Philips Electronics	Netherlands	Lighting	United States
Siemens	Germany	Air-traffic management systems Nuclear medicine and medical equipment	United Kingdom United States

/.....

(Table VI.1, cont'd.)

Parent firm	*Home country*	*Type of headquarters*	*Country/territory of location of headquarters*
		Functional headquarters	
Sony	Japan	***Local procurement/after sales-services***	
		Sony International	Singapore (Asia)
Ford Motor	United States	***Procurement***	
		Mid-size car product development in Europe	Europe
ITT World Directories	United States	***Procurement/local purchasing***	
		Global purchasing headquarters	Belgium
IBM	United States	***Marketing and services***	
		Asia and the Pacific	Japan
		North America and the Caribbean, United States	United States
		Europe, Middle East, Africa	France
		Latin America	United States
Hewlett Packard	United States	***Marketing***	
		Personal computers	Singapore
		Peripherals	Singapore
Mobil	United States	***Exploration and producing operations***	
		North America, Latin America and the Caribbean	United States
		Europe, Africa, Commonwealth of Independent States	United States
		Asia and the Pacific, Middle East	Singapore
		Business development	
		Asia and the Pacific	Singapore
Hewlett Packard	United States	***Manufacturing***	
		Peripherals manufacturing	Singapore

Source: UNCTAD, Programme on Transnational Corporations, based on various sources.

Union Carbide Chemicals and Plastics Technical Center conducts their training programmes for the company's staff in the Asia-Pacific region (Wu, 1991, p. 114). Toyota Motor Management Services Singapore, a wholly owned affiliate of Toyota Motor Corporation (Japan), was established to coordinate transactions in components between Toyota's affiliates in several Asian countries (figure VI.1). It reports directly to the company's headquarters in Japan. Other TNCs pursuing similar strategies include the Ford Motor Company (United States): research and development for the Mondeo and its North American counterpart was carried out by Ford of Europe (an umbrella company for Ford's affiliates in Europe), involving affiliates in Europe and North America and leading to a product that will be sold by Ford on a world-wide basis.

Figure VI.1. The structure of Toyota's arrangements for auto-parts reporting in Asia

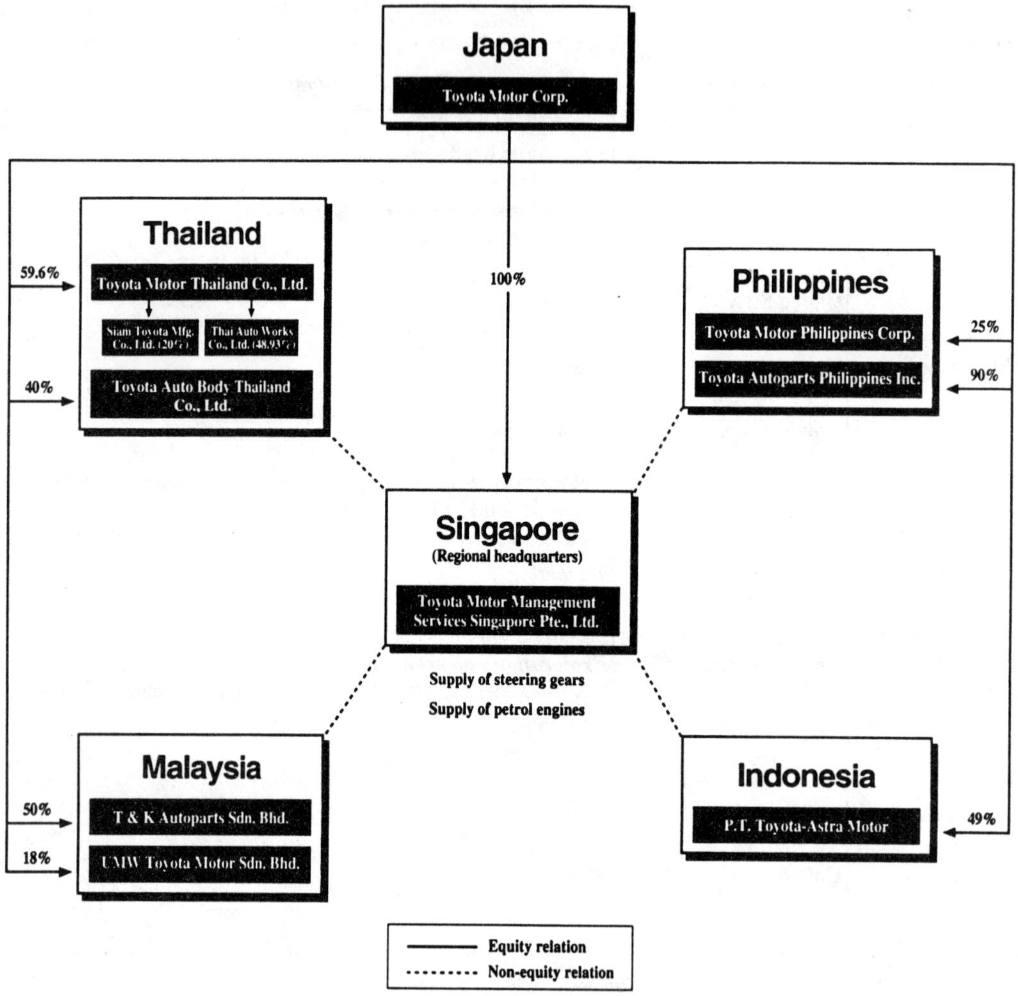

Source: Toyo Keizai Shimpo, 1991.

The main objective of product-line, regional and functional headquarters is to provide coordination more efficiently than can be done from a headquarters at home or one situated in a host country. In practice, the demarcation lines between the three types of headquarters are often not clear. It is not uncommon for TNCs to establish headquarters abroad on the basis of more than one category: IBM (United States), for example, has a regional headquarters in Europe for networking systems, one of its products. While it may be possible to organize TNCs on the basis of the lines of conventional regional or product headquarters when pursuing complex integration strategies, functional headquarters represent a new development in the organizational structure of TNCs that seems to be particularly suitable to these strategies.

The location of a product-line, regional or functional headquarters within a region is determined by a variety of factors, including telecommunication and transportation facilities, the quality of human resources, local operating expenses and fiscal benefits. Since the activities of headquarters often involve a high level of managerial skill and expertise and can have considerable spillover effects on the local economy, Governments are eager to attract them (box VI.1).

Box VI.1. The role of the State in attracting headquarters of transnational corporations: the example of Singapore

Exploiting its sophisticated technological and institutional-support infrastructure, Singapore is actively seeking to attract regional, product-line and functional headquarters of TNCs with activities in Asia and the Pacific. To that end, Singapore is re-adjusting policy measures to address issues, such as resource and credit availability, the development of human resources and the upgrading of infrastructure. In addition, Singapore offers a wide spectrum of services and incentives to TNCs that want to establish headquarters there.

The geographical position and established transportation linkages of Singapore with the rest of the world provide a ready ground for headquarters of TNCs. Having been a major hub for passenger, as well as air-and-sea cargo traffic in South-East Asia, the Government of Singapore has consistently invested in transport infrastructure to maintain its lead as a world-class transportation hub. A second air terminal was completed in late 1990 and the civil aviation authorities plan to build two more terminals at Changi airport increasing the total passenger-handling capacity to 50 million a year and the air cargo capacity to 2.5 million tons. To keep up with a growing regional demand for sea transportation services, the Government has committed $1.1 billion for the expansion of container terminals to expand their capacity to over 15 million twenty-foot equivalent units.

To attract functional headquarters of TNCs for research and development, the Ministry of Trade and Industry of Singapore has recently set up the National Science and Technology Board. Its objective is to oversee the development of research-and-development infrastructure for new industries, such as agro-technology, biotechnology, robotics and automation. Singapore has also established several Government-supported research centres, such as the Singapore Science Park, the Institute of Molecular and Cell Biology, the Institute of Systems Science and the Information Technology Institute. In addition, Singapore inaugurated a new university in mid-1991 with special emphasis on science and technology, thus doubling the national research-and-development expenditure to over half a billion dollars. Singapore has also instituted stricter intellectual property protection for TNCs.

With the inception of the Asian Dollar Market and the Singapore International Monetary Exchange (SIMEX), Asia's first financial futures exchange, Singapore has become a leading financial centre for TNCs in the region. State-of-the-art telecommunications technology allows TNCs to trade in financial centres through the world. In addition, Singapore's location in a time zone that overlaps with that of both European and Asian financial markets allows TNCs to trade in those regions during regular working hours. In order to encourage TNCs to locate their regional or global finance headquarters in Singapore, several fiscal incentives have been introduced. The Finance and Treasury Centre announced in March 1990 a concessionary tax rate of 10 per cent on income received from the provision of treasury and financing services in foreign currencies to affiliates. In addition, dividends from foreign affiliates to the parent firms are exempted from taxes.

The Operational Headquarters initiative, administered by the Economic Development Board of Singapore, grants operational-headquarters status to foreign affiliates that manage related firms outside Singapore. The Government currently offers a concessionary tax rate of 10 per cent (instead of the usual 31 per cent) to income of foreign affiliates arising from the performance of services related to their status of operational headquarters. Some affiliates awarded operational-headquarters status in Singapore are in charge of particular functions for the Asian region and typically engage in planning, procurement, technical assistance, marketing and sales promotion, training, finance and accounting. Through those measures, Singapore seeks to become a business centre for headquarters of TNCs.

Source: Singapore International Chamber of Commerce (1993).

Partly in response to easier regulations for the listing of foreign companies in stock exchanges, TNCs use international capital markets to raise equity. This facilitates a dilution of their ownership by bringing in stockholders world-wide. Thus, the potential for a TNC to be owned by foreign entities increases when it is listed on stock exchanges outside the home country. For the ten largest TNCs (in terms of their foreign assets—see table I.10), the number of foreign countries in which their stock is listed has increased from 58 to 70 over the past decade (table VI.2). Of a sample of the largest United States manufacturing TNCs, 50 per cent were listed on

Table VI.2. Foreign countries in which the stock of the ten largest transnational corporations is listed, 1983 and 1993[a]

Parent firm	*Home country*	*1983*	*1993*
Royal Dutch Shell[b]	The Netherlands and the United Kingdom	Austria, Belgium, France, Germany, Federal Republic of, Luxembourg, Switzerland, United States	Austria, Belgium, France, Germany, Luxembourg, Switzerland, United States
Ford	United States	Belgium, Canada, France, Germany, Federal Republic of, Switzerland, United Kingdom	Belgium, Canada, France, Germany, Japan, Switzerland, United Kingdom
General Motors	United States	Belgium, Canada, France, Germany, Federal Republic of, Japan, United Kingdom	Belgium, Canada, France, Germany, United Kingdom
Exxon	United States	Belgium, France, Germany, Federal Republic of, The Netherlands, Switzerland	Belgium, France, Germany, Japan, The Netherlands, Switzerland, United Kingdom
International Business Machines	United States	Austria, Belgium, Canada, France, Germany, Federal Republic of, Japan, The Netherlands, Switzerland, United Kingdom	Austria, Belgium, Canada, France, Germany, Japan, The Netherlands, Switzerland, United Kingdom
British Petroleum	United Kingdom	France, Germany, Federal Republic of, The Netherlands, Switzerland, United States	Canada, France, Germany, Japan, The Netherlands, Switzerland, United States
Nestlé	Switzerland	Austria, France, Germany, Federal Republic of, The Netherlands	Austria, Belgium, France, Germany, Japan, The Netherlands, United Kingdom
Asea Brown Boveri[c]	Sweden and Switzerland	United Kingdom, United States	Austria, Denmark, Finland, Germany, United Kingdom, United States
Philips Electronics	The Netherlands	Austria, Belgium, France, Germany, Federal Republic of, Luxembourg, Switzerland, United Kingdom, United States	Austria, Belgium, France, Germany, Luxembourg, Switzerland, United Kingdom, United States
Mobil	United States	Canada, France, Germany, Federal Republic of, The Netherlands, Switzerland, United Kingdom	Canada, France, Germany, Japan, The Netherlands, Switzerland, United Kingdom
Total number of countries in which the stock of parent firms is listed		58	70

Source: UNCTAD, Programme on Transnational Corporations, based on company information.

a Largest TNCs ranked by the size of their foreign assets (see table I.10). American Depository Receipts are included.
b Consists of listings of Royal Dutch (the Netherlands) and Shell Transport (United Kingdom) outside of the Netherlands and the United Kingdom.
c Consists of Brown Boveri (Switzerland) listings and ASEA (Sweden) listings outside of Switzerland and Sweden.

stock exchanges outside the United States, of which more than 25 per cent had listed their stocks in more than four countries (Raghunathan, 1992).

Legal ownership structures—especially with the proliferation of layers of ownership—do not necessarily correspond to managerial structures and reporting arrangements within a TNC (box VI.2). Second-tier or third-tier affiliates, for example, may report directly to the parent firm. Nevertheless, as the ownership structure of TNCs becomes more complex, so do questions of coordination, decision-making and reporting. The same goes for policies based on the nationality of a firm (for example, national treatment, investment incentives and performance requirements), an issue discussed in Part Three.

Box VI.2. Multi-tier ownership structures of transnational corporations

Many TNCs now have multi-tiered ownership, with parent firms owning foreign (and domestic) affiliates that are themselves owners of additional affiliates (see also Hedlund, 1993). The first tier consists of affiliates owned by the ultimate parent, the second tier by affiliates owned by first-tier affiliates, and so on. In each tier, minority equity participation by external investors may also be involved.

A 1991 sample of the largest United States manufacturing TNCs shows an average of 2.4 tiers in the structure of ownership of their affiliates, with 46 per cent of those companies having three or more tiers of affiliates abroad (table 1). For example, Mattel, a United States toy producer, has 39 affiliates around the world, 26 of which are directly owned (first-tier affiliates), 11 second-tier affiliates and 2 third-tier affiliates (table 2). Multi-tiered ownership structures are common among mature TNCs. Affiliates that, over time, have acquired the necessary ownership advantages, skills, technology and international experience etc., become parent firms themselves by establishing foreign as well as domestic affiliates.

Indirect ownership of affiliates is sometimes the result of a decision by the parent firm to become more dispersed geographically while retaining control of its affiliates. For example, Nestlé (Switzerland) has more than 95 per cent of its assets abroad in nearly every region of the world, and some 30 per cent of its affiliates are in the second, third and fourth tiers.[a] Mergers and acquisitions may themselves create additional tiers in ownership structures, since they often involve one parent firm taking over another parent firm, which then becomes a first-tier affiliate of the acquirer. The wave of cross-border mergers and acquisitions during the 1980s may therefore have been a factor in the proliferation of multi-tier ownership structures (UNCTAD, 1993f).

Table 1. Multi-tiered ownership structures of United States transnational corporations, 1991[a]

Number of tiers of affiliates	*Percentage of TNCs*
1	32
2	22
3	28
4	12
5	6
Average 2.4	100

Source: Raghunathan, 1992.

a The data are based on a survey of 318 of the largest United States manufacturing TNCs with at least 5 per cent of their total assets or sales abroad and at least $50 million in sales. Of that universe, a total of 51 TNCs responded in full. Those TNCs showed no bias when compared to the universe of 318 TNCs.

/.....

(Box VI.2, cont'd.)

Table 2. The multi-tier ownership structure of Mattel, 1991

Tier of affiliate	*Parent firm*	*Mattel Inc. (United States)*									
		8 United States affiliates, of which:					*18 foreign affiliates, of which:*				
1st-tier affiliates	Mattel G. Inc.	Mattel I. Inc.			Mattel Overseas Inc.		Auritel S.A. (Mexico)	Mattel Toys (HK) Ltd. (Hong Kong)	Mattel France S.A. (France)	Mattel Holdings Ltd. (Canada)	
2nd-tier affiliates	Mattel GmbH (Germany)	Mattel Toys S.R.L. (Italy)	Mattel A.E.B.E. (Greece)	Mattel A.G. (Switzer-land)	Mattel Toys Vendor Operations Limited (Hong Kong)	Mattel Pty. Limited (Australia)	Aurimat S.A. de C.V. (Mexico)	Mattel T Company Ltd. (Hong Kong)	Corolle S.A. (France)	Mattel Canada Inc. (Canada)	Mattel United Kingdom Limited (United Kingdom)
3rd-tier affiliates				Mattel Manufac-turing Europe	S.R.L. (Italy)						

Source: United States, Securities and Exchange Commission, 10-K reports.

In addition to multi-tier ownership structures, affiliates often form what might be termed internal joint ventures, in which the parent and one or two affiliates set up a new company (indirectly owned by the parent). Of the sample of the largest United States TNCs surveyed, only 14 per cent of the parents owned all their affiliates 100 per cent, and 68 per cent had internal and/or external joint ventures in their ownership structure.[b] IBM's Pan-European services affiliate in France, IBM Eurocoordination, is one such example. That affiliate is owned by affiliates of IBM from 15 European countries, each holding a stake roughly in proportion to the size of its operations.[c] The ownership structure highlights the role that the affiliate plays in such areas as marketing, sales, distribution and training in the operations in Europe.

---

a Dun and Bradstreet International, 1992; "Nestlé: a giant in a hurry", *Business Week*, 22 March 1993, pp. 50-51, 54.

b Raghunathan, 1992.

c United States, Securities and Exchange Commission. IBM Eurocoordination is owned by affiliates located in France, Germany, Italy, and the United Kingdom (about 14 per cent each) and by affiliates located in Austria, Belgium, Denmark, Finland, Ireland, The Netherlands, Norway, Portugal, Spain, Sweden and Switzerland (about 4 per cent each); 10-K reports.

2. Inter-firm structures: strategic partnerships

Complex integration covers cross-border transactions not only between companies under common ownership, but also between unrelated firms. International strategic partnerships or alliances, essentially cooperative arrangements mainly between TNCs headquartered in different countries, have become increasingly popular.

Those partnerships are a form of organizing corporate activities across borders so that a TNC, while retaining its core firm-specific advantages, links with other firms to develop new advantages, spread risks and capture economies of synergy. Such relationships typically involve non-equity forms that allow firms to share control over a specific project or activity, but can be accompanied by cross shareholdings.

International strategic partnerships or alliances can occur at various points of the value chain, ranging from research and development to after-sales services. Strategic technology partnerships, estimated to have exceeded 4,000 between 1980 and 1989 (Hagedoorn and Schakenraad, 1991), have become particularly prevalent. For example, IBM (United States) has alliances with Thomson-CSF (France) to market microprocessor chips, with Toshiba (Japan) to cooperate in the development of static random access memory chips, with Siemens (Germany) for work on advanced dynamic random access memory chips, and with Toshiba and Siemens to develop a new 256 megabyte chip (box VI.3). Renault (France) and Volvo (Sweden) have an alliance to produce automobiles and trucks. Nestlé (Switzerland) and Coca-Cola (United States) are cooperating to distribute canned hot drinks through vending machines.[3] An alliance between Sanofi (an affiliate of Elf Aquitaine, France) and Eastman Kodak (United States) was formed to share each other's distribution network.[4] Recently, AT&T announced its plans to form alliances with several major communications companies world-wide (including companies in Europe, Japan, Australia and Singapore), as part of a plan to build a global telecommunications network.[5]

Box VI.3. Functional integration through international strategic alliances in semiconductors: IBM, Toshiba and Siemens

The semiconductor industry is characterized by heavy research and continuous development of new products, a short product life cycle, a high rate of process innovation, the proprietary nature of key technologies and significant economies of scale. The industry comprises highly competitive firms, with new entrants from the Republic of Korea and Taiwan Province of China.

Despite—and, perhaps, because of—the intense competition in the industry, alliances have been formed among rival firms to share the costs and risks involved in developing new products and processes. The alliance between IBM (United States), Siemens (Germany) and Toshiba (Japan) in 1992 to develop a 256 megabyte chip to be introduced by the end of this century is one such example. The trio's objective is to share the huge costs involved in designing the new chip and its fabrication process (estimated at $1 billion) and the risk associated with it.

For the product and fabrication-process design, teams from IBM, Siemens and Toshiba work together to develop sub-products under the supervision of managers from one of the three corporations. Similarly, the three are represented in working groups formed to find solutions to particular problems arising during the design process. Overall, a team of 200 engineers from all three companies work together in IBM's Advanced Semiconductor Technology Center, reporting to a manager from Toshiba. All basic inputs used in developing the 256 megabyte chip are provided by IBM, which then issues invoices to Siemens and Toshiba. Billing and costing are controlled by staff from each company, who are located in the other two, at IBM's Technology Center and at the United States headquarters of Siemens and Toshiba.

In addition to the closely connected functions of product and process design, the three firms are planning to cooperate in production itself.They have plans to build factories and to produce jointly the 256 megabyte chip. At the pre-production phase, they are designing and making the equipment needed for final production. At the same time, they have agreed that the technology they develop jointly can be shared with Motorola (United States), a TNC with which Toshiba has a separate alliance.

Sources: "Talk about your dream team", *Business Week*, 27 July 1992; Siemens, *Annual Report 1992*, Munich: Siemens, 1993.

In advanced-technology industries (for example, biotechnology, information and new materials technology), firms go into partnerships for technological complementarity, to speed up the innovation period and to lower costs and share risks. In other industries, such as automobiles, chemicals, food and beverages and consumer electronics, access to markets appears to be the main motive for partnerships. In services industries, for example, some alliances are aimed at obtaining market access through linking computerized reservation systems (box VI.4). In natural resource industries, cost considerations and risk-sharing have encouraged the formation of alliances among TNCs. The same is true of capital-intensive industries, such as aviation, heavy electrical equipment and telecommunication systems (Hagedoorn and Schakenraad, 1991a). Transnational corporations are increasingly aware that alliances offer access to high value-added resources, such as technology, complex manufacturing processes, skilled labour, marketing and distribution networks and after-sales services. On the other hand, TNCs seldom engage in alliances in areas that they consider to be their core strengths.

Strategic alliances create relationships that are often blurred in terms of authority, with each party expecting to boost the profitability of its own assets or to generate new ones. Such relationships also can blur the traditional boundaries of a firm, creating problems for aspects of national regulatory policy. For example, alliances in high-technology products have made the application of national security guidelines more difficult, and are forcing some Governments to re-evaluate their policies (Graham and Krugman, 1991, pp. 149-155).

3. The emergence of networks

Network structures are matrix relationships along a TNC's value chain combined with horizontal relationships (strategic partnerships or alliances) with other TNCs at a single point in the value chain. Networks combine intra- and inter-firm organizational structures. They are a departure from the hierarchical structures typically found in stand-alone and simple corporate strategies. They involve complex combinations of horizontal and vertical linkages among the firms comprising the network, based on shared authority, goals, expertise, responsibility, accountability, recognition and reward. Information technologies are crucial in managing those links across time zones and countries, and in the need to respond rapidly to changing conditions in a competitive environment.

Networks involve changes in reporting arrangements, flows of information and incentives within the firm away from conventional practices. Information usually flows outside the traditional vertical routes. Monsanto (United States), for example, has tried to foster horizontal lines of communication to offset the "silo" effect, where information flows up one division to its head, and is then passed to the head of a separate division before it flows down to an operational level.

For some corporate-wide functions of a network, decision-making can be centralized. In the case of the Japanese *keiretsu*—a domestically-based network involving parent firms, affiliates, subcontractors, suppliers, financial institutions, wholesale and retail trading companies etc.—the production of components by affiliates or unrelated firms has to comply with standards set by the "core" firm, which coordinates activities so as to ensure compatibility. This is also the way that Toyota and other Japanese automobile TNCs in Asia organize their production networks. The core firm is responsible for transmitting technological advances and innovations to the

Box VI.4. Towards a global distribution system: alliances among airline computer reservation systems

Computer reservation systems (CRS) have radically altered marketing techniques and distribution arrangements in the airline industry. Those systems control the way in which travel is packaged, priced, marketed, sold and delivered to passengers around the world. They play a catalytic role in the gradual integration of the airline industry that is taking place in response to the changing economic environment and regulatory framework. In order to cope with the heightened international competition, and in response to the widespread use of CRS by the major carriers, most large international airlines intend either to join one of these systems through alliances with airlines that own a CRS, or to form regional ownership consortia and turn to a CRS based in the United States for much of the technology. The formation of alliances is therefore becoming increasingly complex in terms of ownership, marketing and technical links, and regional networking (figure 1).

Figure 1. Airlines and their computer reservation systems: marketing and technical links

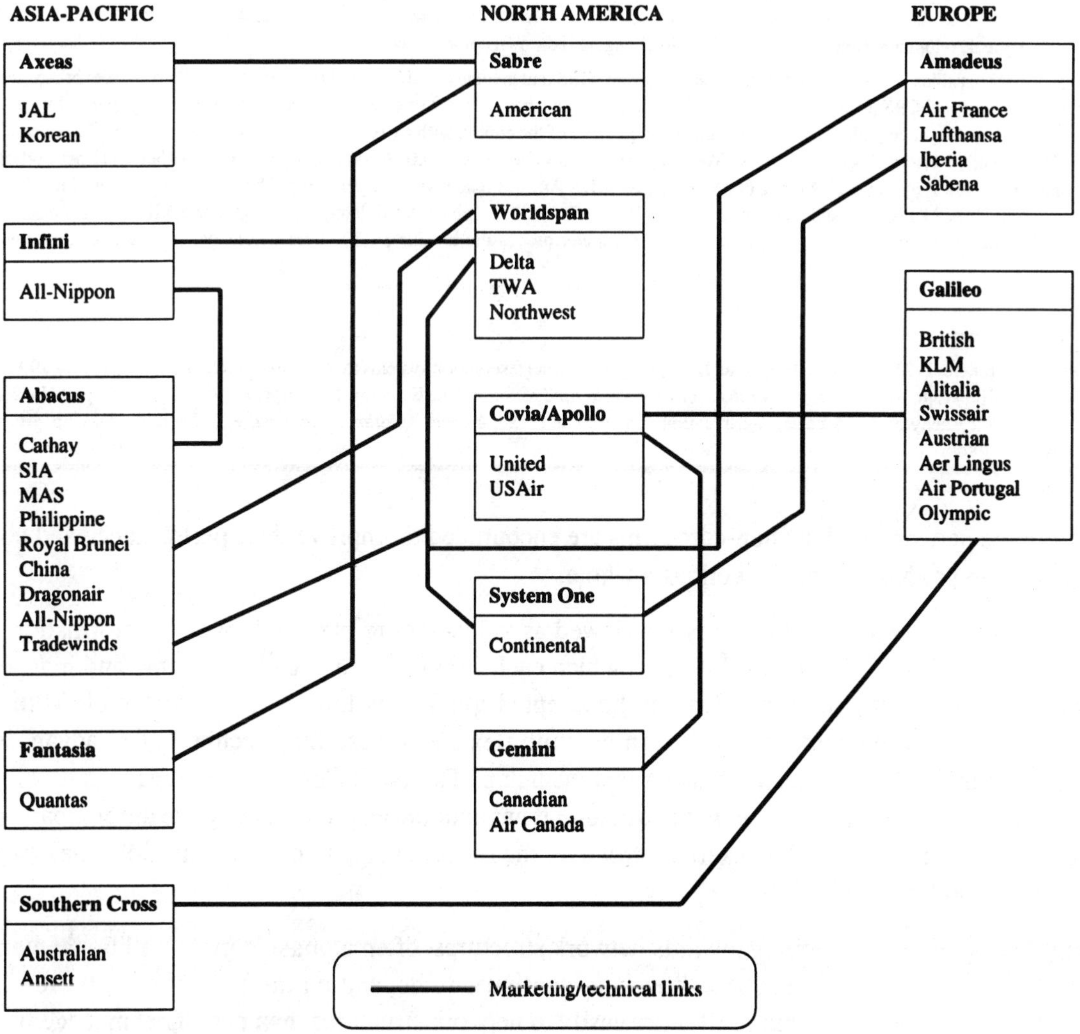

Source: Verchere (1992), based on SRI International.

/.....

(Box VI.4, cont'd.)

Capitalizing on technological advances for computing capacity and the transmission of data, CRS enable airlines to store and change their inventory of products and prices, display them in any market-place served by modern telecommunications, process seat reservations or sales and deliver travel documents. Apart from the products of its owner(s), the more advanced CRS contain the changing schedules and tariffs of hundreds of airlines, as well as information on hotels, car hire, restaurants and cultural events.

Linking the central database to travel agencies or corporate offices has created an electronic distribution network through which airlines can communicate their offers, and agents can obtain information (using microcomputers plugged into local area networks) and then communicate their bookings. For example, in 1991, Sabre (the largest CRS in the United States, wholly owned by American Airlines) served 14,000 locations of subscribing travel agencies in the United States operating through 69,000 terminals; 1,600 agencies in Canada with 5,400 terminals; 2,600 agencies in Europe; and 2,900 agencies in Asia and the Pacific.

Given the cost of establishing and operating such systems and providing the related services, an increasing number of airlines pool their resources and engage in CRS-alliances. These are often cemented by equity stakes from the partner airlines. International airlines establish technical assistance links, code-sharing and other forms of commercial alliances mainly for some complementary strategies: to get access to foreign markets through the marketing and distribution networks of their partners; to capitalize CRS software and services; and to adopt/adapt advanced technology in order to reduce the development time and cost involved in changing their own computer networks.

In early 1993, an alliance was formed between the two largest CRS that include travel information networks, Galileo and Covia-Apollo. Galileo International, the first global CRS group, will have a combined 30 per cent share of the world CRS market and will be jointly owned by airlines from Europe and North America. Each regional group will control 50 per cent of the equity, with shares as follows: American Airlines (38 per cent), British Airways (14.7 per cent), Swissair (13.2 per cent), KLM (12.1 per cent), US Air (11 per cent), Alitalia (8.7 per cent), Air Canada (1 per cent), Olympic Airways (1 per cent), and Aer Lingus, TAP Air Portugal and Austrian Airlines (each with 0.1 per cent). The group will be based in Chicago with offices in Swindon, United Kingdom, and Denver, Colorado, United States. The consolidated data-processing centre will be in Denver. It will use Apollo's principal data complex, which has eight mainframe computer processors handling 1,200 transactions per second and supporting 60,000 terminals.

Sources: Verchere, 1992; Archdale, 1992; Paul Betts, "Biggest airline reservation systems merge", *Financial Times*, 2 February 1993; Stephen Wheatcroft and Geoffrey Lipman, *European Liberalisation and World Air Transport*, The Economist Intelligence Unit, Special Report No. 2015 (May 1990); Feldman, 1992; Anonymous, "Amadeus—tribulation of a political CRS", *Avmark Aviation Economist*, 9, 1 (January 1992), pp. 4-6.

other firms in the network, and the non-core firms are encouraged to improve their performance and contribute new processes and products to the network as a whole.

Decentralized networks of firms may be viewed as value-adding partnerships with information flowing among them (Langlois and Robertson, 1992), in which each firm has a degree of autonomy and independence. In a decentralized network, an innovation can be adopted quickly as long as it is compatible with existing standards. Decentralized network structures can be quite flexible in absorbing technological advances and in fostering initiative and the advancement of entrepreneurship. The NEC Corporation (Japan) is moving in the direction of adopting a decentralized network structure; it has announced plans to integrate the company globally in a decentralized manner, rather than exert control over the firms in the network from its global headquarters in Japan (McGrath and Hoole, 1992).

Many TNCs seem to be moving towards network structures, often alongside more traditional hierarchical structures. The effectiveness of networks, however, continues to depend on the type of activity: research and development, for example, may lend itself more easily to network structures than personnel management, since research and development can generate positive externalities within the network from freer information flows.

B. Integrated international production at the firm level

The complex strategies pursued by TNCs and the structures adopted to carry them out are related to major changes in the world economy and to government policies (chapter V). Heightened competitive pressures, shorter product cycles and the further opening up of the world economy have led TNCs to adopt strategies that involve growing integration both across the functions performed by firms and across a wider geographical area. That combination of greater functional and geographical integration is changing the way that TNCs organize the international production of goods and services, both within the firm and across separate firms in wider organizational networks. A prominent example is Ford Motor Company (United States), which is integrating its operations in Western Europe, establishing strategic alliances and moving towards global strategies.

1. Ford's Western European operations

The Ford Motor Company (United States) was one of the first manufacturing firms to obtain significant competitive advantages through mass production. Because of high transport costs and trade barriers, Ford entered the Western Europe market not through exporting from the United States but via greenfield FDI, in 1911 (United Kingdom) and 1913 (France), and expanded into Germany in the 1920s (Dicken, 1992, p. 248). Ford's affiliates in Western Europe operated on a stand-alone, multi-domestic basis, as trade barriers expanded and nationalist pressures remained high in an era dominated by two major wars and the Great Depression. After the Second World War, Ford's multi-domestic operations extended throughout Western Europe, with the largest facilities in the Federal Republic of Germany and the United Kingdom.

After the establishment of the European Community, Ford began to reorganize its production within Western Europe. A multi-domestic strategy was replaced by a Western Europe-wide strategy. Ford of Europe was established in 1967 as a regional affiliate, and began to integrate the operations of the previously stand-alone national affiliates. Product development, especially between companies in the Federal Republic of Germany and the United Kingdom, was integrated through design and development of the first Europe-wide model, the Capri, in 1969. Falling trade barriers, especially within the European Community, allowed for growing cross-border movements in components and final products. Product development, component manufacturing and final assembly became more integrated throughout Western Europe during the 1970s and 1980s. Ford established multiple assembly plants and both multiple and single-source component plants, to take advantage of specialization and plant-level scale economies, as well as reduced transport and communications costs. Those plants were also supposed to be capable of meeting demand shifts and offsetting work stoppages throughout Western Europe (figure VI.2). In the 1970s, after the demise of the Bretton Woods system, regional integration also provided a hedge against adverse exchange rate movements. Ford's European operations also included subcontractors and suppliers linked across borders.

Ford's models were specific to Western Europe, and Ford of Europe enjoyed considerable autonomy, carrying out its own research and development, marketing, financial management etc. The operation as a whole, therefore, approximated to a regional (intra-Europe) stand-alone structure. During the 1970s and 1980s, as the

Figure VI.2. The Ford Fiesta production network in Western Europe

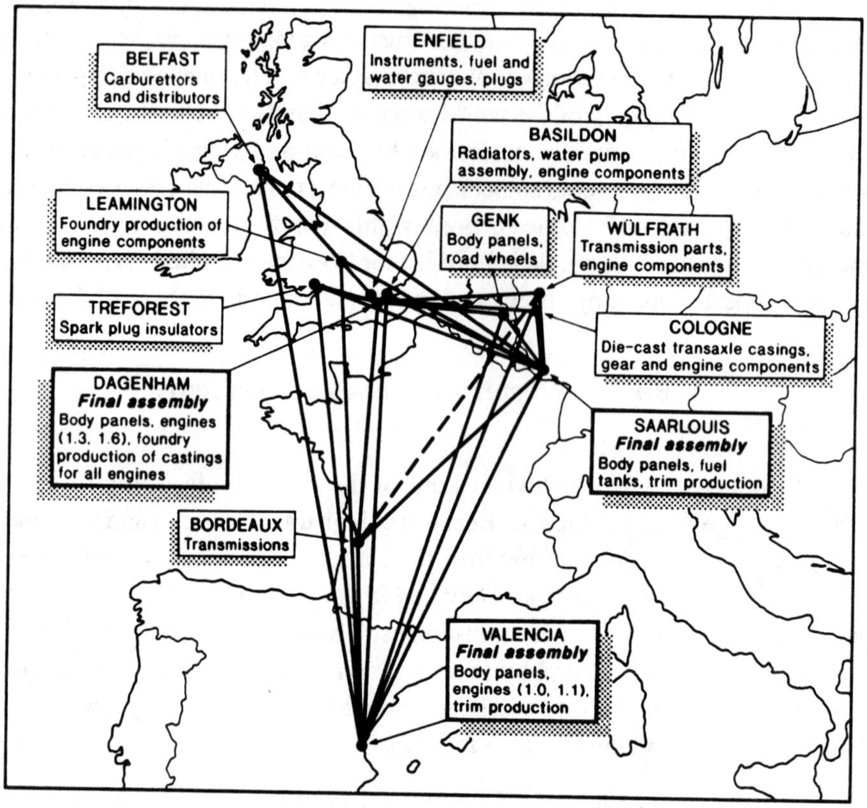

Source: Dicken, 1992, p. 300.

parent corporation was under increasing competitive pressures, the European operations maintained their market position and contributed strongly to firm-wide revenues and profits. The recent experience with developing the Mondeo, discussed below, shows that Ford of Europe has become a source of firm-wide advantages in research and development, coordination and manufacturing technology.

2. The Ford-Mazda strategic alliance

In 1979, Ford acquired a 25 per cent interest in Mazda (Japan). Despite the equity link, the Ford-Mazda relationship has been more like a strategic alliance than an equity relationship, with the two firms collaborating on some projects, but still remaining competitors and maintaining separate management structures. The link has become a strategic alliance that has allowed both parties to achieve valuable strategic and organizational changes (Haigh, 1992).[6]

Part of the arrangement between the two companies is that each produces models for the other to sell in key markets. Several Mazda models are sold under Ford nameplates in Japan and other Asian countries, and Ford has begun producing models for Mazda in the United States. This arrangement has helped Ford become the largest selling foreign automotive nameplate in Japan. As of 1992, several Ford and Mazda models had benefited from the joint efforts of the two firms. Even closer collaboration has occurred in other areas. For example, the two companies linked their expertise in styling (Ford) and engineering (Mazda) which resulted in an updated Escort model for the North American market.[7] Ford styled the exterior and provided components, including the engine (which enabled it to achieve a local content of more than 75 per cent and to continue to use the relatively fuel-efficient Escort to meet government standards on fuel efficiency) and Mazda provided basic engineering. For the Escort, the two companies linked product design and manufacturing expertise at different points on the value chain of each company.

Ford and Mazda also joined forces on the construction and layout of an assembly and stamping plant in Hermosillo, Mexico, using highly efficient team production techniques to produce the Mercury Tracer for the United States market. The Tracer's original design was largely adapted from an existing Mazda model. Ford equipped the plant and designed the production system, drawing heavily upon Mazda practices in Japan. Mazda was involved in training Ford Mexico managers and workers in Mexico and Japan, with additional training conducted by Ford in Belgium, Spain and at headquarters in the United States. Ford and Mazda collaborated on timing and scheduling, although Mazda engineers took the lead as Ford wanted to gain experience with Mazda's scheduling philosophy. Similarly, Ford's legal department took the lead in negotiating contractual arrangements for the project. The result of that collaboration is widely considered to be a success; the Hermosillo plant has been ranked as one of the most efficient in the world (Womack, Jones and Roos, 1991, p. 87).

Despite the success of the Hermosillo alliance and other joint projects, Ford and Mazda were unable to reach agreement on a joint project for the European market and recently agreed to discontinue those discussions. Both companies cited the inability to achieve adequate financial benefits, especially in the deteriorating business environment in Europe. [8] In addition, the Ford-Mazda North American collaboration is limited. For example, Ford provides Mazda with only a two-door version of the Ford-designed and built four-wheel drive, sport-utility Explorer vehicle, sold by Mazda as the Navajo; and Mazda has not shared with Ford its successful sports car, the Miata.

Ford also has limited joint arrangements with other automobile TNCs, largely in research, assembly and marketing. In 1986, Ford and Volkswagen combined their separate operations in Argentina and Brazil into a single joint venture, Autolatina. With the establishment of the four-nation common market, Mercosur (which consists of Argentina, Brazil, Paraguay and Uruguay), Autolatina is well positioned to serve a growing market. Ford and Volkswagen also jointly own a company in Portugal which will produce a multi-purpose people carrier. In addition, Ford is building a minivan for Nissan for the North American market and Nissan is building an off-road vehicle for Ford in Europe.[9]

3. Towards global integration: Ford's world car

Recently, Ford announced plans to revive the notion of a "world car"—a single model, sourced, assembled and sold globally.[11] Ford's world car, to be introduced under the name Ford Mondeo in Europe in 1993 and under the names Ford Contour and Mercury Mystique in North America in 1994 (and, subsequently, to be sold globally), will be assembled at plants in both regions. The main components, including engines and transmissions, will be built in a single location for world-wide needs in either Europe or the United States, with other components from common suppliers either owned by Ford or linked through non-equity arrangements. The world car, under development since the mid-1980s, is a response to the high fixed costs and excess capacity plaguing the industry world-wide and is similar to what other motor manufacturers are doing (box VI.5). It is designed to spread development costs over a larger potential market and to take advantage of flexible production technologies, improvements in transportation and communications, convergence of consumer tastes, safety and emissions regulations, and regional economic arrangements (the United States assembly plant will be supplied from an engine factory in Mexico). Ford's European facilities are producing the world car, the Mondeo, for sale within Western Europe and for export to Eastern Europe, Japan and other countries. Output of the world car from Ford's United States factories located in Kansas City will be aimed primarily at the United States and Canadian markets.

Ford's previous attempt at a world car, the Escort, designed in the 1970s and introduced in 1981, did not succeed, partly because Ford did not establish a single organizational structure for product development and it did not link its European and United States design groups. Although the Escort name was used in both Western Europe and North America, the two cars were different (Dicken, 1992, pp. 298-302).[12]

The design and production of the world car has been led by Ford of Europe—an example of a regional headquarters assuming functional responsibility for a product for the TNC as a whole. The Product Development Group is located in the United Kingdom and in Germany owing to the fact that affiliates in Europe have gained a considerable amount of expertise in developing middle-size automobiles like the Mondeo (e.g., the Capri model); in principle, the group could be located anywhere in the world. The role of the product development group is essentially one of coordinating and having the final say with respect to the development of the car. Specific tasks in design and development have been carried out at different locations in both Europe and North America (figure VI.3). Power steering was developed in North America, the four-cylinder engine in Europe, the six-cylinder engine in North America, the automatic transmission in North America (although the in-vehicle installation was done in Europe), the manual transmission and the body engineering in Europe etc. The vehicle was designed at four separate design facilities in the two regions before the final choice was made.

Ford has developed a communications network for the world car—including extensive use of facsimile, modem and video-conferencing technology—to integrate the work of its research-and-development staff world-wide and to ensure that the project remained truly global. On research and development, staff in Germany and the United Kingdom communicated almost as if they were working side by side. A common system, called world-wide releasing system, has been developed to coordinate engineering development and releases. The system is a complex computerized network with direct online access to engineers and manufacturing activities throughout the world that are involved in the world car programme. With a touch of a button, the staff at Ford's Research and Development Center can communicate with their counterparts around the world—for example, in

Mexico, where some components and the I-4 engine for the United States market are manufactured. All the engineers involved in developing the product release their bits—do the drawings and manufacturing to certain specifications—through that system.

Box VI.5. Is the world car the wave of the future? Strategies of transnational corporations from Japan and Germany

Ford is not the only TNC in the automobile industry to seek wider integration. Japanese TNCs, especially Honda, Nissan and Toyota, have established core networks in each of the three legs of the Triad (UNCTC, 1991a, pp. 44-53). Those networks have integrated many aspects of the manufacture, assembly and distribution of automobiles within their regions. Until recently, models produced for North America and Western Europe were virtually identical to those created for the home market. As the regional affiliates have matured and proved themselves capable of meeting the efficiency and quality standards of the parent firms, they have begun to build upon regional attributes and contribute firm-wide strategies. In the United States, for example, the Japanese TNCs have set up research and design centres to be close to this key market and draw upon its skills. One result was the Mazda Miata, a successful sports car designed in the United States for the North American market.

The Japanese TNCs are now using their foreign affiliates in a more globally integrated fashion.[a] Honda wants its affiliates to increase their specialization so that each can supply its own region and be the primary source of a particular model for the rest of the world. Thus, Honda Accords built in the United States are being exported to Japan, while other models built in Japan are sold in North America. For the Accord, Honda is expanding the role of its United States-based research and design centres. Honda estimates that 80 per cent of the development work on the new version of the Accord station wagon, and 30 per cent of work on the four-door sedan, was done in the United States, compared with 50 per cent and 10 per cent for the earlier versions.[b] Toyota is carrying integration even further. As the originator of "lean production" methods, it has achieved great efficiency in its United States operations. It is now able to balance production between Japan and the United States so that all plants can maintain efficient rates of operations and produce for both markets. Thus, as the United States dollar has fallen against the Japanese yen, Toyota has increased its exports of United States-built Camry's, produced with right-hand drive, to Japan.[c] Both Honda and Toyota expect to extend those aspects of global integration to include operations in Western Europe.

In the case of TNCs from Germany, two firms, BMW and Daimler-Benz, are establishing factories in the United States, and Volkswagen is rumoured to be planning something similar for its Audi division.[d] These firms are responding to several factors: high production costs in Germany, loss of market share in North America, the decline of the dollar, the success of Japanese affiliates with their North American operations, the growth of an extensive supply network of United States, Japanese and European companies located in North America and the benefits of being more closely involved in a critically important market. Both BMW and Daimler-Benz aim for substantial integration of functions between Germany and North America, and across locations within the three-nations covered by the North American Free Trade Agreement. In the case of Daimler-Benz, its United States factory is crucial to a new strategy to move into lower-priced parts of the automobile market. It will produce a sport-utility vehicle which, though initially aimed at North America, is intended to be a major export item as well. Similarly, BMW will produce a new vehicle designed primarily for North America, but including a large export market.[e]

a Krystal Miller and Jacqueline Mitchell, "After years of growth in U.S. car market, Japanese surge is over", *The Wall Street Journal*, 4 March 1993; and Jane Perlez, "Japanese mix and match auto plans and markets", *The New York Times*, 26 March 1993.

b Karen Lowry Miller and Larry Armstrong, "Overhaul in Japan", *Business Week*, 21 December 1992.

c See Perlez, op. cit.

d Krystal Miller, "Mercedes-Benz gears for wider market with sports vehicle to be built in U.S.", *The Wall Street Journal*, 6 April 1993; and Doron Levin, "What BMW sees in South Caroline", *The New York Times*, 11 April 1993.

e Martin Dickson, "Settling down to small talk, *Financial Times*, 24 March 1993.

Figure VI.3. Ford's world car: linkages for purchase of materials, product development and manufacturing

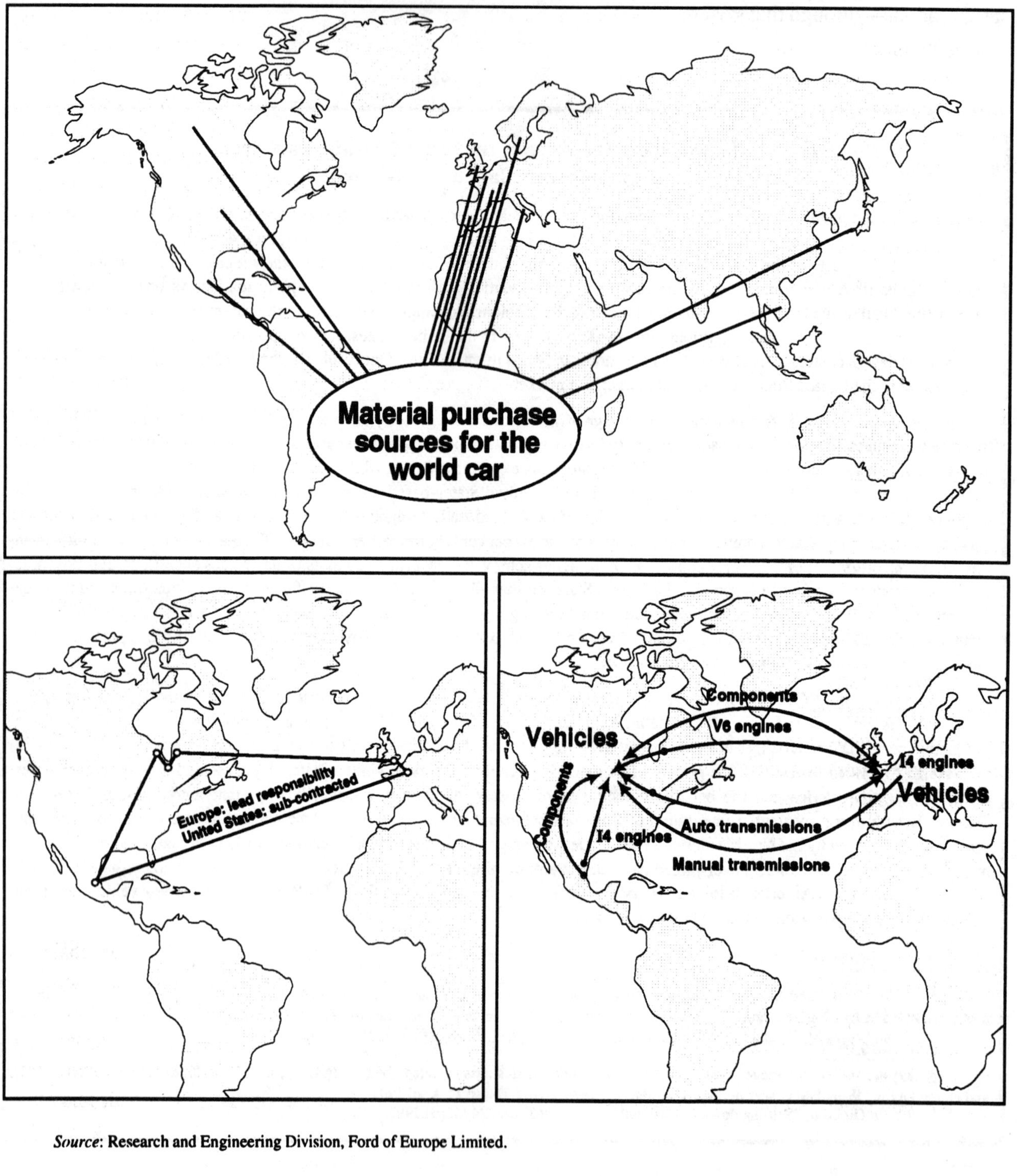

Source: Research and Engineering Division, Ford of Europe Limited.

The design that eventually emerged has been put into production at Ford's assembly plant in Genk, Belgium, early in 1993. Engineers from Genk will help to train staff and design the assembly plant in the United States for a 1994 production start-up. Ford has standardized the manufacturing process, down to minute details, in an attempt to have common processes wherever possible. However, it will bring in some variations in styling and configuration to meet particular market niches. Large components are being manufactured in both Europe and North America (figure VI.3). Similar integration existed earlier, but was confined to Europe. Many components are supplied by affiliates and subcontractors in both regions, while others are single-sourced for both regions. For example, a wiring loom is being sourced in Thailand for both the European and North American assembly operations; and certain electrical components are supplied by a Bosch (Germany) affiliate in the United States for North American assembly and from Bosch in Germany for the Belgian facility (figure VI.3). Sourcing decisions for both regions were being coordinated by Ford of Europe, with the actual procurement being managed by both supply organizations. Sales and marketing responsibilities will remain decentralized, with country affiliates managing their own activities.

The marketing function has largely been kept separate in each of the 15 national markets within Europe, in spite of the integration of production activities. The reason is the flexibility required to respond to differences in language, culture, government regulations etc. among national economies, which requires marketing to be tailored to the specific characteristics of individual markets. Mondeo has in fact been adopted with minor modifications to different markets.

If the Mondeo succeeds, it will be a big step towards greater integration of Ford's work. Ford feels that the project has already borne fruit in terms of achieving engineering efficiencies and economies of scale. Future "world car" projects may depend less on the ability to manage such projects and more on whether cross-national and cross-regional convergence of consumer demands and governmental regulations continues to widen the market for individual models.

As in the past, the extent of future integration of manufacturing activities will be driven by competition and customer convergence of demand. Customer preferences in Europe and North America are still somewhat apart, but are rapidly converging.The demand for fuel-efficient smaller-size cars is still widespread in the former, whereas larger, more comfortable cars are preferred in the latter. In the field of small to middle-size cars, however, there are increasing opportunities for common products and for interregionally integrated production.

C. Conclusions

The combination of complex strategies and greater integration of activities along the value chain, as exemplified by the production of the Ford's Mondeo in Europe, describes integrated international production at the corporate level (figure VI.4). As illustrated by the case of Ford, integrated international production involves several activities in the value chain spread over a wide geographical area. This type of production may be more advanced for some functions and products than for others, although, potentially, every corporate function of a TNC may be carried out that way. Situating different functions in different locations leads to a dispersion of

Figure VI.4. The evolution of corporate strategies and structures towards integrated international production at the firm level

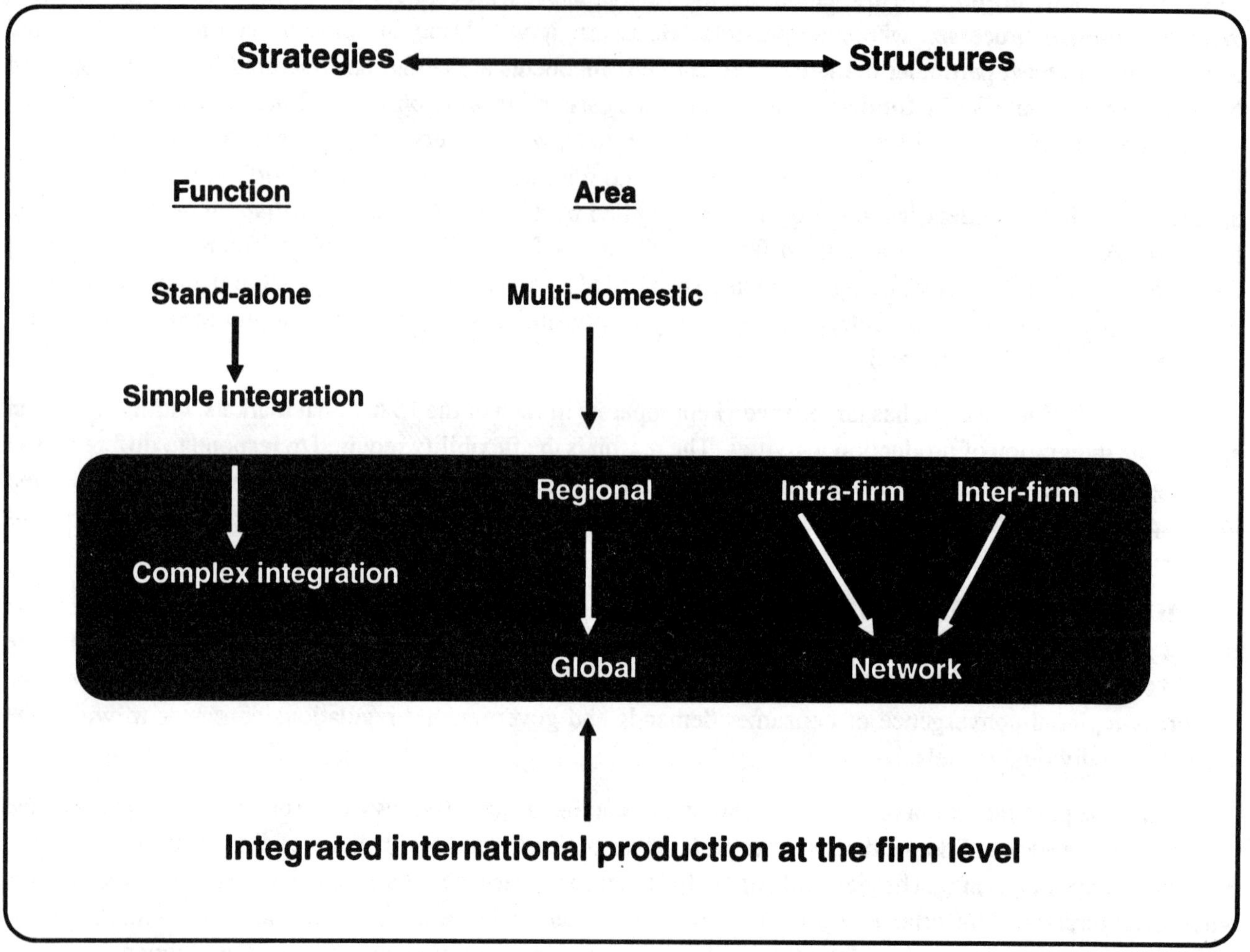

authority and responsibility along the value chain and can make the distinction between parent firms and affiliates increasingly blurred.

Integrated international production allows TNCs to reap the benefits of economies of scale and scope from an increased internal functional specialization and international division of labour. Functional specialization also allows TNCs to make better choices about where to locate a particular function. By finding the lowest-cost site that satisfies its requirements, and by linking the activity carried out there to the rest of its production structure, a TNC can reduce costs and raise the efficiency of its operations. This, in turn, makes this approach to the international organization of production a benchmark for other firms. Competitive pressures are therefore exerted on TNCs to follow the example of those firms that have successfully organized production in an internationally integrated manner. Just as most automobile companies have adopted the lean production methods used by Japanese auto-makers, including just-in-time parts delivery and total quality control, companies may well have to pursue complex integration strategies to remain competitive. In that case, more and more TNCs will follow a course similar to that of Ford in Europe and of other TNCs which are already ahead in terms of integrating individual functions internationally.

As new strategies and structures evolve, the nature of international production changes. Locational advantages become more complex and interrelated, and Governments of host countries, especially in developing countries, need to adapt their FDI regimes. In addition, organizational innovations by firms can alter how they are managed, and raise issues of governance for national and international public policy frameworks. The combination of the growing role of TNCs and the spread of their integrated international production strategies is leading to the emergence of an integrated international production system (chapter VII).

Notes

1 Christopher Lorenz, "When head office goes native", *Financial Times*, 2 December 1992; and Joanne S. Lublin, "Firms ship unit headquarters abroad", *The Wall Street Journal*, 9 December 1992.

2 "GE's new Asia chief sees growth potential in region", *The Asian Wall Street Journal Weekly*, 16 November 1992.

3 Guy de Jonquieres, "Growing taste for alliances in the food industry", *Financial Times*, 22 January 1993.

4 "Managing in an age of anxiety", *The Economist*, 19 January 1991, pp. 59-60.

5 John J. Keller, "AT&T planning to unveil alliances creating a global telephone network", *The Wall Street Journal*, 25 May 1993; "AT&T's global calling-card", *The Economist*, 29 May 1993, p. 66.

6 James B. Treece and Karen Miller, "The Partners: Surprise! Ford and Mazda have built a stray team. Here's How" *Business Week*, 10 February 1992, Issue 3251, pp. 102-107.

7 James B. Treece, "Can Detroit hold its lead in safety", *Business Week*, Issue 3189, pp. 127-130.

8 Michael Williams and Masayuki Kanabayashi, "Mazda and Ford drop proposal to build cars together in Europe", *The Wall Street Journal*, 4 March 1993.

9 See Treece and Miller, op. cit.

10 Oscar Suris, "Big three win joint patent, marking a first", *The Wall Street Journal*, 3 April 1993.

11 Kevin Done, "A model to smash the world", *Financial Times*, 24 March 1993; Richard A. Melcher, "Meet Ford's brand new world car", *Business Week*, 18 January 1993.

12 Robert L. Simison and Neal Templin, "Ford is turning heads with $6 billion cost to design 'world car'", *The Wall Street Journal*, 23 March 1993.

CHAPTER VII

INTEGRATED INTERNATIONAL PRODUCTION AND ITS IMPLICATIONS

The two previous chapters highlighted the growth of complex corporate strategies and organizational forms for transnational corporations (TNCs). They have shown that virtually every function or activity along a TNC's value chain can be performed in various geographical locations in an integrated manner by one or several parts of a transnational enterprise system, depending on what configuration contributes most to the profitability of the entire corporate system. The present chapter looks at the result of these changes: a system of international production, which has important implications for the world economy and for host countries.

A. The characteristics of the system

1. Growth and significance of international production

The growing importance of international production, or the location of value-added activities in a foreign country under the governance of a TNC, is evident from the rapid growth of foreign direct investment (FDI), discussed in chapter I.

The traditional definition of international production, mentioned above, assumes that the foreign and domestic activities of a TNC are quite separate—which is broadly true with respect to the activities of TNCs with stand-alone strategies and structures, even though some linkages (especially ownership) exist—and, therefore, uses only data referring to foreign affiliates for measurement purposes. International production by a TNC pursuing complex integration strategies is, however, more appropriately defined to include value-added activities in both its domestic (that is, home country) and foreign locations. In the case of such a TNC, functional activities are performed by the TNC and its foreign affiliates in an integrated manner for producing a common final output for one or more parts of the international market. In other words, a TNC's activities in the home and host country are closely interlinked and the *entire* value chain under the common governance of the TNC is international in nature.

Defined in this manner, the significance of integrated international production can be measured in terms of the *total* (domestic and foreign) assets, production or similar variables relating to TNC activities. Data for the United States and Japan show that roughly a quarter or more of these countries' productive assets, nearly a third of output in the case of the United States and about a quarter of sales in the case of Japan, are potentially part of integrated international production (table VII.1). In both countries, and particularly in the United States, the shares of total output and sales undertaken by TNCs are considerably higher in manufacturing. Since the United States and Japan are not the most transnationalized economies among the developed countries—those countries that account for the majority of outward and inward FDI as well as world assets and output—the share of world output potentially subject to integrated international production may well be around one third.

As discussed in chapter V, a good deal of international production takes place through the establishment of stand-alone affiliates or through simple integration strategies. In those circumstances, the production links between national economies are weak. Governance is being exercised by the TNC-parent over its affiliates, but the number of areas covered is limited (typically to exercing overall ownership and control or to the provision of technology), and it is geared either towards global markets or outsourcing at lowest cost rather than integration of production as a whole. In other words, governance is fragmented and corporate activities are not integrated at the behavioural level throughout the value chain. As a result, international production by TNCs has limited implications for interrelationships between countries at the aggregated level. With the adoption by TNCs of complex integration strategies and structures, however, the links grow stronger. Integrated international production will increasingly shape the nature of economic life at the national, regional and global levels.

2. The emergence of an integrated system

Although simpler forms of international production are still prevalent, an integrated system is slowly emerging. It is the sum total of the functions and activities of those TNCs that are pursuing complex corporate strategies, either within each firm or in strategic alliances. In response to new technologies, growth and convergence of demand for final output, the opening of increasing portions of the world economy to trade and FDI and the pressures of competition, these companies are seeking to exploit their competitive advantages throughout the value chain in a wide range of locations. They do this both for functions (for example, cash management) and for activities (production of particular goods or services which they sell to a wide market). Advances in information technology permit and facilitate such integration, while other factors, especially competition, push TNCs in the direction of integrated international production.

At the firm level, integrated international production means that any affiliate operating in any foreign location potentially performs functions for the TNC as a whole or in close interaction with other affiliates on the

Table VII.1. The importance of transnational corporations in the economies of United States and Japan

Item	*Assets*[a]		*Gross product/Sales*[b]	
	Total	*Manufacturing*	*Total*	*Manufacturing*
A. United States (Billions of dollars)				
(1) TNC parent firms[c]				
1977	479	..	514[d]	320[d]
1982	934	..	788[d]	423[d]
1989	1 151	..	1 040[d]	590[d]
(2) Foreign affiliates in the United States[c]				
1977	46	..	53	17
1982	153	..	103	47
1989	329	..	226	109
(3) Total (1)+(2)[c]				
1977	525	..	549	337
1982	1 087	..	891	470
1989	1 479	..	1 266	699
(4) Total, all private firms in the United States				
1977	1 824[e]	..	1 534[fg]	465[f]
1982	3 247[e]	..	2 376fg	644f
1989	5 442[e]	..	3 967fg	966f
(5) (3)/(4) (Per cent)				
1977	28.8	..	37.0	72.4[h]
1982	33.5	..	37.5	73.1[h]
1989	27.2	..	31.9	72.4[h]
B. Japan (Billions of yen)[i]				
(1) TNC parent firms[j]				
1980	105	70	185	80
1989	250	126	316	125
(2) Foreign affiliates in Japan[jk]				
1980[j]	11	8	18	12
1989[k]	10	8	17	11
(3) Total (1)+(2)				
1980	116	79	202	92
1989	260	134	332	136
(4) Total, all private firms in Japan				
1980	499	186	820	263
1989	1 061	338	1 308	389
(5) (3)/(4) (Per cent)				
1980	23.1	42.2	24.7	35.1
1989	24.5	39.7	25.4	34.9

Source: UNCTAD, Programme on Transnational Corporations, based on data from the United States Department of Commerce and from the Board of Governors of the Federal Reserve System: Japan, Ministry of International Trade and Industry, *Kaigai Jigyo Katsudo Kihon Chosa: Kaigai Toshi Tokei Soran*, (various issues), *Gaishi-kei Kigyo no Doko* (various issues), and Japan, Ministry of Finance, *Zaisei Kinyu Tokei Geppo* (various issues).

a Figures for the United States relate to net property, plant and equipment. Figures for Japan relate to balance sheet assets.
b Figures for the United States relate to gross product and those for Japan, to sales.
c Figures are slightly overestimated, due to some affiliates of foreign TNCs with FDI of their own being counted as United States (parent) TNCs.
d UNCTAD, Programme on Transnational Corporations estimate.
e Includes the historical cost value of net property, plant and equipment of all United States private businesses. The amount was calculated by applying the ratio of historical cost to current cost of the value of equipment and structures to net property, plant and equipment at current cost. Figure includes the value of land at historical cost which is likely to be overestimated.
f Estimate.
g Excludes banks and private households.
h Differences in methodology for sectoral classification underlying TNC data and data for total manufacturing may result in over- or understatement of the ratio.
i Excludes banking and insurance industries. Data are by financial year ending in March of the following calendar year.
j Data understate the actual values, since the data are based on surveys in which the responses did not cover the whole universe. Also, the number of companies covered and the rate of response are different in the surveys for the two years considered.
k Includes only majority-owned affiliates.

basis of a sophisticated intra-firm division of labour. For example, affiliates have a particular task (such as procurement, component manufacturing, accounting) which they implement for the corporate system as a whole; additions to output resulting from functions performed by affiliates in some host countries are combined with additions from the parent firm and/or affiliates in other countries, to create final products that are assembled in host or home countries, and are for sale in the host country, home country or elsewhere around the world (chapter V). This results in a high degree of interdependence between the processes located in different countries in accordance with firms' strategies aimed at maximizing the profitability of their entire value chains. Integrated international production is also typically organized across a wider geographical area than international production including only limited multi-domestic production or the outsourcing of selected activities. The wider geographical area might be a region or it might be global (chapter V). As discussed in section B below, it is likely to become increasingly global. By no means have all TNCs become, or are becoming, organized—globally or regionally—in a functionally integrated manner. As chapters V and VI showed, however, *each* corporate function *can* potentially be integrated regionally or globally and such integration appears, indeed, to be the most cost-effective method of organization for a growing number of TNCs. More generally, a functionally integrated organization of international production is becoming a benchmark towards which corporations will increasingly move under pressures of competition.

These changes are particularly noticeable in the case of those service functions that have become tradable over transnational computer-communication networks. As a result, the production process of services can not only be split into parts that can be relocated elsewhere but it can also be organized on a real-time network basis, and shifted from one time zone to another. Financial markets are already operating on that basis, allowing a 24-hour trading day moving from east to west. In other industries, individual firms are also beginning to take advantage of this possibility by shifting tasks to different time zones when need arises; for example, at the end of the day a law firm in New York can fax work that needs to be done (for example, data entry and analysis) to a partner firm in Hong Kong and receive the results back the next morning. An increasing number of corporate service functions may well be undertaken in a similar way in the future, and in a much more systematic manner. Functions such as research and development, cash-flow management and data-processing could be performed on a continuing basis by TNCs and their affiliates in different time zones. This would be the equivalent of 24-hour shift-based manufacturing; however, instead of bringing in new shifts of employees to a stationary work place in order to continue production, the materials of production would be sent via computer-communication networks to another set of employees, located in another time zone in another country.

Complex integration by TNCs is deepening the links between national economies and strengthening international economic integration (box VII.1). With shallow integration, international trade results from the division of labour between independent producers in different countries (figure VII.1.a) This integration involves a limited number of relationships that are relatively simple in nature. The main interaction takes place in the international market, where buyers and sellers respond to market prices. The market is governed by a multilateral framework of rules and regulations such as those of GATT, and/or, in some cases, by regional arrangements (for example, the European Community).

International production through FDI and non-equity arrangements deepens integration between countries, because it involves the building of relationships around the FDI package (figure VII.1.b). Even in its simpler

Box VII.1. What is international economic integration?

International integration entails the combination of geographically distinct elements into a larger whole. In the economic field, integration can be seen as proceeding at the microeconomic or macroeconomic levels.

At the microeconomic level, integration describes a process of enterprise expansion through the inclusion of previously distinct activities and geographical units in two or more countries under common governance. Such firm-level integration can involve complementary activities along the same value chain (vertical integration), parallel activities across different value chains (horizontal integration) or expansion in to multiple value chains (diversification). The linkages necessary to establish a more integrated structure have traditionally been pursued through the expansion of ownership relations (mergers and acquisitions or "greenfield" investments); however, various non-equity linkages (such as strategic alliances) are being used increasingly to integrate the activities of independent firms.

At the macroeconomic level, economic integration refers to the elimination of barriers to the flow of goods, services and factors of production between different nation states and the corresponding creation of international linkages of varying intensity and geographical scope. Such cross-national integration can take several forms. The elimination of tariff and non-tariff barriers to trade creates a free trade area (or customs union) among participating countries which can lead to intensified trade linkages. A common market expands the potential linkages to include factors of production and some degree of policy harmonization. Finally, full economic and monetary union implies a more comprehensive harmonization of economic policies and requires the establishment of supra-national institutions to govern the new entity.

In its widest possible sense, economic integration would describe the evolution of a global economy. At least since the gold standard, economists have debated the benefits of this possibility. However, the most prominent examples of integration among countries, such as the European Economic Community established in 1958, have been created at the regional level. The prosperity of Western Europe between the late 1950s and early 1970s was widely attributed to intensified economic links between member countries, particularly through trade. Other countries tried to imitate the success of Western Europe by establishing free trade zones (such as the Latin American Free Trade Association established in 1960), customs or economic unions (such as the West African Customs Union established in 1959) or by introducing other types of institutional arrangements (such as those within the Council for Mutual Economic Assistance). Although those arrangements were commonly referred to as "regional integration", they failed to produce any significant or lasting results. But even when they are successful, there remains considerable uncertainty as to whether these regional blocks represent a stepping stone or an obstacle to global integration.

To accommodate different experiences with integration, it is useful to distinguish between "formal" from "real" integration. The former refers to legislative commitments at the Government level, including to the elimination of barriers to the flow of goods and factors of production. But what matters is real integration—actually increased trade and greater flows of capital, people, technology, services etc. This is where integration at the macroeconomic level links up with integration at the microeconomic level.

In fact, real integration between countries can take place without elaborate intergovernmental agreements. One example is the United States and Canada; already prior to the United States—Canada Free Trade Agreement (1989), extensive trade and FDI in the automotive and other industries had produced significant interlinkages across the two countries. Another example is the close relations now emerging among East Asian countries. In both these cases, international integration has been, to a significant extent, the product of corporate linkages crossing national boundaries at the production level.

Thus, as integration moves from shallow trade-based linkages to deep international production-based linkages under the common governance of TNCs, the traditional division between integration at the corporate and country levels begins to break down. Because TNCs are internalizing activities spanning national boundaries, they encroach on areas over which sovereignty and responsibilities have traditionally been reserved for national Governments. This raises new issues of direct concern to the formation of national laws and regulations. Consequently, deeper international integration is likely to depend upon the interplay of decisions and actions at the corporate and national levels.

Figure VII.1. Economic integration

(a) *Shallow integration as a result of trade*

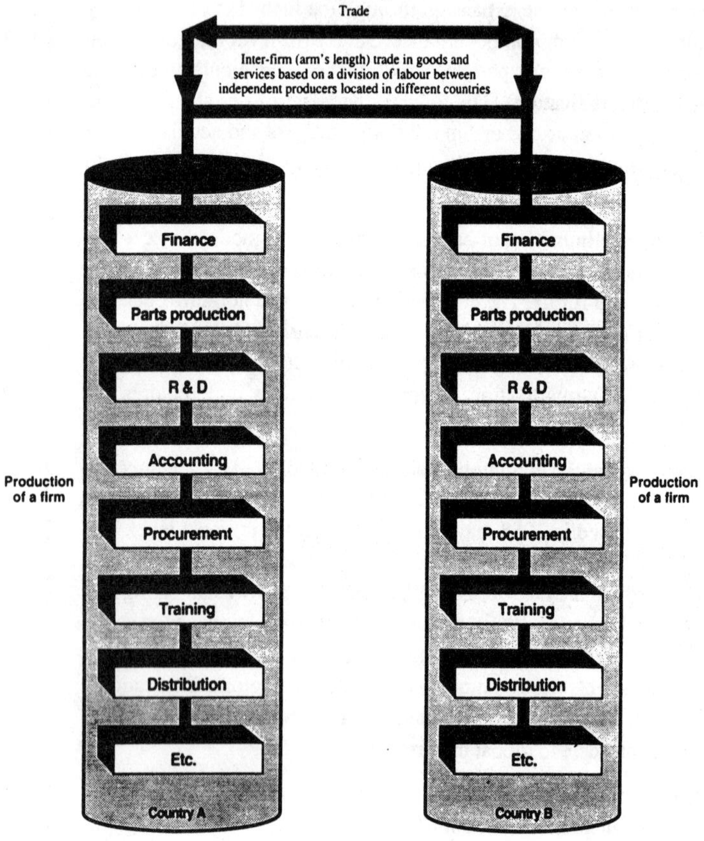

(b) *Deep integration as a result of international production by transnational corporations*

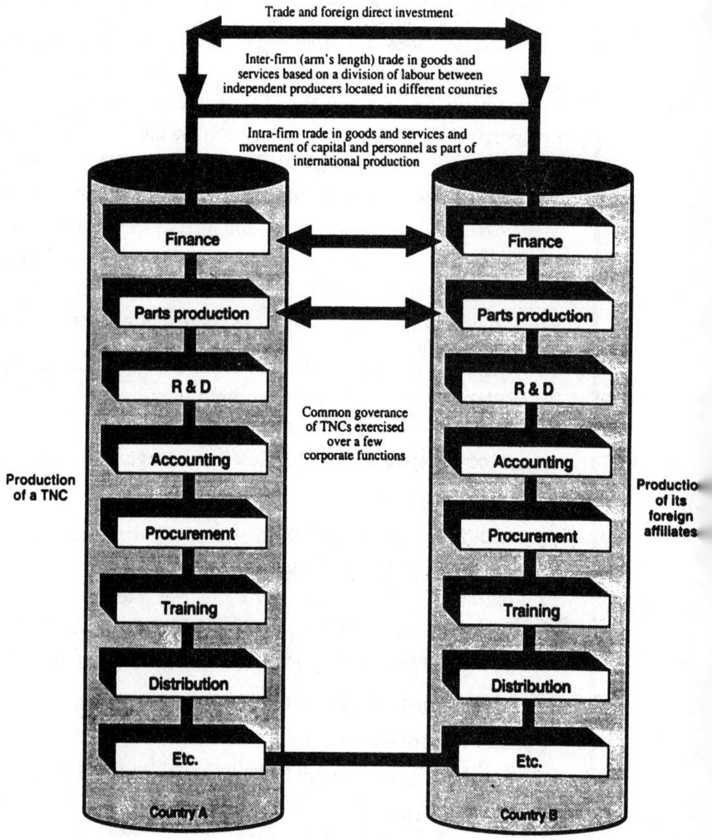

/.....

(Figure VII.1, cont'd.)

(c) Deep integration as a result of functionally integrated international production by transnational corporations

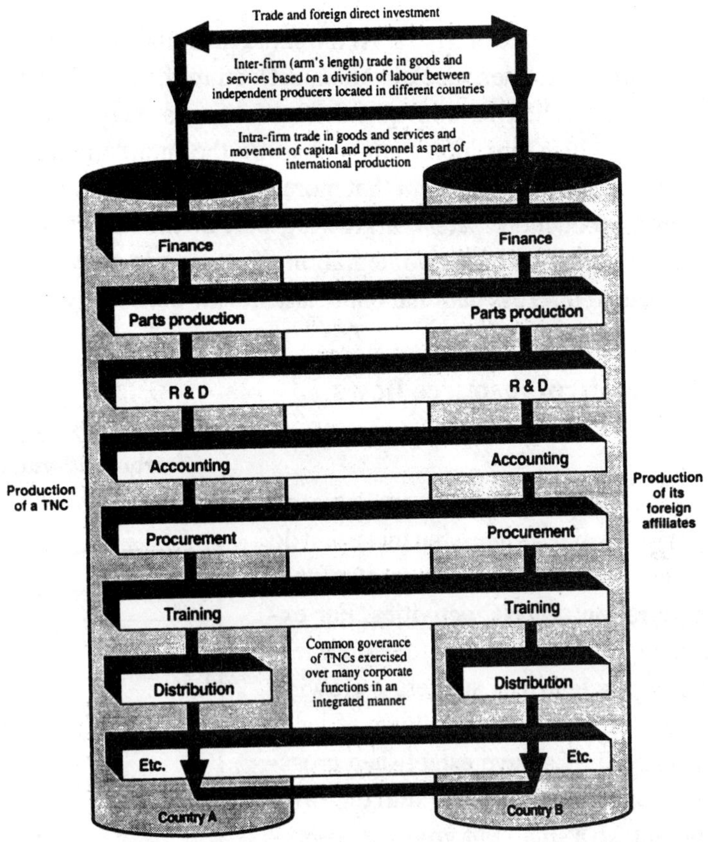

forms, such as stand-alone structures and outsourcing, links between parent firms and foreign affiliates are established through ownership, management, transfer of technology and skills, and sharing of profits. Integrated international production is deep integration *par excellence*, extending these links to many more areas along the value chain. The result is a dense network of production relationships between parent TNCs and affiliates, and among affiliates (figure VII.1.c). Those relationships have implications for trade as well, since they involve intra-firm trade in goods and services and intra-firm flows of resources. Regulatory frameworks for this type of integration are as yet partial—mostly regional. As integrated international production grows, however, pressures for formal arrangements relating to FDI and international production are likely to increase.

As discussed in chapter VI, the nature of governance by TNCs is changing, as a result of the sharing of authority within and among TNCs owing to a shift to network-type arrangements. Networks involve a movement away from hierarchical linkages towards combinations of horizontal and vertical linkages, with resources flowing in both directions between parent firms and their foreign affiliates and among affiliates, and between parents or affiliates and unrelated firms. Networks also involve changes in reporting systems, in resource flows and incentives within firms.

The changes described above result in stronger linkages between countries, through increased exchanges or flows of goods, services and resources, with an increasing share of those flows taking place within the organizational structures of TNCs. At the same time, the composition of these exchanges is undergoing changes in the direction of greater specialization, reflecting the role of TNCs' integrated production strategies. Taken together, these qualitative and quantitative changes suggest that TNCs, with their functionally integrated production activities, are increasingly shaping the international economic system and relationships between national economies. To the extent that more and more international production is reorganized into an *integrated* international production *system*, a growing part of the world economy is undergoing fundamental structural change in the direction of deep integration of economic activities. Value-added activities are becoming more closely interlinked across national boundaries, with TNCs playing the key role as integrators.

3. Intra-firm resource flows

Relatively little data are available on intra-firm flows of resources, but those that do exist show a slow trend towards greater functional integration of TNC activities. For example, data on research-and-development spending and patent fees suggest a growing role of TNCs in international flows of technology. Some TNCs have established cross-border networks for research and development, so a small but growing proportion of their innovations takes place in host countries (TCMD, 1992a, chap. VI). Data for the United States on receipts and payments of royalties and licence fees indicate that, during the 1980s, more than 70 per cent of all receipts and 50 per cent of all payments represented intra-TNC transactions (Young and Steigerwald, 1990, p. 29).

Statistics on the intra-firm trade of United States TNCs also reveal growing cross-border integration. In manufacturing, the share of intra-firm transactions in foreign sales (sales by foreign affiliates, both in host countries and elsewhere) rose between 1977 and 1989 (table VII.2).[1] This growth was marked in transportation equipment, a category that consists largely of motor vehicles. In services, the share of intra-firm trade in-

Table VII.2. Integration index[a] for United States non-bank transnational corporations, by sector and host region, 1977, 1982 and 1989
(Percentage share)

Sector/country	*1977*	*1982*	*1989*
Total	32	24	29
Total, excluding petroleum	25	28	32
Sector			
Primary	42	18	15
Manufacturing	30	32	36
Transportation equipment	45	52	55
Services	8	14	14
Region			
Latin America and the Caribbean	29	26	35
Mexico	20	27	67
Asia and the Pacific	51	35	43
Developed countries	23	22	27
Canada	42	31	38
European Community[b]	24	22	26

Sources: UNCTAD, Programme on Transnational Corporations, based on United States Department of Commerce (1981), tables III.H.1, III.H.2, III.H.6, III.T.1, III.T.2; (1985), tables II.P.1, II.P.2, III.E.1, III.E.2, III.E.6; and (1992a), tables II.Q.1, II.Q.2, III.F.2, III.F.3, III.F.9.

a The integration index is calculated as the value of intra-firm international trade as a share of the value of all sales by the majority-owned foreign affiliates of United States-based TNCs.

b Includes 9 member countries for 1977, 10 member countries for 1982 and 12 member countries for 1989.

trade increased between 1977 and 1982, then remained unchanged. The level of the integration index is much lower in this sector than in the goods sectors, because many services are largely non-tradable. The main exception to the trend of a growing share of intra-firm transactions was petroleum, which was subject to substantial changes in ownership and distribution methods during the period 1977-1982.

Growth in the share of intra-firm trade was marked within the Western Hemisphere, and especially with respect to Mexico, suggesting that regional integration was increasing even before the opening of negotiations on the North American Free Trade Agreement. Indeed, the links between the United States and Mexico, particularly in the automotive industry, are a good example of deep integration through cross-border production by TNCs. Manufactured exports from Mexico have increased steadily since the mid-1980s, a period when FDI also increased, partly because of the debt-equity conversion programme. Exports of transport equipment and parts (with automobiles and auto parts accounting for nearly 50 per cent of the total) were a powerful impetus. They represented 24 per cent of total manufactured exports from Mexico in 1985 and 31 per cent in 1990 (UNCTC, 1992a). Beginning in 1982, United States automobile TNCs invested heavily in Mexico. Their new plants were equipped with highly productive and capital-intensive technology, and were geared strongly to exports—in contrast to the long history of United States TNCs producing for the domestic market in Mexico. By 1987, exports ranged from 48 per cent of total sales in the case of General Motors to 68 per cent for Ford and 82 per cent for Chrysler. Ford and Chrysler export exclusively to North America while General Motors has a more diversified export pattern. The vast majority of exports were intra-firm exports—100 per cent in the case of Ford, and 80 per cent for General Motors and Chrysler (UNCTC, 1991a).

Data on intra-firm trade capture only part of the integration occurring within TNC networks, since they measure only visible flows between parent TNCs and their foreign affiliates and among affiliates controlled by the same parent. Trade between either parent firms or their affiliates and enterprises linked through non-equity arrangements is not properly measured, though it is a further indicator of the integration of international production. Evidence suggests that the incidence of non-equity arrangements has been rising and that they are an integral part of TNC production strategies. In addition, trade data do not reveal many resource flows, that include a significant service component. These include for instance, the exchange of managerial, legal and accounting services between parent firms and their affiliates, as well as among affiliates.

* * * * *

As the above discussion suggests, fundamental changes in the structure of the world economy are likely if more and more international production by TNCs becomes integrated in nature. Economic interrelationships between countries will multiply, involving various production activities falling under the governance of one TNC or another. Transfers of resources and trade, particularly intra-firm trade, will increase. The resulting division of labour among countries should be greater and more specialized than would be the case with international trade alone or TNC activities of a stand-alone or outsourcing type. Among others, since complex integration strategies involve functional integration of value added through services as well as goods-producing activities, the international division of labour in the production of services will increase. An evolution of international production towards integrated international production will therefore lead the global economy towards a new structure with deeper, closer and more complex economic interrelationships among countries.

B. The geographic structure of integrated international production

Traditionally, the patterns of international economic integration were determined largely by the patterns of trade. Integrated international production by TNCs is an additional factor of integration, and its structure is shaped by the pattern of FDI. The fusion of the two both reinforces and alters the existing pattern of international economic linkages.

While all countries participate in FDI flows, there is a tendency for FDI to be concentrated, first of all among the Triad members and then in clusters around each Triad member: the majority of outflows as well as inflows take place to and from the developed countries of the Triad (European Community, Japan and the United States), and the majority of FDI inflows to many developing as well as Central and Eastern European countries originate in a single Triad member, usually in the same or a proximate geographical area, or with other close ties to the host countries in the cluster (UNCTC, 1991a; TCMD, 1992a). The concentration of FDI among the members of the Triad, as documented in chapter II of the present volume (and UNCTC, 1991a) reflects a variety of factors, including the competitive strength of Triad members as outward investors, the effect of high-income levels and large market-size on FDI and, more recently, the strategic responses of TNCs to regional integration movements in Europe and North America.

The clustering of host economies around each Triad member became more pronounced in the mid-1980s. That pattern was consistent with the emerging strategies of TNCs in the Triad to build regional core networks of foreign affiliates centred on their home countries. By the early 1990s (figure VII.2), the United States had become the dominant investor in most Latin American countries, as well as in a few Asian and Pacific countries. The European Community emerged as the dominant investor in an increased number of countries in Central and Eastern Europe, as well as in several countries in other regions. In terms of FDI stocks, Japan accounts for the majority of FDI only in the Republic of Korea, although on the basis of recent inward flow data, it now accounts for the majority of new investments in Fiji, Singapore, Taiwan Province of China and Thailand.

There is also a distinct pattern of FDI from the perspective of home countries, confirmed by an empirical analysis of recent data on outward FDI stock from ten major home countries. Since these ten countries accounted for 88 per cent of world-wide FDI stocks in 1990, the results provide a reasonable approximation of global patterns. They show considerable regional concentration in outward FDI. Intraregional shares of FDI are high in all three major investing regions, and especially so in Europe (table VII.3). To be sure, comparisons among these shares need to be interpreted carefully, since the three investing regions vary greatly in terms of opportunities they offer for intra- and inter-regional investment. For example, from the viewpoint of the United States, North America is a very modest FDI target, since Canada is the only country besides the United States included in this region.

Figure VII.2. Foreign-direct-investment clusters of Triad members, 1990
(Economies in which a Triad member dominates
inward foreign-direct-investment stocks and/or flows)

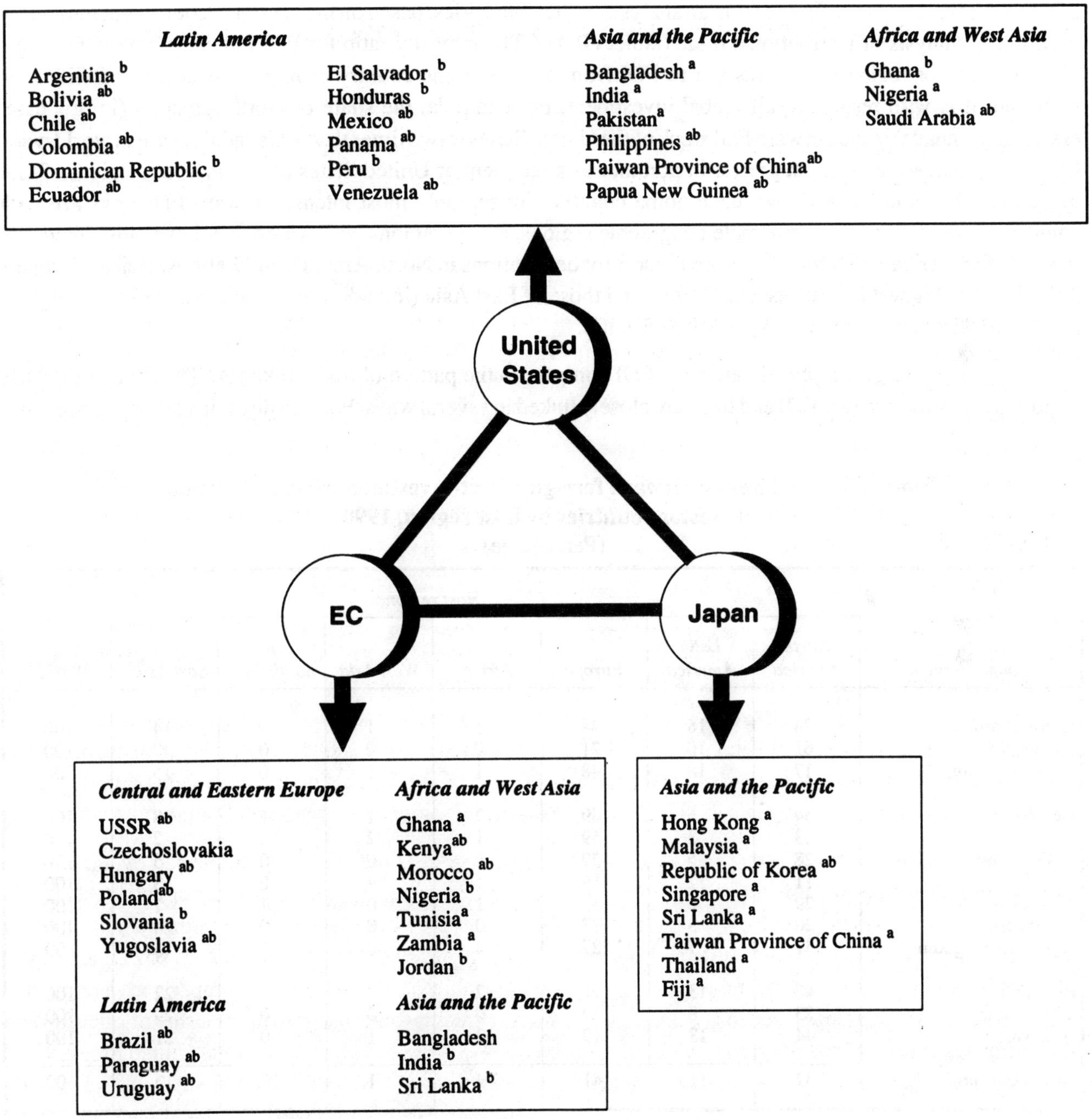

Source: UNCTAD, Programme on Transnational Corporations, foreign-direct-investment database.

a In terms of average inward FDI flow, 1988-1990.
b In terms of inward FDI stock for 1990.

A better way to assess the regional concentration of FDI is to compare the share of FDI in regional host countries with the share of those countries in FDI world-wide. For most of the ten investing countries, the share of FDI directed to host countries within their own respective region is higher than that of those partners in world FDI as a whole. This is confirmed from an analysis of FDI intensities, based on the "gravity" coefficient frequently used in the analysis of international trade (table VII.4).[2] The intensity ratio for FDI indicates how important a given country or region is with respect to FDI from a given home country or region, as compared with how important it is with respect to all global investment. For example, the share of North America (in this case, essentially Canada) in the outward FDI stock of the United States is two times that of Canada's share in world-wide FDI stock, indicating its much greater importance as a recipient of United States FDI than as a recipient of FDI in general. As table VII.4 shows, each home country's or region's most intense outward FDI links are with countries in their own or in proximate geographic regions, and in regions with which they have close historical ties. North America's FDI intensities are highest for destinations in North America and Latin America; Europe's intensities are highest for Europe and Africa; and those of East Asia (including Japan and Australia) are highest for FDI in East and South-East Asia and the Pacific.

How does the geographical pattern of FDI compare to the pattern of trade linkages? This is a particularly important question because FDI and trade are closely linked in several ways. Foreign direct investment sometimes

Table VII.3. Shares of outward foreign-direct-investment stocks of 10 major investor countries by host region, 1990
(Percentage)

Country/region	*Host region*							
	North America	*Latin America*	*Europe*	*Africa*	*West Asia*	*South Asia*	*East Asia* [a]	*World* [b]
North America	24	16	44	1	1	0	14	100
Canada	61	10	21	0	0	0	7	100
United States	17	18	48	1	1	0	15	100
Europe	34	6	49	2	1	1	8	100
France	33	3	59	1	2	0	2	100
Germany	28	6	59	2	0	0	5	100
Italy	11	12	69	1	4	0	3	100
Netherlands	29	6	53	1	0	4	7	100
Sweden	20	3	77	0	0	0	0	100
United Kingdom	47	7	27	4	0	0	15	100
East Asia	42	13	21	2	1	0	22	100
Australia	23	8	39	0	0	0	29	100
Japan	44	13	19	2	1	0	21	100
10-country total	32	11	41	2	1	0	13	100

Source: Based on UNCTAD, Programme on Transnational Corporations, foreign-direct-investment database.

a Including, also, South-East Asia and the Pacific.
b Including the 10 countries shown only.

follows trade, sometimes precedes it, and the two can be substitutes for each other as well as complements, depending upon the conditions that prevail. It is thus important to know whether the two work in the same direction as far as their integrating impact is concerned. For example, there is an overlap between the clustering of host countries with respect to FDI from the Triad and the increasingly regional clustering of trade relationships (UNCTC, 1991a, pp. 72-74). In almost all instances in which a host country was linked to one or more Triad countries in terms of inward FDI stocks in 1988, the relevant home Triad member was also one of the major trading partners of the host country.

An analysis of data for the ten countries considered earlier suggests that international trade is even more regionally concentrated than FDI. That pattern emerges from a comparison of shares of regional and other partners in international trade (table VII.5) with their shares in FDI (table VII.3) and even more clearly, from a comparison of trade intensities (table VII.6) with FDI intensities (table VII.4). For example, North America's trade intensities with North America and Latin America are each more than twice as high as its FDI intensities with those two regions.

Although there is a positive association between bilateral investment and trade intensities, in general, the difference between a region's intraregional and extraregional intensities does not tend to be as great in the case of investment as in the case of trade. Trade linkages are also more intense than investment linkages in the case

Table VII.4. Intensity ratios[a] for foreign direct investment of 10 major investor countries, by host region, 1990

	Host region						
Investor country/region	*North America*	*Latin America*	*Europe*	*Africa*	*West Asia*	*South Asia*	*East Asia*[b]
North America	2.03	1.12	0.84	0.49	0.85	0.32	0.80
Canada	2.23	0.80	0.49	0.13	0.14	0.30	0.53
United States	1.99	1.15	0.88	0.53	0.94	0.32	0.84
Europe	0.97	0.53	1.30	1.13	0.80	1.77	0.55
France	1.00	0.23	1.56	0.33	2.55	0.00	0.14
Germany	0.82	0.52	1.55	1.00	0.16	0.46	0.38
Italy	0.33	1.04	1.76	0.66	4.11	0.00	0.26
Netherlands	0.86	0.54	1.42	0.54	0.00	7.97	0.48
Sweden	0.61	0.31	1.90	0.00	0.00	0.00	0.00
United Kingdom	1.32	0.56	0.79	2.11	0.31	0.72	1.01
East Asia	1.28	1.09	0.50	1.11	1.13	0.28	1.95
Australia	0.70	0.68	0.93	0.17	0.00	0.00	3.06
Japan	1.34	1.13	0.46	1.20	1.23	0.31	1.94

Source: Based on UNCTAD, Programme on Transnational Corporations, foreign-direct-investment database.

a Intensity ratio: share of host region in outward investment stock of a given country, divided by share of host region in world-wide FDI stock, excluding FDI stock in the investor country.

b Including South-East Asia and the Pacific.

Table VII.5. Shares of two-way trade (exports plus imports) of 10 major investor countries, by partner region, 1990
(Percentage)

	Partner region							
Country/region	*North America*	*Latin America*	*Europe*	*Africa*	*West Asia*	*South Asia*	*East Asia* [a]	*World* [b]
North America	30	11	25	3	4	1	30	100
Canada	70	3	12	1	1	0	12	100
United States	19	13	25	3	4	1	35	100
Europe	9	2	72	4	3	1	9	100
France	8	3	71	6	3	1	8	100
Germany	8	2	74	3	3	1	10	100
Italy	7	2	75	6	4	1	7	100
Netherlands	6	2	76	2	3	0	5	100
Sweden	10	2	76	1	2	1	9	100
United Kingdom	14	2	64	3	4	1	11	100
East Asia	29	3	21	2	7	1	35	100
Australia	20	1	22	1	4	1	49	100
Japan	31	4	21	2	8	1	33	100
10-country total	18	5	51	3	4	1	19	100

Source: Based on UNCTAD, Programme on Transnational Corporations, foreign-direct-investment database.

a Including, also, South-East Asia and the Pacific.
b Including the 10 countries shown only.

of unusually *close interregional* relationships, such as those between North America and Latin America, Europe and Africa, and East Asia and North America. More distant interregional relationships, on the other hand, tend to be associated with smaller trade intensities than FDI intensities.

A further comparison of FDI and trade intensities for the three main regional groups of investors is provided in figure VII.3. The comparison uses a logarithmic transformation of the intensity measure, and its value is distributed around zero.[3] An average level of bilateral intensity (the case where the partner's share in a particular country's investment or trade is the same as the partner's global share) appears with the value of 0; positive (negative) values indicate stronger (weaker) relationships. The figure shows that North America's linkages are strongest with North America and Latin America, and somewhat stronger than average (through trade) with Asia. European investor countries are most closely linked to Europe and Africa, and somewhat weakly linked to West Asia (mainly through trade, which reflects purchases of oil) and South Asia (mainly through investment, reflecting former colonial ties). East Asia (including Japan and Australia) has relatively intense links with East and South-East Asia and the Pacific and North America, and (mainly through energy trade) with West Asia. In the case of every intraregional relationship, and nearly every close interregional relationship, however, trade intensity is greater than FDI intensity. On the other hand, if close interregional relationships and those with West Asia are excluded, interregional FDI intensity is greater than trade intensity in the majority of cases.

Thus, despite a shared tendency towards regional concentration, the geographical scope of international production through FDI is more idiosyncratic and less dependent on regional factors than is trade. The ties of FDI are less closely bound to the investor's home region than are those of international trade. In some cases, FDI induced by long-standing political or historical ties can span widely-separated regions. For example, Japan has relatively intense FDI links with Peru, as does the United Kingdom with Kenya and Ghana. Trade links are usually weaker across such wide distances, except in the case of oil trade with West Asia. In sum and on the whole, FDI appears to be better than trade at spanning different regional blocs.

The difference between the geographical concentrations of FDI and trade is an interesting finding, and its causes and implications need to be carefully investigated. One possible explanation is that firms tend to resort more to FDI when impediments to trade are relatively high. This may be the case either because of natural barriers (e.g., high transport costs due to geographical distance) or policy barriers (e.g., a firm faces discriminatory protection because a country offers preferential treatment within its trading bloc). It may also reflect the fact that locational endowments influencing FDI are relatively widely dispersed while, at the same time, transaction costs positively linked to distance are less important for FDI than for trade.

Table VII.6. Intensity ratios[a] for two-way trade (exports plus imports) of 10 major investor countries by partner country/region

	Partner region						
Country/region	*North America*	*Latin America*	*Europe*	*Africa*	*West Asia*	*South Asia*	*East Asia*[b]
North America	4.53	3.03	0.37	0.92	1.33	0.76	1.20
Canada	4.90	0.78	0.23	0.35	0.38	0.31	0.54
United States	4.43	3.64	0.41	1.07	1.59	0.89	1.38
Europe	0.46	0.63	1.49	1.57	1.43	0.65	0.37
France	0.42	0.76	1.46	2.57	1.40	0.53	0.33
Germany	0.39	0.64	1.60	1.06	1.20	0.58	0.40
Italy	0.40	0.71	1.52	2.61	1.85	0.56	0.30
Netherlands	0.33	0.52	1.51	1.00	1.44	0.36	0.24
Sweden	0.54	0.59	1.48	0.46	0.86	0.54	0.40
United Kingdom	0.73	0.51	1.31	1.21	1.68	1.16	0.49
East Asia	1.54	0.99	0.38	0.68	3.31	1.16	2.27
Australia	1.15	0.37	0.42	0.42	1.76	1.34	2.36
Japan	1.60	1.08	0.38	0.72	3.54	1.13	2.25

Source: Based on UNCTAD, Programme on Transnational Corporations, foreign-direct-investment database.

a Intensity ratio: share of partner region in total trade of a given country, divided by share of partner region in world-wide trade excluding trade with the given country.

b Including, also, South-East Asia and the Pacific.

Figure VII.3. Foreign-direct-investment and trade intensities, logarithmic measures, North America, Europe and East Asia [a]

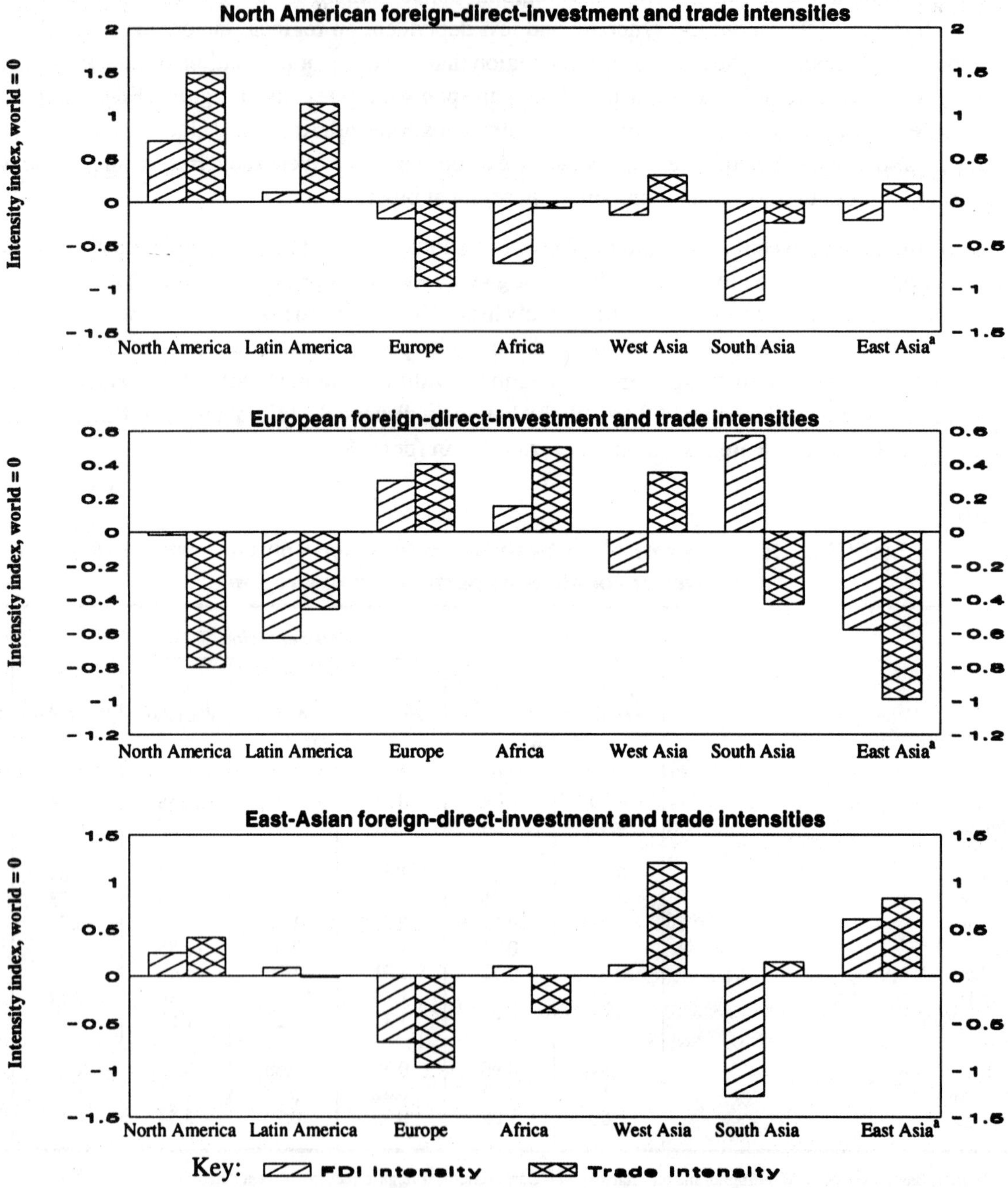

Source: Based on UNCTAD, Programme on Transnational Corporations, foreign-direct-investment database.

a Including, also, South-East Asia and the Pacific.

Be that as it may, the importance of FDI as an agent of integration assumes greater importance with the increasing integration of international production. As discussed in chapters V and VI, many TNCs organize complex integrated production along regional lines. They put their functionally integrated affiliates in several host countries within a single region, and choose non-affiliated companies in the same region as suppliers and subcontractors. Final assembly occurs in countries within the region, which may also be the main market for the product. And, in some cases, regional headquarters may be set up to manage regionally-oriented networks. At the same time, it is important not to overlook the global impact of FDI on integration, as TNCs integrate across regions as well. Furthermore, in any given firm pursuing complex integration strategies, some functions may be organized nationally, some regionally and others globally, thus creating layers of integrated production with varying geographical scope.

As an international production system emerges and is accompanied by increasing intra-firm trade, international trade will also be more widely dispersed. It then becomes an additional force for cross-regional or global integration. In other words, the increasing significance of intra-firm trade in functionally integrated international production, based on the profitability of the entire value chain, widens the geographic scope of trade, as compared with arm's-length trade that is based on the profitability of each separate transaction. Thus, trade as well as FDI may be less subject to regional pressures. The potential links between countries within an integrated international production system are likely to be increasingly global in nature.

C. Implications for host countries

The potential scope of the integrated international production system is global in nature because, in spite of strong tendencies towards regionalization, a significant amount of FDI is interregional and is likely to become more so with the growing importance of complex TNC strategies. The extent to which particular host countries become part of this system depends upon the interaction of their location-specific advantages with the changing firm-specific advantages that TNCs enjoy in the context of integrating their functional activities on a world-wide basis. Some of the implications for host countries, in terms of attracting TNC activities as well as benefiting from their impact on development, are discussed below.

1. Location of economic activities

According to widely accepted theory, TNCs go to a particular economy because of its locational advantages, plus the advantages the company can achieve through internalizing cross-border transactions (Dunning, 1993). The main locational advantages include market size and growth, availability of skilled (and low-cost) labour, natural resources, infrastructure, a favourable policy environment and proximity and access to other large markets (UNCTC, 1992). Integrated international production implies changes in thc nature of the ownership, internalization and location advantages of TNCs.

- Ownership advantages, traditionally considered at least implicitly to emanate from the parent firm, are increasingly becoming firm-wide ownership advantages, reflecting capabilities emanating either from the corporate system as a whole or any part thereof. Internationally-based competitive advantages are generally considered to be developed through cross-national economies of scale, economies of scope and organizational learning (Ghoshal, 1987, pp. 425-440). Those competitive advantages can be gained by firms integrating the activities in their value chain on a world-wide basis. Chapter VI gave examples of affiliates becoming a source of ownership advantages for the firm as a whole.
- To the extent that the above changes cause ownership-specific advantages to become more idiosyncratic or related to the coordination of interrelated activities, the development of internationally-based ownership advantages is accompanied by an increase in the scope of economies of common governance. Thus, there are benefits to firms from internalizing some of their transactions. But, if some ownership advantages can be exploited through markets, then strategic alliances and other interfirm arrangements are likely to grow. In practice, there seems to be an increase in both intrafirm and interfirm transactions.
- As the entire value chain comes to be included in integrated international production, there is a wider range of corporate activities that can be located in host economies. In principle, this gives them a better chance of matching their locational advantages with the needs of TNCs. Attracting FDI may become easier if specific functional activities rather than entire production processes are involved, since the range of skills required will be narrower. At the same time, as TNCs increasingly embody a complex package of attributes in their international production activities, they require a differentiated package of other locational advantages from host economies. Infrastructural support, low factor costs and technological sophistication and adaptability of the workforce are major considerations in the location of foreign affiliates in a country as part of an integrated production system. For countries with financial constraints, such a package of attributes may be easier to develop within specific regions of host countries, suggesting that an integrated international production system involves not only the unbundling of FDI and TNC activities by function, but also of countries by specific locales.

In sum, the emergence of an integrated international production system alters the factors influencing FDI and the location of economic activities abroad. Ownership advantages are becoming system-wide in nature, and exploited through either intra-firm or inter-firm mechanisms, depending upon the nature and costs of the transactions involved. The result is a broader range of opportunities for host countries to attract TNC activities, but also higher requirements in terms of human resources and infrastructure as well as open frameworks for trade and investment.

One factor facilitating the development of an integrated system is the emergence of a global labour force.[4] The availability of skilled labour and professionals in numerous locations around the world, capable of accomplishing work of similar high quality, has enabled TNCs to go to wherever they can perform most economically and efficiently.

It is usually developed countries, however, that are best suited to participate in integrated international production. The newly industrializing and larger developing economies are also likely to succeed in establishing linkages to the emerging system by attracting FDI as part of TNCs' complex strategies, since they offer various levels of labour skills, favourable policy environments, efficient transportation and communications networks and, often, access to a large and growing regional economy. Their increasing role as home countries to TNCs with a potential for establishing their own corporate integrated production systems also strengthens the prospects of their integration into the global economy. However, there is nothing, in principle, to exclude any developing economy from participating in the emerging international production system. One way to do this would be to develop various locational advantages that are a precondition for attracting FDI in higher-value-added activities. Another would be to emphasize or develop specific locational advantages for particular corporate functions of TNCs. Developing countries could also encourage their firms to participate more in interfirm arrangements linking national firms with TNCs for outsourcing by the latter.

It must be recognized, however, that the emerging integrated international production system has left many developing countries so far virtually untouched. Developing appropriate locational advantages takes time. This need not necessarily be a matter of concern to countries not yet in a position to attract integrated production. As emphasized earlier, traditional forms of FDI are still important. Thus, developing countries could attract stand-alone affiliates of TNCs which continue to pursue market-oriented or simple-integration strategies, or natural resource FDI. Given the differentiation that prevails as regards their attributes as host countries (even among the more advanced developing economies), the locational advantages that developing countries offer are likely to differ considerably and the types of investments they can receive are, therefore, likely to differ as well.

2. Impact on development and competitiveness

In the emerging international system, it is increasingly firms—TNCs and their affiliates, rather than arm's-length transactions—that determine a country's participation in the international division of labour. As a result, the growth potential of developing countries will depend to a large extent on their ability to participate in integrated international production and on the nature of their participation. As mentioned earlier, TNCs have been focusing primarily on the three regions of the Triad. Many developing countries have been only partially integrated into the evolving system. However, links to the system are being established in those countries also through interfirm arrangements. To the extent that an integrated international production system creates the primary impulses for global economic growth and development, both the role of TNCs and of countries and regions in determining the impact of this system on developing countries needs to be evaluated.

As mentioned earlier, the expansion of integrated international production implies an increase in cross-border intra-firm flows of resources. It is not clear, however, whether and to what extent flows of foreign capital would increase significantly, especially to host developing countries. Larger FDI may take place because of technology and capital upgrading, but the trend towards functional integration, as well as outsourcing in accordance with overall efficiency, may result in a reduction in the size of affiliate operations and smaller FDI, depending upon the nature of the changes that it involves. In some highly competitive global industries, disinvestment may occur if a TNC fails to keep up with global best practice. More generally, what is taking place is a reorganization of FDI as international production becomes more integrated, with possible implications for the rate of growth and the stability of FDI flows to different host countries.

Integrated international production also implies that competitive conditions in one market increasingly determine the activities of foreign affiliates in all countries, as all of a firm's operations are potentially affected. As such globally-integrated strategies grow in importance, developing countries may increase their leverage with TNCs. However, specialization allows a host country to benefit from the international division of labour, provided it does not specialize so much that it is vulnerable to technical change.

Growth in the integration of production also involves increased flows of goods, services, technology and management know-how, within and between firms. This process is enhanced by applications of information technology throughout the value-added chain which allow the spread of flexible production technologies and new management and research-and-development practices. Increasingly sophisticated work is being parcelled out to distant locations with capable labour forces (box VII.2). Examples in developing countries include the building of steam turbines by Siemens and the production of tapes, chemicals and electrical parts by 3M in India; computer assembly and the design of memory boards by Hewlett-Packard in Mexico; the processing of medical insurance claims by Metropolitan Life in Ireland; and the design and manufacture of electronic pagers by Motorola in Singapore.[5] Moreover, the shift of activities, even to developing countries with low wages, is often accompanied by a shift to more efficient management methods, better technology and heavy investment. Furthermore, foreign affiliates are increasingly likely to buy components from independently owned firms. It has been estimated that at least half of the value of goods shipped from the foreign affiliates of United States TNCs was actually added at independently-owned plants.[6]

Those trends suggest that host countries are likely to improve their productive efficiency and competitiveness. However, they may be less likely to build up their domestic technological capability. Integrated international production by TNCs can mean that host countries receive only a segment of an industry; the possibilities for the transfer of technology and skills may then be narrower than in the case of free-standing affiliates or simple integration. On the other hand, since non-equity forms of TNC participation are available, developing countries with the necessary skills and absorptive capacity will benefit from the transfer of technology.

Box VII.2. Finding a niche: computers and software in India

The tendency for companies to put high-value functions in places where the best and cheapest production capabilities exist is illustrated by the number of computer and software foreign affiliates that are located in India, many of them in Bangalore. Through wholly-owned export operations or joint ventures, Texas Instruments Inc., Motorola Inc., Hewlett-Packard Co., Apple Computer Inc., Sun Microsystems Inc. and Intel Corporation have all set up operations there. Dell Computer Corporation is planning to establish a plant to manufacture computer motherboards for export, and IBM has formed a joint venture with India's biggest industrial firm, the Tata Group (Brauchli, 1993).

Locally-controlled companies are also winning increasingly complex orders for supplying software to foreign clients. Infosys, an Indian software group, provides Holiday Inn with hotel reservation software connecting directly with the computer centre of the Holiday Inn Hotel chain in the United States. Other customers of Infosys include General Electric, Digital Electric and Reebok (United Kingdom). Satellite technology facilitates instantaneous communication with clients (Wagstyl, 1993).

Bangalore is a major research and engineering centre, with some of India's top science, engineering and business schools, as well as high-tech State-sponsored industries and research laboratories. There is thus a concentration of engineers and scientists working in or around the city, and all of them are fluent in English. Bangalore's attractions are completed by its relatively low salaries, reflecting the abundance of labour of all skills.

Those developments make it more important than ever for developing countries to build up their own human and physical infrastructure. In addition to providing the basis for industrialization and development of the domestic economy, it would allow national enterprises to join up with TNCs on a more equal basis. It would raise the quality and sophistication of the FDI a host country could attract, and would strengthen the prospects for technology acquisition. It would also enable host developing countries to build up supplier capabilities that are sometimes a precondition for the location of TNC activities and which, moreover, add to the economic and technological spillovers from foreign affiliates. The building up of such capabilities has been an essential feature of developing countries, including those in Asia and Latin America, that have succeeded in restructuring both their international and domestic production sectors towards higher- value-added activities.

Positive effects on local technological capabilities improve the growth performance of the host economy on a wider basis. The implications for employment, however, may be less favourable. The productivity-boosting technologies and cost-reducing organizational changes that propel deeper integration of TNC activities may be accompanied by little or no growth of employment in the industries concerned, in home as well as host countries. The conflict between efficiency and equity would require domestic action, such as education and training programmes, for absorbing labour into more efficient domestic firms and foreign affiliates, as well as increased domestic investment and social security.

At present, only a few developing countries have attracted sizeable shares of FDI related to functionally integrated TNC activities. For those countries, foreign affiliates linked to TNCs' value chains are a good way to retain competitiveness in industries based on new and costly technologies. Another option is to encourage outward FDI by their own firms, especially in developed countries. This ensures that developing countries will tap into technological developments in advanced host countries. The extent of technological benefits to a home country from such investments is likely to rise with the complexity of the activities in which FDI takes place, the domestic technological capabilities of the firms concerned and the sophistication of industry and technology in the host country (TCMD, 1993c, pp. 71-73).

Other developing countries that do not offer the locational advantages required by regionally or globally integrated firms, such as a skilled labour force, an open trading and investment environment, a developed communication and transport infrastructure and networks of local suppliers on which TNCs can draw, risk being further marginalized. Those countries need to consider how to formulate and coordinate policies so as to maximize the benefits to them from the emerging integrated international production system as well as from FDI in more traditional organizational forms which they may be in a better position to obtain. Issues relevant to the formulation of appropriate policies are discussed in chapter XI.

Notes

1 A slightly different index of integration was developed by Kobrin, 1991.

2 This intensity measure is based on the "gravity index", frequently used in the analysis of international trade. It may be expressed formally as follows:

q_{ab} = $(I_{ab} / I_{a*}) / (I_{*b} / W)$,

where q_{ab} = intensity of country 'a''s investment in or trade with country 'b';

I_{ab} = investment by 'a' in 'b' or trade between 'a' and 'b';

W = world investment or trade, excluding investment in or trade of country 'a';

* = summation across all partners.

3 The logarithmic measure transforms the measure in note 2 as follows:

$Q_{ab} = \ln (q_{ab})$,

where Q_{ab} = logarithmic measure of intensity of 'a''s investment in, or trade with 'b'.

4 Brian O'Reilly, "Your new global labor force", *Fortune* (December 1992), p. 52.

5 O'Reilly, op. cit.

6 Ibid.

PART THREE

PUBLIC POLICY ISSUES

The increasing globalization of transnational corporations (TNCs) and their foreign affiliates[1] has implications for public policy. In particular, the emergence of an integrated international production system is beginning to strain traditional concepts and approaches.

The classical notion of the corporation, initially developed in a different environment but creatively transformed so as to adapt to, and at the same time significantly influence, changing economic and legal conditions, is at the centre of the current *problematique*. As economic boundaries begin to disappear in terms of corporate strategies and TNCs develop complex inter-firm linkages, three interconnected issues, all directly related to the legal effects of the fundamental notions of the legal personality of the corporation, on the one hand, and the functional unity of the enterprise, on the other, appear to need close consideration. They are the subject of the three first chapters of Part Three: corporate nationality, parent-affiliate relations and responsibilities, and the international allocation of taxes on TNCs.

From a legal and public policy perspective, some characteristics of integrated international production are particularly relevant:

- The division of labour between foreign affiliates and their parent firms and among foreign affiliates located in a number of countries, so that specific tasks are the responsibility of particular units of the TNC system.
- The decline of the economic autonomy of each constituent part.
- The increasing difficulty of distinguishing between "parent firms" and "affiliates".

In the light of those changes, it is appropriate to re-examine the concept of the corporate nationality of TNCs since identifying the national origin and attachment of corporations in such a context has become not only more difficult but also less obviously significant. Chapter VIII deals with this subject.

Chapter IX looks at the legal relationship between parent firms and their foreign affiliates, which is becoming increasingly complex as those affiliates lose some of their operational autonomy. In strict legal terms, they remain independent units with limited liability for the results of a production process of which they are an integral part. How far is this still appropriate and realistic?

Nowhere are the consequences of this relationship more clearly felt than in the area of taxation, the subject of chapter X. With business becoming more global, and with more value-adding activities being undertaken by different foreign affiliates spread over many countries, it is increasingly difficult to determine where profits are being earned and what income individual Governments can tax. Moreover, with the integration of value-adding activities among affiliates, the application of methods for the allocation of the business income of TNCs based on arm's-length prices raises complex questions.

Chapter XI discusses, at the level of countries, some of the policy implications of the convergence of foreign-direct-investment policies and the emergence of integrated international production.

Notes

1 As elsewhere in this volume, the term "foreign affiliates" is meant to include subsidiaries (more than 50 per cent equity is controlled by the parent firm) and associates (10 to 50 per cent controlled by the parent firm), which are typically incorporated in their host country as separate legal entities, as well as foreign branches, which are treated in law as integral parts of the parent corporation. In the context of chapters VIII-X, "foreign affiliate" refers only to subsidiaries and associates.

CHAPTER VIII

CORPORATE NATIONALITY

The growth of foreign direct investment (FDI) and the expansion of transnational corporations (TNCs) have been possible partly because of the lowering of national barriers to the movement of goods and services and to the location of factories and offices. More recently, bilateral and multilateral agreements have increasingly held national treatment as the proper standard for foreign affiliates. If this were to become the norm, it would ease the problems associated with the notion of corporate nationality, although the need to determine a firm's nationality would not disappear.

A. The grounds of corporate nationality

In law, it is sometimes necessary to establish a company's national identity in order to determine its legal capabilities, rights and duties. A distinction between domestic and foreign enterprises is also needed where national legislation favours domestic firms or where international law and practice accord a distinctive status to foreign enterprises.

National security considerations are at the root of much of the discrimination against TNCs, such as the closing of certain economic sectors to foreign firms or the privileged treatment of domestic firms for public procurement or subsidies. As long as the international order is based on the existence of sovereign and equal nation states, concern for national security is bound to be at the centre of governmental policies. However, legitimate considerations of national security are sometimes twisted and abused. National security is not a synonym for the national interest; yet it is sometimes construed so broadly as to include most national economic interests. National security is also used as a pretext to justify measures that are, in fact, intended to protect special interests unrelated to security. Beyond these abuses, even a country's genuine national security interests may sometimes conflict with the orderly functioning of the world economy. For example, efforts to expand a home State's jurisdictional grasp to include the foreign affiliates of its corporations may serve legitimate national interests, including national security, but their effects may conflict with the laws and policies of host States. This question of "extra-territoriality" has caused much uncertainty and controversy over the years.

A distinction between domestic and foreign firms is based on several widespread assumptions:

- National borders are deemed of primary importance because they correspond to economic as well as political dividing lines; they separate not only discrete political units, but also discrete national economies. However, this notion is being undermined by the growth of an integrated international production system.
- The economic circumstances of countries (and groups of countries) vary enormously, and these differences should help determine the standards of TNC treatment to which they are held. For developing countries, in particular, the fact that a corporation comes from a developed country may be more significant than its precise national origin. On that basis they may adopt measures to distinguish between domestic and foreign enterprises. However, this conventional wisdom is increasingly being doubted, with many developing countries deciding that equal treatment for all enterprises ("national treatment") is an effective way to attract FDI on appropriate terms.

Whatever the validity of their approach, the fact remains that States still regard nationality as significant, for individuals and for corporations. This fact is so central that it cannot be ignored in a discussion of the topic.

B. Corporate nationality: where and how it matters

In an international order based on the coexistence and cooperation of nation-states, nationality, the legal relationship linking individuals to a particular State plays a pivotal role in law as well as in politics. A person's national identity is an important part of his or her personality. An individual's nationality, the legal manifestation of his or her national identity, is a central part of personal legal status. In international law, nationality (along with territory) constitutes a principal base for the exercise of jurisdiction by States. The general rule, with limited exceptions, is that a State has full jurisdiction over people, goods and activities within its territory—and it also has jurisdiction over people who are its nationals, whether or not they are within its territory.

Since the legal condition of corporations is generally modelled on that of individuals, it is easy to assume that nationality plays a correspondingly large role in their case as well. In fact, corporate nationality raises different legal issues (box VIII.1) and is a significantly different legal notion from nationality. And it is worth noting that, in current policy debate, the term "corporate nationality" is often used to refer to broader notions than the strictly legal one (Reich, 1991; Hu, 1992).

The attribution of nationality to corporations takes place in a variety of policy contexts that reflect the pertinent concerns of States.

Box VIII.1. Legal tests of corporate nationality

No single test of corporate nationality is universally applied today in national and international law. Indeed, in national law there is sometimes no reference to the term or notion of corporate nationality as such, yet the State claims jurisdiction over corporations on the basis of considerations that lead to the same result as nationality. In international law, the issue of corporate nationality arises in relatively few contexts. The criteria most commonly used, separately or in combination, to determine a company's nationality are: the place of incorporation; the location of the "seat" of the corporation; and the nationality of the shareholders who "control" the corporation.

In the *national* legal systems derived from Anglo-American common law, the State of incorporation is the main test of nationality. In most civil law systems of continental Europe and those influenced by them, the test is that of the company's "seat", i.e., the place where the direction and central administration are located. The two tests lead to similar results in the many cases where the seat formally provided for in the corporation's statutes is the place of incorporation. Where the statutory seat does not coincide with the place from which direction is actually exercised, the latter (the "real seat" as distinguished from the statutory one) prevails in many continental legal systems.

The legitimacy of the third test, of "control", is controversial. This test is political in origin, since in many countries it was first used in wartime to deal with locally incorporated companies whose shareholders were enemy aliens. It is still true that the more politically charged an issue, the more likely it is that the test of control will be used. However, the test is used in a variety of regulatory contexts to distinguish between domestic and foreign corporations, in order to restrict the access of foreign companies to particular industries (e.g., air transport, coastal shipping) or to provide privileged treatment (e.g., government subsidies) to local firms. It is also sometimes used by home countries to establish jurisdiction over aspects of the activities of foreign affiliates of corporations owned by their nationals.

The main context in which corporate nationality is relevant in *international* law has traditionally been that of diplomatic protection. The most recent authority, the 1970 decision of the International Court of Justice in the *Barcelona Traction Case* established a rather restrictive test, according to which only "the State under the laws of which [the corporation] is incorporated and in whose territory it has its registered office" has the ability to exercise diplomatic protection (ICJ, 1970). In some of the judges' opinions in this case, and in the extensive analysis of it, other criteria were proposed and discussed (Cafisch, 1971; Ohly, 1983), but they do not seem to have seriously affected established views on customary law. Later decisions, especially the 1989 *Elsi Case*, may have relaxed the standard a little, but the current state of customary law seems to be fairly restrictive (Sacerdoti, 1989; Stern, 1990; Staker, 1991).

The traditional tests have retained their place in the bilateral treaties of some countries and in arrangements for the establishment of TNCs. On the other hand, recent treaty practice in "lump-sum compensation" agreements for nationalized property and in the bilateral investment protection agreements of some large countries has advanced variants of the control test ("substantial interests"), whether independently of the traditional criteria or in combination with them.[a] Outside the strictly legal arena, moreover, classical nationality tests do not count for much. In international relations, where each State seeks to influence the other in order to advance the economic interests of its nationals, the actual control of firms is what counts.

a For earlier treaty practice of a major country, see Walker (1956); for recent bilateral investment treaties, see Laviec (1985); for "lump-sum" agreements, see Lillich and Weston (1975).

- *Determining the law to be applied.* Host countries attribute a specific corporate nationality to TNCs in order to deal with some common legal problems: whether the corporations have been formed in conformity with applicable legal rules; whether they thereby possess the capacity to contract and to sue and be sued; and what legal rules govern their internal structure and the functions and capacities of their organs. These are all concerns that are strongly influenced by private law, and are often subsumed under the rubric of "lawyer's law". In many cases, they involve routine matters of no great overall significance. But they may affect some important public policy issues, especially where there are significant differences between the company laws of home and host countries.

  Laws on the structure and functioning of corporations seek to regulate what firms do, to protect minority shareholders, to determine the rights of creditors and to clarify the status of all those who come into contact with the corporation. Where there are differences in the approach of home and host countries, the hosts may require additional measures to replace the missing company-law regulations or to ensure legal uniformity. For example, a host State may require all banks and insurance companies operating in its territory to be incorporated therein, i.e., that they operate through subsidiaries rather than through branches. This is intended to ensure that they conform to all local requirements on minimum amounts of capital, protection of creditors and clients, etc. The free establishment of foreign affiliates may be allowed where the national laws of the countries concerned are similar enough to permit mutual reliance. In the context of schemes for economic integration, such as the European Community, mutual acceptance and recognition of the effects of company laws are based on the premise of deliberate harmonization of the relevant basic regulations. In other cases, attitudes may be influenced by the type of home regulation that is applied. For example, branches of banks from States with effective supervision may enjoy a competitive advantage in their foreign operations if they are considered safer by prospective customers. On the other hand, if effective regulation imposes additional costs on enterprises or limits their ability to act in a particular way, corporations from home countries with weak supervision may possess, at least temporarily, a competitive advantage of sorts.

- *Restrictions on TNCs.* Corporate nationality may also matter when a State allows only "domestic" firms to operate in certain industries (e.g., civil aviation, coastal shipping, mining) on national security grounds or in order to ensure national control of economic resources. A State may also reserve various kinds of special treatment (e.g., Government subsidies, public procurement) for domestic firms alone. In such cases, Governments may insist not just on local incorporation, but also on full or substantial control by their nationals.

- *Jurisdiction over companies abroad.* Where the unit involved is a branch of a domestic firm, the claim of jurisdiction will normally be based on its "nationality", according to all traditional tests. Where an affiliate incorporated abroad is concerned, the home State may apply the control test, arguing in effect that foreign affiliates have the nationality of the parent corporation. Such claims of jurisdiction, however, are rarely based on a formal claim about a company's nationality. They tend to be simply asserted with the unspoken assumption that the enterprise is a unity. According to that view, the separate legal personality of a foreign affiliate may, for some purposes, be disregarded: its "corporate veil" may be lifted (see also chapter IX). The approach is reversible for sometimes the host State may also want to lift the corporate veil in order to claim jurisdiction over the parent company. However, the nationality approach cannot be used in that way; it cannot be claimed that the parent company has the nationality of the foreign affiliate because it owns its capital. In another variant of the "enterprise-unity" approach, the home State may formally impose its requirements not on the foreign affiliate itself, but on the parent company, expressly expecting it to discipline its foreign affiliates in any manner it chooses, as long as a the desired results are achieved. Whichever approach is followed, however, it often leads to disagreement between home and host Governments.

- *The international law context.* Corporate nationality is important when a State seeks formally to exercise diplomatic protection over a company or invokes relevant provisions of international treaties (box VIII.1). However, the broadening of the ambit of protection, especially in bilateral investment treaties, through often overlapping provisions on independent grounds (covering, for instance, the rights of shareholders and broad categories of assets) may ultimately decrease the importance of the notion of corporate nationality in investment protection.

C. Integrated international production and corporate nationality

The discussion so far has dealt with corporations operating internationally, under any conditions, even if only a single parent company with a single affiliate in another State is involved. However, modern TNCs typically consist of many legal persons, usually incorporated and operating in different countries. The picture becomes even more complicated by present trends towards integrated international production, because current relations between TNC units no longer necessarily reflect the patterns of hierarchy and subordination that may have applied in the past.

To begin with, the TNC as a whole does not possess a legal personality of its own. It does not therefore possess formal nationality. Only in political terms is it associated with a particular country—its home country or, more accurately, the country of nationality of its parent company or of the company that constitutes its decision-making centre. How far it is possible in law to deal with the TNC as a single entity is still very much an open question. The usual legal approaches limit themselves to establishing links between parents and affiliates, even where successive parent-affiliate pairs are involved.

The component parts of a TNC may be subsidiaries, associates or branches. Branches seldom possess any significant autonomy; they are treated in law as parts of the company to which they belong. Subsidiaries and associates do have some autonomy and are typically incorporated in their host countries (or in a third country) as separate legal entities. For some purposes, therefore, each subsidiary has the nationality of the country where it is incorporated and where it has its seat. For other purposes, however, the fact of control by a foreign company means the subsidiary has a "foreign" character. Thus, each subsidiary may, for some purposes, be treated as possessing two (and conceivably more) nationalities.

When the control test is applied, things may be relatively simple where a 100 per cent subsidiary of a foreign corporation is involved. In some complicated cases, difficult problems arise. For instance, it is not clear how far back in the chain of "parent" companies it is appropriate to reach in order to determine a subsidiary's nationality. Nor is it clear whether it is legitimate to apply more than one test to determine the nationality of each unit in that chain of corporations.

Most legal discussions on TNCs (and, in most cases, national law as well) continue to rely on the initial paradigm of a parent company that owns several subsidiaries. Increasingly, however, TNCs develop into networks in which responsibilities for specific tasks are distributed among various units, and the interdependence brought about by a more sophisticated intra-firm division of labour reduces the autonomy of all participating entities. With management and decisions spread among several parts of a TNC, it becomes increasingly difficult to speak of a "parent firm", although it is clear to which corporate system each unit belongs. When the units are incorporated and administered in different countries, and even more when they are owned by shareholders of different nationalities or are linked to one another by contractual arrangements, it may become factually difficult to attribute nationality to a particular subsidiary; perhaps more important, the attribution may have only a distant connection with reality.

The potential for confusion resulting from such complications is great. In the customary international law of diplomatic protection, for instance, the combination of strictly formal criteria and complex business realities brought, for a time, application of the law to a virtual standstill (Fatouros, 1983). Overall, however, the impact in practice has been rather limited. International legal practice has circumvented round many difficulties by means of the skilful structuring of relevant international instruments and transactions. The developments described, moreover, affect today a relatively small number of TNCs, albeit large and important ones, and their impact is not uniform for all countries and regions.

D. Towards more order and clarity

The issue of corporate nationality raises difficult problems, not just for the law, but also for national and international public policy. One way of easing those problems would be to bring the various national laws closer together. That could happen at two interrelated but still distinct levels: public policy and legislation; and the harmonizing of legal methods and techniques of private law approaches by the courts.

Efforts on the first level could be tied to an important current development, the gradually emerging international legal framework for FDI. Recent developments (see chapter I) generally deal with only one aspect of this framework, the liberalization of access and increased legal protection for FDI. Another major dimension, that of developing standards for the activities of TNCs, has had much attention in the past, but is now somewhat neglected. Yet the combination of both approaches might make the emerging legal framework particularly relevant. Liberalization measures tend, by definition, to reduce or eliminate discrimination against TNCs and treat them on a par with domestic companies. And substantial agreement on international standards for TNCs could serve much the same purposes that national regulation of foreign affiliates seeks to achieve. Those aspects of an international legal framework for FDI might be strengthened by adopting a scheme for international incorporation or registration of TNCs (box VIII.2). Even then, however, it would be wrong to suppose that all the issues of corporate nationality would be resolved.

The second approach for dealing with the issue of corporate nationality is harmonization. Two international conventions, the Hague Convention of 1 June 1956 on Recognition of the Legal Personality of Foreign Companies,[1] and the Brussels Convention of 29 February 1968 on the Mutual Recognition of Companies and Legal Persons,[2] have already considered the topic. However, they both avoid using the notion of corporate nationality, they are both narrowly legal in their focus, and neither of them is in force, because they have not been ratified by enough countries.

In the light of those difficulties, other approaches need to be explored. One approach might be developed along the lines of the efforts of OECD in dealing with the problem of "conflicting requirements" imposed on TNCs. Initially, OECD began by considering the possibility of an overall agreement on matters of conflict of jurisdiction between States, but found that this was not feasible. It therefore adopted a set of "general considerations and practical approaches", that is to say, a body of relevant policy principles, intended to guide the practice of Governments, and a series of procedural suggestions for consultations and other arrangements (OECD, 1992c, pp. 57-71, 119-120).

Box VIII.2. Is international incorporation an answer?

The idea of an international company law for the incorporation of TNCs—which would accord to them a truly international status—has been about for several decades (Ball, 1970). However, with the exception of the discussion in the *Institut de Droit International* in 1977, there has been no thorough study of the topic (Goldman, 1977). The lack of interest comes from a general perception that the idea is impractical: it would be too hard to draft such a statute, presumably in the form of an international convention; it would be unlikely that all major home and host States would agree to be bound by it; and TNCs themselves have consistently opposed it. The chief advantage of such a scheme would be that it would deal with the TNC as a whole, filling the gap of legal regulation at the international level. National laws can be fully effective only within the limits of national jurisdiction. They cannot handle all the truly transnational aspects of TNC activities, and run the risk of jurisdictional conflicts, due to differences in policies or legal approaches. An international incorporation arrangement would presumably establish international public policy, and it would simplify the legal treatment of particular issues.

Those advantages, however, presuppose agreement on the policies to be served by the incorporation mechanism as a whole and the particular legal provisions on company law. It is not obvious that such agreement would by feasible, partly because there has been little preparation for it. Even if the technical difficulties are ignored, national company laws reflect significant policy differences that may be difficult to bridge. To take one example, the efforts to create a *societas europea* in the European Community began in the late 1960s, but have been fruitless so far, because of policy disagreements between the member countries (Stein, 1971; Buxbaum and Hopt, 1988). At the same time, the lack of a federal incorporation statute in some federal countries does not appear to have led to serious practical problems (Rubin, 1973; Buxbaum and Hopt 1988).

In view of those difficulties, less intrusive variations of an international scheme have been suggested. The Goldman report at the *Institut de Droit International* explored the possibility of a registration scheme, which might provide some of the advantages of international incorporation, but on a voluntary basis. For such a scheme to work, both States and TNCs would have to be convinced that they could derive advantages from it, while being protected from any untoward consequences.

Such a scheme might also be linked to the emerging international framework for FDI, in terms of both its chief dimensions, i.e., liberalization and protection of investments and the establishment of standards for TNC activities. The interweaving of standards and procedures concerning national and international policies on FDI and TNCs may render more effective any attempt at ordering the issues discussed herein.

To tackle the question of corporate nationality, it may thus be useful to combine prescriptions with procedures. The prescriptions would not be formally binding; rather, they would be suggestions or recommendations, addressed mainly to national decision makers—lawyers, judges and administrators, as well as legislators and policy makers. They would thus be in the broad area of "soft law", although the machinery and procedures supplementing them might be in somewhat "harder" form. Some prescriptions would have to be reasonably specific and, on occasion, deal with common cases that arise in real life.

A set of drafts could thus be prepared in the framework of the appropriate international agencies. They would cover principles and rules of thumb for the attribution of corporate nationality and its effects, as well as for the exercise of jurisdiction. It might be possible to develop some functional criteria to replace or supplement the traditional legal ones, geared to the novel circumstances arising from the globalization of TNC activities. It might also be possible to indicate cases where the use of particular criteria is more appropriate and those where it would be less (or not) appropriate. The drafts could consider the special situation of developing countries and see how far the various prescriptions are appropriate for them. It might even be possible to formulate principles for limiting the incidence of conflicts of jurisdiction.

These standards and prescriptions would have to be supplemented by provisions for procedures of consultation and even for the settlement of disputes. These procedures, too, would have to be flexible and avoid the appearance of a rigid, quasi-judicial approach.

E. Looking ahead

There is today a widening gap between the increasing globalization of TNCs and the notion of corporate nationality. The control and direction of TNCs is now spreading horizontally, and clear hierarchical links are becoming less common or less functionally important. As a result, the fundamental assumption in law of a relationship of subordination between units of a TNC is less and less consistent with reality. Yet, while the law acknowledges, in specific contexts, the impact of the presence of the TNC on the units that constitute it, it has not yet found a way to deal with the TNC as a single unified whole. Absent "legal personality", the TNC has no formal existence in law, and therefore no identity and no nationality.

Thus far, no acute problems appear to have arisen from this changing pattern. The ingenuity of lawyers has helped to invent ways in which established concepts and rules can be applied to new situations. However, this process requires increasingly complicated planning. After a certain point, it becomes confusing and costly—in a word, counter-productive. Use of the notion of corporate nationality to protect or to regulate enterprises begins to cost too much.

In a world of nation-states, even one with globalized TNCs and an integrated economy, the notion of nationality, for individuals and companies, will not readily disappear. But its consequences will become less important: apart from its formal role of identifying the legal rules applicable to a corporation's formation and personality, corporate nationality as a ground for distinguishing between companies will be used less and less frequently. National treatment will become more common, with whatever variations the differing situations of countries may make necessary. This is the way that States seem to be moving, through their national legislation as well as through bilateral and multilateral instruments. But it will take many years for the change to be completed.

Notes

1 For the text of the Convention, see "Treaty Regarding the Jurisdictional Existence of Corporations, Societies, Associations and Foundations", *Journal of Treaties of the Netherlands*, vol. 131 (1956), The Hague: The Government of the Netherlands Publisher, pp. 1-5.

2 Text in *European Communities Bulletin*, Supplement 13/73 (Brussels, Commission of the European Communities, 1973).

CHAPTER IX

PARENT-AFFILIATE RELATIONS AND RESPONSIBILITIES

A. The parent-affiliate dichotomy

The foundation of parent-affiliate jurisprudence is the concept of individual corporate personality, sometimes referred to as "entity law". The recognition of the personality of a corporation, separate from that of the shareholder or investor, is a central feature of all market-oriented legal systems (OECD, 1990).

In those countries that espouse entity law, the traditional view is that, within a group of affiliated companies, each affiliate is a separate legal entity with its own rights and responsibilities. But, as a matter of economic reality, the different affiliates may be engaged in one and the same business, often conducted under a single company logo; the concept of separate corporate personality may therefore strike the observer as somewhat artificial. It raises complications, however, in the attribution of liability to individual members of the corporate group.

Although such complications may arise in any type of corporate group, they are multiplied when a domestic corporate group expands into a transnational corporation (TNC). The legal relationships among corporate affiliates of a TNC traditionally reflect the idea that each is a "native within the country of its incorporation" (Aronofsky, 1985, p. 33). But that approach raises several critical jurisdictional and procedural problems that a strictly domestic company would not encounter (Wallace, 1993). For example, a court must decide whether to exercise jurisdiction over a dispute involving a TNC; whether foreign or domestic law, or some combination, should apply; and what procedure to follow on venue and service of process.

The issue of TNC parent-affiliate relations is taking on new dimensions in the emerging world of globalizing firms and industries. Integrated international production, as discussed in chapter V, is turning stand-alone foreign affiliates into parts of larger corporate systems in which each has a specific role to play within an increasingly sophisticated transnational intra-firm division of labour. In the process, the affiliate may lose part of its autonomy over managerial and operational questions. To the extent that loss of affiliate autonomy does occur, the issue of whether there should be more "parental responsibility" needs to be discussed.

On the other hand, as discussed in chapter VI, intra-firm integration is also producing a network structure, in which the concept of the parent firm can take on a different, more limited meaning, to the extent that the parent becomes more of a coordinating agency for certain corporate activities. The spread of decision-making powers in a TNC is complicating traditional tests for determining which corporate unit is responsible for decisions that have been traditionally associated with the parent company—and thus which firm has parental responsibility. The right issue to consider may therefore be "group responsibility"—the relations and responsibilities among all parts of the group rather than the more familiar parent-affiliate relations and responsibilities. International law is little help to courts adjudicating legal actions involving the allocation of responsibility or liability among a TNC's various parts. Traditionally, of course, "when a state has a recognized basis for prescribing rules to govern a person or activity, international law is usually neutral" (Park, 1978, p. 1,646). It may now be time to reconsider the validity of that approach.

B. National legislative and judicial approaches

1. The traditional approach

The growing discord between legal theory and commercial reality has its roots in history. For many years, it was the original shareholder (who was also the ultimate investor), who granted legal authorization for the development of the corporate structure. Today, the shareholder of one corporation can actually be another company whose ultimate investors were not directly involved in the formation of the new company.

The defining feature of corporate personality is that the corporation is a legal entity distinct from its members. It follows that any personal liability of the members for the acts of the corporation is limited to the extent expressly provided. As originally envisaged, limited liability provided crucial economic advantages to the investors. It allowed them to avoid dangerous exposure to business risks that came from a decision-making process in which they played little or no part. They were therefore able to diversify their portfolios. The management, on the other hand, was encouraged to take appropriate business risks without the constraints of shareholder exposure (Blumberg, 1987).

When corporations themselves were legally authorized to hold the shares of other corporations, however, the distinction between the investor and management began to blur. That raised the spectre of an investor with the powers to manipulate managerial control to the detriment of other parties, particularly creditors, while avoiding responsibility by invoking limited liability. None the less, most jurisdictions around the world stuck to the concept that each corporation in a group is a separate legal entity. Thus, a principle originally designed to distinguish between the ultimate investor and the enterprise was applied for the protection of constituents of the enterprise, even though the ultimate investors of the enterprise were not directly involved in the formation of those constituents (Blumberg, 1987).

In order to deal with the possibility that managerial control by parent companies might be inappropriately used, corporate law again turned to traditional principles. It relied on certain exceptions to the norm originally designed for the traditional investor who became entangled in the management structure. Exceptions to the limited liability rule had long existed to prevent shareholders from achieving illegal or socially intolerable results through the use of a corporate structure. The application of any of those exceptions is commonly referred to as piercing (or lifting) the corporate veil.

In deciding whether to pierce the corporate veil, courts generally review the identities, formalities and status of the corporate affiliates to see how far they are subject to parental control (box IX.1). However, under the same traditional principles, a finding of such control will justify piercing the veil only if, in addition, the court determines that control has resulted in illegality, fraud or injustice. This "analysis-by-checklist", accompanied by the search for fraud or injustice, has increasingly been criticized, because it seems that there are few, if any, rational criteria to guide it (Aronofsky, 1985, p. 39).

Box IX.1. Checklist for veil-piercing

Factors that courts take into account to signify parental control include:

- stock ownership;
- directors and officers common to both parent firm and subsidiary;
- the financial relationship between parent firm and subsidiary, and whether the latter is economically autonomous from the former;
- whether the parent firm incorporated the subsidiary;
- whether the subsidiary is grossly undercapitalized;
- whether the parent firm pays salaries and expenses of subsidiary operations;
- whether the parent firm guarantees or covers any of the subsidiary's financial losses;
- whether the subsidiary has any business apart from that with the parent firm, and whether the subsidiary maintains any separate assets;
- whether the parent firm treats the subsidiary as an unincorporated division or department;
- whether subsidiary directors and officers have any autonomy from parental authority;
- whether the formal legal prerequisites for separate incorporation are observed by the parent firm;
- whether the parent firm treats the subsidiary's assets and property as its own.

Source: Barber, 1981, p. 398.

2. Piercing the veil of the transnational corporation

A reassessment of the adequacy of the traditional liability and veil-piercing concepts has been advocated for a long time, and some judicial systems are beginning to reject the traditional checklist approach. However, change has happened only in those areas of the law where the courts or the lawmakers have found it particularly difficult to achieve appropriate results with traditional concepts. This has been so in bankruptcy, taxation, anti-trust law and tort law. Thus:

- Courts are anxious to establish whether the failure of an affiliate was caused by instructions from central management, and whether the parent company has used its dominating influence to secure itself a position as a privileged creditor in subsequent bankruptcy proceedings. To prevent this happening, the bankruptcy law of some countries automatically disallows any transactions between connected companies which were carried out in a specified period preceding insolvency.[1]
- Although separate taxation of each company is still the general rule in many legal systems, it is qualified by certain exceptions, which are designed to strike a balance between protecting the revenue of a Government and the need to alleviate the tax burden of the corporate group as whole.
- In applying anti-trust law, many courts look at the economic unity of related companies to determine the market power of an enterprise or the abuse of a dominant position.
- It is in tort law that the greatest advances in overcoming limited liability constraints have been made. In particular, tort law in product liability cases has expanded to the point where liability can be imposed on any parts of a group participating in any stage of the interconnected process of designing, manufacturing, distributing, selling or installing dangerously defective products. In some cases, recognition of the effect of integrated international production seems to take the process even further. The degree of economic and operational integration of affiliate operations and the fact that the parent firm may control an affiliate's decision-making processes have sometimes provided a basis for a court to say that the parent firm was directly involved in the offending action.

C. Options for consideration

Despite the trend away from traditional veil-piercing principles, the solutions dealing with parent/affiliate relationships reflect only the specific legal problems that are meant to be tackled. Solutions reached in one area of law are not necessarily applied to other areas, so they do not seem to lead to a uniform concept of parental responsibility. Furthermore, the degree of change varies widely from country to country. To bring a common approach closer, two ideas may be relevant for dealing with the responsibility of the parent firm in the special context of integrated international production: the first is the notion of a TNC's "duty-to-manage responsibly" and the second is group liability for a TNC.

Under traditional veil-piercing jurisprudence, it is the intrusion of the parent firm into the management of the affiliate that justifies piercing the corporate veil of the parent. Underlying this approach is the assumption that the affiliate had the autonomy and the ability to manage its own affairs, but the parent overruled it. However, the autonomy of foreign affiliates is being eroded in several functional areas. It may therefore be better to consider not how much responsibility for affiliates should be attributed to the parent firm because of its intrusion, but rather how much responsibility should be borne by the parent because of an affiliate's limited capacity to manage itself. Cases of environmental disasters illustrate that the moral (and perhaps the legal) charge facing the parent company may not be that it interfered in the affairs of the affiliate, but rather the opposite: that it failed to supervise and control its affiliate management and to minimize risk.[2] It is in that context that the theory of a parent firm's "duty-to-manage responsibly" has been suggested (Westbrook, 1985, p. 326). The idea is to impose a legal duty upon parent firms to manage their affiliates in accordance with some standard of responsible international investment and management.[3]

Such standards would best apply under an international convention that would define and impose them on an agreed basis. As no such convention exists, it will probably be left to the courts to find the "duty-to-manage responsibly" in the investment contracts that TNCs enter into with host countries. For example, many investment agreements provide for an overhead charge for supervisory services provided by the TNC headquarters. Although such clauses are rarely specific about parent company guarantees, they could be construed to include a duty to ensure that the affiliate is managed responsibly. However, it is worth noting that the Governments of host countries sometimes *de facto* constrain the exercise of responsibility by parent firms. For example, they may impose limitations on the import of certain technologies or the employment of expatriates deemed necessary by parent firms.

Accepting that a parent firm has a role in the management of a group of companies is a notion that is already used in veil-piercing law. Indeed, the recent laws of several countries (particularly in Europe) build on the legitimate involvement of parent companies in affiliate affairs (Hofstetter, 1990); Germany, for example, has enacted detailed and comprehensive laws specifically on this issue (box IX.2). Its legislation not only explicitly recognizes the right of a dominating enterprise to direct the activities of companies under its control; it also establishes special responsibilities and safeguards in order to protect the interests of the parties concerned.

If, however, integrated international production blurs the identity of the parent firm (see chapter VIII), and leads to a dispersion of authority within a TNC, then looking for increased parental responsibility may prove increasingly difficult in the future. Instead, an approach that builds upon existing group-liability principles may offer better solutions. Group responsibility, according to legal literature (Hofstetter, 1990), presumes a disregard of the corporate veil for the liability of individual entities in a corporate group, once it is established that there has been common ownership, direction and unity of economic purpose and operation among the affiliates. To overcome this presumption, each of the units would have to show that its conduct and economic status within a TNC system are unrelated to the dispute before a court.

Concepts akin to group liability apply to corporations in several countries. In the United States, for example, the Bank Holding Company Act, the Securities Acts of 1933 and 1934, the Investment Company Act, the Federal Communications Act, the Export Administration Act, the Foreign Boycott Act and the Foreign Corrupt Practices

Act impose some statutory burdens on the group as a whole. In those instances, they tend to brush aside the separate corporate identity of the various components of the group.

In each of those statutes, and in statutes of other legal systems that have adopted some form of group responsibility, the concept of "control" is central to determining whether group responsibility applies. Typically, the test of control is a benchmark of stock ownership. As an alternative, these statutes use a *de facto* or functional standard defined in terms of whether there was a power to "control" or even to exercise a "controlling influence" over management policies and decisions. The statutes concentrate not only on the "controlling company" and the "controlled company" relationship, but also on the relationship of all companies under "common control".

Box IX.2. Special rules of responsibility for parent companies: the case of Germany

German law accepts the principle that each individual company is legally independent and that its liabilities are covered only by its own assets. However, it allows some exceptions to this principle; different provisions apply, depending on whether the subsidiary is a joint stock company *Aktiengesellschaft* (AG) or a private company limited by shares *Gesellschaft mit beschränkter Haftung* (GmbH).

(a) If the subsidiary company is an AG, the provisions of the Joint Stock Companies Act governing groups of enterprises apply. They contain several exceptions to the principle of legal independence:

- Where one company has been fully integrated into another, under Section 322 of the Joint Stock Companies Act, the main company is accountable jointly and severally with the integrated subsidiary for the latter's liabilities.
- Where the connection between enterprises is weaker—i.e., where a contract of domination or a contract providing for the transfer of profits exists—the creditors of the subsidiary company are indirectly protected by the fact that the parent is obliged to compensate for any loss under Section 302 of the Joint Stock Companies Act. Where a contract of domination or a contract providing for the transfer of profits is terminated, the creditors of the subsidiary company can claim from the parent company direct and demand security from it under Section 303 of the Joint Stock Companies Act.
- If what exists between two enterprises is not a contract of domination or a contract providing for the transfer of profits but merely some dependency, the parent company is obliged under Section 311 of the Joint Stock Companies Act to compensate for a subsidiary's financial loss resulting from the fact that disadvantageous directives were given.
- Over and above this, in the case of a contract of domination or a contract providing for the transfer of profits, as well as in the case of a dependency, the law provides for direct claims of the subsidiary company's creditors against transfer of profits. Claims are admissible only if the parent company or its legal representative has caused damage to the subsidiary in violation of their duty and if the creditors of the subsidiary are unable to obtain satisfaction from the latter (Section 309 (4)).

(b) Where the subsidiary company is a GmbH, these provisions of the Joint Stock Companies Act do not apply. But the courts have tried to establish some law appropriate for groups of enterprises. According to their line of decisions, a parent company holding the majority of shares of the subsidiary (GmbH) has a duty of loyalty towards the GmbH. If it breaches that duty, e.g., by giving the GmbH disadvantageous directives, it becomes liable in damages to the minority of shareholders.

Source: OECD, 1990.

Despite those changes, the concept of limited liability of entities within a corporate group is firmly established in law. As a result, public opinion and corporate goodwill may well turn out to be the driving forces behind a greater acceptance by parent firms of some responsibility for their affiliates.

D. Public opinion and corporate good will

Transnational corporations are in business chiefly to earn profits for their shareholders. However, a TNC recognizes the need to be a responsible member of the society in which it operates. Such social responsibility therefore involves more than conformity with the minimum requirements of the law. It implies the acceptance of a "moral imperative" to recognize duties and obligations arising from a TNC's relationship with creditors, suppliers, customers, employees and society at large. Much of the debate about the responsibility of parent firms turns on this question of balance between what is a legal requirement and what the public perceives as a moral obligation. It is not unusual for parent firms to accept a moral obligation while denying legal responsibility.

For example, although neither Union Carbide Corporation in the United States, nor Union Carbide India, Ltd. admitted "legal" guilt for the Bhopal disaster in 1984, Union Carbide Corporation undertook various self-imposed relief measures of an immediate and long-term nature. Its staff visited Bhopal. It sent medical relief teams and supplied medicine and equipment. Its long-term relief efforts were aimed at meeting the health and welfare needs of the survivors. Union Carbide offered to build dwellings, job training centres and schools. The company contributed $1 million to the Victims' Relief Fund (Wilcox, Ault and Agee, 1986, p. 386).

In increasingly global markets, a substantial change in the reputation of an affiliate can significantly affect (for better or worse) the reputation of the parent firm. In the public's mind, the business of a parent company and that of its affiliates is one and the same. For their part, TNCs recognize the potential danger of ignoring such perceptions, so they sometimes translate social or moral responsibility into financial responsibility. Even though they have refused to accept legal responsibility for the actions of their affiliates, they have been actively involved in out-of-court settlements of lawsuits brought against these affiliates, especially in cases concerning environmental catastrophes. For instance, Union Carbide's management said after the Bhopal disaster that a "quick and fair settlement of the legal claims of the victims would serve the company's [Union Carbide's] needs far better than prolonged and expensive litigation" (Trotter, Day and Love, 1989, p. 445).

E. Conclusions

In analysing issues related to group or parental responsibilities, two fundamental factors must be taken into account. First, any proposal for changes in the traditional approach, if they are to be workable and generally acceptable, would have to deal not just with the question of whether a single economic entity really exists; it would also have to consider the extent to which TNCs themselves would benefit from new legal concepts. Transnational corporations have to judge when courts in different countries would impose liability on the parent firm, or on the group, or on neither of them. With a more consistent body of law, their ability to make that judgement might well improve.

The second fundamental factor to keep in mind is that any change must be influenced by the objectives of different areas of the law. Wholesale change could do a great disservice to the issue of corporate liability. The law in action does not deal with problems in terms of a universal conceptualized doctrine. On the contrary, in every field of the law there has to be a separate determination of what best serves its particular objectives.

The increasingly integrated nature of international production might result in a growing number of laws based on enterprise or group concepts. If and when that occurs, the change would inevitably differ from jurisdiction to jurisdiction. That, in turn, could lead to an increase in the conflicting requirements being imposed on TNCs by States—conflicts which international law is currently ill-equipped to handle.

It may be useful, therefore, if those countries already experimenting with aspects of enterprise law and group liability would cooperate in those areas of law where some uniformity is possible. For example, it should be possible to secure common approaches towards such matters as antitrust regulations and provisions for disclosure of information; and common accounting principles and regulations for environmental protection could also be feasible. Given the complexity of the issues involved, considerably more research is needed on the impact of integrated international production on parent-affiliate relations. In the meantime, in those cases that society deems especially deserving, public opinion and corporate goodwill may bring about solutions very akin to international solutions.

Notes

1 The French Bankruptcy Act of 1967 has more far-reaching implications. According to Article 99 of this Act, a parent company that has, in fact, assumed the management of an affiliate can be held accountable for the difference between the assets and debts of the affiliate unless it can prove that it has applied the care of a diligent manager (reversal of the burden of proof). Furthermore, under Article 101 of the Act, which confirms an earlier judicial practice, courts may extend the affiliate's bankruptcy to the parent company if the latter has abused the bankrupt enterprise as a cloak or facade for conducting its own operations or abusively disposed of the affiliate's assets. In Belgium and Italy, case law provides for a similar approach. In the United States, the law invalidates *all* transfers to "insiders" (including all affiliated companies) made within one year of bankruptcy, whether or not the individual case represents any thing otherwise unfair or prejudicial to creditors. For example, this extends to repayments of intercompany indebtedness representing cash advanced and fully recorded and disclosed.

2 See, e.g., "Inspector calls Indian plant below U.S. standard", *The New York Times*, 12 December 1984; "Union Carbide admits problems were known", *Manchester Guardian*, 16 December 1984.

3 In proposing "multinational management responsibility", Westbrook argued: "Whenever a difficult choice is presented, it is natural to look for an accommodating resolution between the poles. One that might be suggested by the Bhopal tragedy would be a theory of "multinational management responsibility". The idea would be to impose a legal duty upon multinationals to manage their subsidiaries—at least those in emerging countries—in accordance with some standard of responsible international investment and management. The duty would include responsibility for training and supervising local management and providing regularly updated technology, at least that technology which is related to safety" (Westbrook, 1985, p. 326).

CHAPTER X

TAX POLICY

In designing a tax system, a Government needs to ensure that it maintains its revenue base while providing a favourable climate for business and investment. That principle also applies to international investment and the taxation of transnational corporations (TNCs), which is the subject of the present chapter. The adoption of different tax systems by Governments may result in the imposition of conflicting tax assessments on TNCs for the same transactions. Ultimately, it can result in double taxation. Both Governments and enterprises therefore have a common interest in devising workable solutions to these issues.

Because of the growth of foreign direct investment (FDI) and the activities of TNCs, an increasing number of transactions in the value-added chain takes place within groups of associated companies in different countries. This raises complex questions about *where* taxable income is *earned* by groups of associated enterprises, ***how*** it is *distributed* among entities located in different countries, and *how* the revenue from taxes imposed on such income is *allocated* among countries.

Those problems are not new, but they matter more and they have become more complex. As long as intra-firm transactions took place in a domestic context only, they could be handled by the same tax authority. When firms acquired control of value-adding activities abroad, more than one tax jurisdiction was affected. But as long as foreign affiliates were stand-alone facilities, it was still relatively simple to judge the tax liability of a TNC and where it arose.

The picture is becoming considerably more complicated with the rise of integrated international production and the growing share of international activities in the total output of firms. The stand-alone nature of foreign affiliates is giving way to an intricate division of labour where a foreign affiliate might not be viable on its own, precisely because it is a specialized unit in a larger transnational system. In addition, linkages are becoming stronger not only between parents and foreign affiliates, but also among affiliates, and the range of linkages has expanded significantly to include various service functions (including research and development).

All these changes make it increasingly difficult to apply the traditional methods of determining where income has been generated and how it should be allocated among the various parts of a corporate system. As in any team effort, the precise contribution of each member is often hard to pin down.

A. Problems of allocating business income

1. The traditional approach

The development of conventional approaches, standards and methods to deal with the international allocation of business income (both by individual States and in international model conventions) began in the 1920s (Langbein, 1986). Since then, successive model conventions for the avoidance of double taxation of income and capital have embodied the conventional approach (United Nations, 1979). At present, the conventions most followed by States are the United Nations Model Double Taxation Convention Between Developed and Developing Countries of 1979 (United Nations, 1980) and the OECD Model Tax Convention on Income and Capital, revised in 1992 (OECD, 1992b). Model conventions deal with the allocation of all types of income[1] and, more generally, with the question of the jurisdictional rights of States to tax (a) income originating within their territories (source or *situs* income) and (b) income of corporations domiciled within their territorial jurisdiction (residence income). The State of residence is generally considered to have jurisdiction to tax the world-wide business income of resident corporations; the source State is normally allowed to tax investment income and income from business conducted in that State through a permanent establishment (e.g., a branch). Consequently, on the basis of the residence principle, the business profits of a foreign affiliate are taxed by the State in which that affiliate is resident (e.g., has its main place of effective management), while, on the basis of the source principle, the profits of a foreign branch are taxed by the country where the branch is located.

In both cases, the conventional approach has been the same: to treat the parent firm and its foreign affiliates or branches as separate and independent enterprises. Accordingly, when a TNC carries out business through a foreign affiliate or branch, the profits attributed to that affiliate or branch are those that it might be expected to make if it were a separate enterprise engaged in the same or similar activities under similar conditions and dealing with the parent on a wholly independent basis. In determining the net taxable profits of such a foreign affiliate or branch, expenses incurred for its benefit (wherever they arise) are frequently allowed as deductions.[2] In the case of a branch, in so far as it has been customary for States to determine its attributable profits by apportioning the total profits of the enterprise, the model conventions uphold that practice, provided that the results are consistent with the overall arm's-length approach.[3]

The arm's-length standard was applied to transactions between related or associated enterprises: for tax purposes, they were to be treated in the same way as similar transactions between independent parties.[4] Indeed, that standard was generally considered to be appropriate for determining the allocation of taxable income for any transaction involving related or unrelated parties (Langbein, 1986; United Nations, 1979; OECD, 1979, 1984, 1992b).

This approach was complemented by measures to protect a corporation from being taxed twice for the same income. This could arise when, for example, an allocation of income made by a TNC or by the tax authority in one country was not recognized for foreign tax purposes. Governments therefore concluded bilateral treaties for the avoidance of double taxation. Those treaties were intended to balance the resulting distribution of revenue between the source country and the residence country. They prescribe common definitions and standards, as well as foreign tax credits, withholding taxes on investment income (i.e., dividends, interest, royalties), tax exemptions, tax sparing and other adjustments. They also provide mutual agreement procedures for resolving discrepancies between tax authorities (see below).

All these standards were introduced at a time when cross-border trade between unrelated parties was the main form of international economic activity, and TNCs were hierarchical organizations firmly rooted in particular countries. The standards were devised for a classic organizational and operational structure and strategy used by TNCs, in which a single parent controlled some largely autonomous foreign affiliates in two or more countries. Most of the elements of the value-added chain of its output were the responsibility of the stand-alone affiliate. For tax purposes, those activities would normally be treated as its production costs, which could be deducted from gross earnings to arrive at its income-tax base.

2. Methods for allocating income under the arm's-length standard[5]

In practice, units of the same TNC have more flexibility than their independent counterparts to enter into arrangements that differ from those that would have prevailed between independent parties. They share a common interest, are part of a common governance structure, and their arrangements may be changed according to the overall strategy of the TNC. As a result, tax authorities have had to develop some tests to establish whether related-party transactions conform with arm's-length standards.

One obvious test is to compare transactions between related parties with similar transactions between unrelated parties. Where direct comparisons are not feasible, other tests were developed (OECD, 1979):[6]

- The *resale price method*. This can be useful for transactions that do not involve substantial value added. The costs and appropriate profit margins are subtracted from the final selling price to arrive at the appropriate allocation of income.

- The *cost plus method*. This is favoured for certain assembly or other value-added production. An appropriate profit margin is added to the initial cost of the goods and services involved.

In addition, a method has been developed known as "*safe harbour*". This is appropriate in situations where the use of a range of arm's-length prices is indicated. It permits tax authorities to establish in advance a methodology for determining a range of profits and costs that would be considered within acceptable arm's-length limits. They then agree to accept allocations made by the taxpayer which fall within the set range. That method can significantly reduce administrative burdens and can give the corporation a higher degree of predictability about its tax liability.[7]

(a) Transfer-of-technology transactions

In principle, the arm's-length standard is applied to transactions involving tangibles, intangibles and services, and the methods described above to varying degrees might be used for all three types. However, those transactions involving a transfer of technology—patents, know-how, industrial designs, trade marks, copyrights etc.—have presented particular difficulties (OECD, 1979, ch. III). They are often the result of research-and-development activities undertaken by one, some or all of the associated corporations within a group, in a process that may require heavy spending over a long period, with uncertain results and considerable risks. If and when research-and-development projects become commercially profitable, there are various ways in which a TNC may seek to recover those costs.

One way is to make the technology available to related parties by intra-firm licensing arrangements. The research-and-development costs of producing an intangible asset can then be offset against the profits of making the patent or know-how available. For tax purposes, these transactions are usually treated in the same way as similar transactions between independent enterprises operating at arm's length. To allow a deduction, the tax authorities normally require that the transaction confers a real benefit to the paying company. They may accept the payment of a fee or royalty based on the output, sales or profits (or similar variables) of the user, provided such arrangements are usual among independent parties. Sometimes a TNC might want to include a technology charge in the price of the sale of unfinished products. In those cases, if it can be assumed that a payment for an unfinished product includes a licensing charge, additional payments for royalties would normally be disallowed by the licensee's jurisdiction. In arriving at the appropriate allocation of costs/profits, the tax authorities will take various factors and special circumstances into account, such as the nature of the patent and the length of time it is likely to maintain its value.

Another form of financing research and development is for the parent TNC to make cost-contribution arrangements with its foreign affiliates. In some cases, the members of the group undertake to share the actual costs and the risks involved. In return, each is entitled to a share of any results. In another type of arrangement, the participants simply pay a fee, the costs are borne by the enterprise doing the research work, and the results are made available to all the contributors. The fees they pay might be related to sales turnover, or to the use of the product developed. Following observations from the OECD (OECD, 1979, ch. III), some countries (e.g., Canada and the United States—see Tang, 1993) have adopted special rules for cost-sharing arrangements. Under certain conditions, enterprises involved in these arrangements are allowed to deduct the actual costs of research and development incurred. However, this approach requires the tax authorities to ensure that the party seeking the deduction has a real interest in, and potential benefit from, the results of the effort.

(b) Payments for intra-firm services

Additional difficulties arise in determining the value and allocation of costs for certain services performed within a group of companies for the benefit of the group as a whole. In some TNCs, technical services are provided to individual companies in connection with new processes or products, or the improvement of existing ones. In others, administrative services might be provided in connection with employment, training, payroll, accounting, auditing, sales control, cash management etc.. In addition, services relating to the role of the parent company as a shareholder, such as annual meetings, distribution of dividends, annual reports and so on, are typically performed by the parent company.

For certain types of services, members of a TNC would normally be charged a fee. The tax authorities would usually agree, provided a real benefit accrues to the paying company. The generally accepted standard is familiar: that prices for services performed between related parties should be those that would be paid between independent companies acting at arm's length (United Nations, 1979; OECD, 1979, 1984). When using cost methods, the arm's-length charge usually includes the direct cost to the supplier of the services, and at least a part of the indirect costs. In certain cases, a profit element may be added. But if the services rendered are an integral part of the business activity of either the supplier or the recipient, the arm's-length charge typically includes a profit element.[8] Services are normally considered an integral part of a firm's business activity if, for example, it performs similar services for unrelated parties, or the provider is peculiarly capable of supplying the services and they are a principal element in the operations of the recipient.

* * * * *

In deciding how to allocate business income in transactions between associated enterprises, most countries use the arm's-length standard, although not all have developed it fully in statutory provisions. The most broadly used model conventions on income allocation also use the arm's-length standard, but do not endorse any particular method for achieving it. However, they may accept the use of a fractional apportionment method for expenses allocation[9] or, generally, if it is the "customary" method, in the context of the permanent establishment provisions.

As regards tax administration practice, "rectifications" are often made to the strict application of methods based on comparables, particularly when arm's-length comparators are not available. These rectifications often resort to apportionment methods, and they may be supplemented by any other method that produces acceptable results.[10] Case law [11] from some countries, where the arm's-length principle has been formally adopted, also tends to deviate from these regulations by relaxing the conditions imposed on the use of comparable uncontrolled transactions methods and/or using alternative methods, such as the profit split (see below).

Lastly, the tax regulations themselves are increasingly embracing *ad hoc* approaches to the allocation of income. This indicates how difficult it is to apply the traditional comparable methods (OECD, 1979). In broad terms, the tax authorities favour a separate-enterprises approach when comparable prices are available; otherwise they tend to use other methods, including apportionment, that look at two or more companies in the TNC system as an economic unit, at least as a cross-check to ensure that the comparable methods have produced the arm's length results.

The allocation of costs and profits between related parties across borders is an area particularly prone to double taxation. Model conventions and bilateral treaties provide that tax authorities make corresponding adjustments to correct their discrepancies. To resolve any potential disagreements between tax authorities relating to these adjustments, the conventions and the treaties have devised the "mutual agreement procedure" to help tax authorities reach satisfactory solutions.[12] Some of these aspects are further discussed in the next sections.

B. Income allocation in an integrated international production system

As corporate activities become more internationally integrated, some of the traditional approaches to taxing TNC profits become increasingly inadequate. It is harder to find comparable transactions taking place between unrelated parties, because a TNC's transactions are becoming more and more integrated. Similarly, when the transactions to be compared take place at different stages in the chain of production, or the volume of the transaction are drastically different, comparability with third-party transactions is seldom satisfactory.

Even where there is an open market for the products and services in question, factors such as the different locations where production takes place may influence the cost-profit ratio. Some activities might be more profitable in some countries than in others, because, for example, they are growing rapidly, whereas elsewhere they are mature; some industries may enjoy monopolistic or oligopolistic power in some countries, but are subject to open competition in others. Government interventions, in the form of subsidies, exchange controls, wage controls etc. will also affect profits and costs. In short, in an internationally integrated production network, it is very difficult to find true comparability.

Under those circumstances, the cost-plus method might be the most appropriate. However, even it must take account of some indirect costs that are not directly attributable to a particular transaction, but are part of intra-group activities. These, too, are increasingly difficult to allocate under conditions of integrated international production.

If it is hard to make all these judgements for the production of goods and services, the same is true for the allocation of research-and-development activities within TNC networks. Indeed, the difficulties are growing, because there is a trend towards decentralizing research and development while, at the same time, integrating it across affiliates and countries (chapter III). It is therefore far from certain which unit of the network has contributed what to the production of an intangible asset. Here again, the efforts of the group as a whole are more significant than any individual contributions. Under those conditions, for the costs of research and development to be allocated fairly, an additional test might be needed. It would look at the overall strategy of a TNC system rather than at individual transactions, and perhaps average some of the calculations in relation to the overall profile of the network.[13]

More and more TNCs are now providing certain functions, such as advisory, research and development, legal, accounting, financial management, and data-processing services, from one or a few international centres for the rest of the group. In other words, functions traditionally performed by the parent company can now be decentralized and spread over several countries. Thus, in order to reduce costs, a TNC might locate its data-processing activities in one country, its accounting in another, training for managers in a third, and group cash management in a fourth. In those circumstances, the challenge for corporate executives and tax authorities is how to value those services (which, as discussed in chapter V, account for a substantial share of a firm's value-added), and how to allocate the costs across countries. This is all the more difficult since the practice differs widely among groups of companies depending on the circumstances, structures and strategies of each group.

Those difficulties are compounded by the fact that associated enterprises may charge a single price for several benefits that are normally treated differently for tax purposes. In the case of the licensing of patents or know-how, for example, tax authorities may require profit charges reflecting fair market value; whereas a related-party service transaction might require only a cost charge. It is very hard to get adequate information and documentation on these issues from different countries. The risk of double taxation also tends to increase under conditions of integrated international production.

C. Alternative methods for dealing with the allocation of income

Although the traditional arm's-length standard remains the principal test in use, others are being used or explored which may be better suited to allocating profits in conditions of integrated international production, or may complement the traditional methods to ensure that they produce the arm's-length result.

1. Mutual agreement procedure

This method is not new; it was originally designed to avoid the risk of double taxation under double-taxation treaties. It provides a mechanism for tax authorities in two or more countries to discuss their adjustments and correct discrepancies. Since allocations of profits between associate enterprises under complex corporate strategies are likely to be adjusted by tax authorities, "mutual agreement procedures" have become increasingly important. Despite the obvious advantages of this mechanism over more formal arbitral or judicial procedures, it does have weaknesses. In particular, it compels the national tax authorities to discuss and negotiate with each other, but not to reach an agreement. However, in a growing number of instances, this mutual agreement procedure includes arbitration of tax disputes between competent authorities. For example, the members of the European Community agreed in 1990 to a convention that provides for binding arbitration in connection with the adjustment of profits of associated enterprises;[14] the same applies for the treaty concluded in 1989 between Germany and the United States.[15] Thus, there are possibilities for improving and adapting this established mechanism to the new realities (Langbein, 1986; Eden, 1985; Wickham and Kerester, 1992).

2. Advance pricing agreements

Another avenue explored in recent years is the possibility for a TNC to obtain advance agreement from the tax authorities on the methodology for allocating its profits. The agreement may be limited to specific affiliates and specific transactions. This is a significant departure from usual tax practice in most States, where such matters have normally been dealt with only in the framework of government audits, which may take place several years after a transaction has occurred. Some countries (e.g., Japan, the Netherlands, the United States) have legitimized advance pricing agreements in recent legislation or administrative practice, and encourage the use of such agreements.[16] To achieve consistency and avoid conflicting adjustments, it would be preferable, of course, that all tax jurisdictions concerned participate in the agreement. Critics of this approach (e.g., Wickham and Kerester, 1992) have argued that the up-front administrative costs for tax authorities are high and that they are affordable only for a few countries and for medium-to-larger TNCs.

For TNCs themselves, advance pricing agreements do have some disadvantages too. They require the firm to submit to an in-depth government review of their allocation policies (which foregoes, at least for smaller companies, the possibility that the Government might not examine those policies for a given year). They carry the risk that the methodology accepted under an agreement might adversely affect earlier audits. And they do involve considerable up-front costs. But this system also has certain advantages—at least for medium to large TNCs, which are anyway already being audited on an annual basis. These include the prospect of obtaining certainty of tax results in advance of transactions; minimizing the risk of double taxation owing to inconsistent positions taken by the countries in which the related parties are located; the ability to use the methodology developed in the advance pricing agreement as a basis for resolving open years; the reduced need for a tax reserve for government audits of profit-allocation practices; and the saving of time and expense (which could be considerable) that might otherwise have to be incurred to defend those practices.

The use of advance-pricing agreements can be helpful for both business and Government. However, given the large number of TNCs and the much larger number of goods and services involved, it is questionable whether that approach can become the predominant method used to solve allocation issues in the years to come.

3. Methods for allocating central management and services costs

For TNCs as much as for tax authorities, it is vital to be able to identify the suppliers and recipients of system-wide services, and to quantify the costs involved. To help in this process, in 1984 the OECD Committee on Fiscal Affairs endorsed a classification of the various types of intra-group services (OECD, 1984):

- activities of the parent firm as a shareholder of the group;
- activities clearly performed for the benefit of one or more affiliates;
- activities benefiting the group as a whole in various degrees.

This classification has become increasingly useful to deal with the new types of TNC structures. It encourages people to start by identifying what functions should be included in each of those categories. Once that is determined, the activities in the third category raise special problems over the allocation of income. For them, several methods are used for charging group members:

- charging directly for individual services;
- apportioning the costs to each of the affiliates (usually on the basis of a cost-benefit ratio);

- contributions in relation to the gross turnover or a similar formula; and
- including a mark-up in the prices of products sold to an affiliate.

In principle, tax authorities prefer the direct method. They consider that it is the easiest for establishing the arm's-length price, and it may reduce the risk of double taxation. For highly integrated groups, however, the indirect methods might be more appropriate. Such groups find it hard to establish how much should be charged, as the inclusion of a profit margin might not always be appropriate.

4. Profit-split method

This method has certain merits, one of which is that it is conceptually simple. Typically, the income of a TNC's various affiliates is shared out in relation to the functions they perform and the risks associated with them. This method is therefore different from the "comparable profits" approach, which looks at the profits of other independent enterprises (OECD, 1993). The difference between the profit-split method and the formulary apportionment methods (which have come to be called "unitary taxation") is that the former tends to focus on a functional analysis unique to the transaction. This said, the profit-split method may occasionally look at the profits of similar enterprises, at least as an additional cross-check.

5. Unitary taxation

One of the approaches to intra-group services that was pursued in 1984 by OECD was for costs to be apportioned according to a predetermined formula. The unitary taxation method (Langbein, 1986; Wickham and Kerester, 1992; Plasschaert, 1992) applies this notion to the allocation of business profits in general.[17] It rests on the assumption that it is too difficult to determine precisely what income is being generated by any particular affiliate and, hence, what should be allocated to it. Instead, a proportion of a TNC's world-wide profits is allocated to the taxing jurisdiction, based on the relationship of assets, payroll and sales (or formulae taking into account several combinations of them) of the foreign affiliate located within that tax jurisdiction to the TNC's world-wide assets, payroll and sales. In effect, this method pierces the corporate veil of foreign affiliates and treats all related affiliates as one corporation. Critics of this method have argued, among other things, that unitary taxation assumes that profit is uniformly related to all stages in an integrated production system and that production costs are the same in different countries; in practice, however, this is not so in the majority of cases. Also, if the operations of a firm in a unitary taxation jurisdiction are more profitable (more efficient) than the rest of its world-wide operations, the affiliate company would be likely to pay less taxes under that method than under a regular arm's-length method; conversely, if the local operations are less profitable (less efficient), the local company is likely to pay more taxes under this method than under the arm's-length method. In effect, unprofitable firms would be more likely to pay more taxes in relation to their real income than profitable ones. To avoid those distortions, a complex analysis would be needed of the different functions of the various associated firms and the different risks and profit opportunities at various different stages of production. Such calculations require complete information about all the activities of the entire TNC. In addition, a number of Governments and TNCs have argued that this approach runs counter to the internationally accepted arm's-length principle and exposes TNCs to double taxation.[18]

D. Some implications for tax policy

The more TNCs engage in integrated related-party transactions, the harder it is for them and the tax authorities to allocate profits and costs among firms in different countries. For tax authorities, the goal is to ensure that the State obtains an appropriate share of the revenues generated by TNC operations. For their part, TNCs want to monitor the performance of their foreign affiliates and avoid double taxation.

Both parties are therefore at one in wanting a "level playing field" for taxation. Both parties, too, want a system that is workable. For TNCs, a system that is stable, clear and simple may be preferable to a cumbersome or unpredictable one, even if their tax burden may occasionally be higher; after all, one helpful influence on international investment is the prospect of being able to predict with some certainty the net return of an investment. At the same time, Governments want to ensure that effective tax rates are competitive internationally, for otherwise this has negative effects on their ability to attract FDI.

With those general observations as a background, the following points deserve more attention:

- *Improving the methods for determining allocation of income and profits in accordance with the "arms's-length" standard.* Where intra-firm transactions can be compared with unrelated ones, the arms's-length standard continues to be a reasonable way to decide how an allocation should be made. The rules should be practical, should take into account how different TNCs actually allocate their profits and be flexible. The full potential of this standard has not yet been exhausted.

- *Alternative methods for the allocation of income.* Although the arm's-length standard remains an acceptable measure for allocating costs and profits across borders, it may suffer from the fact that market characteristics are often unequal. In those cases, or where the standard is difficult to establish because there is no open market for a particular product, it might be better to choose the profit-split method or some pre-agreed formula, including safe harbours. The safe-harbours method, which is still in an experimental stage, can reduce the administrative burden on both TNCs and tax authorities, and it introduces some predictability about tax liability.

- *Use of unitary approaches for allocating income between jurisdictions.* A method that treats the TNC as a unitary enterprise may be more in tune with economic realities than those based on hypothetical market prices. Apportionment methods may gain more acceptance, although, ultimately, such arrangements still need to be tested by reference to benefits obtained and, eventually, the arm's-length price. In any event, for them to be used effectively, they need to gain broad governmental acceptance and to be based on a universal formula. Thus far, the unitary method has been practised only in a very limited way.

- *Use of advance pricing agreements.* These might provide concrete advantages for Governments and TNCs in specific cases, particularly for larger TNCs. To be more effective, agreements should involve all the tax jurisdictions affected. But the use of advance pricing agreements might not be practical for developing countries because of the potential administrative burden involved in negotiating with corporations on a one-to-one basis; in fact, the large number of small- and medium-size TNCs may preclude this approach from becoming generally accepted. It should not be taken as a substitute for clear and transparent rules.

- *Strengthening international cooperation.* Since TNCs often face the risk of double taxation, internationally coordinated approaches could provide better solutions than unilateral ones. Perhaps more could be done to build on the coordination efforts of such organizations as the United Nations and OECD. The model conventions which they have prepared do provide the basis for tackling the problems associated with the allocation of income in an integrated international production system, but they could be addressed more explicitly. If a multilateral approach is not followed, the risk of multiple (not only double) taxation will increase. There have recently been several calls for multilaterally agreed approaches and standards (for example, in 1990, the United Kingdom invited the United States to seek multilateral, rather than bilateral solutions, to the tax problems facing TNCs—see Wickham and Kerester, 1992, p. 361).

- *Improving mechanisms and procedures for mutual agreement among tax authorities.* This approach is already included in model tax conventions and bilateral treaties. Despite the limitations of mutual agreement, it has been useful in reaching negotiated solutions on an informal basis. It should therefore be encouraged by Governments, which should consider compelling tax authorities to reach agreement, rather than just to negotiate.

- *Improving information and accounting systems.* Too little is known about the way the modern TNC operates. More research and disclosure are needed, and they should be complemented by efforts to improve and standardize accounting practices in different countries.

In summary, it is necessary to adapt the ways of allocating and taxing TNC income to take account of the growing integration of international production. This is certainly a challenging task for policymakers. It is easy for a Government to assume that it is competing against other Governments for a share of TNC tax revenues, but that conclusion is superficial. All Governments would gain if their tax authorities were to pool the information on TNC costs, prices and profits.

Notes

1 This chapter deals with the allocation of business income only. Consequently, other types of investment income, such as dividends, interest, royalties or income from immovable property are not discussed here.

2 See, Article 7 (3) of the United Nations Model Convention (United Nations, 1980), and Article 7 (3) of the OECD Model Convention (OECD, 1992).

3 Article 7 (4) of the United Nations Model Convention (United Nations, 1980), and Article 7 (4) of the OECD Model Convention (OECD, 1992).

4 See, Article 9 (1 and 2), United Nations Model Convention (United Nations, 1980), and Article 9 (1 and 2) OECD Model Convention (OECD, 1992).

5 The various tests and approaches for the determination of the arm's-length standard in related-party transactions were discussed at length in a report prepared by the OECD (OECD, 1979). The report was approved by the Committee on Fiscal Affairs of the OECD in January 1979. The Council of Ministers of the OECD endorsed the report and adopted the recommendation annexed to it on 16 May 1979.

6 The "comparable uncontrolled transactions" method was set down in the 1979 OECD Report as the primary method and has been widely recognized as having that status.

7 This method was not endorsed by the above-mentioned OECD report (1979).

8 It appears that a mark up over the costs is not taken into account in the majority of countries except perhaps in special circumstances (Langbein, 1986).

9 See Article 7 (4) of the United Nations Model Convention (United Nations, 1979) and Article 7 (4) of the OECD Model Convention (OECD, 1992).

10 Such an approach was recommended in the 1979 OECD Report.

11 See, Langbein, 1986, for a review of trends in the United States courts.

12 See Article 25, United Nations Model (United Nations, 1980), and Article 25, OECD Model (OECD, 1992b). For an in-depth discussion of this procedure, see OECD, 1984, pp. 9-40.

13 This approach was already suggested by the 1979 OECD report; see OECD, 1979, p. 62.

14 Section 3 of the "Convention on the Elimination of Double Taxation in Connection with the Adjustment of Profits of Associated Enterprises", 33 *Official Journal of the European Communities*, 19, L225/10 (90/463 EC) (of 20 August 1990). Thus far, only four member States of the European Community have signed this Convention.

15 Article (25) of the Treaty for the Avoidance of Double Taxation, Germany, United States, T.I.A.A.S. Treaty Doc. no. 101-10, 101st Congress, 2d. session (5 February 1990).

16 In the Netherlands, for example, the administrative practice for many years has been that tax inspectors are authorized to enter into advance agreements with tax payers about matters of interpretation of both law and factual circumstances. The tax courts have confirmed the binding character of these agreements.

17 For a full discussion of the unitary method, see also, OECD, 1979, 1984, 1993; United Kingdom Inland Revenue and United States Treasury, "Joint report: unitary tax, review of progress towards resolving the problems", December 1991 (London and Washington, 1991), mimeo.

18 See, United Kingdom Inland Revenue and United States Treasury Deparment Joint Report, "Unitary Tax, review of progress towards resolving the problems", December 1991, chap. 5, para. 5.4, which quoted the Appeals Court of California in *Barclays Bank International Ltd. v. Franchise Tax Board*: "every single nation in the industrialised Western world has sent letters to the United States Government protesting the use of worldwide combined reporting by American States and it took note of the United Kingdom's enactment of retaliatory legislation and the cancellation of several trade missions to the United States".

CHAPTER XI

INVESTMENT POLICIES

World economic interdependence today is increasingly production-based, not just trade-based as it was in the 1950s and 1960s. The change owes much to advances in transport, information and communications technology, and the liberalization of financial markets. Those advances also propelled the spread of transnational corporations (TNCs) which, in turn, have become prominent agents of integration. Today, TNCs in the largest home countries have internationalized their value-added activities and internalized the exchange of goods and services to such a degree that global sales of affiliates are considerably larger than exports in delivering goods and services to markets world-wide. In addition, the functional breakdown of the value-added chain is creating a new enterprise-level division of labour spanning national boundaries. Equally significantly, research and development is more and more carried out through intra- and interfirm technology networks on a regional or world scale (TCMD, 1992a, ch. VI). Increasingly, therefore, international economic transactions need to be seen from the perspective of foreign direct investment (FDI) (TCMD, 1992a, part III), and Governments have to adapt to this new reality. Some of the challenges for public policy were discussed in chapters VIII to X; here, the focus is on policies influencing FDI flows.

The tendency of TNCs to integrate their activities globally presents opportunities for a new pattern of production among nations. As discussed in chapter VII, the potential is considerable for developing countries, many of which are still marginal to world investment flows: two thirds of the recent expansion in FDI flows to developing countries went to just 10 countries (chapter I). However, the projections in chapter IV suggest that FDI in developing countries will increase substantially over the next decade. In principle, all of them have greater opportunities to attract investment.

New strategies are needed, however, to realize that potential. Many developing countries lack the range of locational advantages required by globally-integrated TNCs. Unless they correct that deficiency, they will be handicapped in the global competition for FDI, high technology and world export markets. Breaking this vicious circle should be a paramount concern for policy makers, at both national and international levels. How this could be done is the subject of this final chapter. It begins with a discussion of the convergence of FDI policies (section A) and then considers the need for more sophisticated policies by developing countries, going beyond the current liberalization trend, to more pro-active measures (section B). It concludes by considering the extent to which integrated international production extends the range of policies that may require international treatment (section C).

A. Competition for investment and the convergence of investment policies

A growing consensus holds that the benefits of FDI outweigh the conceivable costs of hosting TNCs (TCMD, 1992a). This has heightened competition to attract FDI. With the recent changes in Central and Eastern Europe, competition for FDI has become truly global. The regulatory framework for FDI is one tool being used in this competition. As more countries liberalize their FDI policies, they are converging towards common standards (box XI.1) which, in general, cover the following:

- Right of establishment;
- Fair and equitable treatment, including non-discrimination in the application of the law;
- Protection against nationalization (except under clearly defined conditions), and standards of payment of compensation;
- International dispute settlement, including arbitration;
- Assurances for the repatriation of earnings and capital.

These standards are often subject to various derogations and exceptions; but, overall, they characterize a new national approach towards FDI. Bilateral investment treaties further encourage such convergence, especially by stipulating many of these standards, in addition to national treatment. At the same time, the openness to FDI does not, of course, imply that TNCs are no longer constrained by national laws and regulations that provide standards for the conduct of business in general.

With FDI policy regimes converging, the remaining differences in these regimes exercise less and less influence on the locational decision of TNCs. Instead, the appeal of any host country to potential investors is determined by other factors. In an increasingly integrated world economy, the relative attractions of developing countries versus developed countries is of more and more importance. For many developing countries, that is stiff competition. It means that their Governments should play an active role in improving their economies as locations for FDI. Finding appropriate pro-active measures to attract FDI in an emerging international production system is one of the key policy challenges facing many developing countries.

B. Investment policies in developing countries

1. The new openness

The liberalization of FDI regimes has been part of a sea-change in the policies of developing countries, from inward- to outward-looking development strategies. In addition, the growing recognition that TNCs offer

Box XI.1. Namibia's code on foreign direct investment: a legislative example of the trends in convergence

On 28 December 1990, Namibia's parliament passed the Foreign Investments Act,1990. The Act provides for an open regime for FDI and covers the main issues that are often critical for investment decisions: establishment, national treatment, compensation in case of expropriation, international arbitration and the ability to remit profits.

The Act gives effect to three basic principles:

- There is no requirement for screening foreign investments. Apart from a few defined exceptions, a foreign national or foreign-owned company may engage in any business activity in Namibia that may be lawfully undertaken by a Namibian or a Namibian company;
- The Act guarantees national treatment for all foreign investors;
- For major investments, where capital expenditure is above a minimum figure prescribed in the Act and which are designed to be responsive to the economic and social priorities of Namibia, the Act offers special guarantees;

The Act makes clear that:

- A foreign investor would not normally enjoy any special rights or have the benefit of any fiscal or other incentives to which a Namibian citizen or a Namibian company engaged in similar business activity would not also be entitled;
- The foreign investor would be obliged in all respects to abide by the law of Namibia.

A foreign investor whose project may be eligible for special incentives may apply to the Minister of Trade, who will consider the case. However, such an investor has the option to invest without undergoing any approval test and would therefore operate under national treatment.

Those deemed eligible for special treatment are guaranteed foreign exchange availability for loans, and the transfer of profits or proceeds of sale of the investment. Although the Constitution of Namibia guarantees "just compensation" in case of any expropriation, they have the further guarantee that compensation will be made without undue delay and in convertible currency. They are also given the right to refer disputes, including disputes about compensation, to international arbitration.

When an investor has been granted special incentives, they will remain in force only so long as the firm complies with two reciprocal obligations:

- The investor is required to make specific proposals acceptable to the Government for training of Namibians and localization and then to implement them;
- The investor's plan for the investment itself are also set down in detail, and must be honoured, in accordance with an agreed timetable.

Source: Foreign Investments Act, 1990; Act No. 27; published in the official *Gazette of the Republic of Namibia*, No. 129.

a variety of benefits to a host country (TCMD, 1992a) has replaced various concerns with disadvantages potentially associated with TNCs.

In particular, innovation and technological change are now understood as powerful causes of economic growth and dynamic comparative advantage,[1] and TNCs are recognized as the main channels for technological change in many developing countries. Thus, government policy is geared more to capturing the dynamic spillovers of technology transfer, than to reducing its possible costs. Since joint ventures tend to involve less up-to-date technologies than do fully-owned investments, limits on foreign ownership have been greatly relaxed. The same is true of the ceilings on technology licensing fees. Similarly, since the possession of proprietary knowledge matters less than actually using it, Governments in developing countries are now more willing to accept legislation and enforcement of intellectual property protection.

In short, it is more important to host technology than to own it. But this goes along with another maxim: the greater the national ability to innovate, the more a country will be able to use imported technology. The building up of national capabilities should therefore proceed in an open policy framework. This applies particularly to services. Modern financial services, telecommunications, transportation and utilities are essential for developing countries, not only to bolster the efficiency of the wider economy and improve the competitiveness of the export sector, but to insert themselves into the system of integrated international production. Many developing countries have already responded by opening their service sectors to FDI (see chapter III).

Overall, outward orientation is becoming central to development strategy. In pursuing import-substitution, many developing countries used to allow TNCs to invest in protected domestic markets. In the future, developing countries will still want to host market-seeking (import-substituting) investments, but in an open, outward-oriented framework. This is already happening in Latin America and South and South-East Asia.

For most developing countries, however, the new openness and the liberalization of their FDI policies have not yet led to a substantial increase of investment inflows. Partly this is because freer FDI policies are not on their own enough to attract FDI. Partly, there are lags before investors respond to policy change—and, the more dramatic the change, the longer the lag. But the biggest factor is that the differentiating effects of policy regimes count for much less, as the general policy framework and the imperatives of economic factors become the main determinants for choosing where to invest. It is here that the role of Governments is important.

2. Enhancing national capabilities and competitiveness for foreign direct investment

The new openness does not necessarily imply a *laissez-faire* approach to the functioning of markets. Governments still have much to do to ensure that markets are established, and maintained efficiently. This may be particularly difficult when markets operate across borders and are thus affected not only by the decisions of buyers and sellers, but also by external factors, including the policies of other Governments (Dunning, 1992).

By assuming a pro-active role, Governments can help to decrease the costs of market deficiencies. They can remove any entry-barriers and other obstacles that raise transaction costs for TNCs. They can encourage the creation of tangible and intangible assets (e.g., infrastructure assets, technological know-how and organizational capabilities) that determine where TNCs invest. And they can affect the costs of research and development through training grants and tax exemptions, and stimulate domestic entrepreneurship through incentives and the provision of information. To do all this, Governments may need to change their own internal structure, from a hub-and-spoke system to a spider's web of relationships between the central coordinating body and the various ministries/departments (Box XI.2).

(a) The national enabling framework

Policies to enhance national capabilities must be framed in the context of sound macroeconomic policy and a credible development strategy. Social policies also matter, for they contribute to political stability. And Governments must invest in physical infrastructure and in education, training and health.

To put it bluntly, an efficient private sector is unlikely without an efficient public sector. In most developing countries, public institutions do not adequately support the functioning of markets or reward entrepreneurial activities. They must be restructured according to modern organizational and management practices. Governments also need to bring in modern accounting practices; allow for the development and deepening of capital markets, including an efficient banking system; and encourage an appropriate range of business services. With the current trend towards liberalization and privatization, the market-enabling role of Government and the need for functional regulatory regimes have become more, not less, relevant.

(b) Building linkages

Beyond general development, successful strategies for attracting FDI require the establishment of a virtuous growth circle between FDI, technology diffusion and market expansion. External ties can help developing countries become insiders in a global network. Strategies should aim at participating in global trading networks, at strengthening the links between domestic and foreign firms and at developing policies for attracting foreign firms.

Given the role of technological capabilities in maintaining international competitiveness, links with TNCs are particularly important to strengthen national systems of innovation. Government support for innovation has been particularly successful in Japan, the Republic of Korea, Taiwan Province of China and in Europe, where the "European archipelago of innovation" links research laboratories, universities and knowledge-intensive enterprises. Moreover, the European Community has extended its programmes that support and finance such networks to its less developed regions (OECD/TEP, 1992); a similar approach could be used to embrace developing countries.

There is also another kind of external linkage for Governments of developing countries to explore: their own TNCs. Outward FDI can have a number of benefits for the home country, including access to markets, acquisition of technology, training and, generally, exposure to the rigours of international competition (TCMD, 1993b). The liberalization of foreign exchange controls promotes FDI, as has happened in the case of the Republic of Korea and Taiwan Province of China. Since 1989, firms from the Republic of Korea need no longer obtain official approval for outward investments of up to $2 million; in the case of Taiwan Province of China, the threshold is $5 million per year. Both countries are now net foreign direct investors. Fiscal policies that stimulate

Box XI. 2. Governing the process of deep integration

Deeper economic integration may force Governments to reexamine their culture and structure of governance. Just as TNCs have adopted new organisational arrangements to promote deeper economic integration at the firm level, a similar response may be required from Governments to ensure the effective implementation and coordination of policy at the national level.

Existing Government structures tend to encourage a series of independent objectives, each pursued by an individual ministry or agency. These agencies compete with each other for available resources, whose allocation is ultimately decided at the executive level. This "hub and spoke" structure is illustrated in figure 1.a. By contrast, a more integrated approach implies a network of vertical and horizontal decision-making relationships between a central coordinating body responsible for the formation and outcome of broad economic strategy and individual departments responsible for advising on and implementing strategy, and ensuring the complementarity and consistency of a chosen strategy across areas. This "spider's web" structure is illustrated in figure 1.b.

Figure 1. Two kinds of intra-government administration[a]

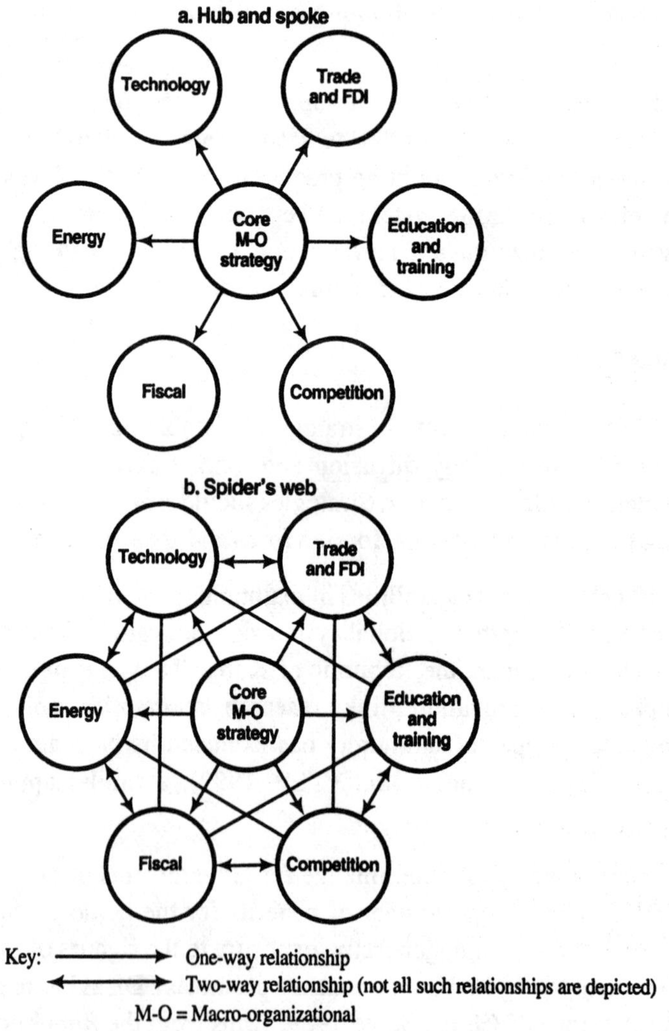

a These diagrams are for illustrative purposes only and do not embrace all areas of government macro-organizational strategy.

Source: Dunning (1992).

FDI from developing-country firms include concessionary loans, tax measures and insurance for FDI. For example, firms based in the Republic of Korea are provided concessionary loans of up to 60 per cent of the FDI amount (80 per cent in the case of FDI by small and medium-size enterprises). They can reserve up to 15 per cent of the amount of FDI for losses, and are offered insurance of up to 90 per cent of FDI against war, expropriation or restrictions on remittance.

(c) *Investment promotion*

Governments can pursue many approaches to attract FDI (FIAS, 1990; Wells and Wint, 1991; Encarnation and Wells, 1985; Lall and Streeten, 1977). However, all have a common goal: to convince TNCs of their locational advantages. This section identifies a few relatively specific measures that may influence the locational decisions of foreign investors and deserve more attention by policy makers. Since TNC strategies have become more complex, Government policies to attract FDI need to become more sophisticated as well. In particular, they need to take into account the emergence of an integrated international production system.

- Since the implementation of more complex strategies by TNCs means that all parts of the value chain are potential areas for FDI, Governments wishing to attract foreign investment should go beyond general, broad-based efforts and focus on particular functions (e.g., regional headquarters, research and development, accounting) for which they believe they have certain advantages. The measures adopted by the Government of Singapore are an instructive example (box VI.1).

- Countries must learn to market themselves attractively. Some of the best strategies for attracting investment have involved well-funded promotion agencies that use a combination of advertising, direct calling and investment missions. Those activities may best be done by quasi-government organizations, as in the case of Ireland's Industrial Development Authority, or by subcontracting those activities to private agencies, as Thailand's Board of Investment has done with Arthur D. Little, Inc.

- Government agencies should also monitor changes in the structure of FDI, in order to focus their promotion campaigns properly. They should be particularly aware of the growing share of services in the stock of FDI and the role that non-equity ventures play for many TNCs.

- Small and medium-size enterprises are increasingly investing abroad, and their needs are often different from those of large TNCs (UNCTAD, 1993g). They have often been neglected by Governments. As they generally invest smaller amounts than large firms, it helps them not to have to obtain approval if the investment is below a certain size (as in Mexico), or if minimum investment values are abolished (as in Indonesia), or investment requirements lowered (as in Chile and the Republic of Korea). More generally, measures intended to encourage *domestic* small- and medium-size enterprises can also attract their counterparts from abroad, as long as these measures apply to TNCs as well. Fiscal incentives in such countries as Brazil, Cameroon, Chile, Côte d'Ivoire, Malaysia, the Republic of Korea, Sri Lanka, Venezuela and Zaire favour smaller undertakings; so does access to credit in Chile and Singapore (table XI.1.).

- Many countries set up export processing zones as special areas, with favourable regulatory and administrative conditions. Typically, the Government also provides the basic infrastructure, including

Table XI.1. Policy and promotional measures to attract small and medium-size enterprises to host developing countries

Country	*Measure*
Brazil	Corporate income tax of 25 per cent for small and medium-size enterprises, as opposed to 30 per cent for other firms.
Cameroon	Investments with a more than 65 per cent local equity share and a value of less than CFAF 500 million are offered not only a 5 per cent deduction of import tax and duties over 10 years (which are also allowed for other firms), but exemption from capital tax, credit distribution tax, registration duties, company tax and the tax on industrial and commercial profits is granted over an eight year period.
Chile	A 2 to 4 per cent reduced income tax rate for small mining firms is granted; 20 per cent of sales are exempted from corporate tax for certain investments by small and medium-size enterprises in the southern regions. Firms with assets up to $750,000 are eligible for loans through a World Bank/Corporacfon de Fomento (holding company for state enterprises) programme. The minimum FDI level was lowered from $100,000 to $25,000 in 1986.
Côte d'Ivoire	Investments with a value of between CFAF 40 million and 200 million and local employees between five and 50 are offered tax incentives in more industries.
Indonesia	Abolition of the minimum FDI level in 1988.
Malaysia	Manufacturing firms of less than M$ 0.2 million in shareholder's funds and less than M$1 million in fixed assets are allowed a 5 per cent deduction from taxable income for five years and another 5 per cent deduction if they comply with the New Economic Policy. A 50 per cent tax credit on all expenditures on capital equipment is allowed as opposed to 25 per cent for other firms.
Mexico	Foreign direct investment by firms with less than $8 million annual sales, less than 500 employees and whose affiliates are in manufacturing, with net annual sales less than M$4.5 billion (as of November 1988, revised yearly) and export more than 35 per cent of output, needs no approval by the National Foreign Investment Commission as of September 1986.
Republic of Korea	The minimum FDI level was lowered from $0.5 million to $0.1 million in September 1980; in the case of joint ventures with local small and medium-size enterprises it was further reduced to $50,000 in September 1986. Tax incentives for small-scale operations by both foreign small and medium-size enterprises and foreign large firms (but, for the latter, the foreign equity share should be less than 50 per cent) in 74 industries (under six digits of Korean Standard Industrial Classification).
Singapore	Firms with less than S$8 million in fixed assets, that are at least 30 per cent local-owned and have less than 50 employees are eligible for a small-industries finance scheme by the Economic Development Board as of 1976.
Sri Lanka	Firms with less than SL Rs 0.5 million capital in issued shares are eligible for an exemption of corporation tax (it applies to both local and foreign firms).
Venezuela	Small and medium-size enterprises are offered tax and loan incentives without having to comply with the plan for the decentralization of industries (which applies to both local and foreign firms).
Zaire	Firms with a capital of less than Z10 million are offered an extension of duration of exemption from the income tax due on salaries paid to workers to five years in Economic Zone A or two years in Economic Zone B. Additional incentives are: exemption from the tax on revenues of capital assets, the tax on acquisition of land, and import tax and duties (which is also offered to other firms); deduction of expenditures on training of managers and personnel from taxable profits; and exemption from duties on capital increases, duties on registration and duties on acts to form a company or co-operative.

Source: Fujita, 1990.

factory halls etc. (UNCTC, 1990a). Although many of those zones have not lived up to expectations, some have been quite successful. Some may be gradually upgraded into science and technology parks.

- Governments can seek help from their diasporas abroad. A good part of the FDI in China originates from the Chinese overseas community. Expatriate managers and entrepreneurs often have a good knowledge of international markets and their requirements, which can be of great value to host countries.

- Governments can also make their countries more welcoming by cutting the transaction and "hassle" costs that accompany any investment, especially in an unfamiliar place (Dunning, 1992). Measures could include minimizing the risk and uncertainty associated with FDI by encouraging the use of futures markets and of finance investment guarantee schemes; providing good international telecommunication services; supplying information, for example, with respect to FDI regulations and export markets; ready access to government agencies and reducing red tape; and helping in negotiating with clients or suppliers.

- In this context, more could be done about post-approval services, an analogue to after-sales services (Wint, 1993). In some countries, one-stop agencies are meant to provide such services, but they often neglect the post-approval side. Once an investment has been approved, TNCs typically still face various bureaucratic hurdles before they can actually begin production. Work and import permits need to be obtained, relations with financial intermediaries (including the Central Bank), have to be established, permission needs to be obtained to buy or lease land and telecommunications equipment must be installed. All this can take much precious time and thus obstruct the implementation of an investment project (box XI.3).

- Although the protection of intellectual property rights is, overall, not one of the main determinants of FDI, stronger protection is likely to boost the flow of FDI to some industries, such as pharmaceuticals, micro-electronics and the copyright industries (TCMD, 1993f).

- Countries establish embassies to advance their *political* interests in countries of special political importance to them. Perhaps countries should take a similar approach to advance their economic interests regarding those actors that are of special economic importance to them. More specifically, countries may wish to make extra efforts to cultivate relationships with those TNCs that, for instance, control a substantial part of domestic assets

(d) Upgrading

Although FDI is concentrated in only a few developing countries, every developing country is a recipient of some FDI. In short, investment opportunities do exist everywhere—just as every country has some sort of comparative advantage (such as cheap labour or abundant natural resources). Moreover, market-seeking and export-oriented FDI is common in many developing countries.

Much of this FDI, however, offers limited technology and skills, which must be upgraded along the value chain. For example, mining can be upgraded into processing; labour-intensive inputs and offshore assembly can be upgraded into component sourcing; and market-seeking FDI can be upgraded from trading and marketing to assembly of subcomponents, or full assembly and even production of complete product lines for domestic and world markets (Eden, 1991). Although traditional FDI is not insignificant, the big new flows of FDI are along, or (in the case of integrated international production) cut across, these higher links of the value chain (see chapter III).

Few developing countries, however, have achieved a significant upgrading in the composition of their inward FDI (TCMD, 1993e). This is because international production is increasingly determined by factors that go beyond cheap labour and depend on overall national competitiveness. Consequently, a strategy for upgrading needs to combine policies that strengthen national capabilities with specific measures to encourage FDI of a higher value-added nature (box XI.4).

Developing countries have often aimed for particular industries on well-founded economic grounds, e.g., economies of scale, learning economies and externalities. But their targets have sometimes been obscured by demands for a shift of ownership, including direct expropriation. Nowadays, expropriation is far less likely than privatization (box I.1), but this new emphasis is not inconsistent with targeting. Instead, it should be taken as an

Box XI.3. Post-approval problems

Some investors have learned that, even as it is becoming easier to obtain approval to invest, it is not necessarily any easier to implement an approved investment. The following examples illustrate the types of difficulties TNCs often encounter:

- A United States service firm was interested in establishing operations abroad. Like many other countries, its chosen host had simplified its system for approving FDI projects. The company received approval for its investment within four months of filing the application with the Foreign Investment Department of the Ministry of Finance, which collects applications and sends them to the various relevant departments of the Government for their independent approval. Shortly after formal approval was granted, the company's managers went to another government department to obtain an operating licence. Since the company had already obtained approval to invest, and indeed it had already begun the process of shipping equipment to the country, it was expected that the granting of the operating licence would be virtually a formality. Instead, the Department questioned the approval that had been obtained from the Foreign Investment Department. It was only after many months, and the costly engagement of a local law firm, that the company was able to acquire the operating licence and implement its project.
- In another country, a United States manufacturing firm applied to the Board of Investment for permission to invest and qualify for incentives. The firm received permission to invest quickly—within two months of the submission of its application. To its consternation, however, it found that this was only the beginning. It had difficulty getting work permits for expatriate staff, getting permission from the central bank to import machinery and, once the equipment was imported, clearing this equipment through customs. One year after receiving approval from the Board of Investment, the project was still not fully operational. The president of the company said that its "problems began when its investment application was approved by the Board of Investment".
- A Japanese agricultural-processing firm seeking to set up operations in a third country received permission to invest from the Board of Investment. The firm was informed by the Board that the Department of Agriculture had been represented during the investment-approval process and that its project had the Department's approval. Shortly after the company began implementation of the project, however, its operations were halted by the Department of Agriculture. The Department said it had not been able to examine the project adequately during evaluation by the Board of Investment and that it now believed the project would harm local agricultural firms.

Source: Wint, 1993, pp. 76-77.

opportunity to establish more cooperative links between public agencies and TNCs. The approach should be to improve the basic conditions for business even if this is difficult and time-consuming. Countries that seek to rely excessively on a much easier way to attract FDI, namely, by offering various kinds of fiscal and financial incentives, are unlikely to realise unlikely desired long-term results (see section C).

At the same time experience shows that certain incentives work better than prohibitions (Bhagwati, 1988). In the past, many developing countries allowed FDI on a selective basis through licensing and quantitative controls. However, the more successful countries relied chiefly on incentives (particularly production, export or interest-rate subsidies), on moral suasion, and on improving the overall economic climate. In recent years, many developing countries (including the Republic of Korea) have revised their incentives to extend privileges to cover both domestic and foreign enterprises. For example, the Board of Investment in Thailand grants incentives to both domestic and foreign firms in promoted industries and/or areas. Although that approach has met with less success in Africa, the main lesson is that targeting works best in an open FDI framework.

Aside from the issue of how to achieve particular targets, there is the question of what they should be. Developing countries can still make special efforts to attract particular industries—in which they can reasonably expect to acquire comparative advantage; those with large externalities for the rest of the economy; and, perhaps those industries seeking large markets in neighbouring countries. But for many developing countries, the answer is still defined by their technology gaps. Governments often seek out producers of high-technology goods with the expectation of dramatic benefits from technology transfer. However, long-term benefits do not exclusively

Box XI.4. Upgrading foreign direct investment through public-private sector cooperation

Founded in 1976 as a joint venture between the Government of Chile and ITT, the *Fundación Chile* has overcome the learning hurdles of a promotional agency, and the initial distrust of the private sector. It is now a successful model of technological upgrading that complements the natural resource base of the country.

In its formative years, the *Fundación* had close links with ITT, and therefore ready access to the human resources, finance, technology and research departments of a large TNC. These represented a temporary advantage and the initial goal of providing service support quickly expanded into setting up new industries. However, the purpose of the *Fundación* has not been to establish and run an industry for its own sake; rather, it followed an incubator approach aiming eventually to sell facilites to the private sector.

One particularly successful example has been the establishment of a salmon-farming industry. Chile has one of the world's largest fishing industries, but most of the catch has been processed into low-grade, low-value-added fish meal. A small fresh-water salmon farm in southern Chile was acquired, renamed *Salmones Antartica*, and used as a pilot site. The *Fundación* tapped national and international expertise to choose an appropriate technology and solve the formative problems. In particular, it acted as an innovative centre to produce a high-quality fish-feed mixture using local resources. Following the success of the initial pilot, *Salmones Antartica* bought four new farms and expanded production to 400 tons by 1986-1987. The firm was sold to a Japanese processing firm, Nippon Suisan Kaisha, in 1988. The salmon-farming project has met a significant response in Chile. The number of new farms has expanded to create a profitable industry (Huss, 1988, pp. 110-113). In 1990, production had reached 5,600 tons.

More recently, and following the model established by salmon farming, the *Fundación* has initiated a project to upgrade the use of Chile's timber resources. It has already improved the information network to bolster technological and organizational know-how and raise product standards. Training schemes have been organized to ensure the upgrading of skills. A furniture factory was established by the *Fundación* in 1992, and it is hoped that the venture will have a similar catalytic effect on domestic and foreign investor's as did the salmon-farming project (Messner, 1992).

depend on the technology-content of the final product, but on the purchasing needs of the targeted industry in both product and factor markets. Upgrading, including through FDI, cannot proceed independently of existing technological capabilities and supply structures, but must embody a creative tension between inherited conditions and future market prospects.

In any event, Governments must establish and sustain a coherent strategy to promote the long-term competitiveness of firms within their jurisdictions (Tyson, 1992). The nature of international production implies that investment, technology and competition policy are best approached as an integrated package and employed in unison to strengthen markets.

(e) Policy integration

For TNCs, investment, trade, technology transfer and the movement of staff are often interrelated ways of expanding abroad. In fact, integrated production strategies typically require that each of these channels is open to a firm, depending on its needs and the nature of a market. Accordingly, a rounded and outward-oriented development strategy is indispensable if a country wants to become part of the emerging system of international production.

But more is required. In the same manner in which TNCs consider FDI, trade, technology transfer and the movement of technical personnel as interrelated, so too must Governments consider their policies in these areas as interrelated. In other words, Governments must reexamine each policy proposal for its impact on the other policy areas and its implications for the wider strategy; table XI.2 indicates a few interrelationships between FDI and trade.

Table XI.2. Policy interdependencies: the effects on foreign direct investment

Policy	*Effects on FDI*
Trade agreements: including free trade agreements and common markets	Encourages FDI for regional markets and promotes inclusion of TNCs in regional integration of production
Stable exchange rates	Encourages all FDI
Investment in physical infrastructure and human capital	Encourages all FDI and can be used to upgrade FDI
Tariffs, quotas, technical standards	Encourages market-seeking FDI, but restricts most other FDI
Tariff drawback schemes	Encourages labour-seeking and component-sourcing FDI
Prohibitions to operate in domestic markets, including restrictions on joint ventures	Restricts all FDI, but may discriminate heavily against FDI in the service sector and against TNCs from developing countries.
Visa requirements, work permits, import licences and domestic content agreements	Restricts all FDI, but particularly damaging to FDI in high technology industries, which use intangible assets
Full access to domestic markets for services producers	Encourages FDI in services and consequently all FDI
Preferential tax treatment for TNCs	Used to target FDI with desired attributes
Preferential tax treatment for TNCs with selected performance requirements	Used to encourage FDI upgrading
Export processing zones	Encourages labour-seeking and component-sourcing FDI
Export subsidies	Encourages labour-seeking, component-sourcing and resource-seeking FDI, but may discourage export-oriented FDI if subsidies are a substitute for needed currency devaluations or where retaliation is feared

C. International production, competitiveness and systemic convergence

The advent of global markets and integrated international production has direct consequences for competitiveness. In a closed economy, competitiveness is very much determined at the firm level. In an open economy (engaging in arm's-length trade), the competitiveness of companies is affected by the comparative strength of national capabilities. In an economy moving towards integrated international production, competitiveness of a firm depends upon the combined locational advantages of each of the nations in which it has affiliates. Consequently, the competitiveness of companies and nations is becoming increasingly interdependent. The previous section suggests that government policies to strengthen locational advantages can play an important role in attracting increasingly footloose economic activities. However, those developments also raise new issues for international economic management.

In such a world, it is very tempting for Governments to rely on fiscal incentives to attract FDI (table XI.3). However, such incentives tend to distort the functioning of the market and the flow of investment and trade. Moreover, they are costly for host countries (and put developing countries at a particular disadvantage), and they are not among the main reasons why TNCs invest. It may therefore be desirable to set some international limits to the use of incentives (box XI.5).

But more generally, as FDI frameworks become broadly similar among countries, economic factors and conditions of production assert themselves as the primary determinants for the location of economic activities. Integrated international production, therefore, shifts the level of competition from the trade and FDI regimes more and more to the level of all national policies and institutions directly affecting the production process. This, in turn, widens the range of issues that are within the realm of international discussions and negotiations (Ostry, 1992a).

Indications of a movement from a trade-based to a production-based regime are already visible in the negotiations over regional integration schemes. The obvious examples are the 1992 single market programme of the European Community, the Canada-United States Free Trade Agreement and NAFTA. All three began by seeking more liberal trading regimes, but have expanded into free production agreements, including various measures directly related to FDI. In fact, these negotiations suggest that a more fundamental "re-think" is required. In a world where FDI is more important than trade in delivering goods and services to foreign markets, where a sizeable part of trade itself is intra-firm and where TNCs are central economic actors, international economic negotiations need to be seen more and more from the perspective of FDI as opposed to trade alone (TCMD, 1992a). Finding the right policy framework to facilitate the growth of integrated international production will be a continuing policy challenge for many years to come.

Table XI.3. Investment incentive measures adopted by selected developing countries during 1992

	Type of measure		*Geographical scope*		*Coverage*		*Targeting to specific industries/activities*	
Country	*Fiscal*	*Other*	*Local/ Regional*	*National*	*Targeted to FDI*	*Domestic and foreign firms*	*Target*	*Untargeted*
Africa								
Burundi	x		x			x	Exports	
Egypt	x		x			x		x
Ethiopia	x		x			x		x
Malawi	x			x		x	Exports	
Morocco	x		x		x		Banks	
Tunisia	x	x	x			x	Exports	
Asia								
China	x		x		x		Exports	
Democratic People's Republic of Korea	x	x	x		x		High-tech	x
Malaysia	x			x	x			x
Republic of Korea	x			x	x		High-tech services	
Viet Nam	x	x		x				
Central and Eastern Europe								
Azerbaijan	Customs			x	x			x
Lithuania	x			x	x			x
Romania	x		x		x			x
Tajikistan	x		x		x			x
Turkmenistan	x	x	x					x
Ukraine	Customs			x	x			x
Uzbekistan	x			x	x		Industrial equipment	
Latin America and the Caribbean								
Argentina	x		x			x	x	
Peru	x			x			Mining	
Sao Tome and Principe	x			x				x

Source: UNCTAD, Programme on Transnational Corporations, drawing from various national sources.

Box XI.5. Incentives and foreign direct investment

There is widespread agreement that incentives are not among the key determinants of the total supply of FDI (Wells, 1986; UNCTC, 1991b). Moreover, evidence collected by OECD suggests that tax incentives are not cost effective, and do not produce an efficient allocation of investment (UNCTC, 1992c). Foreign investors are themselves acutely aware of the difficulties associated with investment incentives and often express reservations about projects whose potential profitability relies on host-country incentives (Reuber, 1973; Group of Thirty, 1984; Kerdpibule and Ramsetter, 1987).

There is also a persistent belief, however, that once a company has narrowed its choice of sites, incentives do count for some industries (UNCTC, 1991b, pp. 42-43). A World Bank study on incentives and performance criteria found that, in two-thirds of the 74 cases studied, the final decision on where to invest was influenced by incentives (Guissinger *et al.*, 1985). A study of the petrochemical industry (Gray and Walter, 1983) found that, although incentives were secondary to corporate strategic planning, in at least one case, in Belgium, the decision to invest was contingent upon an attractive subsidy package. Dunning's (1986) survey of Japanese FDI in the United Kingdom also found incentives to have a modest influence on decisions. In addition, unlike other factors, incentives have the advantage of being under the direct control of Governments.

Although there is some indirect evidence to suggest that subsidies were reduced between 1982 and 1989, many developing countries continue to favour incentive legislation. Moreover, for many industries in developed countries, incentives have continued to grow.[a] In the automobile industry, for example, the evidence from States within the United States suggests that the size of incentives required to induce FDI lies between $120 million and $325 million, well in excess of the financial capacities of many developing countries (UNCTC, 1991b, p. 74).

It is clear, however, that an incentive competition between Governments is very costly, particularly for developing countries, and can generate inefficient investments with disappointing results. If it goes too far, not even the "winning" country obtains a net benefit.

Reducing incentives requires cooperation among Governments. Efforts to date have focused on the regional level. In particular, the OECD has long sought closer harmonization of investment policies among its members, including the reduction of incentives to a minimum level. The European Community has also sought a ceiling on total incentive packages, while allowing for some regional variation. A reduction in trade-related investment measures as a result of the Uruguay Round will reduce those financial subsidies that might be punishable under GATT rules, i.e., those that can be shown to distort trade. However, once the Uruguay Round has been completed, there will still be considerable scope for further improvements.

It might be possible for host developing countries that have already reduced subsidies to domestic producers to extend this approach on a cooperative basis within a region. The need to disclose incentive measures fully and assess their effectiveness, as a first step towards broader harmonization, might also be best achieved at the regional level. As the experience of the existing schemes shows, international harmonization of incentives is a very difficult thing. But, given the limited effectiveness of incentives, their tendency to distort FDI, trade flows and the danger of an incentives war, a concerted effort in this area would be desirable.

---

a While figures from the benchmark surveys on United States FDI abroad for 1982 and 1989 show a decline in the total subsidies received by foreign affiliate from $1.3 billion to $1.2 billion, those in manufacturing rose from $947 million to $965 million over the same period. The share of total subsidies provided in developed countries rose from 73 per cent to 80 per cent over this period.

Notes

1 There is an extensive literature on the new growth theory. For a survey, see Grossman and Helpman, 1992.

REFERENCES

Agarwal, Jamuna Prasad (1992). Effect of EC 92 on foreign direct investment in developing countries. Kiel: Kiel Institute of World Economics, mimeo.

Alter, Rolf (1993). Foreign direct investment in Eastern Europe. Paris: OECD, mimeo.

Aoki, Akira and Dennis S. Tachiki (1992). Overseas Japanese business operations: the emerging role of regional headquarters. *RIM Pacific Business and Industries*, 1, pp. 28-39.

Archdale, Gilber (1992). World tourism organization report on CRS. *WTO News*, 7 (July/August), pp. 12-13.

Aronofsky, David (1985). Piercing the transnational corporate veil: trends, developments, and the need for widespread adoption of enterprise analysis. *North Carolina Journal of International Law*, 10, pp. 31-38.

Aspe, Pedro, Andres Bianchi and Domingo Cavallo (1992). *Sea Changes in Latin America.* Washington, D.C.: Group of Thirty.

Astbury, Sid (1991). Malaysia: making it big and fast. *Management Today* (December), p. 83.

Balk, Alfred (1991). Asia power: East Asia's power crescent. *IEEE Spectrum*, 28 (June), pp. 24-29.

Ball, G. (1970). Cosmocorp: the importance of being stateless. In *World Business: Promise and Problems*, C.C. Brown ed. New York: Macmillan, pp. 330-338.

Barber, David H. (1981). Piercing the corporate veil. *Williamette Law Review*, 17, pp. 371-404.

Basle Committee on Banking Supervision (1992). *Minimum Standards for the Supervision of International Banking Groups and Their Cross-border Establishment*, Basle: Basle Committee on Banking Supervision.

Behrens, Roberto (1992). Inversion extranjera y empresas transnacionales en la economía chilena: el papel del capital extranjero y la estratégia nacional de desarrollo. *Estudios e Informes de la CEPAL*, 86, Santiago: ECLAC.

Bhagwati, Jagdish (1988). *Protectionism*, Cambrige: The MIT Press.

Bidlake, Suzanne (1992). Nestlé adopts the personal touch. *Marketing*, 19 (November), pp. 24-26.

Bielschowsky, Ricardo (1992). Transnational corporations and industrial modernization in Brazil: results of a questionnaire administered to the largest foreign-owned companies in the manufacturing sector during November 1991/January 1992. Santiago: ECLAC (14 September), mimeo.

Blomström, M. and H. Norberg (1990). *Are Diamonds Forever? Botswana Facing the 1990s*. Stockholm: Stockholm School of Economics.

Blumberg, Phillip I. (1987). *The Law of Corporate Groups: Tort, Contract, and the Other Common Law Problems in the Substantive Law of Parent and Subsudiary Corporations*. Boston: Little, Brown and Company.

Buckley, Peter J. and P. Artisien (1987). Policy issues of intra-EC direct investment: British, French and German multinationals in Greece, Portugal and Spain with special reference to employment effects. In *Multinationals and the European Community*, John H. Dunning and P. Robson, eds. Oxford: Blackwell, pp. 105-128.

Buckley, Peter and Michael Z. Brooke (1991). *International Business Studies: An Overview*. Oxford: Basil Blackwell.

Buxbaum, R., and K. Hopt (1988). *Legal harmonization and the Business Enterprise: Corporate and Capital Market Law Harmonization Policy in Europe and the United States*. Berlin: de Gruyter.

Cable, Vincent (1988). 1992 and its implications for developing countries. London: Commonwealth Secretariat, mimeo.

Caflisch, L. (1971). The protection of corporate investments abroad in the light of the Barcelona Traction case. *Zeitschrift fur Auslandisches Offentlishes Recht und Volkerrecht*, 31, pp. 162-196.

Cantwell, John (1991a). Foreign multinationals and industrial development in Africa. In *Multinational Enterprises in Less Developed Countries*, P. Buckley and J. Clegg, eds. London: Macmillan, pp. 183-224.

__________ (1991b). The technological competence theory of international production and its implications. In *Foreign Investment, Technology and Economic Growth*, D. McFetridge, ed. Calgary: University of Calagary Press, pp. 33-70.

Caves, Richard E. (1982). *Multinational Enterprise and Economic Analysis*. Cambridge: Cambridge University Press.

Chandler, Alfred D., Jr. (1962). *Strategy and Structure: Chapters in the History of the American Industrial Enterprise*. Cambridge: The MIT Press.

Coase, Ronald H. (1988). The nature of the firm. In *The Firm, the Market, and the Law*, R. H. Coase, Chicago: University of Chicago Press, pp. 33-56.

Cowhey, Peter F. and Fonathan D. Aronson (1993). *Managing the World Economy: the Consequences of Corporate Alliances*, New York: Council on Foreign Relations Press.

Crumley, Bruce (1992). Ideally imperfect. *Air Transport World* (August), pp. 42-44.

Daoust, Didier (1992). Air transport liberalization: the European dilemma. *European Avianews* (September), pp. 22-23.

David, P. (1992). Knowledge, property, and the systems dynamic of technological change. In *Proceedings of the World Bank Annual Conference on Development Economics, 1992*. Washington D.C.: The World Bank, pp. 215-248.

Davis, Edward, Jeff Coates, Paul Collier and Steven Longden (1991). *Currency Risk Management in Multinational Companies*. New York: Prentice Hall.

de Andrés, Arturo et al. (1993). *Mondeo: The Story of the Global Car*. Luxembourg: World Publishing and Publicity.

de Maria y Campo, Mauricio (1992). Reestructuración y desarrollo de la industria automotriz mexicana en los años ochenta: evolución y perspectivas. *Estudios e Informes de la CEPAL*, 83, Santiago: ECLAC.

Deutsche Bundesbank. *Monthly Report of the Deutsche Bundesbank*, various issues.

__________ (1992). *Statistical Supplements to the Monthly Reports of the Deutsche Bundesbank, Series 3, Balance of Payment Statistics*, No. 4, April 1992.

Dicken, Peter (1992). *Global Shift: The Internationalization of Economic Activity*. New York: The Guilford Press.

Donogue, J.A. and Douglas W. Nelms (1993). Power and persuation. *Air Transport World* (May), pp. 37-38, 41-42 and 46.

Douglas, Susan P. and Yoran Wind (1987). The myth of globalization. *Columbia Journal of World Business*, 22 (Winter), pp. 19-29.

Dun and Bradstreet International (1992). *Who Owns Whom 1992, Continental Europe, Volume I*. Bucks: Dun and Bradstreet.

Dunning, John H. (1985). International business, the recession and economic restructuring. University of Reading Discussion Papers in International Investment and Business Studies, 88 (September).

__________ (1986). *Japanese Participation in British Industry*. London: Croom and Helm.

__________ (1988). *Explaining International Production*. London: Unwin Hyman.

__________ (1992). The global economy, domestic governance strategies and transnational corporations: interactions and policy implications. *Transnational Corporations*, 1, 3 (December), pp. 7-45.

__________ (1993). *Multinational Enterprises and the Global Economy*. Wokingham: Addison-Wesley.

Eden, Lorraine (1985). The micro-economics of transfer pricing. *Multinationals and Transfer Pricing*. Beckenham: Croom Helm, pp. 13-46.

__________ (1991). Multinational responses to trade and technology changes: implications for Canada. In *Foreign Investment, Technology and Economic Growth*, D. McFetridge, ed., Calgary: the University of Calgary Press, pp. 133-171.

Eliasson, Gunnar, *et al.* (1990). *The Knowledge Based Information Economy*. Stockholm: The Industrial Institute for Economic and Social Research.

Encarnation, Dennis and Louis T. Wells, Jr. (1985). Soverignty en garde: negotiating with foreign investors. *International Organization*, 39, 1 (Winter), pp. 47-78.

Ericsson, Magnus and Andreas Tegen (1993). The corporate structure in the international mining industry: the present situation and outlook for the mid 1990s. *Raw Material Report*, 8, 4, pp. 4-11.

Erzan, Refik and Alexander Yeats (1992). Free trade agreements with the United States: what's in it for Latin America?. *The World Bank Policy Research Working Papers*, 827 (January), Washington, D.C.: The World Bank.

Fahim-Nader, Mahnaz (1992a). Capital expenditures by majority-owned foreign affiliates of U.S. companies, plans for 1992. *Survey of Current Business*, 72 (March), pp. 43-50.

__________ (1992b). Capital expenditures by majority-owned foreign affiliates of U.S. companies, latest plans for 1992. *Survey of Current Business*, 72 (September), pp. 48-55.

Fatouros, Arghyrios A. (1983). Transnational enterprise in the law of State Responsibility. In *International law of State Responsibility for Injuries to Aliens*, R.B. Lillich ed. Charlottesville: University Press, pp. 361-403.

__________, ed. (1993). *Transnational Corporations: The International Legal Framework. United Nations Library on Transnational Corporations*. London: Routledge (forthcoming).

Feinerman, James V. (1991). Enter the dragon: Chinese investment in the United States. *Law and Policy in International Business*, 22, 3, pp. 547-569.

Feldman, Joan M. (1992). Complicated kinships. *Air Transport World*, 8 (August), pp.49-51.

Ffrench-Davis, Ricardo, Patricio Leiva and Roberto Madrid (1991). La apertura comercial en Chile. *Estudios de política comercial*, 1, New York: UNCTAD.

Flint, Perry (1993). What's wrong with the airlines. *Air Transport World* (May), pp. 58-59, 61 and 64.

Foreign Investment Advisory Service (FIAS) (1990). *Marketing a Country*. Washington, D.C.: FIAS.

Fritsch, Wilson and Gustavo Franco (1991). *Foreign Direct Investment in Brazil: Its Impact on Industrial Restructuring*. Paris: OECD Development Centre.

Froot, Kenneth A. and Jeremy C. Stein (1991). Exchange rates and foreign direct investment: an imperfect capital markets approach. *The Quarterly Journal of Economics*, 106 (November), pp. 1191-1217.

Fujita, Masataka (1990). Small and medium-sized TNCs. *The CTC Reporter*, 30 (Autumn), pp. 37-42.

__________ (1993). Small- and medium-sized enterprises in foreign direct investment. In *Technology Transfer to Developing Countries by Small and Medium-sized Enterprises*, P. Buckley et al., eds. London: Macmillan (forthcoming).

Gestrin, Michael and Alan M. Rugman (1993). The NAFTA's impact on the North American investment regime. *C.D. Howe Institute Commentary*, 42 (March), pp. 1-19

Ghoshal, S. (1987). Global strategy: An organizing framework. *Strategic Management Journal*, 8, pp.425-440.

Gialloreto, Louis (1992). Survival in Europe: strategy part 2. *Airline Business* (September), pp. 52-55 and 57-58.

Goldman, B. (1977). *Les entreprises multinationales. Annuaire de l' Institut de Droit International*, 57, vol. I, pp. 266-385; vol. II, pp. 192-263, 338-343 (reports, discussion and resolution).

Graham Edward M. and Paul R. Krugman (1991). *Foreign Direct Investment in the United States*. Washington, D.C.: Institute for International Economics.

Gray, Peter H. and I. Walter (1983). Investment-related trade distortions in petrochemicals. *Journal of World Trade Law*, 17,5 (July/August), pp. 283-307.

Griffiths, Michael (1992). Angola-peace opens up new prospect for investment. *Multinational Business*, 3 (Autumn), pp. 30-36.

Gross, Thomas F. (1989). Europe 1992: American firms blaze the hottest frontier. *Management Review*, 78, 9 (September), pp. 24-29.

Grossman, Gene and Elhanen Helpman (1992). *Innovation and Growth in the Global Economy*. Cambridge: The MIT Press.

Group of Thirty (1984). *Foretin Direct Investment: 1973-87*. New York: Group of Thirty.

Guissinger, S. *et al.* (1985). *Investment Incentives and Performance Requirements*. New York: Praeger.

Hagedoorn, John (1992). Catching up or falling behind: patterns in international inter-firm technology partnering. Paper presented at the Workshop on Global Trends in Foreign Direct Investment and Strategies of Transnational Corporations, organized by the United Nations, Transnational Corporations and Management Division and Centro de Estudos das Relacoes Economicas Internacionais, San Paulo, 3-6 November 1992, Sao Paulo, Brazil, mimeo.

Hagedoorn, John and Jos Schakenraad (1991a). The internationalization of the economy, global strategies and strategic technology alliances. *Nouvelles de la Science et des Technologies*, 9, pp. 29-41.

__________ (1991b). *The Role of Interfirm Cooperation Agreements in the Globalisation of Economy and Technology*. Brussels: Monitor Fast Programme. Commission of the European Communities.

Haigh, Robert W. (1992). Building a strategic alliance: the Hermosillo experience as a Ford-Mazda proving ground. *Columbia Journal of World Business*, 27 (Spring), pp. 60-74.

Harvey, C. (1991). Botswana: is the economic miracle over? *Journal of African Economies*, 1, 3, pp. 335-368.

Hebditch, David (1990). Opening up CIM Opportunities. *Datamation*, 36, 11 (June), pp. 111-113.

Hedlund, Gunnar, ed. (1993). *Organization of Transnational Corporations. United Nations Library on Transnational Corporations.* London: Routledge.

Henderson, Jeffrey (1989). *The Globalisation of High Technology Production: Society, Space, and Semiconductors in the Restructuring of the Modern World.* London and New York: Routledge.

Herrera, Alejandra (1992). La privatizaci6n de la telefonia argentina. *Revista de la CEPAL*, 47 (August), pp. 163-176.

Hill, C. (1992). Managing Commodity Booms in Botswana. *World Development*, 19 (September), pp. 1185-1196.

Hobday, Mike (1992). Foreign investment, exports and technology development. University of Sussex (November), mimeo.

Hoffman, Kurt and Raphael Kaplinsky (1988). *Driving Force: The Global Restructuring of Technology, Labor and Investment in the Automobile and Components Industries.* Boulder: Westview Press.

Hofstetter, Karl (1990). Parent responsibility for subsidiary corporations: evaluating European trends. *International and Comperative Law Quarterly*, 39 (July), pp. 576-598.

Hoole, Richard W. (1992). Manufacturing's new economics of scale. *Harvard Business Review*, 70, 3 (May-June), pp. 94-114.

Howard, Robert (1992). The CEO as organizational architect: an interview with Xerox's Paul Allaire. *Harvard Business Review*, 70, 5 (September-October), pp. 104-124.

Howelles, J. and M. Wood (1991). The globalisation of production and technology. *Commission of the European Communities*, Commission Dossier 2 (October), pp. 77-78.

Hu, Yao-Su (1992). Global corporations are national firms with international operations. *California Management Review*, 34, 2 (Winter), pp. 109-123.

Huss, Torben (1988). Transfer of technology: the case of the Chile Foundation. *CEPAL*, 43, pp. 97-115.

International Centre for Settlement of Investment Disputes (ICSID), (1992). *Report on the Twenty-sixth Annual Meeting of the Administrative Council.* Washington, D.C.: ICSID.

International Court of Justice (ICJ) (1970). *Barcelona Traction, Light & Power Ltd (Belgium v. Spain), (1970).* International Court of Justice Reports: The Hague: ICJ, p.3.

International Monetary Fund (IMF) (1988). *Direction of Trade Statistics, Yearbook 1988.* Washington D.C.: International Monetary Fund.

__________ (1990). Tax Policy Division. Tax policy and reform for foreign investment in developing countries. In *Taxation and International Capital Flows.* Paris: OECD. pp. 169-180, 191-195.

__________ (1992). *Direction of Trade Statistics, Yearbook 1992.* Washington D.C.: International Monetary Fund.

James, Harvey S., Jr. and Murray Weidenbaum (1993). *When Businesses Cross International Borders: Strategic Alliances and thier Alternatives,* Westport and London: Preager Publishers.

Japan, Ministry of International Trade and Industry (MITI) (1983). *Dai-Ikkai Kaigai Jigyo Katsudo Kihon Chosa: Kaigai Toshi Tokei Soran.* Tokyo: Toyo Hoki Shuppam.

__________ (1986). *Dai-Nikai Kaigai Jigyo Katsudo Kihon Chosa: Kaigai Toshi Tokei Soran.* Tokyo: Keibun Shuppan.

__________ (1992a). *Dai-Nijuikkai Wagakuni Kigyo No Kaigai Jigyo Katsudo.* Tokyo: Printing Bureau, Ministry of Finance.

__________ (1992b). *Dai-Yonkai Kaigai Jigyo Katsudo Kihon Chosa: Kaigai Toshi Tokei Soran.* Tokyo: Printing Bureau, Ministry of Finance.

__________ (1992c). *Dai-Nijugokai Gaishi Kei Kigyo No Doko.* Tokyo: Printing Bureau, Ministry of Finance.

Jenster Per V. and David Hover (1992). How to focus marketing intelligence to serve strategy. *Planning Reviews,* 20, 4 (July/August), 32-36.

Julius, DeAnne (1990). *Global Companies and Public Policy.* London: Pinter Publishers.

__________ (1993). Liberalisation, foreign investment and economic growth. London: Shell Selected Paper, mimeo.

Kasper, Daniel M. (1988). *Deregulation and Globalization: Liberalizing International Trade in Air Services.* Washington, D.C. and Cambridge: American Enterprise Institute and Ballinger.

Kennedy, Charles R., Jr. (1992). Relations between transnational corporations and Governments of host countries: a look to the future. *Transnational Corporations,* 1, 1 (February), pp. 67-92.

Kerdipule, U. and E. D. Ramsetter (1987). Foreign investment theories and policy issues. In *Direct Foreign Investment and Export Promotion: Policies and Experiences of Asia,* Seiji Naya, V. Vichit-Vadakean and Udom Kerdipule, eds., Honolulu: East-West Center (Resource Systems Institute), pp. 1-24.

Klein, Peter R. (1991). Global advertising: does research find accross-cultural effect? *Applied Marketing Research,* 31, 1 (Spring-Summer), pp.17-26.

Kline, John (1993). International regulation of transnational business: providing the missing leg of global investment standards. *Transnational Corporations,* 2, 1 (February), pp. 153-164.

Kobrin, Stephen (1991). An empirical analysis of the determinants of global integration. *Strategic Management Journal,* 12, pp. 17-31.

Konopacki, Ron (1992). Tips on working in a developing country and an Asian culture. *Industrial Management,* 34, 2 (March/April), pp. 2-3.

Kozlow, Ralph (1982). Capital expenditures by majority-owned foreign affiliates of US companies, 1982. *Survey of Current Business,* 62, 2 (March), pp. 32-36 and 64.

Krugman, Paul and Edward Graham (1992). The surge in foreign direct investment in the late 1980s: conceptual issues. Paper presented in the NBER conference *Foreign direct investment today,* Boston, 15-16 May 1992.

Lall, Sanjaya (1991). Asia's emerging sources of foreign investment: Hong Kong, Singapore, Taiwan, Korea. *East Asian Executive Reports*, 13, 6 (June), pp. 7, 19-25.

__________ and P. Streeten (1977). *Foreign Invetment, Transnationals and Developing Countries*, Boulder: Westview Press.

Langbein, Stanley L. (1986). The unitary method and the myth of arm's length. *Tax Notes*, 30 (January, March), pp. 625-281.

Langlois, Richard N. and Paul Robertson (1992). Network and innovation in a modular system: lesson s from the microcomputer and stereo component industries. *Research Policy*, 21, 4 (August), pp. 297-313.

Laviec, J.P. (1985). *Protection et Promotion des Investissements*. Paris: P.U.F.

Lawrence, Robert Z. (1992). Why is foreign direct investment in Japan so low? *Transnational Corporations*, 1,3 (December), pp. 41-69.

Leben, Charles (1977). Une tentative de perception globale: le recours a la nationalité des sociétés. In *L'Enterprise Multinationale Face au Droit*, Berthold Goldman and Phocion Francescakis, eds. Paris: Litec, pp. 187-235.

Lecraw Donald J. and Allen J. Morrison, eds. (1993). *Transnational Corporations and Business Strategy. United Nations Library on Transnational Corporations*. London: Routledge.

Levin, Michael (1991). How Asians invest in Asia. *Global Finance*, 5, 6 (June), pp. 43-45.

Levitt, Theodore (1983). The globalization of markets. *Harvard Business Review*, 61 (May-June), pp. 92-102.

Levy, Laurent (1984). *La nationalité des Sociétés*. Paris: L.G.D.J.

Lewis, S. (1988). Primary sector exporting countries. In *Handbook of Development Economics*, vol. II, H. Chenery and T. Srinivasan, eds. Amsterdam: Elsevier, pp. 1542-1600.

Lillich, R.B. and B.H. Weston, B.H. (1975). *International Claims, Their Settlement by Lump Sum Agreements*, part I. Charlottesville: University Press of Virginia.

Maljers, Floris A. (1992). Inside Unilever: the evolving transnational company. *Harvard Business Review*, 70, 5 (September-October), pp. 46-52.

Marton, Katherin (1993). Foreign direct investment in Hungary. *Transnational Corporations*, 2, 1 (February), pp. 111-134.

Maxcy, George (1981). *The Multinational Motor Industry*. London: Croom Helm.

McGrath Michael E. and Richard W. Hoole (1992). Manufacturing's new economies of scale. *Harvard Business Review*, 70, 4 (May-June), pp. 94-114.

McKern, Bruce (1993). *Transnational Corporations and the Exploitation of Natural Resources. United Nations Library on Transnational Corporations*. London: Routledge (forthcoming).

Messner, D. (1992). Shaping industrial competitiveness in Chile: the case of the Chilean wood-processing industry. In *International Competitivesness in Latin America and East Asia*, K. Esser et al. eds. Berlin: German Development Institute, pp. 33-65.

Ministry of Economic Affairs, Investment Commission (Taiwan Province of China) (1992). *Statistics on Overseas Chinese and Foreign Investment, Technical Cooperation, Outward Investment, Outward Technical Cooperation*. Taipei: Ministry of Economic Affairs.

Minor, Michael S. (1993a). Privatization: A worldwide survey. Paper prepared for United Nations, Transnational Corporations and Management Division, New York.

__________ (1993b). The demise of expropriation as an instrument of LDC policy, 1980-1992. Department of Marketing School of Business Administration, University of Texas - Pan American, mimeo.

Monczka R. and R. Trent (1992). Worldwide sourcing: assessment and execution. *International Journal of Pruchasing and Materials Management*, 28, 4 (Fall), pp. 9-19.

Mortimore, Michael (1991). Debt-equity conversion. *CEPAL Review*, 44 (August), pp. 79-96.

__________ and Torben Huss (1991). Industrial modernization in Mexico: results of a questionnaire administered to the largest foreign-owned companies in the manufacturing sector during May/June 1990. Santiago: ECLAC, LC/L.613.

Morton, Michael S. Scott, ed. (1991). *The Corporation of the 1990s: Information Technology and Organizational Transformation*, Oxford and New York: Oxford University Press.

Murrell, P. (1992). An antidote to shock therapy: an evolutionary approach to East European economic transition. The Woodrow Wilson Center, Occasional Paper 37, Washington, D.C.

Odle, Maurice (1993). Foreign investment as part of the privatization process. *Transnational Corporations* (forthcoming).

OECD, *OECD Economic Outlook*, Paris: OECD, various issues.

__________ (1979). *Transfer Pricing and Multinational Enterprises*. Paris: OECD.

__________ (1984). *Transfer Princing and Multinational Enterprises: Three Taxation Issues*. Paris: OECD.

__________ (1990). *International Investment and Multinational Enterprises: Responsibility of Parent Companies for Their Subsidiaries*, Paris: OECD.

__________ (1992a). Committee on International Investment and Multinational Enterprise. Feasibility study of a wider investment instrument: Note by the Secretariat. Paris: OECD, mimeo.

__________ (1992b). *Model Tax Convention on Income and Capital: Report of the Committee on Fiscal Affairs*. Paris: OECD.

__________ (1992c). *The OECD Declaration and Decisions on International Investment and Multinational Enterprises, 1991 Review*. Paris: OECD.

__________ (1993). *Tax Aspects of Transfer Pricing Within Multinational Enterprises*. Paris: OECD.

OECD, Technology/Economy Programme (TEP) (1992). *Technology and the Economy: The Key Relationships*. Paris: OECD.

Ohly, D. C. (1983). A functional analysis of claimant elegibility. In *International Law of State Responsibility for Injuries to Aliens*, R.B. Lillich, ed. Charlottesville: University Press of Virginia, pp. 281-319.

Ohmae, Kenichi (1985). *Triad Power: The Coming Shape of Global Competition*. New York: The Free Press.

Oman, Charles, ed. (1984). *New Forms of International Investment in Developing Countries*. Paris: OECD.

Ostry, S. (1992a). The domestic domain, the new international policy arena. *Transnational Corporations*, 1,1 (February), pp. 7-26.

__________ (1992b). The new international order: the regionalization trend. Paper presented at the International Conference on the New International Order, Rio de Janiero, 13-14 April.

Otaki, Shunichi (1992). Toyo Keizai Survey: Is Japan's overseas corporate expansion winding down. *Tokyo Business Today*, 60, 7 (July), pp. 30-35.

Ozawa, T. (1982). A newer type of foreign investment in third world resource development. *Internazionale di Scienze Economiche e Commerciali*, 29, (December), pp. 1133-1151.

__________ (1992). Foreign direct investment and economic development. *Transnational Corporations*, 1, 1 (February), pp. 27-54.

Park, William W. (1978). Fiscal jurisdiction and accrual basis taxation: lifting the corporate veil to tax foreign company profits. *Colombia Law Rebiew*, 78, pp. 1609-1662.

Perez, Wilson N. (1990). *Foreign Direct Investment and Industrial Development in Mexico*. Paris: OECD Development Centre.

Plasschaert, Sylvain, ed. (1993). *Transfer Pricing and International Taxation. United Nations Library on Transnational Corporations*. London: Routledge (forthcoming).

Porter, Michael E. (1990). *The Competitive Advantage of Nations*. New York: The Free Press.

Prahalad, C. K. and Gary Hamel (1993). The core competence of the corporation. In *Organization of Transnational Corporations. United Nations Library on Transnational Corporations*, Gunnar Hedlund, ed. London: Routledge, pp. 359-382.

Raghunathan, Sankaran P. (1992). Ownership strategies of multinational corporations: towards designing global networks. Philadelphia: Temple University, mimeo.

Rapp, Lucien and François Vellao (1988). *Airline Privatization in Europe*. ITA Studies Reports, 10. Paris: Institute of Air Transport.

Reich, R. (1991). *The Work of Nations*. New York: Knopf.

Reuber, G. (1973). *Private Foreign Investment in Development*, Oxford: Oxford University Press.

Rozas, Patricio (1992). Inversión extranjera y empresas transnacionales en la economía de Chile: proyectos de inversión y estratégias de las empresas transnacionales. *Estudios e Informes de la CEPAL*, 85, Santiago: ECLAC.

Rubin, Seymour J. (1973). Corporations and society: the remedy of federal and international incorporation. *American University Law Review*, 23, pp. 262-311.

__________ and Don Wallace, Jr., eds. (1993). *Transnational Corporations and National Law: United Nations Library on Transnational Corporations*. London: Routledge (forthcoming).

Rutter, John (1992). Recent trends in international direct investment. Washington, D. C.: International Trade Administration, U.S. Department of Commerce, mimeo.

Sacerdoti, G.(1989). Barcelona Traction revisited: foreign-owner and controlled companies in international law. In *International Law at a Time of Perplexity, Essays in Honour of Shabtai Rosenne*, Y. Dinstein ed. Dordrecht: Nijhoff, pp. 699-716.

Saghafi, Massoud and Chin-shu Davidson (1989). The new age of global competition in the semiconductor industry: enter the dragon. *Columbia Journal of World Business*, 24, 4 (Winter), pp. 60-70.

Sauvant, Karl P. (1990). The tradability of services. In *The Uruguay Round, Services in the World Economy*, The World Bank and UNCTC, Washington, D.C. and New York: The World Bank and UNCTC.

Schapiro, Alen C. (1989). *Multinational Financial Management*. Boston: Allyn and Bacon.

Scholl, Russell B., Raymond J. Mataloni, Jr. and Steve D. Bezirganian (1992). The international investment position of the United States in 1991. *Survey of Current Business*, 72 (June), pp. 46-59.

Secretaria de Comercio y Fomento Industrial, UNCTAD and UNDP (1991). *Mexico: Una Economia de Servicios*. UNCTAD/ITP/58.

Singapore International Chamber of Commerce (1993). *The Investor's Guide to Singapore: 1993 Edition*. Singapore: Singapore Chamber of Commerce.

Small and Medium Enterprise Agency. *Chusho Kigyo Hakusho*, various issues. Tokyo: Printing Bureau, Ministry of Finance.

Staker, C. (1991). Diplomatic protection of private business companies: determining corporate personality for international law purposes. *British Yearbook of International Law*, 61, pp. 155-174.

Statistisches Bundesamt (1991). *Statistisches Jahrbuch 1991*. Wiesbaden: Statistisches Bundesamt.

Stein, E. (1971). *Harmonization of European Company Law, National Reform and International Coordination*. Indianapolis: Bobbs-Merrill.

Steindel, Charles, (1992). Manufacturing productivity and high-tech investment. *Federal Reserve Bank of New York Quarterly Review*, 17, 2 (Summer), pp. 39-47.

Stern, B. (1990). La protection diplomatique des investissements internationaux. De Barcelona Traction a Elettronica Sicula ou les glissements progressifs de l'analyse. *Journal du Droit International*, 117, pp. 897-948.

Stopford, John. M., ed. (1992). *Directory of Multinationals*. London: Macmillan.

Tanaka, Tomoyoshi (1992). Japan's buildup in the EC: going strong. *Tokyo Business Today*, 60, 3 (March), pp. 12-15.

Tang, Roger Y.W. (1993). *Transfer Pricing in the 1990s: Tax and Management Perspectives*. Westport: Quorum Books.

Taylor, William (1991). The logic of global business: an interview with ABB's Percy Barnevick. *Harvard Business Review*, 69, 2 (March-April), pp. 90-105.

Thompsom, Grahame, Jennifer Frances, Rosalind Levacic and Jeremy Mitchell, eds. (1991). *Market, Hierarchies and Networks*, London: Sage Publications.

Thuermer, Karen E. (1992). Exports breathe fire on the little dragons. *Global Trade*, 112, 8 (August), pp. 34-38.

Tolentino, Paz Estrella E. (1993). *Technological Innovation and Third World Multinationals*. London: Routledge.

Toyo Keizai Shimpo (1991). *Kaisha-betsu Kaigai Shinshutsu Kigyo Soran, 1991/1992*. Tokyo: Toyo Keizai Shimpo.

Trotter, R. Clayton, Susan G. Day and Amy E. Love (1989). Bgopal, India and Union Carbide: the second tragedy. *Journal of Business Ethics*, 8 (June), pp. 439-454.

Tyson, Laura (1992). *Who's Bashing Whom?* Washington, D.C.: Institute for International Economics.

Unger, Kurt (1990). *Las exportaciones mexicanas ante la reestructuración industrial internacional*. Mexico: El Colegio de Mexico/Fondo de Cultura Econ6mica.

United Nations (1979). *Manual for the Negotiation of Bilateral Tax Treaties Between Developed and Developing Countries*. United Nations publication, Sales No. E.79.XVI.3.

__________ (1980). *United Nations Model Double Taxation Convention Between Developed and Developing Countries*. United Nations publication, Sales No. E.80.XVI.3.

United Nations Centre on Transnational Corporations (UNCTC) (1983). *Transnational Corporations in World Development: Third Survey*. United Nations publication, Sales No. E.83.II.A.14.

__________ (1986). *Transnational Corporations in the International Semiconductor Industry*, United Nations publication, Sales No. E.86.II.A.1.

__________ (1988a). *Transnational Corporations in World Development: Trends and Prospects*. United Nations publication, Sales No. E.88.II.A.7.

__________ (1988b). *Bilateral Investment Treaties*. United Nations publication, Sales No. E.88.II.A.1.

__________ (1989). *The Process of Transnationalization and Transnational Mergers*. United Nations publication, Sales No. E.89.II.A.4.

__________ (1990a). *The Role of Free Economic Zones in the USSR and Eastern Europe*. United Nations publication, Sales No. E.90.II.A.5.

__________ (1990b). *Regional Economic Integration and Transnational Corporations in the 1990s: Europe 1992, North America, and Developing countries*. United Nations publication, Sales No. E.90.II.A.14.

__________ (1991a). *The World Investment Report, 1991: The Triad in Foreign Direct Investment*. United Nations publication, Sales No. E.91.II.A.12.

__________ (1991b). *The Impact of Trade-related Investment Measures on Trade and Development*, United Nations publication, Sales No. E.91.II.A.19.

__________ (1992a). *Foreign Direct Investment and Industrial Restructuring in Mexico*. United Nations publication, Sales No. E.92.II.A.9.

__________ (1992b). *World Investment Directory 1992, volume I: Asia and the Pacific.* United Nations publication, Sales No. E.92.II.A.11.

__________ (1992c). *The Determinants of Foreign Direct Investment: A Survey of the Evidence.* United Nations publication, Sales No. E.92.II.A.2.

United Nations Centre on Transnational Corporations and the International Chamber of Commerce (UNCTC and ICC) (1992). *Bilateral Investment Treaties, 1959-1991.* United Nations publication, Sales No. E.92.II.A.16.

United Nations Conference on Environment and Development (UNCED) (1992). *Report of the United Nations Conference on Environment and Development (Rio de Janeiro, 3-14 June 1992),* United Nations Document A/Conf. 151/26 of 13 August 1992, volumes I, II and III.

United Nations Conference on Trade and Development (UNCTAD), Programme on Transnational Corporations (1993a). *Explaining and Forecasting Regional Flows of Foreign Direct Investment.* New York: United Nations (forthcoming).

__________ (1993b). *Transnational Investment and Operations: A Compendium of Multilateral and Regional Instruments.* New York: United Nations (forthcoming).

__________ (1993c). *World Investment Directory 1992, volume IV: Latin America and the Caribbean.* New York: United Nations (forthcoming).

__________ (1993d). *World Investment Directory 1992, volume V: Africa and Western Asia.* New York, United Nations (forthcoming).

__________ (1993e). *World Investment Directory 1992, volume VI: Global Volume.* New York: United Nations (forthcoming).

__________ (1993f). *International Cooperation Agreements and International Mergers and Acquisitions in the 1980s: Central Measures in the Strategies of Transnational Corporations.* New York: United Nations (forthcoming).

__________ (1993g). *Small and Medium-Sized Transnational Corporations: Role, Impact and Policy Implications.* New York: United Nations (forthcoming).

United Nations, Department of Economic and Social Affairs (DESA) (1973). *Multinational Corporations in World Development.* United Nations publication, Sales No. E.73.II.A.11.

United Nations, Department of International Economic and Social Affairs (DIESA) (1991). *World Economic Survey 1991: Current Trends and Policies in the World Economy.* United Nations publication, Sales No. E.91.II.C.1.

United Nations, Transnational Corporations and Management Division (TCMD) (1992a). *World Investment Report 1992: Transnational Corporations as Engines of Growth.* United Nations publication, Sales No. E.92.II.A.19.

__________ (1992b). *The East-West Business Directory 1991/1992.* United Nations publication, Sales No. E.92.II.A.20.

__________ (1993a). *From the Common Market to EC92: Regional Economic Integration in the European Community and Transnational Corporations.* United Nations publication, Sales No. E.93.II.A.2.

__________ (1993b). *Transnational Corporations from Developing Countries: Impact on Their Home Countries.* United Nations publication, Sales No. E.93.II.A.8.

__________ (1993c). *World Investment Directory 1992, volume III: Developed Countries.* United Nations publication, Sales No. E.93.II.A.9.

__________ (1993d). *Debt-Equity Swaps and Development.* United Nations publication, Sales No. E.93.II.A.7.

__________ (1993e). *Foreign Investment and Trade Linkages in Developing Countries.* United Nations publication, Sales No. E.93.II.A.12.

__________ (1993f). *Intellectual Property Rights and Foreign Direct Investment.* United Nations publication, Sales No. E.93.II.A.10.

United Nations, Transnational Corporations and Management Division and Economic Commission for Europe (TCMD and ECE) (1992). *World Investment Directory 1992, volume II, Central and Eastern Europe*. United Nations publication, Sales No. E.93.II.A.1.

United States Department of Commerce (1981). *U.S. Direct Investment Abroad: 1977*. Washington, D.C.: Government Printing Office.

__________ (1985). *U.S. Direct Investment Abroad: 1982 Benchmark Survey Data*. Washington, D.C.: Government Printing Office.

__________ (1992a). *U.S. Direct Investment Abroad: 1989 Benchmark Survey, Final Results*. Washington, D.C.: Government Printing Office.

__________ (1992b). *U.S. Direct Investment Abroad: Operations of US Parent Companies and Their Foreign Affiliates*. Washington, D.C.: Government Printing Office.

United States, International Trade Commission (1991). *The Likely Impact on the United States of a Free Trade Agreement with Mexico*. USITC Publication 2353 (February), Washington, D.C.: USITC.

Van Oldenborgh, Marita (1992). Riding the big Pacific rim boom. *International Business*, 5, 2 (February), pp. 36-42.

Vascianne, Stephen (1992). The PTA Charter on Multinational Industrial Enterprises. *Transnational Corporations*, 1, 2 (August), pp. 97-110.

Verchere, Ian (1992). Is CRS bias still a cause of concern? *Interacia Aerospace Review*, 47 (July), pp. 41-44.

Vernon, Raymond. (1971). *Sovereignty at Bay*, New York: Basic Books.

Wälde, T. (1991). Investment policies and investment promotion in the mineral industries. *Foreign Investment Law Journal*, 6, pp. 94-113.

Walker, H., Jr. (1956). Provisions on companies in United States commercial treaties. *American Journal of International Law*, 50, pp. 373-393.

Wallace, Cynthia Day (1993). *Legal Control of the Multinational Enterprises*, Hague: Martinus.

Warrant, F. (1991). Le deploiement mondial de la R&D industrielle. *Commission of the European Communities*, 4, Perspective Dossier 2 (October), pp.77-78.

Wells, Louis T. (1986). Investment incentives: an unnecessary debate. *The CTC Reporter*, 22 (Autumn), pp. 58-60.

__________ and Alvin G. Wint (1990). Marketing a country: promotion as a tool for attractig foreign investment. Foreign Investment Advisorty Services Occasional Paper 1, Washington, D.C.: International Finance Corporation.

__________ (1991). The public-private choice: the case of marketing a country to investors. *World Development*, 19, pp. 749-761.

Westbrook, Jay Lawrence (1985). Theories of parent company liability and the prospects for an international settlement. *Texas International Law Journal*, 20, pp. 321-331.

Wickham, Dale W. and Charles J. Kerester (1992). New directions needed for solution of the international transfer pricing tax puzzle. *Tax Notes* (20 July), pp. 339-361.

Wilcox, D. L., P.H. Ault and W.K. Agee (1986). *Public Relations: Strategies and Tactics*. New York: HarperCollins.

Williamson, Peter J. (1992). European Single Market: the toughest test yet for sales and distriubution. *Multinational Business*, 3 (Summer) pp. 57-76.

Wint, Alvin G. (1993). Promoting transnational investment: organizing to service approved investors. *Transnational Corporations*, 2, 1 (February), pp.71-90.

Womack, James P., Daniel T. Jones and Daniel Roos (1991). *The Machine that Changes the World*. New York: Macmillan.

The World Bank (1991). Privatization: The lessons of experience. Washington, D.C.: The World Bank, Country Economics Department, mimeo.

__________ (1992a). Annual Report. Washington D.C.: The World Bank.

_________ (1992b). World Bank Conference on the Welfare Consequences of Selling Public Enterprises: Case Studies from Chile, Malaysia, Mexico and the United States. Washington, D.C.: Public Sector Management and Private Development Division, Country Economic Department, mimeo.

_________ (1992c). *World Development Report, 1992.* Washington D.C.: The World Bank.

_________ (1993). *Global Economic Prospects and the Developing Countries 1993.* Washington, D.C.: The World Bank.

The World Bank Group (1992a). *Foreign Direct Investment in the States of the Former USSR.* Washington, D.C.: The World Bank.

_________ (1992b). *Legal Framework for the Treatment of Foreign Investment, volume II, Guidelines.* Washington, D.C.: The World Bank.

_________ (1992c). *World Bank Debt Tables 1992-1993, volume I: Analysis and Summary Tables.* Washington, D.C.: The World Bank.

Wu, Friedrich (1991). The ASEAN economies in the 1990s and Singapore's regional role. *California Management Review,* 34, 1 (Fall), pp. 103-114.

Yip, George S. and George A. Coundouriotis (1991). The world chocolate confectionery industry. *Planning Review,* 19, 1 (January-February), pp. 4-14.

Young, Kan H. and Charles E. Steigerwald (1990). Is foreign investment in the U.S. transferring U.S. technology abroad? *Business Economics,* XXV (October), p. 28-30.

ANNEX TABLES

Page

Annex table 1. Foreign-direct-investment inward flows, by region and economy, 1981-1991
(Millions of dollars)

Host region/economy	*1981-1986 (Annual average)*	*1987*	*1988*	*1989*	*1990*	*1991*
Developed regions/countries	41 797	109 455	129 856	167 504	171 907	107 793
Western Europe	17 402	41 482	60 489	88 250	108 822	84 065
European Community	15 478	37 644	57 263	81 069	99 020	75 186
Belgium and Luxembourg	1 053	2 355	5 212	7 057	8 056	9 377
Denmark	97	85	503	1 090	1 132	1 553
France	2 338	5 140	8 487	10 313	13 223	15 235
Germany, Federal Republic of	1 395	1 480	870	10 630	8 390	6 590
Greece	466	683	907	752	1 005	1 135
Ireland	143	89	92	85	99	98
Italy	860	4 188	6 789	2 191	6 441	2 403
Netherlands	1 840	2 891	5 046	8 233	11 554	4 308
Portugal	195	466	922	1 737	2 610	2 448
Spain	2 051	4 571	7 021	8 428	13 841	10 502
United Kingdom	5 041	15 696	21 414	30 553	32 669	21 537
Other Western Europe	1 924	3 838	3 226	7 181	9 802	8 879
Austria	267	486	511	850	1 008	607
Finland	130	265	532	490	979	-233
Iceland	19	2	-15	-27	6	35
Norway	309	187	279	1 519	876	-439
Sweden	398	578	1 514	1 522	1 972	6 348
Switzerland	802	2 320	405	2 827	4 961	2 561
North America	21 249	62 418	61 065	70 753	52 158	16 034
Canada	-173	4 198	3 795	2 883	7 018	4 534
United States	21 422	58 220	57 270	67 870	45 140	11 500
Other developed countries	3 145	5 555	8 302	8 502	10 927	7 694
Australia	2 270	3 899	7 715	7 345	6 577	4 833
Israel	98	270	225	181	157	244
Japan	317	1 170	-520	-1 060	1 760	1 370
New Zealand	296	176	412	1 365	1 754	444
South Africa	77	-75	116	8	-5	-7
Turkey	89	115	354	663	684	810
Developing regions/economies	13 270	25 303	30 204	28 644	31 345	38 768
Africa	1 709	2 344	2 795	4 814	2 085	2 514
Oil-exporting countries	1 440	1 813	2 079	3 526	1 317	1 928
Algeria	-6	4	13	12	6	10
Angola	141	119	131	200	-335	665
Cameroon	136	12	67	5	9	-16
Congo	32	43	9	3	7	5

/.....

(Annex table 1, cont'd.)

Host region/economy	*1981-1986 (Annual average)*	*1987*	*1988*	*1989*	*1990*	*1991*
Africa						
Oil exporting countries (cont'd.)						
Egypt	777	948	1 190	1 250	734	253
Gabon	72	90	133	-31	74	125
Libyan Arab Jamahiriya	-256	-98	98	125	159	24
Nigeria	361	603	377	1 882	588	712
Tunisia	184	92	61	79	75	150
Other countries	269	531	716	1 289	769	586
Benin	-	-	-	-	-	-
Botswana	53	114	40	42	38	3
Burkina Faso	2	-	2	2	2	2
Burundi	3	1	1	1	1	1
Central African Republic	6	12	-4	1	1	-5
Chad	15	8	1	19	-	-2
Comoros	-	8	4	3	-	3
Côte d'Ivoire	40	88	52	41	48	46
Djibouti	-	-	-	-	-	-
Equatorial Guinea	2	2	1	-	10	42
Ethiopia	1	-3	2	-	12	1
Gambia	-	1	1	15	1	..
Ghana	8	5	5	15	15	1
Guinea	1	6	7	4	-	1
Guinea-Bissau	1	-	1	1	2	2
Kenya	19	43	-	62	51	43
Lesotho	4	6	21	13	17	8
Liberia	15	39	290	656	276	-7
Madagascar	4	4	3	13	22	14
Malawi	1	-	-	-	-	-
Mali	2	-6	1	25	8	4
Mauritania	8	2	2	4	..	..
Mauritius	4	17	24	36	41	19
Morocco	42	60	85	167	165	320
Mozambique	-	-	-	-	-	-
Niger	3	-	-	-	-	-
Rwanda	16	18	21	16	8	5
Senegal	5	-4	14	10	3	22
Seychelles	11	19	23	23	27	22
Sierra Leone	-25	39	-23	21	-	1
Somalia	-4	-	-	-	-	-
Sudan	1	-	-	4	-	-
Swaziland	11	56	51	69	45	20
Togo	7	7	13	-7	-1	7
Uganda	-	-	5	-2	-	1
United Republic of Tanzania	6	-1	4	6	-2	1
Zaire	-14	-55	-4	-6	-12	14

/.....

(Annex table 1, cont'd.)

Host region/economy	*1981-1986 (Annual average)*	*1987*	*1988*	*1989*	*1990*	*1991*
Africa						
Oil exporting countries (cont'd.)						
Zambia	21	75	93	38	-9	..
Zimbabwe	1	-31	-18	..	..	..
Latin America and the Caribbean	5 759	10 950	11 451	8 326	9 950	15 235
Oil-exporting countries	1 523	3 413	2 816	3 454	3 302	6 982
Bolivia	23	38	-10	-24	27	52
Ecuador	55	75	80	80	82	85
Mexico	1 226	3 246	2 594	3 037	2 632	4 762
Trinidad and Tobago	113	33	63	149	109	169
Venezuela	105	21	89	213	451	1 914
Other countries/territories	4 236	7 537	8 635	4 871	6 649	8 252
Antigua and Barbuda	15	29	59	61	85	36
Argentina	502	-19	1 147	1 028	2 008	2 439
Bahamas	-3	11	37	25	-16	..
Barbados	5	7	12	8	11	7
Belize	1	7	14	19	17	13
Bermuda	736	3 466	1 272	-769	1 139	2 180
Brazil	1 709	1 225	2 969	1 267	901	1 680
Cayman Islands	264	1 661	2 075	1 884	935	160
Chile	205	230	141	184	249	576
Colombia	588	319	203	576	500	457
Costa Rica	58	80	122	101	163	142
Dominican Republic	47	89	106	110	133	145
El Salvador	12	18	17	13	2	25
Dominica	1	9	7	9	8	..
Grenada	3	13	13	10	13	..
Guatemala	70	150	330	76	48	91
Guyana	1	4	2	-2	8	12
Haiti	6	5	10	9	8	14
Honduras	18	39	48	51	44	45
Jamaica	-8	53	-12	57	138	127
Netherlands Antilles	-84	2	7	17	..	..
Nicaragua	..	..	..	..	..	..
Panama	14	57	-52	36	-30	-62
Paraguay	13	5	8	13	68	80
Peru	24	32	26	59	41	-7
Saint Kitts and Nevis	6	9	15	30	49	48
Saint Lucia	20	22	16	18	45	72
Saint Vincent and the Grenadines	2	6	10	6	8	10
Suriname	2	-73	-96	-168	-43	..
Uruguay	17	50	47	38	39	30
Virgin Islands	6	38	90	117	148	14

/.....

(Annex table 1, cont'd.)

Host region/economy	1981-1986 (Annual average)	1987	1988	1989	1990	1991
Western Asia	418	255	690	447	494	794
Oil-exporting countries	259	154	476	298	250	651
Bahrain	50	-36	222	181	-4	-7
Iran (Islamic Republic of)	-49	-308	61	-19	-362	23
Iraq	1	13	-	3	-	-3
Kuwait	-2	-6	16	4	-1	..
Oman	143	35	92	112	144	7
Qatar	-1	-3	-21	-1	16	43
Saudi Arabia	86	411	-83	-20	572	657
United Arab Emirates	31	41	189	39	-116	-69
Other countries	159	101	214	148	244	143
Cyprus	63	52	62	70	130	82
Democratic Yemen[a]	-	1	8	5	..	..
Jordan	60	40	24	-1	38	-12
Lebanon	4	1	-	2	6	2
Syrian Arab Republic	17	7	121	74	71	71
Yemen [a]	16	1	..	..	..	..
East, South and South-East Asia	5 230	11 636	15 025	14 774	18 454	19 967
Oil-exporting countries	1 225	808	1 296	2 350	3 424	5 554
Brunei Darussalam	1	-	1	-	-1	-1
Indonesia	240	385	576	682	1 093	1 482
Malaysia	984	423	719	1 668	2 332	4 073
Other countries/territories	4 004	10 828	13 729	12 424	15 030	14 413
Afghanistan	-	-	-	-	-	-
Bangladesh	-	3	2	-	3	1
China	1 021	2 314	3 194	3 393	3 489	4 366
Hong Kong	646	3 298	2 675	1 076	2 173	961
India	69	212	91	252	162	149
Korea, Republic of	170	601	871	758	715	1 116
Lao People's Democratic Republic	-	-	-	-	-	-
Macao	1	-	-	-1	-	11
Maldives	-	-	-	-	8	..
Myanmar	-	-2	-	-	5	..
Nepal	-	1	1	-	6	2
Pakistan	82	129	186	210	244	257
Philippines	74	307	936	563	530	544
Singapore	1 409	2 836	3 655	2 770	3 861	3 584
Sri Lanka	40	60	46	20	43	105
Taiwan Province of China	212	715	959	1 604	1 330	1 271
Thailand	277	352	1 105	1 775	2 444	2 014
Viet Nam	5	-	8	4	16	32

/.....

(Annex table 1, cont'd.)

Host region/economy	*1981-1986 (Annual average)*	*1987*	*1988*	*1989*	*1990*	*1991*
Oceania	127	92	180	222	250	106
Fiji	26	-11	24	13	75	7
Kiribati	-	-	-	-	-	..
Papua New Guinea	100	93	154	203	155	77
Western Samoa	-	1	-	-	7	3
Solomon Islands	1	8	3	6	13	19
Tonga	-	-	-	-	-	..
Vanuatu	5	13	11	9	13	18
Other	27	27	63	61	113	152
Malta	25	19	41	52	46	34
Yugoslavia	2	7	22	9	67	118
Central and Eastern Europe	18	12	15	11	89	1 793
Hungary	-	-	-	-	-	1 462
Poland	18	12	15	11	89	291
Romania	-	-	-	-	-	40
All countries	55 084	134 771	160 075	196 159	203 341	148 353

Sources: UNCTAD, Programme on Transnational Corporations, based on International Monetary Fund, balance-of-payments statistics tape, retrieved in March 1993; OECD estimates; and UNCTAD, 1993e.

a Yemen was admitted to membership in the United Nations on 30 September 1947 and Democratic Yemen on 14 December 1967. On 22 May 1990 the two countries merged and have since been represented as one Member with the name "Yemen".

Annex table 2. Foreign-direct-investment inward and outward stock, 1980, 1985 and 1990
(Millions of dollars)

Region/country	Inward stock			Outward stock		
	1980	1985	1990	1980	1985	1990
Total stock	448 248	685 293	1 496 114	515 537	690 227	1 612 980
Developed countries	352 369	509 719	1 230 215	513 346	684 856	1 602 199
European Community	167 614	197 549	563 329	194 489	254 334	666 426
Belgium and Luxembourg	7 306	8 840	28 588[f]	6 037	4 688	22 651[f]
Denmark	4 193	3 613	9 192	2 065	2 178	10 441
France	15 457	19 194	51 121[f]	12 205	20 258	74 833[f]
Germany	36 630	36 926	93 456	43 127	59 909	155 133
Greece	4 524	8 309	13 011	..	..	..
Ireland	2 714[a]	4 609[c]	5 405[f]	..	..	..
Italy	8 892	18 976	57 985	6 970	16 301	56 105
Netherlands	19 167	24 791	54 982[f]	42 116	47 647	87 325[f]
Spain	5 141	8 939	41 951[f]	1 226	2 076	14 987
Portugal	576	791	2 019[g]	14	83	199[g]
United Kingdom	63 014	62 561	205 618[g]	80 729	101 195	244 753
Western Europe	14 917	20 370	46 634	31 365	43 145	89 768
Austria	3 163	3 580	6 816[g]	530	1 079	1 360[g]
Finland	445	1 339	4 112[f]	743	1 842	8 188[f]
Norway	775	993	2 450[g]	559	1 093	2 757[g]
Sweden	2 028	4 399[c]	7 309[g]	8 041	13 868[c]	24 850[g]
Switzerland	8 506	10 058	25 946[f]	21 491	25 263	52 613[f]
North America	134 697	247 031	511 758	242 750	289 762	497 886
Canada	51 651	62 416	108 023	22 572	38 728	74 703
United States	83 046	184 615	403 735	220 178	251 034	423 183
Other developed countries	35 142	44 769	108 494	44 742	97 615	348 119
Australia	13 173	25 049	74 451[h]	2 260	6 653	27 357[h]
Japan	2 979	6 397	18 432	36 497	83 649	310 808
New Zealand	2 363	2 043	3 242[f]	263	809	2 322[f]
South Africa	16 519	10 919	11 048[g]	5 722	6 504	7 632[g]
Turkey	107	360	1 320	..	..	..
Developing regions/economies	95 878	175 574	265 899	2 190	5 371	10 781
Africa	23 307	22 489	19 404	419	390	441
Algeria	734	572	366[f]	99	139	106
Botswana	321	181	618	..	..	..
Cameroon	69	115	110[i]	196	60	61[i]
Congo	210	291	440[g]	..	..	..
Côte d'Ivoire	650	550	1 039[f]	..	..	..
Egypt	1 901	5 345	4 467	27	79	65
Ethiopia	..	5[c]	6f	..	..	..
Gabon	803	774	1 458	79	71	175
Gambia	31	16	21[f]	..	..	..

/.....

(Annex table 2, cont'd.)

Region/country	*Inward stock* 1980	*Inward stock* 1985	*Inward stock* 1990	*Outward stock* 1980	*Outward stock* 1985	*Outward stock* 1990
Africa (cont'd.)						
Ghana	288	332	375	..	..	..
Kenya	669	375	376	18	42	35
Lesotho	9	13	69	..	..	..
Liberia	1 230	1 334	1 356[i]	..	..	..
Malawi	106	55	45[i]	..	..	..
Mauritius	4[a]	19	66[g]	..	..	..
Morocco	714	656	1 110[g]	..	..	..
Nigeria	6 649	6 817	2 118[g]	..	..	..
Senegal	337	230	319[i]	..	..	..
Seychelles	26	78	175[f]	..	..	..
Sierra Leone	79	..	..	..	..	..
Somalia	100	4	..	..	..	..
Tunisia	548	1 422	2 554[g]	..	..	..
United Republic of Tanzania	154	77	11	..	..	..
Zaire	511	181[d]	..	..	..	..
Zambia	414	99	226[g]	..	..	..
Zimbabwe	6 749[a]	2 959	2 122[f]	..	..	..
Asia and the Pacific	34 009	65 401	120 901	938	2 064	6 087
Bangladesh	63	112	144[g]			
China	670[a]	3 444	10 648[f]	39[a]	131	1 659[f]
Fiji	358	393	310[f]	..	..	..
Hong Kong	1 729	3 520	11 685[f]	..	..	..
India	1 177	1 075	1 179[g]	..	96	76g
Indonesia	10 274	24 971	38 883	..	..	..
Malaysia	6 076	8 510	10 117[g]	406	826	1 878[g]
Pakistan	690	1 079	1 254[g]	40	126	228[g]
Papua New Guinea	748	683	1 353[f]	25	22	9[f]
Philippines	1 225	1 302	1 568[f]	171	168	154[g]
Republic of Korea	1 140	1 806	3 956[g]	142	476	1 119[g]
Singapore	6 203	13 016	26 780[f]	..	..	..
Sri Lanka	231	517	618[g]	..	..	..
Taiwan Province of China	2 405	2 930	6 801[g]	102	204	705[g]
Thailand	981	1 999	5 536[f]	13	14	258[f]
Vanuatu	40[b]	44	68[g]	..	..	..
Western Asia		27 484	28 446	..	1 075	1 189
Bahrain	..	281	815	..	..	..
Cyprus	310	520	1 046	..	..	..
Iran (Islamic Republic of)	1 214	857	665[g]	..	..	..
Iraq	153	149	167[f]	..	..	..
Israel	35	420	1 352	..	524	550
Jordan	155	455	306[f]	22	24	32[f]
Kuwait	348	342	349[f]	..	..	..
Lebanon	12	11	7	..	..	..

/.....

(Annex table 2, cont'd.)

Region/country	Inward stock			Outward stock		
	1980	1985	1990	1980	1985	1990
Western Asia (cont'd.)						
Oman	266	985	1 407	..	..	..
Qatar	174	167	157	..	..	..
Saudi Arabia	..	22 422	20 965[f]	..	508	551[i]
United Arab Emirates	719	792	1 137[g]	..	19	55[g]
Yemen[j]	56	83	74[i]	..	..	..
Latin America and the Caribbean	39 488	60 201	97 148	833	1 841	3 064
Argentina	5 344	6 563	6 942[f]	..	..	..
Bolivia	420	592	806	..	..	..
Brazil	17 480	25 664	37 143	652	1 400	2 397
Chile	886	2 321	6 175	42	102	201
Colombia	1 061	2 231	3 500	137	301	402
Costa Rica	672	957	1 447	..	..	..
Dominican Republic	239	265	572	..	..	..
Ecuador	719	982	1 370	..	..	..
El Salvador	154	181	212	..	..	..
Guatemala	44	71	..	..	..	..
Honduras	..	231[e]	258[f]	..	..	..
Mexico	8 459	14 629	30 310	..	..	..
Panama	387	533	491[f]	..	..	..
Paraguay	..	245[e]	253[g]	..	..	..
Peru	898	1 152	1 254	3	38	63
Trinidad and Tobago	1 080	1 719	2 093	..	..	..
Uruguay	43[b]	319[e]	459[f]	..	..	..
Venezuela	1 604	1 548	3 865	..	..	..

Source: UNCTAD, 1993e.

a 1981.
b 1978.
c 1986.
d 1983.
e 1984.
f 1989.
g 1988.
h 1991.
i 1987.
j Yemen was admitted to membership in the United Nations on 30 September 1947 and Democratic Yemen on 14 December 1967. On 22 May 1990 the two countries merged and have since been represented as one Member with the name "Yemen".

Annex table 3. The ratio of foreign-direct-investment inflows to gross domestic capital formation and the ratio of gross domestic capital formation to gross domestic product (in parentheses)
(Percentage)

Region/economy	*1971-1975*	*1976-1980*	*1981-1985*	*1986-1991*
Developed countries				
Australia	4.5	4.6	4.6	9.5
	(24.8)	(24.6)	(24.5)	(23.0)
Austria	1.8	0.9	1.7	2.3[a]
	(29.0)	(27.3)	(23.7)	(25.0)
Belgium/Luxembourg	7.1	5.8	7.6	16.0[a]
	(22.9)	(21.8)	(16.3)	(18.4)
Canada	3.6	1.7	-0.7	3.7
	(24.4)	(24.2)	(20.6)	(21.5)
Denmark	3.0	0.3	0.9	3.7
	(24.1)	(21.4)	(17.1)	(18.3)
Germany, Federal Republic of	2.1	0.8	0.6	1.8
	(23.4)	(22.4)	(20.3)	(21.0)
Finland	0.6	0.4	0.7	1.4
	(31.8)	(25.5)	(24.9)	(26.1)
France	1.8	1.9	2.0	4.4
	(26.1)	(24.1)	(20.6)	(21.1)
Greece	1.0	5.4	6.0	8.0
	(30.0)	(28.0)	(21.8)	(19.0)
Iceland	4.4	1.3	3.0	0.2
	(33.6)	(33.6)	(28.6)	(18.9)
Ireland	3.8	6.7	4.0	1.0
	(25.7)	(29.0)	(24.7)	(18.8)
Israel	2.9	1.1	1.6	2.7
	(29.0)	(23.2)	(20.3)	(18.3)
Italy	1.8	0.8	1.1	2.0
	(22.6)	(23.2)	(23.1)	(20.9)
Japan	0.1	0.05	0.1	0.1[a]
	(35.8)	(31.9)	(29.2)	(31.0)
Netherlands	6.1	4.5	6.1	12.3
	(30.2)	(21.5)	(18.7)	(20.5)
New Zealand	4.8	6.1	4.9	8.6
	(29.6)	(27.2)	(26.2)	(22.2)
Norway	3.1	3.2	1.2	2.6
	(32.2)	(30.7)	(25.3)	(24.6)
Portugal	3.1	1.5	3.0	10.7
	(25.7)	(29.6)	(28.4)	(27.8)
Spain	1.9	2.8	5.3	9.2
	(27.8)	(23.8)	(20.1)	(23.6)
Sweden	0.6	0.5	1.6	5.9
	(23.1)	(20.4)	(17.6)	(19.2)
Switzerland	..	..	3.9	4.9
	(29.2)	(23.3)	(24.6)	(27.9)
United Kingdom	7.3	8.4	5.4	14.4
	(19.0)	(20.1)	(19.0)	(18.4)
United States	0.9	2.0	3.0	5.6
	(19.0)	(20.0)	(18.4)	(16.7)

/.....

(Annex table 3, cont'd.)

Region/economy	*1971-1975*	*1976-1980*	*1981-1985*	*1986-1991*
Developing economies				
Asia and the Pacific				
Bangladesh	..	..	-0.01	0.1[a]
	(7.5)	(13.6)	(13.0)	(12.0)
China	0	0.08	0.9	2.3
	(33.6)	(32.0)	(32.5)	(38.3)
Fiji	12.2	6.7	10.7	11.4[a]
	(21.6)	(26.8)	(24.0)	(15.7)
Hong Kong	5.9	4.2	6.9	12.1[b]
	(24.7)	(31.9)	(28.0)	(26.8)
India	0.3	0.1	0.1	0.3
	(19.2)	(22.2)	(24.2)	(22.8)
Indonesia	4.6	2.4	1.0	2.4
	(18.3)	(20.7)	(27.8)	(33.4)
Malaysia	15.2	11.9	10.8	9.7
	(24.0)	(27.2)	(34.1)	(29.3)
Nepal	0.3	0.1	0.04	0.33
	(9.8)	(16.7)	(19.2)	(20.9)
Pakistan	0.5	0.9	1.3	2.3
	(15.3)	(13.9)	(17.8)	(18.6)
Papua New Guinea	..	8.7	15.1	16.0
	(18.9)	(22.7)	(28.3)	(24.4)
Philippines	1.0	0.9	0.7	5.7
	(25.3)	(30.1)	(24.0)	(17.9)
Republic of Korea	1.9	0.4	0.5	1.1
	(26.5)	(31.3)	(29.2)	(34.2)
Singapore	15.0	16.6	17.4	29.4
	(41.4)	(42.0)	(46.8)	(37.7)
Sri Lanka	0.1	2.6	2.9	3.0
	(14.9)	(22.1)	(27.5)	(22.2)
Taiwan Province of China	1.4	1.2	1.5	3.5
	(30.5)	(31.2)	(23.5)	(22.0)
Thailand	3.0	1.5	3.1	6.3
	(24.7)	(27.3)	(23.5)	(32.1)
Latin America and the Caribbean				
Argentina	0.1	2.1	5.0	14.5[a]
	(21.7)	(24.4)	(14.8)	(10.5)
Barbados	20.4	4.1	2.5	3.3
	(21.7)	(23.5)	(20.0)	(17.5)
Bolivia	4.6	2.3	5.8	2.4
	(19.7)	(20.4)	(12.9)	(11.8)
Brazil	4.2	3.9	4.3	1.7[a]
	(29.3)	(24.2)	(18.5)	(22.4)
Chile	-7.3	4.2	6.3	5.7
	(15.2)	(17.6)	(15.1)	(18.3)
Colombia	1.7	2.2	7.7	6.1
	(18.8)	(18.5)	(19.8)	(18.9)

/.....

(Annex table 3, cont'd.)

Region/economy	*1971-1975*	*1976-1980*	*1981-1985*	*1986-1991*
Latin America and the Caribbean (cont'd.)				
Costa Rica	11.3	6.0	7.1	8.8
	(23.7)	(24.9)	(25.2)	(25.6)
Dominican Republic	9.4	5.0	2.8	9.6
	(22.1)	(23.8)	(21.2)	(18.1)
Ecuador	13.6	1.8	1.9	3.5
	(24.3)	(26.1)	(20.3)	(20.9)
El Salvador	4.0	1.7	1.7	2.4
	(19.0)	(19.4)	(12.3)	(13.3)
Guatemala	10.0	7.9	5.7	12.2
	(15.4)	(19.2)	(13.0)	(12.8)
Guyana	-9.1	-4.3	2.1	0.8[a]
	(26.2)	(29.4)	(26.4)	(34.9)
Honduras	2.5	2.6	3.0	5.1
	(19.8)	(24.5)	(17.3)	(18.6)
Jamaica	12.9	1.6	-1.4	6.6
	(27.7)	(16.0)	(22.1)	(26.4)
Mexico	3.5	3.6	2.7	7.0
	(21.2)	(24.3)	(22.8)	(21.6)
Panama	4.8	0.03	3.1	-2.9
	(32.1)	(27.5)	(21.8)	(13.2)
Paraguay	6.2	3.9	1.2	2.3
	(19.8)	(27.3)	(24.2)	(24.3)
Peru	3.3	2.0	0.4	0.3
	(21.7)	(22.4)	(26.7)	(21.6)
Suriname	1.5	-2.6	4.9	-23.6
	(25.9)	(30.6)	(18.8)	(21.4)
Trinidad and Tobago	22.3	10.7	7.3	9.4
	(27.0)	(28.9)	(24.8)	(19.0)
Uruguay	..	15.7	1.5	4.1
	(12.4)	(16.5)	(12.5)	(12.5)
Venezuela	-0.9	-0.9	1.0	4.3
	(34.8)	(39.7)	(19.5)	(20.4)
Western Asia				
Cyprus	13.8	11.1	9.3	6.1
	(26.4)	(35.3)	(32.1)	(27.3)
Jordan	4.6	2.9	4.5	1.7
	(24.3)	(37.7)	(38.7)	(21.3)
Kuwait	0.02	0.02	0.01	0
	(9.6)	(16.6)	(20.5)	(18.8)[b]
Oman	3.6	8.9	6.4	6.9[a]
	(29.7)	(27.3)	(27.1)	(18.2)
Yemen	..	2.6	1.9	0.9[b]
	(18.7)	(36.9)	(25.9)	(30.4)
Africa				
Algeria	1.9	1.4	-0.01	0.05
	(41.6)	(44.4)	(36.3)	(30.8)
Botswana	24.3	24.1	16.1	15.9[a]
	(47.6)	(40.1)	(33.9)	(19.3)

/.....

(Annex table 3, cont'd.)

Region/economy	*1971-1975*	*1976-1980*	*1981-1985*	*1986-1991*
Africa (cont'd.)				
Congo	31.6	3.9	4.0	3.5
	(30.6)	(30.9)	(40.3)	(17.9)
Côte d'Ivoire	5.4	2.5	2.3	5.3
	(22.2)	(27.3)	(18.2)	(11.5)
Egypt	..	7.1	6.9	7.8
	(20.6)	(29.9)	(28.2)	(22.1)
Gabon	10.8	3.2	5.0	7.6
	(44.3)	(38.8)	(35.6)	(29.9)
Ghana	9.7	1.8	2.4	0.9
	(11.4)	(6.8)	(5.8)	(14.0)
Kenya	2.9	4.4	1.0	2.1
	(22.9)	(25.9)	(24.0)	(22.4)
Liberia	37.3	18.7	13.8	--
	(26.1)	(33.6)	(17.8)	(11.0)[a]
Madagascar	4.2	-0.6	0.6	4.1
	(14.0)	(19.9)	(14.5)	(12.4)
Mauritius	1.1	1.2	1.8	4.0
	(27.7)	(21.6)	(17.3)	(28.0)
Morocco	0.4	1.6	1.7	2.6
	(18.8)	(25.6)	(22.4)	(22.9)
Nigeria	4.9	0.5	3.6	16.3
	(26.6)	(34.8)	(32.1)	(27.3)
Rwanda	4.6	2.9	4.5	1.7
	(24.3)	(37.7)	(38.7)	(21.3)
Senegal	0.02	0.02	0.01	0
	(9.6)	(16.6)	(20.5)	(18.8)[b]
Seychelles	3.6	8.9	6.4	6.9[a]
	(29.7)	(27.3)	(27.1)	(18.2)
Sierra Leone	..	2.6	1.9	0.9[b]
	(18.7)	(36.9)	(25.9)	(30.4)
Somalia	4.3	2.4	-2.00	
	(9.8)	(10.5)	(12.2)	(22.7)[a]
Sudan	-0.2	..	0.4	0.1
	(0.6)	(16.1)	(0.7)	(0.07)[a]
Swaziland	16.1	18.8	4.3	31.3[a]
	(21.5)	(38.4)	(32.4)	(34.0)
Togo	-5.3	11.7	3.5	1.2
	(21.6)	(41.3)	(24.6)	(23.6)
Tunisia	5.2	6.1	8.4	3.5
	(24.6)	(30.0)	(30.3)	(22.9)
Uganda	-0.8	1.0	-0.3	0.2
	(4.8)	(7.3)	(16.3)	(10.5)
Zimbabwe	..	0.02	0.02	-0.8
	(24.5)	(16.4)	(20.1)	(17.5)[a]

Sources: UNCTAD, Programme on Transnational Corporations, based on International Monetary Fund, balance-of-payments statistics tape, retrieved in March 1993; OECD estimates; and United Nations Department of Economics and Social Development database on major economic indicators showing historical developemnt trends.

a 1986-1990.

b 1986-1989.

Annex table 4. Average annual inflows of foreign direct investment to the 10 largest developing economies
(Millions of dollars and percentage)

Host economy	*1970-1980*	*Host economy*	*1981-1991*
Brazil	1 390	Singapore	2 287
Mexico	743	Mexico	2 148
Singapore	386	China	2 080
Malaysia	381	Brazil	1 663
Nigeria	219	Malaysia	1 374
Egypt	205	Hong Kong	1 278
Indonesia	194	Argentina	874
Hong Kong	162	Thailand	850
Argentina	121	Egypt	821
Algeria	120	Taiwan Province of China	650
Percentage share of total flows to developing countries	67		66

Source: UNCTAD, Programme on Transnational Corporations, based on International Monetary Fund, balance-of-payments statistics tape, retrieved in March 1993, and OECD estimates.

Annex table 5. New bilateral treaties for the promotion and protection of foreign direct investment signed or entered into force in 1991 and 1992[a]

Countries	*Date of signature* [b]	*Date of entry into force* [c]
Albania		
Italy	12 September 1991	..
Germany	31 October 1991	Provisional application
Finland	7 November 1991	16 April 1992
Turkey	1 June 1992	..
Switzerland	22 September 1992	..
Algeria		
Belgium-Luxembourg	24 April 1991	..
Argentina		
Germany	9 April 1991	..
Switzerland	12 April 1991	6 November 1992
Spain	2 October 1991	..
Canada	5 November 1991	..
United States	14 November 1991	..
Sweden	22 November 1991	28 September 1992
Turkey	8 May 1992	..
Austria	7 August 1992	..
Netherlands	20 October 1992	..
Denmark	6 November 1992	..
Armenia		
United States	23 September 1992	..
Australia		
Papua New Guinea	3 September 1990	20 October 1991
Viet Nam	5 March 1991	11 September 1991
Poland	7 May 1991	27 March 1992
Czechoslovakia[d]	29 July 1991	..
Hungary	15 August 1991	10 May 1992
Indonesia	17 November 1992	..
Austria		
USSR[e]	8 February 1990	1 September 1991
Czechoslovakia	15 October 1990	1 October 1991
Republic of Korea	14 March 1991	1 November 1991
Cape Verde	3 September 1991	..
Argentina	7 August 1992	..
Morocco	2 November 1992	..
Bahrain		
United Kingdom	30 October 1990	30 October 1991
Belarus		
Finland	28 October 1992	..

/.....

(Annex table 5, cont'd.)

Countries	*Date of signature* [b]	*Date of entry into force* [c]
Belgium-Luxembourg		
Poland	19 April 1987	2 August 1991
Bulgaria	25 October 1988	29 May 1991
USSR[e]	9 February 1989	13 October 1991
Czechoslovakia[d]	24 April 1989	13 February 1992
Algeria	24 April 1991	..
Uruguay	4 November 1991	..
Mongolia	3 March 1992	..
Chile	15 July 1992	..
Paraguay	6 October 1992	..
Bolivia		
Sweden	20 September 1990	3 July 1992
Netherlands	10 March 1992	..
Bulgaria		
Belgium-Luxembourg	25 October 1988	29 May 1991
United States	23 September 1992	..
Canada		
USSR[a]	20 November 1989	27 June 1991
Poland	26 October 1990	22 November 1990
Czechoslovakia[d]	15 November 1990	9 March 1992
Uruguay	16 May 1991	..
Hungary	3 October 1991	..
Argentina	5 November 1991	..
Cape Verde		
Austria	3 September 1991	..
Switzerland	28 October 1991	6 May 1992
Netherlands	11 November 1991	25 November 1992
Chile		
Spain	2 October 1991	..
Germany	19 October 1991	..
Belgium-Luxembourg	15 July 1992	..
France	July 1992	..
China		
Czechoslovakia[d]	4 December 1991	1 December 1992
Portugal	3 February 1992	..
Spain	6 February 1992	..
Republic of Korea	30 September 1992	4 December 1992
Ukraine	31 October 1992	..
Cyprus		
Belgium-Luxembourg	26 February 1991	..
Romania	16 June 1991	..
Greece	30 March 1992	..

/.....

(Annex table 5, cont'd.)

Countries	*Date of signature* [b]	*Date of entry into force* [c]
Czechoslovakia		
Belgium-Luxembourg	24 April 1989	13 February 1992
United Kingdom	10 July 1990	26 October 1992
Italy	1 August 1990	..
France	13 September 1990	27 September 1991
Germany	2 October 1990	2 August 1992
Austria	15 October 1990	1 October 1991
Finland	6 November 1990	23 October 1991
Sweden	13 November 1990	23 September 1991
Canada	15 November 1990	9 March 1992
Spain	12 December 1990	28 November 1991
Denmark	6 March 1991	19 September 1992
Netherlands	2 April 1991	1 October 1992
Norway	21 May 1991	6 August 1992
Greece	3 June 1991	31 December 1992
Australia	29 July 1991	..
Thailand	16 October 1991	..
United States	22 October 1991	19 December 1992
China	4 December 1991	1 December 1992
Republic of Korea	27 April 1992	..
Turkey	30 April 1992	..
Denmark		
Turkey	7 February 1990	1 August 1992
Czechoslovakia[d]	6 March 1991	19 September 1992
Malaysia	6 January 1992	18 September 1992
Ghana	13 January 1992	..
Latvia	30 March 1992	..
Lithuania	30 March 1992	..
Ukraine	23 October 1992	..
Argentina	6 November 1992	..
Estonia	6 November 1992	..
Egypt		
United States	11 March 1986 (modified)	27 June 1992
Ukraine	21 December 1992	..
Estonia		
Finland	13 February 1992	2 December 1992
Sweden	31 March 1992	20 May 1992
Norway	15 June 1992	15 June 1992
Netherlands	27 October 1992	..
Denmark	6 November 1992	..
Germany	12 November 1992	Provisional application
Switzerland	21 December 1992	..
France	1992	..

/.....

(Annex table 5, cont'd.)

Countries	*Date of signature* [b]	*Date of entry into force* [c]
Finland		
Czechoslovakia[d]	6 November 1990	23 October 1991
Albania	7 November 1991	16 April 1992
Indonesia	7 February 1992	..
Estonia	13 February 1992	2 December 1992
Latvia	5 March 1992	7 December 1992
Romania	26 March 1992	..
Ukraine	14 May 1992	..
Lithuania	12 June 1992	..
Kazakhstan	29 September 1992	..
Uzbekistan	1 October 1992	..
Belarus	28 October 1992	..
France		
Yemen Arab Republic	27 April 1984	October 1991
USSR[e]	5 July 1989	18 July 1991
Kuwait	27 September 1989	16 May 1991
Laos	12 December 1989	8 March 1991
Nigeria	27 February 1990	19 August 1991
Czechoslovakia[d]	13 September 1990	27 September 1991
United Arab Emirates	9 September 1991	..
Mongolia	8 November 1991	..
Estonia	1992	..
Latvia	1992	..
Lithuania	1992	..
Viet Nam	26 May 1992	..
Chile	July 1992	..
Kazakhstan	25 September 1992	..
Germany		
Czechoslovakia[d]	2 October 1990	2 August 1992
Argentina	9 April 1991	..
Mongolia	26 June 1991	..
Chile	19 October 1991	..
Albania	31 October 1991	Provisional application
Lithuania	28 February 1992	Provisional application
Kazakhstan	22 September 1992	..
Jamaica	24 September 1992	..
Estonia	12 November 1992	Provisional application
Ghana		
United Kingdom	22 March 1989	25 October 1991
Denmark	13 January 1992	..
Greece		
Czechoslovakia[d]	3 June 1991	31 December 1992
Romania	16 September 1991	4 October 1992
Cyprus	30 March 1992	..

/.....

(Annex table 5, cont'd.)

Countries	*Date of signature* [b]	*Date of entry into force* [c]
Hungary		
Norway	8 April 1991	4 December 1992
Australia	15 August 1991	10 May 1992
Canada	3 October 1991	..
Thailand	18 October 1991	..
Morocco	12 December 1991	..
Turkey	14 January 1992	..
Portugal	28 February 1992	..
Indonesia	20 May 1992	..
Indonesia		
Republic of Korea	16 February 1991	..
Italy	25 April 1991	..
Viet Nam	25 October 1991	..
Finland	7 February 1992	..
Tunisia	13 May 1992	..
Hungary	20 May 1992	..
Sweden	17 September 1992	..
Poland	7 October 1992	..
Australia	17 November 1992	..
Israel		
Romania	2 September 1991	26 August 1992
Italy		
Republic of Korea	1 January 1989	26 June 1992
Czechoslovakia[d]	1 August 1990	..
Indonesia	25 April 1991	..
Albania	12 September 1991	..
Jamaica		
Switzerland	11 December 1990	21 November 1991
Netherlands	18 April 1991	1 August 1992
Germany	24 September 1992	..
Japan		
Turkey	12 February 1992	12 March 1993 (proposed)
Jordan		
Romania	2 July 1992	..
Kazakhstan		
Turkey	1 May 1992	..
United States	19 May 1992	..
Germany	22 September 1992	..
France	25 September 1992	..
Finland	29 September 1992	..

/.....

(Annex table 5, cont'd.)

Countries	*Date of signature* [b]	*Date of entry into force* [c]
Kuwait		
France	27 September 1989	16 May 1991
Romania	21 May 1991	26 July 1992
Kyrgyzstan		
Turkey	28 April 1992	..
Lao People's Democratic Republic		
France	12 December 1989	8 March 1991
Thailand	22 August 1990	..
Latvia		
Denmark	30 March 1992	..
Finland	5 March 1992	7 December 1992
Norway	16 June 1992	1 December 1992
Sweden	10 March 1992	6 November 1992
France	1992	..
Switzerland	22 December 1992	..
Lithuania		
Germany	28 February 1992	Provisional application
Sweden	17 March 1992	1 September 1992
Denmark	30 March 1992	..
Norway	16 June 1992	19 December 1992
Switzerland	23 December 1992	..
France	1992	..
Malaysia		
Denmark	6 January 1992	18 September 1992
Mongolia		
Republic of Korea	28 March 1991	30 April 1991
Germany	26 June 1991	..
France	8 November 1991	..
Belgium-Luxembourg	3 March 1992	..
Ukraine	5 November 1992	..
Morocco		
Hungary	12 December 1991	..
Austria	2 November 1992	..
Netherlands		
Jamaica	18 April 1991	1 August 1992
Czechoslovakia [d]	29 April 1991	1 October 1992
Venezuela	22 October 1991	..
Cape Verde	11 November 1991	..
Bolivia	10 March 1992	..
Poland	7 September 1992	..

/.....

(Annex table 5, cont'd.)

Countries	*Date of signature* [b]	*Date of entry into force* [c]
Netherlands (cont'd.)		
Argentina	20 October 1992	..
Estonia	27 October 1992	..
Paraguay	29 October 1992	..
Nigeria	2 November 1992	..
Nigeria		
France	27 February 1990	19 August 1991
Netherlands	2 November 1992	..
Norway		
Hungary	8 April 1991	4 December 1992
Czechoslovakia[d]	21 May 1991	6 August 1992
Romania	11 June 1991	23 March 1992
Estonia	15 June 1992	15 June 1992
Latvia	16 June 1992	1 December 1992
Lithuania	16 June 1992	19 December 1992
Papua New Guinea		
Australia	3 September 1990	20 October 1991
Paraguay		
Switzerland	31 January 1992	..
Belgium-Luxembourg	6 October 1992	..
Netherlands	29 October 1992	..
Republic of Korea	22 December 1992	..
Peru		
Thailand	15 November 1991	..
Poland		
Belgium-Luxembourg	19 April 1987	2 August 1991
Canada	26 October 1990	22 November 1990
Australia	7 May 1991	27 March 1992
Turkey	21 August 1991	..
Netherlands	7 September 1992	..
Russian Federation	2 October 1992	..
Indonesia	7 October 1992	..
Portugal		
China	3 February 1992	..
Hungary	28 February 1992	..
Republic of Korea		
Italy	1 January 1989	26 June 1992
USSR[e]	14 December 1990	10 July 1991
Indonesia	16 February 1991	..

/.....

(Annex table 5, cont'd.)

Countries	*Date of signature* [b]	*Date of entry into force* [c]
Republic of Korea (cont'd.)		
Austria	14 March 1991	1 November 1991
Mongolia	28 March 1991	30 April 1991
Turkey	14 May 1991	..
Czechoslovakia[d]	27 April 1992	..
Uzbekistan	17 June 1992	20 November 1992
China	30 September 1992	4 December 1992
Paraguay	22 December 1992	..
Republic of Moldova		
Romania	14 January 1992	..
Romania		
Turkey	24 January 1991	..
Kuwait	21 May 1991	26 July 1992
Norway	11 June 1991	23 March 1992
Cyprus	16 June 1991	..
Israel	2 September 1991	26 August 1992
Greece	16 September 1991	4 October 1992
Republic of Moldova	14 January 1992	..
Finland	26 March 1992	..
United States	28 May 1992	..
Jordan	2 July 1992	..
Russian Federation		
Belgium-Luxembourg	9 February 1989	13 October 1991
United Kingdom	6 April 1989	3 July 1991
France	5 July 1989	18 July 1991
Canada	20 November 1989	27 June 1991
Austria	8 February 1990	1 September 1991
Republic of Korea	14 December 1990	10 July 1991
United States	17 June 1992	..
Poland	2 October 1992	..
Singapore		
Viet Nam	29 October 1992	25 December 1992
Spain		
Czechoslovakia[d]	12 December 1990	28 November 1991
Argentina	2 October 1991	..
Chile	2 October 1991	..
China	6 February 1992	..
Uruguay	7 April 1992	..
Sri Lanka		
United States	20 September 1991	..

/.....

(Annex table 5, cont'd.)

Countries	*Date of signature* [b]	*Date of entry into force* [c]
Sweden		
Bolivia	20 September 1990	3 July 1992
Czechoslovakia[d]	13 November 1990	23 September 1991
Argentina	22 November 1991	28 September 1992
Latvia	10 March 1992	6 November 1992
Lithuania	17 March 1992	1 September 1992
Estonia	31 March 1992	20 May 1992
Indonesia	17 September 1992	..
Switzerland		
Jamaica	11 December 1990	21 November 1991
Argentina	12 April 1991	6 November 1992
Paraguay	31 January 1992	28 September 1992
Viet Nam	3 July 1992	3 December 1992
Albania	22 September 1992	..
Estonia	21 December 1992	..
Latvia	22 December 1992	..
Lithuania	23 December 1992	..
Thailand		
Republic of Korea	24 March 1989	..
Laos	22 August 1990	..
Czechoslovakia[d]	16 October 1991	..
Hungary	16 October 1991	..
Viet Nam	30 October 1991	..
Peru	15 November 1991	..
Tunisia		
United States	15 May 1990	..
Indonesia	13 May 1992	..
Turkey		
Denmark	7 February 1990	1 August 1992
Romania	24 January 1991	..
Republic of Korea	14 May 1991	..
Poland	21 August 1991	..
Hungary	14 January 1992	..
Japan	12 February 1992	..
Kyrgyzstan	28 April 1992	..
Uzbekistan	28 April 1992	..
Czechoslovakia[d]	30 April 1992	..
Kazakhstan	1 May 1992	..
Turkmenistan	2 May 1992	..
Argentina	8 May 1992	..
Albania	1 June 1992	..
Turkmenistan		
Turkey	2 May 1992	..

/.....

(Annex table 5, cont'd.)

Countries	*Date of signature* [b]	*Date of entry into force* [c]
Ukraine		
United States	6 May 1992	..
Finland	14 May 1992	..
Denmark	23 October 1992	..
China	31 October 1992	..
Mongolia	5 November 1992	..
Egypt	21 December 1992	..
United Arab Emirates		
France	9 September 1991	..
United Kingdom	8 December 1992	..
United Kingdom		
Ghana	22 March 1989	25 October 1991
Russian Federation	6 April 1989	3 July 1991
Czechoslovakia[d]	10 July 1990	26 October 1992
Bahrain	30 October 1990	30 October 1991
United Arab Emirates	8 December 1992	..
United States of America		
Egypt	11 March 1986 (modified)	27 June 1992
Tunisia	15 May 1990	7 February 1993
Sri Lanka	20 September 1991	..
Czechoslovakia[d]	22 October 1991	19 December 1992
Argentina	14 November 1991	..
Ukraine	20 November 1992	..
Kazakhstan	19 May 1992	..
Romania	28 May 1992	..
Russian Federation	17 June 1992	..
Armenia	23 September 1992	..
Bulgaria	23 September 1992	..
Uruguay		
Belgium-Luxembourg	4 November 1991	..
Spain	7 April 1992	..
Uzbekistan		
Turkey	28 April 1992	..
Republic of Korea	17 June 1992	20 November 1992
Finland	1 October 1992	..
Venezuela		
Netherlands	22 October 1991	..
Viet Nam		
Australia	5 March 1991	11 September 1991
Indonesia	25 October 1991	..
Thailand	30 October 1991	..

/.....

(Annex table 5, cont'd.)

Countries	*Date of signature* [b]	*Date of entry into force* [c]
Viet Nam (cont'd.)		
France	26 May 1992	..
Switzerland	3 July 1992	3 December 1992
Singapore	29 October 1992	25 December 1992
Yemen Arab Republic		
France	27 April 1984	October 1991

Source: UNCTAD, Programme on Transnational Corporations, based on information provided by member countries.

a This table updates the list of bilateral investment treaties in UNCTC and ICC (1992).

b The following bilateral investment treaties were signed since 1 January 1993: Algeria/France, 13 February 1993; Germany/Ukraine, 15 February 1993; Ukraine/Poland, 12 January 1993; Ukraine/United Kingdom, 10 February 1993; United States/Kyrgyzstan, 19 January 1993.

c The following bilateral investment treaties have entered into force since 1 January 1993: Austria/Cape Verde, 1 April 1993; Denmark/Estonia, 24 February 1993; Finland/Romania, 6 January 1993; Finland/Ukraine, 1 January 1993; Finland/Lithuania, 8 January 1993; Hungary/Turkey, 12 March 1993; Indonesia/Sweden, 8 February 1993; Japan/Turkey, 12 March 1993 (proposed); Tunisia/United States, 7 February 1993; United Kingdom/Ukraine, 10 February 1993.

d Temporarily applicable to the successor States via exchange of notes. The Czech Republic and Slovak Republic have upheld all bilateral treaties for the promotion and protection of FDI concluded by the Czech and Slovak Republic by 31 December 1992.

e Temporarily applicable to the successor States. New negotiations are in progress or planned.

Annex table 6. Changes in main national legislation relating to foreign direct investment in 1992 [a]

Country	*Law/Regulation*	*Content*
Africa		
Burundi	Law No. 1/30 on the Creation of a Free Zone in Burundi, of 31 August 1992	Creates a free-zone regime for export-oriented enterprises covering the entire territory of Burundi and open to local investment and FDI; prescribes procedures for obtaining free enterprise status: foreign investors may create such companies or purchase their shares; establishes fiscal advantages, including a 10-year tax holiday, exemption from taxes on dividends and from customs duties; allows free transfer of income and repatriation of capital; permits approved free enterprises to hold accounts in foreign currency without foreign exchange controls and to export without a license; labour legislation is flexible.
Congo	Investment Code, of March 1992	Lifts most previous criteria to benefit from legal advantages it creates. Nationality of firms no longer a determinant to take part in priviledged customs duty rates. Creates new tax breaks to promote investment in general and special tax incentives to firms operating in certain areas. Mandates the national investment commission to improve investment climate.
Egypt	Amendments to the Executive Regulations issued under Investment Law No. 230, issued by General Authority for Investment and Free Zones, of April 1992	Includes permission for foreign bank subsidiaries to operate in local currency; branch banks still limited to foreign currency transactions.
	Decree issued by General Authority for Investment and Free Zones, of April 1992	Further streamlines investment procedures applying to FDI; also, permits TNCs to form joint stock holding companies; allows repatriation of capital gains without prior approval of Investment Authority; opens new activities to FDI, including sea and air transport as well as water and wastewater consulting services; reduces requirement of distribution of profits to employees.
	Banking Law No. 37/1992, of 1 June 1992	Creates eight new investment zones open to both domestic companies and TNCs, two of which are free zones where companies are completely tax-exempt; in other zones, projects are exempt from taxes for 10 years from the commencement date of their activities.

/.....

(Annex table 6, cont'd.)

Country	*Law/Regulation*	*Content*
Africa (cont'd.)		
Ethiopia	Proclamation No. 15/1992 to Provide for the Encouragement, Expansion and Coordination of Investment, of 25 May 1992.	Aims at encouragement of FDI by opening some areas to private investment, while reserving some spheres to the Government and other spheres to Ethiopian investors; requires minimum FDI of $500,000 with 25 per cent in cash deposits and registration of imported capital by foreign investors; establishes investment incentives in qualified areas, including partial exemption on custom duties and tax holidays for new investments and expansion of established ones; precludes nationalization except upon payment of adequate compensation; allows establishment of foreign currency accounts by investors earning foreign currency; allows remittances of dividends and payments and repatriation of capital in approved currency at prevailing rates; guarantees access to land use and water; establishes procedures for approval of investment applications and registration: requires registration of imported capital and approval of technology agreements.
Ghana	Amendment of the Investment Code of 1985, effective September 1992.	Removes previous restrictions to FDI, including requirement of Ghanaian participation in enterprises unless these were not foreign-exchange earners; reduction of minimum FDI equity participation for joint ventures and for wholly-owned foreign enterprises; reduces number of sectors closed to FDI from 24 to 2. Offers favoured treatment to investors in agriculture, manufacturing, tourism and construction.
Malawi	Investment Promotion Act, Act No. 28 of 1991, assented to by the President on 24 January 1992, effective 16 March 1992.	Establishes the Malawi Investment Promotion Agency, to encourage and facilitate both local investment and FDI, giving priority to certain sectors; permits FDI, with no ownership restrictions; replaces industrial licenses with simple registration; plans assistance to develop industrial sites; states commitment to availability of foreign exchange, local financing and land; provides for tax and import duty incentives for export-oriented investments; states assurance of investment protection and access to international arbitration.

/.....

(Annex table 6, cont'd.)

Country	*Law/Regulation*	*Content*
Africa (cont'd.)		
Morocco	Offshore Financial Centres Law, Law No. 58-90, Dahir No. 1-91-131, of 26 February 1992.	Authorises creation of offshore financial centre in Tangier, where non-resident banks are permitted to offer services to non-residents and to offer loans in convertible currency, without being subject to Moroccan banking laws; requires authorisation by the Finance Minister; offers incentives for banks including exemptions from certain fees and charges for 15-year period, as well as corporation tax rate of only 10 per cent; even more liberal rules apply to offshore bank-holding companies.
Tunisia	Law 92-81, of 3 August 1992.	Authorises creation of free zones within which companies, including TNCs, which export 100 per cent of their production benefit from a wide range of incentives, including tax relief, services, infrastructure and access to customs facilities.
Asia		
China	Measures to Control and Tax Exemption for Import and Export Goods of Foreign Enterprises, issued on 22 August 1992, effective since 7 September 1992.	Allows qualified enterprises with foreign investment to set up bonded warehouses and bonded factories; establishes customs clearance procedures; allows tax and customs reductions and exemptions for foreign enterprises or Sino-foreign joint ventures, subject to time limits on preferential tax treatment for imported goods.
	Interim Provisions on the Establishment of Foreign Law Firms in China, issued jointly by Ministry of Justice and State Administration for Industry and Commerce, effective July 1992.	Allows foreign law firms to establish offices in China; requires approval from Ministry of Justice and registration with the State Administration for Industry and Commerce; establishes operating guidelines for foreign law firms.
	Decision of the State Council of China, of March 1992.	Approves the use of foreign capital to develop Hainan's Yangpu Economic Development Zone.
	Decision of State Council of China, of December 1992.	Permits five cities and five special economic zones to each run one or two Sino-foreign joint venture commercial retail enterprises; scope of business limited to general merchandise and import and export of commodities, but not permitted to engage in wholesale business or act as agent for import or export.

/.....

(Annex table 6, cont'd.)

Country	*Law/Regulation*	*Content*
Asia (cont'd.)		
Democratic People's Republic of Korea	Decision No. 17, Foreign Investment Law, of 5 October 1992.	Establishes general principles and rules for foreign-funded enterprises; TNCs permitted to establish wholly-owned enterprises or contractual joint ventures within the free economic and trade zone; offers incentives for companies located in these zones, including low tax rates and tax concessions during first five years of operation for companies in high-technology industries, resource development and infrastructure construction; allows partial profit remission; includes guarantee of certain legal rights and interests; promises compensation in case of unavoidable expropriation; allows lease of land for up to 50 years in the zones and exemption from tariffs on imported goods.
	Decision No. 18, Contractual Venture Law, of 5 October 1992.	Establishes framework for joint ventures between local investors and TNCs, with management assumed by host partner; sets out application, approval and registration procedures; establishes significant controls, including requirement of approval for transfer of rights, employment of third country technicians and import or export activities; grants some investor protection, notably requirement of dispute settlement through court or arbitration agency of the Democratic People's Republic of Korea; provides for wind-up of venture by Administrative Council in case one party fails to perform.
	Decision No. 19, Law on Foreign Enterprises, of 5 October 1992.	Allows TNCs to establish and manage their own wholly-owned enterprises, but only within the free economic and trade zone and only in certain sectors; sets out registration procedures; imposes significant controls on business activities, including requirement of submission of production, export and import plans to state authorities and purchase of local goods and services; allows remission of profits subject to exchange control laws; protects capital and income.
India	Exemptions under Foreign Exchange Regulation Act, of January 1992.	Removes restrictions on domestic borrowing, trading, acquisition and transfer of immovable property, intercorporate borrowing, acceptance of fixed deposits and establishment of branch offices, with aim of putting FERA companies (with over 40 per cent foreign equity) on a par with Indian companies and newly approved 51 per cent foreign equity firms.

/.....

(Annex table 6, cont'd.)

Country	*Law/Regulation*	*Content*
Asia (cont'd.)		
India (cont'd.)	Amendment to Executive Regulations, of March 1992.	The condition that repatriation of dividends be balanced by export earnings earlier imposed on all FDI now applies only to 22 industries.
	Ministry of Industry Amendment to Executive Regulations, of April 1992.	Allows foreign ownership of up to 51 per cent in electronic software.
	Presidential Ordinance No. 9, of May 1992, repealing Capital Issue (Control) Act, 1947.	Indian companies, subject to disclosure and investor protection guidelines issued by the Securities and Exchange Board of India, are free to make public issues of capital, with or without any premium hereafter.
	Ministry of Industry amendment to Executive Regulation, of May 1992.	Removes prohibition on use of foreign brand names/trade marks by industry both for domestic sales and for exports.
	Ministry of Finance Guidelines on Investment by Foreign Institutional Investors, of September 1992.	Opens up India's capital market to foreign institutional investors with no limit on investment; no lock-in period; 20 per cent tax on long term capital gains (for one year), 5 per cent holding limit by single investment institution and 24 per cent overall portfolio holding in single company.
Indonesia	Presidential Decree No. 17 of 1992 on Share Ownership Requirements in Foreign Investment Companies, effective 16 April 1992.	Lengthens period during which companies may be majority foreign-owned; permits 100 per cent foreign equity ownership of certain investments and, subject to partial fade-out requirements, these investments may remain majority-owned; foreign investors may also make smaller initial investments than previously permitted in certain types of businesses, subject to partial fade-out requirements.
	Presidential Decree No. 32/1992 concerning the list of Sectors that are closed to Capital Investment, of 6 July 1992, revoking Presidential Decree No. 23 of 1991.	Lists 51 sectors closed to FDI and domestic capital investment and 37 sectors reserved for small-scale industry.
	Presidential Decree No. 33/1992 concerning the procedure for capital investment.	Establishes detailed procedures for domestic and foreign investment.

/.....

(Annex table 6, cont'd.)

Country	*Law/Regulation*	*Content*
Asia (cont'd.)		
Indonesia (cont'd.)	Presidential Decree No. 34/1992 concerning the utilisation of land and building rights for joint ventures.	Grants land-holding rights for joint ventures for a maximum period of 35 years that can be extended for a maximum of 25 years.
Malaysia	1992 Budget Proposal of the Ministry of Finance, of November 1991.	Liberalises equity ownership requirements for FDI by permitting 100 per cent foreign ownership for companies exporting 80 per cent or more of production or if 50 to 80 per cent of production exported and investment of 50 million ringgit or more or project has over 50 per cent value-added.
	Legislative amendments to Income Tax Act, of 20 February 1992.	Improves tax incentives for operational establishments of TNCs.
Republic of Korea	Ministry of Finance Revision of its administrative regulations, effective 1 January 1992.	Simplifies procedures for FDI in service industries, by requiring only notification rather than approval in 95 service businesses if foreign share is 50 per cent or less.
	Ministry of Finance Plan to simplify administrative regulations governing management of foreign investment enterprises, effective 29 June 1992.	Relaxes some restrictions on TNC acquisition and disposition of stockholdings; allows TNCs to reduce invested capital at any time and repatriate full amount of investment.
	Ministry of Finance Revision of its Regulations on Foreign Technology Inducement, effective 1 November 1992.	Requires technology licensing agreements to be reported to the relevant ministry when payment of a royalty on a licensing fee is over a certain threshold amount; sets an additional 33 categories of high-technology projects that are eligible for tax exemption on licensing fees or royalties received by a foreign licensor.
	Ministry of Finance Revision of its Regulations on Foreign Investment, effective 1 November 1992.	Adds 12 more activities in which foreign investment is permitted; abolishes 4 activities in which joint-ventures are required; expands tax benefits to 22 additional manufacturing projects accompanied by advanced technology; abolishes the Korea Development Bank assessment of financial plans of foreign investment applicants.
	Ministry of Finance Norm Implementing Improvements to the Foreign Investment System and its Environment, effective 1 December 1992.	Adds two more business activities permitted to FDI; abolishes the residual performance requirements; allows high-tech services and insurance firms.

/.....

(Annex table 6, cont'd.)

Country	*Law/Regulation*	*Content*
Asia (cont'd.)		
Republic of Korea (cont'd.)	Ministry of Finance Amendments to Foreign Capital Inducement Act and Revision of its Regulations on Foreign Investment and on Foreign Technology Inducement, of December 1992, effective 1 March 1993.	Expands coverage of tax benefits to include all foreign investments, not merely those in high technology computer software and telecommunications; simplifies the application procedures for FDI and technology licenses; reduces the scope of foreign investment review.
Viet Nam	Amendments to Foreign Investment Law, of 23 December 1992.	Extends duration of enterprises with foreign ownership to 50 years and for "necessary cases" to 70 years; allows enterprises with foreign capital to open bank accounts in Vietnamese and foreign currency and to obtain loans from overseas banks "under special circumstances"; allows foreign investors to engage in infrastructure projects; guarantees government protection of investors' interests in event of changes in Vietnamese law affecting enterprises with foreign capital; allows investment promotion through incentives and tax concessions on a case-by-case basis for enterprises with foreign capital; defines responsibilities of State Organ for Management of Foreign Investment.
Central and Eastern Europe		
Albania	Foreign Investment Act No. 7498, of August 1992. [c]	Permits 100 per cent foreign ownership; requires authorisation of all foreign investments and special authorisation only for those investments over a certain amount in major sectors of the economy; provides for equal treatment of foreign and local investors; gives legal guarantees upon expropriation of foreign investments including standards of compensation; provides limited right to transfer of funds and repatriation of capital; permits employment of qualified technical personnel; provides for dispute resolution by international arbitration or competent court albeit with limited scope.

/.....

(Annex table 6, cont'd.)

Country	*Law/Regulation*	*Content*
Central and Eastern Europe (cont'd.)		
Azerbaijan	Law on the Protection of Foreign Investments, of 15 January 1992. [c]	State guarantees full legal protection for FDI including against changes in the law; allows restriction or prohibition of foreign investment for national security reasons or as stated by law; allows foreign investors to participate in privatization; provides that tax and other concessions are to be further defined in future laws; provides certain guarantees of transfer of profits and other sums by foreign investors; allows foreign investment enterprises with over 30 per cent foreign capital to export without a license; states that intellectual property rights are protected in accordance with the laws of the Republic; permits nationalisation only in public interest, with compensation; requires resolution of disputes by domestic courts, domestic or foreign arbitration or certain specialized institutions.
Belarus	Council of Ministers Decree No. 100, February 1992.	Establishes free economic zone in Brest.
Bulgaria	Law on the Economic Activity of Foreign Persons and the Protection of Foreign Investment, of 16 January 1992, effective 1 February 1992, repealing Law on Foreign Investment of 17 May 1991.	Eliminates requirement of minimum amount of investment; requires prior approval of investment only with respect to defense, banking, insurance, exploitation of natural resources and a few other activities; abolishes restrictions on repatriation of profits; eliminates or eases some restrictions on foreign investment, including easing of restrictions on foreign ownership or lease of real property, except that only companies with Bulgarian majority-ownership may own land; safeguards against expropriation; provides for equal treatment of foreign investors.
	Banking Law, of 4 March 1992.	Requires license from Bulgarian National Bank for establishment of new banks; sets minimum capitalization requirements, including requirement of minimum capitalization of $20 million for foreign banks; requires investors, both foreign and domestic, to obtain central bank approval for acquisition of over 5 per cent of a bank's assets.
	Privatization Law, of 23 April 1992.	Allows foreign investors to participate in the acquisition of state-owned enterprises.
	Ordinance No. 74 of the Council of Ministers, of May 1992.	Ordinance No. 74 of the Council of Ministers, of May 1992.
Lithuania	Amendments to the Law on Foreign Investments, 11 February 1992.	Offers new incentives for TNCs, especially tax concessions; allows long-term lease of rental property; allows state to sell shares to non-citizens without prior approval by the Government.

/.....

(Annex table 6, cont'd.)

Country	*Law/Regulation*	*Content*
Central and Eastern Europe (cont'd.)		
Republic of Moldova	Law on Foreign Investment, of 19 May 1992.[c]	Establishes general legal regime for FDI; aims to attract FDI by permitting 100 per cent foreign ownership of enterprises; allows repatriation of profits (within constraints of non-convertible ruble); establishes legal and organizational forms of companies with foreign investment; prescribes standards for compensation upon expropriation and allows foreign participation in privatization.
Romania	Law No. 84 on Free Economic Zones, of 21 July 1992.	Permits creation of free zones regime in sea ports and river ports; permits TNCs operating in free economic zones to receive exemption from turnover tax, excise duties and profits tax for duration of their activities.
	Law Providing Advantages for Investment of Foreign Capital in the Field of Oil and Gas Prospecting and Exploitation, of 8 July 1992.[c]	Provides fiscal advantages to foreign investors in that field, regarding taxes on profits; exemption from customs taxes on certain imports and on exports of oil and gas from their share in production results; free transferability of revenues from the sale of petroleum or gas in convertible currency.
Russian Federation	Law on Mineral Rights, of February 1992.	Provides for concessions and production-sharing for all investors, as well as for licences for exploration and operating rights through tenders and auctions; establishes ceiling of five years for exploration permits and 20 years for exploitation rights.
	Presidential Decrees on Privatization 1 July 1992.	Permits foreign investors to purchase shares in certain state enterprises, subject to various restrictions.
Tajikistan	Law on Foreign Investments, of 10 March 1992.	Allows TNCs to establish wholly-owned companies, to form joint ventures, to buy shares and securities and to participate in privatization; allows any TNC activity not specifically banned; permits TNCs to lease land and exploit natural resources under government licence; reduces profits tax by 50 per cent for enterprises with foreign ownership located in free economic zones; the cabinet of Ministers can reduce profits tax on a case by case basis.
Turkmenistan	Decision of Supreme Soviet, effective 15 December 1992.	Introduces six economic zones for free entrepreneurial activity for all investors; all entrepreneurs in the zones exempted until 1996 from paying lease charges for land and reduction in their payments for water, electricity and gas; exemption from taxation of profits for first three years of profitable work.

/.....

(Annex table 6, cont'd.)

Country	*Law/Regulation*	*Content*
Central and Eastern Europe (cont'd.)		
Turkmenistan (cont'd.)	Law on Foreign Economic Activity, of 4 July 1992. [c]	Introduces the basic legal principles governing foreign economic activity in the country including generally accepted international standards; establishes system of registration and disclosure of pertinent information on the enterprise and its economic activity. Restrictions on FDI may be imposed only by law. Settlement of disputes might be established by agreement between the parties.
Ukraine	Law on Foreign Investments of March 1992, effective 31 March 1992.[c]	Allows 100 per cent foreign ownership of business or property; establishes registration requirements; provides for exemption from customs duties and import taxes, as well as 3 or 5 year tax holidays for TNCs; allows exports and imports without license and free disposition of foreign exchange; permits TNC bank accounts and conversion of local currency; subjects repatriation of profits to 15 per cent duty; permits expropriation only in exceptional circumstances and with compensation; provides for dispute settlement.
	Law on Free Economic Zones, December 1992.	Aims to attract FDI by establishing framework for creation of free economic zones; provides that both foreign and domestic legal entities engaged in economic activities on the territory of such zones enjoy customs, foreign-exchange, financial, tax and other preferences; State guarantees property and non-property rights will remain intact in event of dismantling of zones; requires disputes arising from dismantling of zone to be heard by judicial and arbitral bodies, with the consent of the parties, including foreign judicial and arbitral bodies.
Uzbekistan	Uzbek Foreign Investment Law, of July 1992.	Relaxes requirements concerning reinvestment of profits from FDI; provides guarantees against nationalisation; grants two-year tax exemption for imports and exports of industrial equipment.
Latin America and the Caribbean		
Argentina	Resolution No. 72 of the Ministry of Economy and Public Works, of 7 January 1992.	Establishes regime of temporal admission for the promotion of export processing zones.
Cuba	Constitutional amendments, of July 1992.	Allows private investment in selected state enterprises; recognises foreign ownership of property in joint ventures.

/.....

(Annex table 6, cont'd.)

Country	*Law/Regulation*	*Content*
Latin America and the Caribbean (cont'd.)		
Honduras	Decree No. 80-92 on an Investment Law, of 29 May 1992; and Agreement No. 345, of 10 September 1992.	Establishes registration and authorisation procedures; reserves small-scale industry and commerce for Hondurans; requires equal treatment of all private enterprises, whether they have foreign ownership or not; provides guarantees of access to foreign currency and financing; states guarantees of property rights and of freedom to determine production and pricing.
Mexico	Mining Law, of 24 June 1992.	Maintains current limitations on foreign equity participation; opens up new areas, previously restricted (sulphur, potassium, phosphates, iron and coal) and opens up to private exploitation mining rights on 2 million acres of national reserves; allows for sale of three state-owned mining companies; contains new incentives including longer concession terms; also, simplifies applications and approval process and more legal protections to concession holders.
Nicaragua	Decree Law No. 30-92, adopting Law No. 127 on Foreign Investments, of 1992.	Establishes procedures, including requirement of authorisation; sets out basic guarantees and rights of investors, including guarantee of equal treatment of foreign and local investors; establishes right to net capital repatriation after 3 years and right to repatriation of payments; requires adequate and effective compensation in case of expropriation in the social interest.
Paraguay	Investment Law No. 117/91, of 7 January 1992.	Guarantees free repatriation of capital and remission of payments abroad; provides for equal treatment of foreign and local investors.
Peru	Supreme Decree No. 014-92-EM, of 3 June 1992 on a General Mineral Law.	Includes tax and other incentives for foreign investment in mining activities.
	Fishing Law, Decree Law No. 25977, of 22 December 1992.	Promotes private investment, domestic and foreign, in fishing activities, offering benefits, including free remission of profits and dividends.
Sao Tome and Principe	Law No. 13/92 establishing the Investment Code, promulgated on 15 October 1992.	Allows admission of foreign capital in any activity where private investors are permitted; refers to procedures for registration and approval; establishes incentives regime, including 50 - 70 per cent tax reductions for certain projects and access to credit; provides benefits in case of capital reinvestment; promotes foreign investment through equal treatment; allows remission of profits subject to a ceiling and subject to other restrictions.

/.....

(Annex table 6, cont'd.)

Country	*Law/Regulation*	*Content*
Latin America and the Caribbean (cont'd.)		
Venezuela	Decree No. 2095 of 13 February 1992 on Foreign Investment, implementing Andean Pact Decisions 291 and 292 of March 1991.	Following Decisions 291 and 292 of the Commission of Cartagena, it eliminates most previous restrictions on foreign investment; provides for equal treatment of FDI and local investment under the law. FDI subject to certain limitations including exclusion of FDI in communications, national defense and some professional services; provides for registration of FDI and technology transfer agreements; allows free repatriation of capital and remittance of profits; opens Andean Pact tariff incentives to TNCs.
West Asia		
Iran (Islamic Republic of)	Decision of Supreme Council for Investment, 5 May 1992.	Lifts nearly all restrictions on share ownership and repatriation of profits (free transfer of principal and interest); provides guarantees against expropriation.
	General Framework of Policies and Criteria adopted by the High Council of Informatics for the Operation of Foreign Computer Companies, 1992.	Bars foreign computer firms from direct operation in Iran; requires channelling of hardware and software services through representative Iranian companies; allows joint ventures with FDI in qualified Iranian companies within approved ceiling; allows branch offices for limited activities, subject to authorisation and registration.
United Arab Emirates	Dubai Law No. 9 of 1992.	Allows establishment in the Jebel Ali Free Zone of 100 per cent foreign-owned enterprises, with characteristics of limited liability company, except that can have a single shareholder; requires only licence from the free zone authority, and not the municipal authority.

/.....

(Annex table 6, cont'd.)

Country	*Law/Regulation*	*Content*
Developed countries [b]		
Australia	Amendments to Foreign Investment Review Board policy guidelines, of 26 February 1992.	Raises threshold for requirement of Board approval of a foreign investment from $3-10 million to $50 million in most sectors.
	Broadcasting Services Act, 1992.	Establishes restrictions that foreign person may not be in position to exercise control of a television license or have more than 15 per cent interest. Also establishes that two or more foreign persons must not have more than 20 per cent aggregate interests in such a license.
Canada	Bank Act, of 1 June 1992.	Allows foreign subsidiaries of foreign banks to establish banking operations. Reintroduces reciprocity requirement with respect to operations of foreign subsidiaries.
	Trust and Loan Companies Act, of 1 June 1992.	Allows foreign trust and loan companies to establish banking operations under the conditions established in the Bank Act of 1992.
	Insurance Companies Act, of 1 June 1992.	Allows foreign insurance companies to establish banking operations under the conditions established under the Bank Act of 1992.
Finland	Foreign Investment Act, effective 1 January 1993, repealing Restrictions Act of 1939; Act Restricting Foreigner's Right to Carry on a Trade; as well as relevant provisions in the Act on Insurance Companies and the Act Restricting Foreigner's Ownership of Shares in Banks.	Removes restrictions on foreign ownership in existing Finnish firms; eliminates supervision of transfers of shares or entire undertakings into foreign ownership; lifts requirement of permit to own real property.
	Act on the Monitoring of Foreigners' Corporate Acquisitions in Finland, effective 1 January 1993.	Supervision system over transfers into foreign ownership of shareholdings in larger Finnish companies to be phased out at the end of 1995; requires Defence Ministry to carry out permanent monitoring of defence companies; requires Ministry of Trade and Industry authorisation (or the Ministry of Finance, in case of commercial banks and credit institutions) for TNCs to buy more than one-third of the voting power in the company.

/.....

(Annex table 6, cont'd.)

Country	*Law/Regulation*	*Content*
Developed countries [b] **(cont'd.)**		
France	Decree No. 92-134, of 11 February 1992.	Eases rules governing foreign investment in France by extending the free EC investment regime to the vast majority of FDI; requires prior notification instead of authorisation regime for investments of less than FF 50 million affecting French companies with turnover of up to FF 500 million.
Japan	Amendments to Nippon Telegraph and Telephone Law, of 29 May 1992, effective 1 August 1992.	Allows foreigners to own up to 20 per cent of the shares in the domestic telecommunications firm, Nippon Telegraph and Telephone Corp.
Sweden	Law on Right for Foreigners to Transact Business in Sweden, of 1 July 1992, repealing existing law.	Eliminates authorisation requirement for foreign citizens and corporations seeking to transact business in Sweden; requires only registration procedure for FDI.
	Amendment of Swedish Companies Act, Swedish Banking Companies Act and Swedish Insurance Business Act, of December 1992, effective 1 January 1993.	Swedish Companies Act, Swedish Banking Companies Act and Swedish Insurance Business Act, of December 1992, effective 1 January 1993.

Sources: UNCTAD, Programme on Transnational Corporations, based on various sources.

a This table contains information, according to available sources, on laws and regulations directly addressing foreign direct investment. In addition, it contains some legal statutes that are not directly addressed to foreign investors, but contain important provisions affecting their operations. Occasionally, laws addressing specific sectors are also included. Some legal texts were provided by the International Centre for Settlement of Investment Disputes.

b Information on developed countries is based primarily on various sources provided by the OECD secretariat.

c The original text of the law was obtained in the United States Department of Commerce, National Technical Information Service.

Select list of publications of the United Nations Conference on Trade and Development Programme on Transnational Corporations

A. Individual studies

Foreign Investment and Trade Linkages in Developing Countries. 108 p. Sales No. E.93.II.A.12. $18.

World Investment Directory 1992, Volume III, Developed Countries. 532 p. Sales No. E.93.II.A.9. $75.

Transnational Corporations from Developing Countries: Impact on Their Home Countries. 116 p. Sales No. E.93.II.A.8. $15.

Debt-Equity Swaps and Development. 150 p. Sales No. E.93.II.A.7. $35.

From the Common Market to EC 92: Regional Economic Integration in the European Community and Transnational Corporations. 134 p. Sales No. E.93.II.A.2. $25.

World Investment Directory 1992, Volume II, Central and Eastern Europe. 432 p. Sales No. E.93.II.A.1. $65. (Joint publication with ECE.)

The East-West Business Directory 1991/1992. 570 p. Sales No. E.92.II.A.20. $65.

World Investment Report, 1992: Transnational Corporations as Engines of Growth: An Executive Summary. 30 p. Sales No. E.92.II.A.24.

World Investment Report, 1992: Transnational Corporations as Engines of Growth. 356 p. Sales No. E.92.II.A.19. $45.

World Investment Directory 1992, Volume I, Asia and the Pacific. 356 p. Sales No. E.92.II.A.11. $65.

Climate Change and Transnational Corporations: Analysis and Trends. 110 p. Sales No. E.92.II.A.7. $16.50.

Foreign Direct Investment and Transfer of Technology in India. 150 p. Sales No. E.92.II.A.3. $20.

The Determinants of Foreign Direct Investment: A Survey of the Evidence. 84 p. Sales No. E.92.II.A.2. $12.50

The Impact of Trade-Related Investment Measures on Trade and Development: Theory, Evidence and Policy Implications. 108 p. Sales No. E.91.II.A.19. $17.50. (Joint publication with UNCTAD.)

Transnational Corporations and Industrial Hazards Disclosure. 98 p. Sales No. E.91.II.A.18. $17.50.

Transnational Business Information: A Manual of Needs and Sources. 216 p. Sales No. E.91.II.A.13. $45.

World Investment Report, 1991: The Triad in Foreign Direct Investment. 108 p. Sales No.E.91.II.A.12. $25.

Transnational Corporations: A Selective Bibliography, 1988-1990. 618 p. Sales No.E.91.II.A.10. $65. (English/French.)

Transnational Corporations in South Africa: A List of Companies with Investments and Disinvestments. 282 p. Sales No. E.91.II.A.9. $50.00.

*University Curriculum on Transnational Corporations:**

Vol. I	*Economic Development.*	188 p.	Sales No. E.91.II.A.5. $20.00.
Vol. II	*International Business.*	156 p.	Sales No. E.91.II.A.6. $20.00.
Vol. III	*International Law.*	180 p.	Sales No. E.91.II.A.7. $20.00.
* The Set:			Sales No. E.91.II.A.8. $50.00.

Directory of the World's Largest Service Companies: Series I. 834 p. ISSN 1014-8507. (Joint publication, UNCTC/Moody's Investors Service, Inc.) $99.

The Challenge of Free Economic Zones in Central and Eastern Europe. 444 p. Sales No. E.90.II.A.27. $75.

Accountancy Development in Africa: Challenge of the 1990s. 206 p. Sales No. E.91.II.A.2. $25. (Also available in French.)

Transnational Banks and the International Debt Crisis. 157 p. Sales No. E.90.II.A.19. $22.50.

Transborder Data Flows and Mexico: A Technical Paper. 194 p. Sales No. E.90.II.A.17. $27.50.

Debt Equity Conversions: A Guide For Decision-Makers. 150 p. Sales No. E.90.II.A.22. $27.50.

Transnational Corporations and Manufacturing Exports from Developing Countries. 124 p. Sales No. E.90.II.A.21. $25.

Transnational Corporations in the Transfer of New and Emerging Technologies to Developing Countries. 141 p. Sales No. E.90.II.A.20. $27.50.

Transnational Corporations, Services, and the Uruguay Round. 252 p. Sales No. E.90.II.A.11. $28.50.

The Uruguay Round: Services in the World Economy, 220 p., ISBN 0-8213-1374-6. (Joint publication, UNCTC/World Bank.) $13.50.

Transnational Corporations in the Plastics Industry. 167 p. Sales No. E.90.II.A.1. $20.

Objectives and Concepts Underlying Financial Statements. 32 p. Sales No. E.89.II.A.18. $8.

Services and Development: The Role of Foreign Direct Investment and Trade. 187 p. Sales No. E.89.II.A.17. $20.

Transnational Corporations in South Africa and Namibia: A Selective Bibliography. 98 p. Sales No. E.89.II.A.13. $12.

Transnational Corporations in the Construction and Design Engineering Industry. 60 p. Sales No. E.89.II.A.6. $9.

Foreign Direct Investment and Transnational Corporations in Services. 229 p. Sales No. E.89.II.A.1. $26.

Data Goods and Data Services in the Socialist Countries of Eastern Europe. 103 p. Sales No. E.88.II.A.20. $13.50.

Conclusions on Accounting and Reporting by Transnational Corporations: The Intergovernmental Working Group of Experts on International Standards of Accounting and Reporting. 58 p. Sales No. E.88.II.A.18. $7.50. (Also available in Arabic, Chinese, French, Russian, Spanish.)

Transnational Corporations in World Development: Trends and Prospects. 628 p. Sales No. E.88.II.A.7. $56. (Also available in Arabic, Chinese, French, Russian, Spanish.)

Executive Summary. Transnational Corporations in World Development: Trends and Prospects. 66 p. Sales No. E.88.II.A.15. $3.

Transnational Corporations: A Selective Bibliography, 1983-1987.

Vol. I	441 p.	Sales No. E.88.II.A.9. $45.
Vol. II	463 p.	Sales No. E.88.II.A.10. $49.

Joint Ventures as a Form of International Economic Co-operation: Background Documents of the High-Level Seminar Organized by the United Nations Centre on Transnational Corporations in Co-operation with the USSR State Foreign Economic Commission and the USSR State Committee on Science and Technology, 10 March 1988, Moscow. 210 p. Sales No. E.88.II.A.12. $21.

International Income Taxation and Developing Countries. 108 p. Sales No. E.88.II.A.6. $13.50.

Transnational Corporations in Biotechnology. 136 p. Sales No. E.88.II.A.4. $17.

Foreign Direct Investment in the People's Republic of China: Report of the Round-Table Organized by the United Nations Centre on Transnational Corporations in Co-operation with the Ministry of Foreign Economic Relations and Trade, People's Republic of China, Beijing, 25 and 26 May 1987. 115 p. Sales No. E.88.II.A.3. $15.50.

Bilateral Investment Treaties. 194 p. Sales No. E.88.II.A.1. $20.

UNCTC Bibliography, 1974-1987. 83 p. Sales No. 87.II.A.23. $12.

Licence Agreements in Developing Countries. 108 p. Sales No. E.87.II.A.21. $13.50.

Consolidated List of Products Whose Consumption and/or Sale Have Been Banned, Withdrawn, Severely Restricted or Not Approved by Governments, Second Issue (UNCTC in collaboration with FAO, WHO, ILO and other relevant intergovernmental organizations). 655 p. Sales No. E.87.IV.1. $60.

Transnational Corporations and Non-fuel Primary Commodities in Developing Countries. 89 p. Sales No. E.87.II.A.17. $10.

Transnational Corporations in the Man-made Fibre, Textile and Clothing Industries. 154 p. Sales No. E.87.II.A.11. $19.

Transnational Corporations and Technology Transfer: Effects and Policy Issues. 77 p. Sales No. E.87.II.A.4. $11.

Analysis of Engineering and Technical Consultancy Contracts. 517 p. Sales No. E.86.II.A.4. $45.

Transnational Corporations in the International Semiconductor Industry. 471 p. Sales No. E.86.II.A.1. $41.

Trends and Issues in Foreign Direct Investment and Related Flows. 96 p. Sales No. E.85.II.A.15. $11.

Environmental Aspects of the Activities of Transnational Corporations: A Survey. 114 p. Sales No. E.85.II.A.11. $12.50.

Transnational Corporations and International Trade: Selected Issues. 93 p. Sales No. E.85.II.A.4. $11.

B. Serial publications

UNCTC Current Studies, Series A

No. 1 Patrick Robinson, *The Question of a Reference to International Law in the United Nations Code of Conduct on Transnational Corporations.* 22 p. Sales No. E.86.II.A.5. $4.

No. 2 Detlev Vagts, *The Question of a Reference to International Obligations in the United Nations Code of Conduct on Transnational Corporations: A Different View.* 17 p. Sales No. E.86.II.A.11. $4.

No. 3 *Foreign Direct Investment in Latin America: Recent Trends, Prospects and Policy Issues.* 28 p. Sales No. E.86.II.A.14. $5.

No. 4 *The United Nations Code of Conduct on Transnational Corporations.* 80 p. Sales No. E.86.II.A.15. $9.50.
(Also published by Graham & Trotman, London/Dordrecht/Boston. $31.50)

No. 5 *Transnational Corporations and the Electronics Industries of ASEAN Economies.* 55 p. Sales No. E.87.II.A.13. $7.50.

No. 6 *Technology Acquisition under Alternative Arrangements with Transnational Corporations: Selected Industrial Case Studies in Thailand.* 55 p. Sales No. E.87.II.A.14. $7.50.

No. 7 *Foreign Direct Investment, the Service Sector and International Banking.* 71 p. Sales No. E.87.II.A.15. $9. (Also published by Graham & Trotman, London/Dordrecht/Boston. $25).

No. 8 *The Process of Transnationalization and Transnational Mergers.* 91 p. Sales No. E.89.II.A.4. $12.

No. 9 *Transnational Corporations and the Growth of Services: Some Conceptual and Theoretical Issues.* 96 p. Sales No. E.89.II.A.5. $12.

No. 10 *Transnational Service Corporations and Developing Countries: Impact and Policy Issues.* 50 p. Sales No. E.89.II.A.14. $7.50.

No. 11 *Transnational Corporations and International Economic Relations: Recent Developments and Selected Issues.* 50 p. Sales No. E.89.II.A.15. $7.50

No. 12 *New Approaches to Best-practice Manufacturing: The Role of Transnational Corporations and Implications for Developing Countries.* 76 p. Sales No. E.90.II.A.13. $12.50.

No. 13 *Key Concepts in International Investment Arrangements and Their Relevance to Negotiations on International Transactions in Services.* 66 p. Sales No. E.90.II.A.3. $9.

No. 14 *The Role of Free Economic Zones in the USSR and Eastern Europe.* 84 p. Sales No. E.90.II.A.5. $10.

No. 15 *Regional Economic Integration and Transnational Corporations in the 1990s: Europe 1992, North America and Developing Countries.* 52 p. Sales No. E.90.II.A.14. $12.50.

No. 16 *The New Code Environment.* 54 p. Sales No. E.90.II.A.7. $7.50.

No. 17 *Government Policies and Foreign Direct Investment.* 68 p. Sales No. E.91.II.A.20. $12.50.

No. 18 *Foreign Direct Investment and Industrial Restructuring in Mexico.* 114 p. Sales No. E.92.II.A.9. $12.

No. 19 *New Issues in the Uruguay Round of Multilateral Trade Negotiations.* 52 p. Sales No. E.90.II.A.15. $12.50.

No. 20 *Foreign Direct Investment, Debt and Home Country Policies.* 50 p. Sales No. E.90.II.A.16. $12.

No. 22 *Transnational Banks and the External Indebtedness of Developing Countries: Impact of Regulatory Changes* 48 p. Sales No. E.92.II.A.10. $12.

No. 23 *The Transnationalization of Service Industries: An Empirical Analysis of the Determinants of Foreign Direct Investment by Transnational Service Corporations,* 62 p. Sales No. E.93.II.A.3. $15.

No.24 *Intellectual Property Rights and Foreign Direct Investment,* 108 p. Sales No. E.93.II.A.10. $20.

No.25 *International Tradability in Insurance Services,* 54 p. Sales No. E.93.II.A.11. $20.

UNCTC Advisory Studies, Series B

No. 1 *Natural Gas Clauses in Petroleum Arrangements.* 54 p. Sales No. E.87.II.A.3. $8.

No. 2 *Arrangements Between Joint Venture Partners in Developing Countries.* 43 p. Sales No. E.87.II.A.5. $6.

No. 3 *Financial and Fiscal Aspects of Petroleum Exploitation.* 43 p. Sales No. E.87.II.A.10. $6.

No. 4 *International Debt Rescheduling: Substantive Issues and Techniques.* 91 p. Sales No. E.89.II.A.10. $10.

No. 5 *Negotiating International Hotel Chain Management Agreements,* 60 p. Sales No. E.90.II.A.8. $9.

No. 6 *Curricula for Accounting Education for East-West Joint Ventures in Centrally Planned Economies.* 86 p. Sales No. E.90.II.A.2. $10.

No. 7 *Joint Venture Accounting in the USSR: Direction for Change.* 46 p. Sales No. E.90.II.A.26. $12.

No. 10 *Formulation and Implementation of Foreign Investment Policies: Selected Key Issues.* 84 p. Sales No. E.92.II.A.21. $12.

The United Nations Library on Transnational Corporations (published for and on behalf of the United Nations by Routledge, London and New York):

Set A (Boxed set of 4 volumes. ISBN 0-415-08554-3. £350):

Volume One:	*The Theory of Transnational Corporations.*	464 p.
Volume Two:	*Transnational Corporations: A Historical Perspective.*	464 p.
Volume Three:	*Transnational Corporations and Economic Development.*	448 p.
Volume Four:	*Transnational Corporations and Business Strategy.*	416 p.

Set B (Boxed set of 4 volumes. ISBN 0-415-08555-1. £350):

Volume Five:	*International Financial Management.*	400 p.
Volume Six:	*Organization of Transnational Corporations.*	400 p.
Volume Seven:	*Governments and Transnational Corporations.*	352 p.
Volume Eight:	*Transnational Corporations and International Trade and Payments.*	320 p.

International Accounting and Reporting Issues:

1984 Review.	122 p.	Sales No. E.85.II.A.2. $13.50.
1985 Review.	141 p.	Sales No. E.85.II.A.13. $15.
1986 Review.	158 p.	Sales No. E.86.II.A.16. $15.
1987 Review.	140 p.	Sales No. E.88.II.A.8. $17. (Also published by Graham & Trotman, London/Dordrecht/Boston. $65).
1988 Review.	95 p.	Sales No. E.88.II.A.3. $12.
1989 Review.	152 p.	Sales No.E.90.II.A.4. $12.
1990 Review.	254 p.	Sales No. E.91.II.A.3. $25.
1991 Review.	244 p.	Sales No. E.92.II.A.8. $25.
1992 Review	328 p.	Sales No. E.93.II.A.6. $25.

National Legislation and Regulations Relating to Transnational Corporations:

Vol. I (Part One)	302 p.	Sales No. E.78.II.A.3. $16.
Vol. I (Part Two - Supplement)	114 p.	Sales No. E.80.II.A.5. $9.
Vol. II	338 p.	Sales No. E.83.II.A.7. $33.
Vol. III	345 p.	Sales No. E.83.II.A.15. $33.
Vol. IV	241 p.	Sales No. E.85.II.A.14. $23.
Vol. V	246 p.	Sales No. E.86.II.A.3. $23.
Vol. VI	322 p.	Sales No. E.87.II.A.6. $45.
Vol. VII	320 p.	Sales No. E.89.II.A.9. $36.

Transnational Corporations in South Africa and Namibia: United Nations Public Hearings:

Vol. I	*Reports of the Panel of Eminent Persons and of the Secretary-General.*	242 p.	Sales No. E.86.II.A.6. $65.
Vol. II *	*Verbatim Records.*	300 p.	Sales No. E.86.II.A.7.
Vol. III	*Statements and Submissions.*	518 p.	Sales No. E.86.II.A.8. $54.
Vol. IV *	*Policy Instruments and Statements.*	444 p.	Sales No. E.86.II.A.9.

Four-volume set — $200.

* May not be purchased separately.

Transnational Corporations in South Africa: Second United Nations Public Hearings, 1989

Vol. I	*Report of the Panel of Eminent Persons, Background Documentation.*	162 p.	Sales No. E.90.II.A.6. $19.
Vol. II	*Statements and Submission.*	209 p.	Sales No. E.90.II.A.20. $21.

Transnational Corporations (formerly ***The CTC Reporter***). Published three times a year. Annual subscription price: $35; individual issues $15.

Transnationals, a quarterly newsletter, is available free of charge.

United Nations publications may be obtained from bookstores and distributors throughout the world. Please consult your bookstore or write to:

United Nations Publications

Sales Section	OR	Sales Section
Room DC2-0853		United Nations Office at Geneva
United Nations Secretariat		Palais des Nations
New York, N.Y. 10017		CH-1211 Geneva 10
U.S.A.		Switzerland
Tel: (212) 963-8302/(800) 253-9646		Tel: (41)(22) 917-1234
Fax: (212) 963-3489		Fax: (41)(22) 917-0123
Telex: 422311 UN UI		Telex: 23711 ONU CH

All prices are quoted in United States dollars.

For further information on the work of the UNCTAD Programme on Transnational Corporations, please address inquiries to:

United Nations Conference on Trade and Development
Programme on Transnational Corporations
United Nations, Room DC2-1329
New York, N.Y. 10017, U.S.A.

Telephone: (212) 963-3352
Telefax: (212) 963-3062
Telex: UNCTNC 661062

QUESTIONNAIRE

World Investment Report 1993:
Transnational Corporations and Integrated International Production

In order to improve the quality and relevance of the work of the UNCTAD Programme on Transnational Corporations, it would be useful to receive the views of readers on this and other similar publications. It would therefore be greatly appreciated if you could complete the following questionnaire and return it to:

Readership Survey
United Nations Conference on Trade and Development
Programme on Transnational Corporations
United Nations, Room DC2-1329
New York, N.Y. 10017, USA

1. Name and address of respondent (optional):

____
____
____

2. Which of the following best describes your area of work?

Government	☐	Public enterprise	☐
Private enterprise	☐	Academic or research institution	☐
International organization	☐	Media	☐
Non-profit organization	☐	Other (specify) __________	

3. In which country do you work? ____________________

4. What is your assessment of the contents of this publication?

Excellent	☐	Adequate	☐
Good	☐	Poor	☐

5. How useful is this publication to your work?

Very useful ❐ Of some use ❐ Irrelevant ❐

6. Please indicate the three things you liked best about this publication:

____

____

____

7 Please indicate the three things you liked least about this publication:

____

____

____

8. If you have read more than the present publication, what is your overall assessment of them?

Consistently good ❐ Usually good, but with some exceptions ❐

Generally mediocre ❐ Poor ❐

9. On the average, how useful are these publications to you in your work?

Very useful ❐ Of some use ❐ Irrelevant ❐

10. Are you a regular recipient of ***Transnational Corporations*** (formerly ***The CTC Reporter***), the tri-annual publication of the UNCTAD Programme on Transnational Corporations?

Yes ❐ No ❐

If not, please check here if you would like to receive a sample copy sent to the name and address you have given above ❐

Litho in United Nations, New York
38140—July 1993—6,100
ISBN 92-1-104417-0

United Nations publication
Sales No. E.93.II.A.14
ST/CTC/156